THE MAKI
A STATE

MEMORIES AND OBSERVATIONS
1914-1918

BY

Dr. THOMAS GARRIGUE MASARYK

President of the Czechoslovak Republic

AN ENGLISH VERSION, ARRANGED AND PREPARED
WITH AN INTRODUCTION

BY

HENRY WICKHAM STEED

Author of "The Hapsburg Monarchy" and "Through Thirty Years"

ISHI PRESS
INTERNATIONAL

The Making of a State: Memories and Observations, 1914-1918

by Dr. Thomas Garrigue Masaryk
President of the Czechoslovak Republic

With an Introduction by
Henry Wickham Steed

First Printed in 1927

Current Printing May, 2009
Ishi Press in New York and Tokyo

Copyright © 1927 by Thomas Garrigue Masaryk

Copyright © 2009 by Sam Sloan

All rights reserved according to International Law. No part of this book may be reproduced by any mechanical, photographic or electronic process or otherwise copied for public or private use without the written permission of the publisher.

ISBN   0-923891-33-1
978-0-923891-33-6

Ishi Press International
1664 Davidson Avenue, Suite 1B
Bronx NY 10453
USA
1-917-507-7226

Printed in the United States of America

Thomas Masaryk, The Making of a State: Memories and Observations, 1914-1918

Foreword by Sam Sloan

Tomáš Garrigue Masaryk (7 March 1850 – 14 September 1937), sometimes called Thomas Masaryk in English, was an Austro-Hungarian and Czechoslovak statesman, sociologist and philosopher, who was the most prominent advocate of Czechoslovak independence during World War I and became the first President and founder of Czechoslovakia.

This book describes those events leading up to the creation of the State of Czechoslovakia.

The name "Garrigue" was the maiden name of his wife, a Protestant American, from whom he took his middle name.

The main street in Mexico City, Avenida Presidente Masaryk, is named after him.

Although World War I was a great tragedy for everybody, Czechoslovakia did better than most other countries because they got their independence, due primarily to the efforts of Thomas Masaryk. Prior to that, it had been part of the Austro-Hungarian Empire.

At the time of the writing of this book, Thomas Masaryk was the President of the country. He continued as president until 14 December 1935, when he resigned for health reasons. He was succeeded as President by Edvard Beneš.

This story did not have a happy ending. It was said that as long as Thomas Masaryk ruled Czechoslovakia, Hitler would never attack.

However, promptly after Thomas Masaryk died on 14 September 1937, that happened. In September 1938, the Sudetenland of Czechoslovakia was occupied by German forces, an event that started World War II. The rest of the country was taken by Hitler by March 1939.

His son, Jan Garrigue Masaryk (14 September 1886 – 10 March 1948), became Foreign Minister in Exile, and spent World War II in England, where he made radio broadcasts to his people. When the war was over, he returned to his country as Foreign Minister.

Although the Communist Party was a minority party in Czechoslovakia, its members gradually took the most important positions in the government. Finally, Jan Masaryk was left as the only non-Communist minister. On 25 February 1948, Edvard Beneš, fearful of civil war and Soviet intervention, capitulated and appointed a Communist dominated government. The only important portfolio held by a non-Communist was foreign affairs, which went to Jan Masaryk. The presence of Jan Masaryk gave the government the facade of being a National Front, but he was found dead two weeks later.

On 10 March 1948, Jan Masaryk was found dead, dressed in his pajamas, in the courtyard of the Foreign Ministry below his bathroom window. The initial investigation stated that he had committed suicide by jumping out of the window, although ever since it has been believed that he may have been murdered by the Communist government. The question is: "Did he fall or was he pushed?" The conclusion of death by suicide was reaffirmed by a second investigation taken in 1968 during the Prague Spring and a third one in the early 1990s after the Velvet Revolution. Despite the outcomes of all three investigations, discussions about the mysterious circumstances of his death are still continuing.

In any case, his death enabled the Soviet Union to complete their takeover of the country.

Then, when they finally got their freedom from the Soviet Union, the Czechs and the Slovaks decided that they could not live together any more, so they broke up and the country disappeared.

On January 1, 1993, Czechoslovakia peacefully split into the Czech Republic and the Slovak Republic.

And that is the end of the Story.

Sam Sloan

PREFACE

WRITTEN by President Masaryk as an authoritative record of the efforts by which the freedom of Czechoslovakia had been won, this book was originally published at Prague in 1925 under the title "The World Revolution." It is a discerning historical interpretation both of the process of Czechoslovak redemption from Hapsburg servitude, and of the war as a whole. Wider in range than any "war book" yet written, it is a comprehensive examination of the philosophy of national, international and social life by a philosopher-statesman whose principles experience has vindicated. It deserves not only to be read but to be studied throughout the English-speaking world.

In the preparation and arrangement of this English version some changes of sequence have been made in parts of the narrative, and a few minor details have been omitted. Otherwise it is an accurate and faithful rendering of the original. I wish gratefully to acknowledge the help given by President Masaryk himself in revising the greater part of the manuscript. My acknowledgments are also due to M. Camille Hoffmann, of the Czechoslovak Legation in Berlin, who prepared the German edition, as well as to Messrs. Lawrence Hyde and J. C. C. Johnstone, and to M. Paul Selver and Dr. Jaroslav Cisař, of the Czechoslovak Legation in London, for the assistance I have received from their painstaking work.

No attempt has been made to transliterate Czech names. They have been printed with the original accents and spelling of which the following English equivalent may, however, be given:—

c = ts.
č = tch.
ch = the Scottish guttural "ch" as in "loch."

ě = ye.
ř = rzh.
š = sh.
ž = zh or the French "j."

The stress usually falls on the first syllable. The acute accent " ' " as in "Palacký," (which is pronounced "Palatskee") denotes the length of a vowel, not the accentuation of the word.

H. W. S.

CONTENTS

PAGE

PREFACE v
INTRODUCTION xi

CHAPTER I

THE TESTAMENT OF COMENIUS 1
    (*August–December* 1914)

The Outbreak of War—A Balance Sheet—The Position in
Austria—And in Germany—Russia and the Slavs—How
long will the War last?—In the Lion's Den—Dr. Beneš—
The Pan-German Plan—Our Task.

CHAPTER II

ROMA AETERNA 35
    (*December* 1914–*January* 1915)

My Escape to Italy—Work in Rome—In Touch with the
Allies—Personal Relationships—Allied Military Plans—The
Position of the Vatican.

CHAPTER III

IN ROUSSEAU'S BIRTHPLACE 47
    (*Geneva. January–September* 1915)

Slav Differences—The Organization of Czech Colonies—The
Treaty of London—Italy Joins the Allies—Action against
Austria—The Standard of Hus—The Meaning of the Fight
—The Question of War Guilt—Intrigues in Switzerland.

CHAPTER IV

IN THE WEST 71
    (*Paris and London. Sept.* 1915–*May* 1917)

Paris and London—Czech Colonies Abroad—The National
Council—The Art of Propaganda—The Work in England—
The Military Outlook—The Work in France—Isvolsky and
the Slavs—tefánik—Views on France—Views on England
—The Cinema Spirit—The American Declaration of War—
The Southern Slavs and Italy—Peace Feelers—A Disavowal.

Contents

CHAPTER V

PAGE

PAN-SLAVISM AND OUR REVOLUTIONARY ARMY 130
    (*May 1917–April 1918*)

The Russian Revolution—The Russian Anarchy—Russia
and the Slavs—Supilo—Our Army in Russia—Military Difficulties—Ups and Downs—Russian Anomalies—Organization—My Own Plan—The Bolshevist Revolution—My
View of Bolshevism—Communism and Bolshevism—The
Ukraine—In Roumania—Why We Were Neutral in
Russia—Across Siberia—Vladivostok.

CHAPTER VI

IN THE FAR EAST 201
    (*Tokio. April 6–20, 1918*)

Memorandum to President Wilson on the Bolshevists—On
the Way to Canada.

CHAPTER VII

AMERICAN DEMOCRACY 207
    (*Finis Austriae. Washington, April 29–Nov. 20, 1918*)

In America—American Democracy—American Literature—
The Political Aspect—Cooperation with the Yugoslavs—The
Poles—The Mid-European Peoples—The Ruthenes—Mr.
Voska—The Breaking up of Austria-Hungary—The Siberian
"Anabasis"—A Summary—The Decisive Hour—The Last
Days of Austria—My Relations with President Wilson—
President Wilson and Professor Herron—Incipit Vita Nova.

CHAPTER VIII

GERMANY AND THE WORLD REVOLUTION 313
    (*From Washington to Prague. Nov. 20–Dec. 20, 1918*)

The Errors of Germany—Why the War Came—The Rival
War Aims—Germany and Europe—Goethe or Bismarck?—
The Decline of German Thought—German Decadence—
Militarism and Suicide—The Psychology of Suicide—War
and Religion—A Philosophy of the War—In London Again
—Paris, Padua—and Home.

Contents

CHAPTER IX

PAGE

THE RISE OF THE CZECHOSLOVAK REPUBLIC 368

The Work at Home—"De Facto" and "de Jure"—The
Legal Birth of our State—The Prague Revolution—Republic
or Monarchy?—The Policy of Vienna—The Germans of
Bohemia—Allied Sincerity—Intentions.

CHAPTER X

DEMOCRACY AND HUMANITY 409

The "Balkanization" of Europe—The Grouping of Small
Peoples—The Influence of the West—Our Relations with
the East—The Slav Question—The Problem of Minorities—
Democracy at Home—Economic Democracy—The Thral-
dom of Habit—Political Education—Democracy and
Publicity—Democracy and Theocracy—The Value of
Morality—The Good and the Beautiful—Democracy and
Anarchy—Democracy and Revolution—Democracy and
Dictatorship—The Problems of a President—Ends and
Means—The Humane Ideal—Our Relation to Catholicism
—Church and State—The Law of Love.

APPENDIX 498

INDEX 511

INTRODUCTION

A GENERATION hence, when the war and its antecedents are seen in perspective, who will be held to have won abiding fame? Among military commanders, perhaps Marshal Foch. Among political leaders, perhaps President Wilson. But I have long thought that, when all accounts are closed and all reputations critically assessed, the man who will stand foremost as a creative statesman will be Thomas Garrigue Masaryk, the first President of the Czechoslovak Republic.

Partiality may, it is true, affect my judgment. For twenty years Masaryk has allowed me to think of him as a friend; and though, from the spring of 1907 onwards, I have sought coolly to estimate the man and his work, I may be biased by personal affection and admiration. Yet some knowledge of his deliberate aims and positive achievements leads me to think him peerless among the agents of Destiny who, between 1914 and 1918, wrought in her smithy and forged the framework of Europe anew.

None of the statesmen on either side of the contest entered into it with so keen a sense of its meaning as Masaryk. None saw so clearly from the beginning what its outcome must be if Europe, and all that Europe stood for in the world, were to survive. Where is a parallel to be found to the Prague professor who went open-eyed into exile, determined to return only when he should bring with him the freedom and the restored independence of his own people—a people whose very name was strange to Allied Governments and peoples?

And if, in vision and lofty resolve, Masaryk was thus pre-eminent, no less notable was he in his divination of the historical forces which the war had brought into play. He counted, as with a practical reality, upon the power of the spirit of John Hus, Wyclif's disciple, who was burned at the stake for heresy in July 1415. Who, save Masaryk, understood that, in raising the Hussite standard in the Hall of the Reformation at Geneva on July 6, 1915, the fourth centenary of the Czech martyr's death, he was consciously challenging the whole work of the Hapsburg Counter-Reformation and was setting out to reverse the sentence of death passed upon the Czech nation after the Battle of the White Mountain in 1620? Even he could hardly then foresee that the fire of his faith would presently burn in every Allied country or that it would guide the Czechoslovak Legions on their epic march from the shores of the Black to the shores of the Yellow Seas. Nor could he have imagined, when he reached London later in 1915, an almost unknown professor of "enemy" nationality whose doings aroused the suspicions of the British police, that, on his return to England in November 1918, a company of the Coldstream Guards would render him military honors as the head of an Allied and belligerent State.

The thought of personal advantage was ever alien to him. Time and again, in the years before the war, he had risked all to bear witness to the truth. When war came, what stirred him to his depths and possessed him wholly was the idea that, after three centuries of servitude, his people might be reborn to freedom, to spiritual and democratic unity as Hus and the Bohemian Brotherhood had conceived them, and that to him it might be given to fulfil the seer's vision of his illustrious prototype, Comenius: "I, too, believe before God that, when the storms of wrath have passed, to thee shall return the rule over thine own things, O Czech people!"

Those who may wish to learn the story of Masaryk's effort will find it in this book. It is truly the story of "The Making of a State," and of much besides. It is the work of a philosopher-historian, whom Fate made a constructive statesman. His broad learning and sense of history run through it. His analyses of pan-Germanism, of Communism and of Bolshevism are masterly. His critical faculty is ever alert, even when his own people are its object. Written by a Czechoslovak for Czecho-slovaks in order that they may learn how they were redeemed, it nevertheless contains so much of enlightenment for others, it betrays so penetrating a discernment of the deep things of life, that it is indispensable to an understanding of the Europe which the war transformed and of the process of transformation itself.

Thus it is no mere literary record of the war, drawn up at leisure by one of the chief actors in it. As literature it may have less value than as a living document—or as a monument inadvertently raised by Masaryk to himself. In form, and lack of form, it is a complication of notes and reminiscences, reflections and observations, put together while he was actually engaged in building up the State of which he writes. If he has unwittingly raised his own monument he has not built it as a trained architect with a nice sense of proportion and embellishment, but rather as a hewer of stone in a quarry, winning block after block from its reluctant flanks and scarcely pausing to think how best they might be arranged in organic symmetry. Chips and fragments lie all about him; but the stone is there, rough hewn and enduring, raw material for a finished temple of fame. Yet of the temple and of the fame the least careful is he who hewed, builded and writes.

The Masaryk revealed in these pages is a standing refutation of the shallow view that the Great War brought forth no great man. To me, who had experience of the Austria in which he grew up, of the deadening spell she cast over her children, of the Hapsburg system that was a perennial negation of political morality, the emergence of Masaryk seems well-nigh as miraculous as his triumph in the fight he fought, all but single-handed, against inveterate oppressors. Without some knowledge of Hapsburg Austria, the intensity of his repeated injunction to his fellow-citizens can hardly be understood: that they must, above all, de-Austrianize themselves.

To Masaryk and to the Czechs the name "Austria" meant every device that could kill the soul of a people, corrupt it with a modicum of material well-being, deprive it of freedom of conscience and of thought, undermine its sturdiness, sap its steadfastness and turn it from the pursuit of its ideal. Since the Hapsburgs, with their Army, their Church, their Police and their Bureaucracy were the living embodiment of this system,

Masaryk, after long hesitation, turned against them and opposed them in the name of every tradition, conviction and principle he held dear. He knew the dimensions of the venture. For his people, the price of failure would have been oppression more fierce, demoralization more dire; for him it would have meant a choice between death on a Hapsburg gallows and lifelong exile.

He knew, too, that Allied statesmen did not, could not, feel as he felt or see as he saw. Genuine though their sympathy might be with the cause he upheld, it was not to be expected that they would pledge their own peoples to support a Quixotic crusade for Czechoslovak freedom, all the less since the Hapsburgs commanded the resources of a powerful Monarchy and might perchance be detached, by political skill, from the Allies' main foe, Germany. In comprehending this position, despite his own conviction that they were wrong, Masaryk proved himself a greater statesman than they; for an essential quality of statesmanship is the power to understand the position of others better than they themselves understand it. Therefore, as soon as he had given them an inkling of his purpose, he set about making an army. To make it he went to Russia, where the main body of Czechoslovak prisoners of war was to be found. Having made it, he resolved to remove it from the Russian chaos and to place it alongside of Allied armies on the Western front. For this reason, he preceded it through Siberia to Japan and the United States in order to seek means of transporting it to Europe. Before it could reach Europe the war was over. Yet its work had been done. A vagrant professor who could put fifty thousand men into the field was obviously a more considerable personage in the eyes of Allied Governments than the ablest advocate of humanitarian ideals. Thanks to his army in Siberia and to the Czechoslovak Legions simultaneously organized in France and Italy, Masaryk and his devoted helpers, Beneš and Štefánik, won formal recognition for their people as belligerent Allies. They had gained freedom. It remained for them to make a State—a workaday task that might well prove harder than the heroic work of war and revolution.

A man less steeped than Masaryk in the traditions and

history of his people, or a man whose authority as a leader had been less firmly established, might have found this task beyond his powers. For nearly three centuries the people, mainly of peasant stock, had been subjugated and Germanized. The native nobility of Bohemia had been executed or driven into exile at the beginning of the Thirty Years War after the over-throw of the Bohemian forces by the arms of the Hapsburg-Jesuit Counter-Reformation at the White Mountain on November 8, 1620. Czech lands and fortunes had been confiscated, the Czech language proscribed, the Czech faith condemned, Czech Bibles and books burned and the people themselves decimated. What had been a flourishing State of 3,000,000 inhabitants was reduced to a devastated province with a population of barely 800,000. "Better a desert than a country full of heretics," exclaimed Ferdinand II of Hapsburg, who followed to the letter the advice of his preachers: "Thou shalt break them with a rod of iron, thou shalt dash them in pieces like a potter's vessel." Among themselves, their Church and the swarm of foreign Catholic adventurers who joined their standards, the Hapsburgs distributed the confiscated Czech lands. So extensive were the confiscations that an alphabetical catalogue of them, compiled from Hapsburg and Jesuit archives, covers 1,468 pages. No effort was spared to re-Catholicize the nation of Hus. Its fate was what the fate of England would have been had the Spanish Armada triumphed in 1588.

It is sometimes argued that persecution serves to strengthen the persecuted. That depends upon the efficacy of the perse-cution. The Czech people was re-Catholicized by fire and sword, and its national spirit all but extinguished. Its learned men and spiritual leaders were driven to take refuge in England, in the Protestant parts of Germany, in Holland and in Scandi-navia. Greatest among them was Comenius the Educator, the last Bishop of the Bohemian Brotherhood Church. Within the country itself, no breath of life could stir. Yet memories of the past were tenaciously cherished in the hearts of the people; and when, in the "Era of Enlightenment" toward the end of the eighteenth century, the Emperor Joseph II eased the pressure and issued an Edict of Toleration, more than fifty thousand Czech Bibles emerged from secret hiding-places. The French Revolution and the Napoleonic armies stimulated the national spirit in Bohemia as elsewhere. But to such straits were her people reduced that Goethe, who looked upon their efforts with a friendly eye, doubted whether they would ever be able to revive their national tongue. Thanks to a handful of ardent "awakeners," most of whom were Protestants, the process of rebirth was nevertheless carried on. Palacký, chief among them, expounded the meaning of Czech history and, in the spirit of Comenius, taught that through education alone could the way of salvation be found. Throughout the nineteenth century, amid ceaseless struggles with the Hapsburgs and their system, the work of education went on. The Czechs secured High Schools and a University of their own, and established so excellent a school system that, by the end of the century, illiteracy had fallen to a fraction of one per cent.

In the later stages of this educational work, Masaryk himself took a prominent part. Born in Moravia, on March 7, 1850, of humble Slovak stock—his father was a coachman on one of the Imperial Estates—he studied ardently, learning Czech, German and afterwards Polish. Despite the quickness of his intelligence, his parents apprenticed him first to a locksmith and then to a blacksmith, though they presently yielded to the protests of his schoolmaster and allowed him to be trained as a teacher. Thus, in 1865, he began the secondary and university studies which led to his appointment to a minor professorship at the University of Vienna which he held until 1882 when he joined the staff of the Czech University at Prague. Thence his fame as a philosopher and historian quickly spread throughout the Slav world, and, with it, his influence over the younger generation of Czechs and Slovaks, Serbs, Croats and Slovenes of Austria-Hungary. In a description of the reconciliation between the Serbs and Croats of Dalmatia which marked the revival of the Southern Slav movement, Hermann Bahr, the well-known Austrian-German writer, said in 1909:—

It is remarkable that, when one inquires into this reconciliation and looks for the intermediaries who brought it about, one comes across, almost invariably, a pupil of Masaryk. It is nearly always somebody who, as a young man, once went to Prague, sat in his class-room and, awakened by him, returned home to proclaim the gospel of concord. Masaryk's pupils have united the Serbs and Croats of Dalmatia and are now bringing that distracted province to have faith in the future—so strong is the influence of the lonely Slovak in Prague who seems to some a mixture of Tolstoy and Walt Whitman, to others a heretic, to others again an ascetic, and to all an enthusiast.

"The lonely Slovak in Prague" was a not unfair description of Masaryk in the spring of 1909. His independence of judgment, his strength of character had gained him deep respect but few friends. He had once been returned to Parliament, yet had quickly resumed his literary and academic life. Twice he had stood out against public opinion—once when he had exposed as forgeries some "historical" manuscripts which were regarded as Czech national heirlooms; and once when he had fought the battle of a Jewish tramp who was falsely accused of ritual murder. In his eyes, truth came first. Popularity he held of little account.

Returned again to the Austrian Parliament after the introduction of universal suffrage in 1907, as the leader of a tiny group, he speedily became one of the outstanding figures in Bohemian and Austrian public life. During the crisis which followed the annexation of Bosnia-Herzegovina in 1908, he was a severe critic of Austro-Hungarian policy; and, in the autumn of 1909, he gave evidence for the prosecution in a libel suit begun by the Serbo-Croat Coalition in the Croatian Diet against the Austrian historian, Dr. Friedjung, and others who, on the strength of official documents, had accused the Coalition leaders of being in the pay of Serbia. The trial proved the Austro-Hungarian official documents to have been forged. Then, greatly daring, Masaryk went to Belgrade to procure the originals of the forgeries and, on the strength of them, publicly indicted Count Aehrenthal, the Austro-Hungarian Foreign Minister, for complicity in their fabrication. His action did more than that of any man to discredit the Hapsburg system in the eyes of the civilized world.

Yet no man strove harder than he to avert the catastrophe which he felt to be impending. He knew what sufferings it would bring upon his own people, what course it would compel him to follow, and to what risks it would expose him—a lonely professor, past his sixtieth year, without pecuniary resources and an object of official hatred. Though he foresaw that his choice would lie between exile and the gallows, he never wavered or flinched. The Bosnian Annexation crisis of 1908-1909 and its sequel had convinced him that the Hapsburg Monarchy was doomed; that its policy was leading straight toward a European war in which victory would make of it a mere vassal of Germany while defeat would sound its death-knell; and that the fate of his own people hung in the balance.

Conscious of their peril, the majority of Czechs placed their hopes in Russia, counting that she would not again submit to humiliation such as she had suffered at the close of the Bosnian Annexation crisis and believing that she would never allow a Slav people to perish. Masaryk thought otherwise. Unlike his fellow-countrymen, he knew Tsarist Russia through and through. He did not await Czech national redemption at her hands. The Czechs, he held, must work out their own salvation in the spirit of Hus and of the Czech Reformation. He believed in democratic freedom and moral uprightness as twin factors in national rebirth, and he could not imagine that either would be fostered by Russia. A nationalist he was, in the sense that national freedom seemed to him an indispensable postulate of the international cooperation for humane ideals of which he dreamed; but in his nationalism there was neither vainglory nor racial intolerance. Here, again, he was at variance with other prominent Czech leaders, if not, indeed, with popular feeling.

With the outbreak of the war came the call to action. In December 1914 he escaped from Austria to begin abroad, primarily in the West, his fight for national redemption. In this book he tells the story of his struggles, and recounts his steps along the stony path to triumph, for the enlightenment of a people still largely ignorant of the means by which its freedom had been won, still bearing, in spite of itself, the Austrian stamp on mind and body, still unaware of the political and moral demands of independent national life. It is as Masaryk's testament to the nation that his book must be judged, not solely as a history of the making of a Czechoslovak State.

In Bohemia and Moravia, indeed, the framework of public administration, if not of a State, was already in existence. It had been taken over from Austria, with all its defects. But, in Bohemia especially, there were some 3,000,000 Germans, historically Bohemian and, in any event, too important, too wealthy and too educated a minority not to be accounted first-class citizens. Could they be reconciled to Czechoslovak rule? Would they, who had been the spoiled children of Austria, resenting every economic or educational advance of the Czechs as derogatory to the privileged German position, be satisfied with a position of equality, or would they look upon it as a species of persecution?

To the East, some millions of Hungarian Slovaks had joined the Republic. They had long been oppressed by the Magyars, deprived of education and deliberately kept in a backward, nay, a primitive condition. In general culture and political maturity they were decades, perhaps generations, behind the Czechs; and, despite the presence of a Protestant leaven among them, they were apt to be fanatically Catholic and priest-ridden.

Still further to the East and extending to the Roumanian border were the Ruthenes, or Little Russians, of what had been Hungarian Ruthenia. Now, as an autonomous "Sub-Carpathian Russia," they had adhered to the Czechoslovak Republic. If, in point of general culture and political maturity, the Hungarian Slovaks were decades behind the Czechs and Germans of Bohemia and Moravia, the Ruthenes were decades behind the Slovaks.

Upon all these difficulties Masaryk touches with discerning hand. He looks upon them as aspects of the great moral and educational task that awaits his people. Few of his pages reveal his mind so clearly as those in which he examines the entire problem of democracy and of fitness for a democratic system of public life. He treats it as a whole, not exclusively in its relation to Czechoslovakia. Against autocracy or dictatorship in any form he sets his face like flint. The cooperation of enlightened peoples for the realization of a humanitarian ideal is still his chief aim. But he is no visionary. Rather is he a practical mystic. He is fully alive to the world-wide significance of the new order in Central Europe. He knows that it stands as a political barrier against any revival of pan-Germanism, that is to say, of German ambitions to attain political mastery in Europe and the world. He sees that such ambitions could not be fulfilled without a fight to the death in which Europe herself might perish; but he believes that there may be found a more excellent way of merging national aims in a higher synthesis of international endeavor. In this endeavor he wishes his own people to play their full part, drawing inspiration from the heroes of their own history and from the spirit of their Reformation. After having led them from Hapsburg servitude to the green pastures of freedom, he would fain teach them the Law and show them that it is written in the story of their past. The examples of Hus and of Žižka, of Chelčický, Comenius and Palacký he holds up before them as worthy of reverent emulation.

Not least does he set them, albeit unconsciously, the example of his own life and work, a life of utter devotion to truth and to truthfulness, of steady faith in an ideal and of self-sacrifice for a cause transcending any individual aim. If he be a mystic, if religious feeling penetrates his every fiber, the story of his achievement stands as proof that, when a man seeks righteousness for its own sake, other things shall be added unto him. Having vindicated the faith of Comenius, he hands it on as a greater testament to the people he redeemed, a testament written in every line and between the lines of one of the most notable interpretations of past and contemporary history.

H. W. S.

THE MAKING OF A STATE

THE MAKING OF A STATE

CHAPTER I

THE TESTAMENT OF COMENIUS

(AUGUST–DECEMBER 1914)

I WAS on holiday with my family at Schandau, in Saxony, when the Archduke Francis Ferdinand and his wife were assassinated at Sarajevo on June 28, 1914. Even before this outrage I had, in my heart of hearts, expected war though I dreaded the final decision which war would force upon me—the decision to translate into action my antagonism to Austria and Austrianism. After the Austro-Hungarian ultimatum to Serbia on July 23, I was therefore in a state of constant tension. Yet I still hoped for peace. I assured my acquaintance that even mobilization was merely a threat and that the responsible statesmen would meet and settle the conflict. From mobilization to the actual waging of war the way might be long. Not even the declaration of war did I take to be the last word. People called me an incorrigible pacifist and idealist. But my last hope vanished when England declared war on Germany (August 4) though I still fancied there were traces of hesitation in the German ultimatum to Belgium, and afterwards in the German proposals of August 9 to the Belgian Government for a peaceful settlement. I thought they showed a certain respect for the opinion of the world. Of course, all these fancies were born of futile reluctance to take the plunge. Even a politician sets store by his neck.

After the second Balkan war, in the summer of 1913, I had worked on a scheme to reconcile the Serbians and the

Bulgarians, whose animosity alarmed me; for, as I have said, I expected a great war at no distant date. From time to time I urged this upon many Serbians and Bulgarians; and in the spring of 1914 I agreed upon a complete plan with an intimate Serbian acquaintance, who was staying at Prague. He went home and came back again, with good reason to think that the leading men in Belgrade were ready for peace and would be willing to make concessions. Then I was to have gone to Paris and London in order to get influential Western statesmen to put pressure on Belgrade and Sofia and in order also to awaken the interest of the French and English press. There might have been no need for me to go to St. Petersburg. It might have sufficed to talk things over with the Russian Ambassadors and to influence St. Petersburg through Paris and London. From Paris I was to have gone to Sofia by way of Constantinople since—so I was advised from Belgrade—the Bulgarians would be less suspicious if I came to them direct from London and Paris. The idea was good; but the Sarajevo outrage and the Austro-Hungarian ultimatum to Serbia brought my scheme of conciliation to naught.

There had been a similar and more important effort in the same direction during the first Balkan war in December 1912. I was in Belgrade and discussed the war and the whole political outlook with the Prime Minister, M. Pashitch. As a result he sent for me next day and sketched the conditions on which Serbia would come to terms with Austria; and, as proof of his wish for peace, he was ready to pay his respects personally in Vienna to Count Berchtold, the Austro-Hungarian Foreign Minister, so as to satisfy the Viennese craving for prestige. I was to tell Berchtold of his proposal. This I did, but he did not understand it and would not hear of a reconciliation. When I complained of Berchtold's bearing to several Austrian public men like Dr. von Baerenreither, Dr. de Biliński (the Joint Austro-Hungarian Finance Minister and Secretary of State for Bosnia-Herzegovina) and others, they were horrified at Berchtold's senselessness and tried vainly to put things right. More than ever did I become convinced of the superficiality and worthlessness of the Viennese Balkan policy. Think of it: During a victorious war the Serbian Prime Minister shows moderation and offers his hand in reconciliation to the Austro-Hungarian Minister for Foreign Affairs; with the arrogance of a Great Power the latter rejects it and adds fresh guilt to the old Austrian sin of provocation. This episode strengthened the expectation of a great war to which I had been led by historical studies and by observation of Europe. Thus the Viennese attack on Serbia at the end of July 1914 did not surprise me.

During the mobilization the railways were reserved for soldiers and recruits, and we could not get back at once from Schandau to Prague. Masses of Austrians and Hungarians were also returning from Germany. The stay in Saxony enabled me, however, to see the German mobilization at Dresden and elsewhere and to compare it with the Austrian, which I witnessed when I did get home, towards August 10. The Germans were much more orderly in everything, and their men were far better equipped; and I was pained to see numbers of the Austrian recruits drunk, especially the Austrian Slavs who came home from Germany or by way of Germany.

On my way back to Prague I observed the Czech soldiers more closely and spoke to a sergeant-major. We were near Melnik, and I dropped a few skeptical remarks about the way the war might go. I can still see the poor fellow's big eyes as he looked at me and asked sadly, "What can we do?" Yes, indeed, what could we, what must we do? I knew what we, what I, had to do; it was becoming daily clearer.

Prague was politically deserted, all individual and party activity being suspended, but we Members of Parliament met and talked about trifles, for our minds were far away from the Chamber. On leaving Prague our Czech soldiers had given vent to their anti-Austrian feelings, and we heard that, in the army, there was insubordination among them. Soon came reports of military severity and even of executions. Our men were being punished for what I, a Member of Parliament, had advocated. Could I, ought I to do less than the simple soldier-citizen whose anti-Austrian and Slavonic feelings I had encouraged?

To find out how my fellow-members and their Parties felt I began to talk things over with them—often with M. Švehla, whom I saw at Hostivař and at Karlsbad, and then with Dr. Stránský (the elder), M. Kalina, Dr. Hajn, M. Klofáč (with whom I was in touch before and during his imprisonment), Dr. Soukup and Dr. Šmeral. Once or twice I asked several of them to my house. I approached M. Choc also, but he was so scared that I left him out of account. From these talks I concluded that the great majority in all the parties whose leaders I had consulted would remain anti-Austrian, even if individual leaders or groups should side with Austria.

At first I was not suspected by the police and the authorities, for I was prudent and tried not to compromise anybody. In such a position it is important to do as much as possible one-self and to say little to others, so that, in case of arrest and judicial inquiry, they can give simpler evidence. Therefore I hid my plans even from those nearest to me. Some guessed, of course, what I was about and what my going abroad would really mean; but I was careful to say nothing to them.

THE DECISION

My mind was made up, for good—Austria must be opposed in grim earnest, to the death. This the world-situation demanded.

The only question was how to begin and what tactics to adopt. At home, neither armed revolution nor even thorough-going opposition was possible. Of this I was quickly per-suaded. Outbreaks might have been fomented here and there, but I would have nothing to do with that sort of thing.

It would probably be just what people in Vienna, particularly the Archduke Frederick, would like. After careful consideration it was clear that we should have to leave the country and organize abroad our fight against Austria.

While still at Prague, I tried to get into touch with friends in the Entente countries. To this end Mr. Voska, whom I had known in America and who had come to Bohemia on a visit before the war, served me well. As soon as I was sure of his discretion, I arranged with him the raising of a big fund by our fellow-countrymen in the United States for the purpose of assisting the victims of Austrian persecution at home. Then we discussed politics. As a citizen of neutral America he could enter all belligerent countries; therefore I asked him to go home by way of England and to take messages and letters to my friends in London. He assented, and started at the end of August. Several other American citizens went with him so as to allay suspicion. He took verbal messages; what was written were mainly figures and jottings. The messages referred to the persecution of our people and also of the Southern Slav leaders, to the financial position of Austria-Hungary and, finally, to military matters. They were delivered immediately upon Mr. Voska's arrival in London on September 2, 1914, to Mr. Wickham Steed, then Foreign Editor of "The Times," who conveyed them the same day to the quarters for which they were intended, including the Russian Embassy. I asked Mr. Steed also to have a hint sent to Russia not to impede our soldiers from passing over to the Russian lines and to receive them well, for the Russians looked upon Czech soldiers simply as "Austrians" and treated them accordingly. Mr. Steed did this through the Russian Ambassador, Count Benckendorff; and for his own part, sent me word that our soldiers should make themselves known to the Russians by singing the song "Hej Slované."

Mr. Voska carried out his mission well. He organized, besides, a service of special couriers, chosen among citizens of neutral States and among our own people who were returning home. In this way we established regular connections with the Entente countries. Towards the end of September Mr. Kosák, one of our fellow-countrymen living in England, brought me news from Mr. Steed. This news, which I supplemented soon afterwards by a personal meeting with political friends in Holland, was highly important for me and very serious.

It was that, in the opinion of Lord Kitchener, the war would last at least three or four years. For me this question was very weighty, since the character of the work I meant to do abroad depended largely upon the duration of the war. I heard also that the British military commanders thought the fate of Paris sealed, but that nevertheless England would hold out to the last man and to the last ship, and that we ought to keep our spirits up and hold out with the Allies.

Equally important was it for me to know approximately the military plans of the Allies. Their idea was that Russian armies should pass through Silesia, Moravia and Bohemia, so as to cut Austria-Hungary off from Germany strategically. The plan was to be carried out during 1914. The Russians, I was informed, could provide arms for our people so as to enable them to keep order at home.

As later developments were to convince me, the Allies stuck to this idea of separating Austria-Hungary from Germany. Indeed, as we shall see, they worked at it with the help of Austria right up to the spring of 1918. Neither militarily nor politically did I like it. Militarily I saw in it a certain lack of confidence in their own resources; and politically it meant coming to terms with the Hapsburgs, and the preservation, perhaps even the aggrandizement, of Austria. It seemed to me not a plan but planlessness, and it increased my fears about Russia.

Meanwhile I took advantage of my sister-in-law's visit from America to see her on to her boat at Rotterdam. This was between the 12th and the 26th of September, 1914. From Rotterdam I wrote to Professor Ernest Denis in Paris and to my friends Steed and Seton-Watson asking the latter to come from England to see me or to send me somebody trustworthy. But time was too short and I had to think of a second journey to Holland. Yet, as I passed twice through Germany and saw something of Holland, even this first trip was not in vain.

At home things were getting clearer. The anti-Austrian feeling of our people increased. The question was how to organize ourselves and what to do. From various quarters I got proof of the animosity of the Court and of the military leaders, especially the Archduke Frederick, towards us, and learned of their plans against the Czech and the Southern Slav Sokol, or gymnastic, organizations. Action was soon taken against them, the Sokol at Jičin being among the earliest victims. Trustworthy information often enabled me to give a timely hint to those in danger.

Then I managed to go once more to Holland (October 14-29). Again I went through Germany and watched things in Berlin for some days. In Holland I stayed at Rotterdam, The Hague, Amsterdam and elsewhere studying, as could only be done in a neutral country, the foreign press and war literature generally. This time I got into touch with my friends. Seton-Watson came to Rotterdam where, in the course of two days, I gave him an account of the whole Austrian situation and of my views upon the war and the international position. I explained to him our national program and our plan of action in so far as it was already defined. He seemed surprised that I should lay stress upon the historical State rights of Bohemia, and hinted that in England we and the other Austro-Hungarian peoples were expected to put the principle of nationality into the foreground. On his return to London our trusty friend drew up a Memorandum on what I had told him and caused it to be laid before the Allied Governments in London, Paris and St. Petersburg. The Oxford Professor, Sir Paul Vinogradoff, who was going to St. Petersburg, gave it personally to the Russian Foreign Minister Sazonof. While in Rotterdam I was able to correspond with Professor Denis, and I met there also Dr. Kastiliansky, a Russian with whom I had already had literary and political intercourse. He moved afterwards to London and helped us in all sorts of ways. In Holland he was of assistance to Dr. Beneš when, later on, we set up a branch propaganda establishment there. I myself established a provisional propaganda center with the help of the correspondent of "The Times" in Holland. Money began already to reach me from our fellow-countrymen in America; and Mr. Charles Crane sent me personally a considerable sum. With Mr. Steed's help these transactions were carried out by cable.

In the comparative solitude of Holland I was able quietly to think out and to review our future tasks. Any lingering trace of doubt or hesitation was dispelled by the memory of Comenius—revived by his grave in Dutch soil—the example of his propaganda in the political world of his time, his political prophecy and the program laid down in his will. In my subsequent journey round the world, the will of Comenius, together with the Kralicka Bible of the Moravian Brethren, was for me a daily memento, national and political.

Once again I stayed in Berlin on the way back from Holland and saw several leading politicians and writers. I told the Socialists that they had suffered a defeat when they voted the German war credit on August 4, and said that the Social Democratic Party would soon split. It was already uneasy. On December 2 one of its members (Liebknecht) voted against the new war credit and, on December 20, twenty others followed his example. What I heard in Berlin about the course of the war strengthened my belief in Austro-Hungarian and German guilt.

At home and in the army persecution was increasing. On November 23 the execution of Kratochvil of Prerov showed that it was time to get away, though before I went Matějka was executed on December 15. I was ready to escape to the Allies, the only question being how to manage my final departure. It took some time to make sure whether the police suspected me, for in Holland I had an impression that

I was being watched. What I had already done was enough to bring me to the gallows, though, on the whole, little seemed to be known of it. Besides my other foreign relationships I had, while still in Prague, established contact with official Russia through M. Svatkovsky—of whom I shall have more to say—and I had arranged to procure German and Allied newspapers, which were forbidden in Prague. By this means I learned many details that had failed to reach our press.

After my second journey to Holland I spoke somewhat more openly to my Parliamentary colleagues, and I asked them to sanction verbally the work to be done abroad. This was because of Seton-Watson's hint that politicians in Allied countries would want to know whether I was speaking and acting in my own name or in that of our political parties, and, if so, which parties.

THE OUTLOOK

The course of the war made me feel uneasy. Who would win it?—a question hard to answer definitely, then or afterwards. As soon as it broke out, I had begun to study a number of works on modern warfare which I had not read before. The problem was whether the struggle would be long or short, because our chances had to be reckoned and our work arranged according to its probable duration. The experts differed. On the whole, the opinion prevailed on both sides that a modern war could not last long. Foch, for instance, held this view. The well-known French writer, Leroy-Beaulieu, thought it would be over in seven months, while Hanotaux and Barrès expected the Russian "steam roller" to end it. The Germans predicted a speedy collapse of the French army, as in 1870; and their rapid advance through Belgium and Luxemburg in the North, and through Lorraine and Alsace in the South, bore out their forecast at first. The earliest hostilities went badly for France—Paris was threatened, and on September 2 the French Government migrated to Bordeaux. I hoped that Kitchener might be right, though from what I knew of him I was inclined to doubt the soundness of his judgment.

Until I left Prague I was doubtful, too, about the actual position at the fronts. The battle of the Marne puzzled me especially. I took the French and English view that the Germans had lost it, since they had gone back to a new line; but the French had likewise withdrawn from the Moselle to behind the Marne—a retreat that looked like a defeat. Why had the French not gone forward after the victory? The Germans claimed that two of their army corps had been removed from France and thrown against the Russians in East Prussia, and that therefore the battle of the Marne was not decisive. From the outset the Allies had been numerically superior; consequently, the French retreat was all the more discouraging. I knew several good military experts in the Austrian army but I could not get at them. Not until I went abroad was I able to consult the soldiers and get details. Then I understood that on the Marne the Germans had really been beaten.

This hopeful impression was deepened by the protracted fighting round Ypres—from October 20 to November 11, 1914 —for the shore of the English Channel. Here also the Germans were unable to carry through their plan and to get control of the Channel and its harbors (Dunkirk, Calais and Boulogne), whence they could have threatened England. They had to fall back along the whole line and to resign themselves to a war of position. Their offensive had miscarried, their reckoning had proved wrong and their whole plan of campaign was compromised.

On November 12, however, Turkey sided with the Triple Alliance. Asia Minor, Egypt and the Balkans thus acquired great political and military importance. What would Bulgaria, Greece and Roumania do? British policy towards Turkey (two cruisers built for the Turkish Navy in England had been seized) was severely condemned in "The Times"; and on

December 18 the position in Asia Minor was rendered more acute by the British declaration of a Protectorate over Egypt. The war was becoming more complicated—hence it was likely to last longer. Proof of my views on the war at that moment may be found in an article which I wrote for "Naše Doba" (Our Era), in which I pointed out its military, economic and political significance and set forth the problems that worried me, as well as my hopes. The Austrian censor passed the article; though, in the same issue, he suppressed part of an older article on the Balkans, and portions of an essay by Professor Denis on our position in "The International League for the Defense of the Rights of Nations." In these articles, and in other reflections called "The Warriors of God," I defined my political aims from the very outset; and, in subsequent numbers, I continued to analyze critically the objects of the war for the benefit of the thoughtful. Day by day I studied the war maps closely. It was on the battle fronts that political issues were now being, and probably would be, decided for a long time to come. The behavior of friend and foe indicated their war aims as well as their respective strength and capacity.

Our hopes of victory were encouraged by the Austrian reverses in Serbia, by the defeat of General Potiorek and, finally, by the Austrian evacuation of Belgrade on December 15, 1914. On the other hand, the Russian advance to Cracow and to the mountain passes of Slovakia could not offset Hindenburg's victories in East Prussia, at Tannenberg and on the Masurian Lakes. Though the Austrians and Germans were certainly wrong in underestimating the Russian army and especially its artillery, what I knew of the Russian forces and of the Russian Command filled me with apprehension. Russian vacillation in front of Cracow troubled me. The articles published at that time in my paper, the "Čas," on the fighting and on the advance and retreat of the Russians, were widely read. They were the outcome of editorial conferences in which conclusions were worked out according to the news and the positions of the armies. Some of the staff were optimistic, far too optimistic, whereas I was reserved and even skeptical; it was said jokingly that, when the Russians entered Prague I should be the first to hang. From time to time I alluded in the "Čas" to the unpreparedness of Russia and dealt critically both with the incompetent War Minister, Sukhomlinov, and with the Commander-in-Chief, the Grand Duke Nicholas, despite his patriotic and pro-Slav manifestos. After all, I was right; and I think that one of my soundest political judgments and decisions was in not staking our national cause on the Russian card alone and in seeking, on the contrary, to win the sympathies of all the Allies instead of sharing the mood of uncritical and passive Russophilism then prevalent.

The "Czech Throne"

This mood was everywhere apparent. The market women, it was said, were keeping the best geese for the Russians. How eagerly the manifestos of the Grand Duke Nicholas, and reports of the audience granted to Russian Czechs by the Tsar, were copied and circulated is well known, as is the punishment incurred by those found in possession of them. I remember a scene in what was then Ferdinand Street. A well-known Radical journalist stopped me and, in high spirits, showed me a copy of a report of the first audience the Tsar had granted to the Russian Czechs. He was sorely disappointed when I handed it back to him saying that, politically, it meant little. In fact, the Tsar said nothing definite. I admitted, however, that the audience itself was a success; and, as could be seen in the case of this journalist, it helped to keep up the hopes of our people. Of such reports there were many. The story was that Russian airmen dropped them at night; but it seemed to me, from their style and substance, that many of them were spurious. Austria, for her part, was treating with especial severity both the Russian prisoners of war and the Russians who had been staying in Austria when hostilities began. This I recognized when I sought to secure the release of the Russian writer, Maxim Kovalevsky, whom the war caught at Karlsbad, and of the Russian lady journalist, Madame Zvezditch. True, the Serbians were treated still worse.

I often met and discussed matters with M. Kalina, a Czech Member of Parliament, whom I had already told something of what I had done secretly abroad; and I mentioned to him the danger to which our Sokol organizations were exposed from the Austrian Commander-in-Chief. We considered the part the Sokols might play in the immediate future and particularly during the expected Russian occupation of the country. Through him I met Dr. Scheiner, the head of the Sokols, with whom we agreed that, in case of a Russian occupation, the Sokols should act as a Public Safety Guard and, should need arise, as a national army. But I did not hide from him my doubts of the Russian army and of Russian policy, and I alluded to the possibility that, if the Germans should advance through Saxony and the Austrians from the South, the Russians might be compelled to retreat. There was a serious possibility; nay, a probability that, should the Russians push forward as far as Moravia and, perhaps, Bohemia, they would be obliged to withdraw. We were bound in conscience to exercise the greatest prudence lest the Austrians take cruel revenge after a Russian retreat in order to terrorize the people for the future.

In the spring of 1914 Dr. Scheiner had been in Russia, and had realized that Russo-Czech political relations were so slight as to be practically non-existent. M. Sazonof, the Russian Foreign Minister, had complained to him that Czech politicians took no account of Russia and were therefore unknown to the Russians. He had said frankly that we were not to count upon Russia and that the Russian army was not yet ready for a decisive war. Earlier in the year Sazonof had said much the same thing to Klofáč, another Czech Member of Parliament, whom he had assured that the Great Powers wanted no war. But these things were not said or known openly. Our public opinion was uncritically pro-Russian, in the expectation that the Russians and their Cossacks would set us free. Not only did I repeat to Dr. Scheiner my misgivings on the subject of the Russian army, but I expressed my fears of the Russian dynasty and even of a Russian Governor, since Russian absolutism and indolence, as well as Russian ignorance of things and men among us, would soon demolish our Russophilism.

To these arguments Dr. Scheiner replied that, under existing conditions, a Russian would be the most popular candidate for the "Czech Throne," and that we were obliged to take this into account. I agreed, for it was certainly not the moment to expound to the public the true state of Russia. But I made my conviction clear to Seton-Watson, who explained it in the memorandum which, as I have said, he drew up and caused to be sent to Sazonof. In the interest of our relationship to Russia I wished official Russia to know. My propaganda abroad, and especially the memoranda submitted to the Allied Governments, mentioned the prevalence of pro-Russian feeling among us, though, for my own part, I should have preferred, as a candidate for the "Czech Throne," a member of some Western dynasty or one having influence with Western dynasties, had no other solution been possible.

Yet I must say at once that nowhere while I was abroad did I negotiate with any one about such a candidate. My own opinion I expressed only to my most intimate foreign friends, so that, in case of need, they might know it; but all reports that I negotiated with English or other Princes are totally false. I favored a Republic, though I knew that the majority of our people were then monarchist. Moreover, the behavior of the Social Democrats in Austria and in Germany and their attitude towards the dynasties, no less than the murder of Jaurès in France, enjoined prudence upon us in considering the future form of the State, all the more because the question was not then urgent. Republicanism was first strengthened among our people, as elsewhere, by the Russian Revolution in 1917. By that time, it seemed to me, the confidence of our people in the Russian dynasty had been shattered.

I discussed also with Dr. Scheiner the financing of our work abroad, and he gave me at once a sum to begin with. We thought of using the Sokol funds for the purpose; but later on, through some legal arrangement, an embargo was placed upon them. For the time being I was to appeal to the Czechs in America, and Dr. Scheiner gave me the address of Mr. Štěpina in Chicago.

Pro-Russian Feeling

Of the pro-Russian feeling of our people—it was hardly a policy—something more must be said. It was serious, and unforeseen developments made it more serious still.

Though our pro-Russians favored a maximum Slav policy, their ideas were vague. After a Russian triumph, which they never doubted, a great Slav Empire was to arise, the small Slavonic peoples being linked with Russia. As far as I could make out, most of our Russophils contemplated a sort of analogy to the planetary system in which the planets—the Slavonic peoples—were to revolve round the Russian sun. A section of the Russophils desired, indeed, a degree of autonomy within the Russian Federation, with a Grand Duke of sorts as Viceroy or Imperial Lieutenant in Prague. Now I had made a lifelong study of Russia and of the Slav peoples individually and, in the light of it, I could not look to Tsarist Russia for salvation. On the contrary, I expected a repetition of the Russo-Japanese war. Therefore I favored vigorous action abroad, not in Russia alone but also in the other Allied countries, so as to gain for us the goodwill and the help of all. I insisted that, like me, Dr. Kramář should get away, so that we could share the work abroad; but he, I was told (for I had no chance of approaching him personally), was determined to stay at home since he expected that the Russians would themselves settle the Czechoslovak question once for all. The lessons of the Russo-Japanese war made me fear, however, that Russia would not win and that a new revolution would break out among her people. Then, I apprehended, our own people would lose heart if salvation by Russia had been generally awaited and Russia should prove powerless to help us.

The evolution of modern Russia and of the Russian army I had watched very closely. I had last visited Russia in 1910, when I had got good information of the state of the army. The decay and demoralization which had been so frightfully revealed in the Japanese war had not been overcome and, though reforms had been introduced and weapons provided, progress was insignificant. Of this I had confirmation during the Balkan wars of 1912-1913, and subsequently up to the beginning of the Great War. I distrusted the Russian army administration and the various Grand Dukes. Indeed, the light-mindedness of Tsarist Russia was soon shown by the terrible fact that Russian soldiers had to withstand the Germans with sticks and stones; and it was no compensation that the Archdukes in the Austro-Hungarian army were little better than the Grand Dukes of Russia. In the spring of 1914, about May, I think, a leading Russian journal, the "Novoe Vremya," had written of Russian unpreparedness for war in the same way as Sazonof had spoken to our fellow-countrymen. This was reported in the Czech press, but soon forgotten, and a miraculously rapid Russian victory was expected. Our optimists are, however, entitled to plead that the Allies were no less optimistic than they.

I could understand that our people should be enthusiastic over the official Russian pronouncements, which spoke of "Slavs and brothers." That was enough for our public opinion. It had not been educated in practical foreign policy, which, for us, really began with the war. I read all the Russian pronouncements attentively. The Russian war manifesto of August 2 spoke of Slavs related by blood and faith—in the eyes of official Russia the Orthodox Slavs of the Balkans had long been "Slavs and brothers." On August 9 the Tsar, speaking to the Members of the Duma, referred again to "co-religionist brethren." For this reason his further phrase, "the complete and inseparable union of the Slavs with Russia," did not strike me as particularly precise, since he was silent on the question whether Poles, Bulgars and Serbs, as well as Croats, Slovenes and Czecho-slovaks, could be so closely united with Russia. At the Moscow war celebration on August 18, the representative of the nobility declared the war to be a defense of Slavdom against pan-Germanism, and the Tsar replied that it was a question of defending Russia and Slavdom. He said nothing about the Orthodox faith because, for him, that was a matter of course.

In the Duma, Sazonof as Foreign Minister announced that it was the historical task of Russia to protect the Balkan peoples —not the Slav peoples—and that the will of Austria and of Germany must not be the law of Europe. Sazonof, as I heard later, also wrote the manifesto to the Poles on August 15. It was a fine declaration which the Poles accepted with grateful emotion; but I felt misgivings because it was signed by the Grand Duke Nicholas, not by the Tsar, just as the Austrian Emperor had not spoken to the Poles directly but through his Commander-in-Chief. Before long the old enmity between Poles and Russians blazed up again, by no means through the fault of the Poles alone. In fact, Tsarist Russia showed, little by little, that it had no thought of real independence for Poland but only of some sort of autonomy; and Trepoff presently blurted it out and the Tsar repeated it.

Besides, the bombastic vagueness of the Grand Duke Nicholas's war manifestos displeased me, especially the one addressed to the Austro-Hungarian peoples. Many copies of it were circulated in nine languages. The Slovak text, however, differed from the Czech and other texts in that the Slovaks were expressly appealed to. A special manifesto to the Czech people was also put into circulation, but it struck me as having been forged either by some of our own fellows or by the Austrian police. I could not find it in the Russian files of documents or in the Russian newspapers.

None of these manifestos and proclamations availed to modify the opinion of official Russia that I had formed by study and observation; moreover, very little was said of the Slavonic peoples in the speeches made by members of the Russian Duma. The Polish representative, indeed, mentioned them so as to avoid naming the Russians; and Milyukoff, the Cadet leader, spoke of the fight against German mastery over Europe and the Slavs. Nevertheless, the Tsar's bearing towards the Czechs in Russian encouraged our people, who knew nothing of details and were not in a position to form a critical estimate of the Russian or of the European situation. They were unhesitatingly Russophil, awaiting redemption from mighty Russia and persuading themselves that there was no need for active opposition —a state of mind fostered by Austrian political pressure and by the weariness of futile beating against Viennese prison bars.

How vague the Russian press, for its part, was in regard to Slavonic matters, may be judged from an article in the "Russkoye Slovo" which the "Čechoslovan" (a Czech journal published at Kieff) reproduced on September 20, 1914. Commenting upon the manifesto of the Grand Duke Nicholas to the Austro-Hungarian peoples, the "Russkoye Slovo" wrote:—

The great hour strikes. The varied races of Austria-Hungary are called to new life. Bosnia, Herzegovina, Dalmatia and Croatia will unite with Serbia; Transylvania and Southern Bukovina with Roumania; Istria and the Southern Tyrol with Italy. More complicated is the question as to the fate of the Czechs, Slovenes, Magyars and Austrian Germans. Against a German Austria, within ethnographical limits, nothing can be said, but it is inadmissible that German districts should be added to Germany, who would thus come out of the war stronger than ever. Germany must be separated from the Near East by an independent Austria. On the way to the creation of an independent Czech State arises the question of Czech access to the sea, a question not to be solved within the ethnographical or the historical boundaries of the Czech people. Hungary will be given independence, the fatal blunder of 1849 being thus made good, though the Hungarians must be confined to Magyar territory.

I need not dwell upon the uncertainty and haziness of this article, especially as regards our people—to say nothing of an Austria which was to separate Germany from the "Near East"! A little study of the map will show how foggy were its notions about Poland, Bohemia and the Slovenes; indeed, its only definite features were those relating to Serbia and Roumania.

While I was assuredly right in looking upon Russia with a skeptical eye, it was too late to criticize her publicly or to reduce our pro-Russianism to proper proportions. Even before the war my "open-eyed love" of Russia—as our poet Neruda might have termed it—had often been misunderstood. Now, amid the war excitement, it would not have been understood at all. Yet I was no whit behind our pro-Russians in my love of Russia, that is to say, of the Russian nation and people; but love cannot and ought not to silence reason. A cool, clear head is needed in war and revolution, for wars are not waged or revolutions made by imagination and enthusiasm, feeling and instinct alone. I trod in the footsteps of Havlíček,[1] who first showed us Russia as she is, and I would let no man and nothing lead me astray. I knew well when, how and how far even a democratic politician—precisely because he is democratic—could and should go with the majority and be guided by general opinion.

Russia, especially official Russia in whose hands lay the decision to make war, was confronted with a Slavonic problem of her own. In her aspirations to Constantinople, aspirations strengthened and even hallowed by old religious tradition, she had encountered the resistance of Austria who, in the service of Rome and of the pan-German idea, was likewise pressing towards the Balkans. For Austria, as for Russia, the small Balkan peoples were but means to an end. Here the Catholic Austrian and the Orthodox Russian tendencies collided. Austria and Russia competed for influence and supremacy in Serbia, Roumania and Bulgaria—countries bordering on the territories of the two rivals, nearest to them in historical development and therefore objects of their special attention.

To the north also—in Galicia and Poland—political and religious antagonism had long made rivals of Austria and Russia. It was here that official Russia saw her main Slavonic problem,

---

[1] Karel Havlicek (1821-1856), one of the leaders of the national reawakening of the Czech people. A disciple of Mazzini, he looked upon national freedom as synonymous with political freedom and as a necessary condition of democratic liberalism.

though it had been, from time immemorial, subordinated to political and ecclesiastical ambitions. Really, in its broader, racial, pan-Slav sense, the Slavonic problem was understood by few in Russia—only by some Slavonic specialists and historians and by a part of the *intelligentsia,* who nevertheless looked upon it largely from a Russian religious standpoint. For this reason Russian interest in us Czechs, as in the Catholic Croats and Slovenes, lacked keenness. The Russian people had heard only of their Orthodox brethren in the Balkans. Nor were the radical elements in the Russian *intelligentsia*—the Socialists in particular —who were in opposition to the Government and its official Nationalism and Slavophilism, well disposed towards our endeavors. This we learned by experience in Russia during the war.

Such was, and is, Russia really—a reality too little known among us, for most of our Russophils were satisfied with hazy notions. To them Russia seemed great and mighty; and, since we sorely needed foreign help against Austria and Germany, brotherly Russia was to deliver us—a policy and a state of mind alike comprehensible. Did not Kollár [1] explain why the idea of inter-Slav reciprocity arose in tiny Slovakia!

A BALANCE SHEET

Of Russia and our relationship to her I shall have occasion to speak more fully. At the beginning of the war our business was very carefully to weigh the assets and liabilities of the belligerents on both sides and to make up our minds upon the truly fateful situation. I reckoned thus:—

Germany has a big army of good quality; a definite plan (pan-Germanism) for which she has gained the support not only of the com-

---

[1] J. Kollár, the first modern Czech poet (1793-1853). By birth a Slovak, and a Protestant by religion, he was deeply influenced by the philosophy of Herder and by the ideas of Rousseau. He was a pan-Slav idealist, and explained that Slovakia, in the center of the Slav world, was the natural birthplace of idealistic pan-Slavism.

mon people but of the more cultured classes; she is well prepared, has efficient commanders (a view I soon modified), is wealthy and has a strong war industry.

The Austrian army and its command are weaker. The various Archdukes (with an impossible fellow like the Archduke Frederick as Commander-in-Chief) and jealousy of Berlin and of the German command are debit items. In Vienna, as I knew, one current ran in favor of a unified Austro-German and the other in favor of an independent Austrian command. Of Conrad von Hoetzendorf, the Chief of General Staff, I had my doubts. Vienna, I expected, would reluctantly submit to and obey Berlin; and the separatist tendencies in Hungary would make themselves felt. Thus the Central Powers, though neighbors, would not get an entirely unified political and military leadership. In the Austrian army our men and the Italians would be untrustworthy, perhaps also the Roumanes and the Yugoslavs.

The Allies, on the other hand, are stronger in man-power (even in 1914), are richer and industrially more powerful. True, France alone has a well-trained army of any size. The Russian army is half-trained, and altogether Russia is an uncertain quantity militarily, politically, economically and financially. England has still to create and train an army. The Serbian troops are excellent but few, and the Turks will give them trouble (Turkey had declared war on November 12). Italy will at least be neutral, perhaps Roumania also, despite her pro-German King (Italy declared her neutrality on July 31, Roumania on August 3). The geographical distance between the Allies and the consequent lack of unity in their military and political plans will be a serious drawback, making for uncoordinated action. In the East, communications are very disadvantageous to Russia. On the other hand, the battles of the Marne and of Ypres are promising. The Entente is resolute against Germany but less resolute against Austria—a danger for us. To sum up:—A victory of the Allies is possible but every ounce of their strength will be needed to win it. The German failure to smash France at once and to checkmate Russia awakens hopes of victory. A long war would give us time to develop our revolutionary propaganda.

In December 1914, when I was preparing to go abroad, feeling was depressed at Prague and in Bohemia generally. Our people began to be uncertain about Russia and the Allies and also about themselves. Vienna declared and Berlin confirmed that the mobilization had gone smoothly, all races rallying round the Throne. I was convinced that this was not true. At Prague and elsewhere there had been some loyal mummery, but feeling was anti-Austrian. Though some were weak and some ill-disposed, the deliberate resistance offered by a comparatively large number of individual soldiers and the mood of the people warranted, in my view, organization for an active struggle. While our people, especially the educated classes, had long been schooled in the idea that Austria was necessary to us as a dam against the Germanic flood, and while it was to be expected that some leading men would be determined partisans of Austria, the feelings and the convictions of the majority of our people were decidedly anti-Austrian. If only the Czech Parliamentary representatives, as a body, do not disavow me, I said to myself, individual disavowals and newspaper articles extorted by the police matter little. Therefore: Go abroad and get to work, with God's help! And if Germany and Austria manage to win, or if the war is indecisive, stay abroad and carry on revolutionary opposition to Austria for the future.

Our people abroad had already shown their feelings by demonstrations against Austria. As early as July 27 the Paris Czechs had pulled down the Austrian flag at the Embassy, and on July 29 they resolved to enter the French army. On July 27 also the Czechs in Chicago got up a manifestation against Austria-Hungary, as did the London Czechs on August 3. In Russia our people laid before the Government, on August 4, a scheme for a Czech Legion. On August 20 the Czechs in France were admitted to the Foreign Legion, and on the same day the Czechs in Russia were received by the Tsar. On August 28 the "Družina," or League of Czechs in Russia, was formed. News of its formation was brought to Prague by messengers. All this was in keeping with our program and with my feeling: Go abroad! Go abroad!

As I knew that I should need facts and figures to convince people abroad of the feasibility of a Czechoslovak State, I took long and frequent counsel of Professor Koloušek upon its economic and financial bases, for it was necessary to have as clear an idea as possible of what such a State (including Slovakia) would be. My program was a synthesis of Czech aspirations in the light of our constitutional, historical and natural rights; and I had kept the inclusion of Slovakia constantly in view, for I am by descent a Slovak, born in Moravia. Hungarian Slovakia I knew, as I had often been there, and I had a border line between Slovakia and the Magyar country clearly in my mind. Nevertheless, for greater certainty I asked Dr. Anthony Hajn to get one of his friends, a staff officer, to sketch the Southern boundary of Slovakia on a map. This sketch and a list of the chief points on the frontier I took with me.

A CZECH-YUGOSLAV CORRIDOR

I must mention also the idea, warmly supported by many of our people and by some Southern Slavs, of creating a territorial corridor between Czechoslovakia and the Southern Slav country. This idea was not mine. It seemed to me impracticable to establish a narrow corridor or strip of territory 120 miles long from north to south, between the Magyars and the Austrians, completely isolating the Magyars. Unless I am mistaken, it was Dr. Lorkovitch, a Croatian Member of Parliament, who carried to Zagreb the idea of this corridor. I had invited him to Prague, as I wished to learn all I could of the position in Croatia before going abroad. The old animosity between the Austro-Hungarian Croats and Serbs might, I feared, break out again, since Vienna and Budapest would do their utmost to foment it. From Dr. Lorkovitch I gathered that not a few Croats believed in the possibility of setting up an independent Croatian State, either as a Republic or as a Monarchy with a foreign (preferably an English) dynasty, such a State to include Croatia, Dalmatia, Istria and the Triestine littoral. The question of Bosnia and of the Slovene country was left open. I was in favor of the greatest possible degree of Southern Slav unity, both territorial and political. Italy, I must repeat, was then neutral. Trieste, I thought, might be an independent free port, like Hamburg. At the same time, no detailed plan could be made; but I gave Dr. Lorkovitch my views so that he might inform my Southern Slav friends, whom I expected to meet abroad and with whom I wished closely to cooperate. I met Dr. Lorkovitch again in Vienna before going to Italy; he gave me a map and a statistical table of the Croat settlements in the projected corridor. As to the Slovenes I conferred with Dr. Kramář who, as I expected, told me that the progressive Slovenes were in favor of union between all three branches of the Southern Slav race—Slovenes, Croats and Serbs.

In the Lion's Den

Before starting I wanted to have another good look at Vienna and Austria; and I went right into the lion's den.

At Prague the story ran that Count Thun, the Lord Lieutenant or Viceroy of Bohemia, had already received from Vienna a list of the people whom he was to arrest, and that my name was on it. Therefore I had gone to him after returning from my first journey to Holland, ostensibly because my review, the "Naše Doba," had been confiscated and because official pressure was being put on my paper, the "Čas." Thun was a decent fellow with whom one could talk pretty frankly; but, this time, he appeared more reserved than usual. Without shaking hands, he took me to a room alongside of his reception-room, where, it seemed to me, somebody behind a curtain was taking down what I said. I had one or two things to tell him—that, for instance, during the recent Balkan wars of 1912-13 the Austrian Government had allowed us to make collections for the Serbians and Bulgarians, and that our Czech soldiers could not be expected to forget this so soon. As to our pro-Russian feelings, we were certainly Russophil, which did not necessarily mean that we were quite enamored of the Tsar and his system of Government. In any case, people in Vienna ought to treat our soldiers with a little political tact. I said further that our wounded men who had been sent back from the Russian front complained of the inadequacy of the Army Medical Service (to which, indeed, army doctors, and Germans at that, had drawn attention even before the war), and that the condition of this service had been influenced by the Archduke Francis Ferdinand, who had looked upon army doctors as atheists and Jews. I added that the military administration had not kept its supply of medicines fresh or its medical appliances up to date, that there were not enough surgical instruments and no X-ray apparatus in the field. Thus I managed to tell him a good deal, including what I had seen in Holland and Germany, and to let him see that things in Austria were not perfect. Politically, I suggested that, if people in Vienna were less biased, they might even be thankful to the Czechs for not wishing Austria to come entirely under German control; and I cited several instances of the unseemly anti-Czech and anti-Slav conduct of German officers attached to the Austro-Hungarian General Staff.

The Lord-Lieutenant was obviously surprised and embarrassed. I felt that, in his heart of hearts, he agreed with me on many points. When I left he thanked me for my visit, said that he had been much interested by what I had told him, and though he did not offer me his hand, he remarked that he had not taken any special measures against me. From this I gathered that I should be able to go abroad a third time without difficulty. I asked him to do one thing—to advise the German Jews in Prague to moderate their Austrophilism, for feeling was strong against them in Prague and there had been talk of wrecking the German newspaper offices. I myself gave similar advice to the more reasonable German Jews. I feared that anti-Jewish outbreaks might make a bad impression abroad and hamper my work. Thun promised to do what he could.

A few days later I wrote to draw his attention to several other matters. This was partly a tactical move to allay suspicion. Then I went to Vienna to talk things over with a number of political men and in order to give a finishing touch to my views on Austria. Among others I saw the former Prime Minister,

Dr. von Koerber, with whom I had often talked freely. This time our conversation lasted more than two hours and covered the whole situation. I inquired especially about some of the people at Court; and my chief question was, "If Austria wins, will Vienna be capable of carrying out the necessary reforms?" After much reflection and consideration of the persons involved, Koerber said decidedly: "No! Victory would strengthen the old system, and a new system under the young heir-apparent, the Archduke Charles Francis Joseph, would be no better than the old. The soldiers would have the upper hand after a victorious war and they would centralize and Germanize. It would be absolutism with parliamentary embellishments." "What about Berlin?" I asked. "Will Germany be wise enough to make her ally adopt reforms?" "Hardly," was Koerber's reply.

If necessary, I could quote from Koerber's experience of the Austrian Court and its surroundings many an anecdote to illustrate its incapacity and moral degeneracy. But his Memoirs will certainly not get lost. From a purely political point of view his diagnosis was all the more striking because he did not look upon the Hapsburg Dynasty, Vienna and Austria as I did or judge them from an ethical standpoint.

I hunted up also a number of my Austrian-German Parliamentary acquaintances. They merely confirmed what Koerber had said and what I had foreseen; but, before carrying out so grave a decision as that which I had taken, I wanted to hear for a last time what the Austrian-Germans themselves thought about Austria. I discovered, however, that even quiet and peaceable Germans had been turned against us by military influence. Several of them hinted at impending prosecutions and they, like Koerber, knew of the administrative and political schemes that were to be carried through after victory. Dr. Kramář (the leader of the Young Czech Party), I learned, was in for trouble. His pro-Russian policy was a thorn in the flesh of the Archduke Frederick, while pan-Slavism of every shade was a nightmare in Vienna and Budapest. I let some intimate acquaintance of Dr. Kramář know what I had heard.

DR. BENES

After this trip to Vienna the only thing was to get ready to start; and, at this point, I must say a word about Dr. Beneš.

Up to the war my personal knowledge of him was slight. I had noticed the articles he had sent from Paris and his other writings. In him I could detect the influence—albeit as yet undefined—of my own "Realist" philosophy, of French Positivism and of Marxism. After the outbreak of war he offered his services to my paper the "Čas," as a volunteer, and we met often in the "Čas" office. One day, before the regular conference at the office, he came to my house in an earnest mood. He had reached the conclusion that we could not remain passive spectators of the war but must do something. He was restless and wanted to get to work. I said: "Good. I am at it already." On the way to the office I confided in him and we agreed at once. I can remember the scene as we reached the top of the steps that lead down to the Elizabeth Bridge. I stopped, leant against the wooden railing and mused over the view of Prague, thoughts of our future passing through my mind, and the prophecy of Libuša—and of money, for money would be the sinews of political war. Dr. Beneš reckoned up his resources and promised at once several thousand crowns. He had enough to begin work abroad on his own account; and, in fact, he afterwards lived abroad at his own expense. To me, American friends sent what was necessary for my family and myself, nor did they forget us afterwards. Thus Beneš and I felt no anxiety about our own needs.

We discussed the situation at home, as well as in Austria and Germany and among the Allies, in a word, everything that mattered. We agreed upon our whole plan of campaign and also about our helpers at home and abroad. As long as possible Beneš was to remain at home and to organize communications with me after the fashion of the Russian Secret Societies. What I knew of this business was helpful; the rest we worked out—successfully, as I soon found after my departure. Before Beneš himself was obliged to leave Prague for good, he came twice to see me in Switzerland, once in February and once in April 1915.

Work with him was easy and efficient. There was little need to talk. Politically and historically he was so well trained that a word was enough. He thought out and executed plans in detail; for he was soon able to act by himself. As long as I was in Western Europe we met often and worked out everything minutely. By telegram and letter we kept up a lively correspondence. Later, when I could write or telegraph little from Russia, Japan and America, our thought and our work ran on parallel lines. As things developed, Beneš grew. While keeping strictly to our agreed policy, he dealt very independently with the main issues. He had great initiative and was an untiring worker. For both of us it was good that we had led what is called a "hard life." We had made our own way, worked ourselves up from poverty, which means acquiring practical experience, energy and boldness. This was true also of Štefánik, to whom I shall refer later. Twice as old and experienced as Beneš and Štefánik, I naturally took the lead, helped by the power of our common ideal and by our good understanding. Beneš and Štefánik soon realized that my knowledge of men, at home and abroad, was valuable. Indeed, there was no misunderstanding between us during my whole stay abroad, and our cooperation was exemplary. We were few— but neither were the Apostles legion. Clear heads, knowledge, firm wills, fearlessness of death give giant strength. Devoted helpers soon gathered round us, united with us by the cause. Good, strong men there were, too, in touch with us at home and, indeed, everywhere in the Bohemian lands, as our soldiers showed. Before leaving Prague I invited some of them to attend meetings at Dr. Bouček's house so as to initiate, in addition to Members of Parliament, others whom the police would not so readily suspect. As far as I can remember their names were Dr. Bouček; Dr. Veselý; Architect Pfeffermann; two journalists, Dušek and Herben; Dubský, a publisher; Dr. Šámal and, of course, Dr. Beneš. So arose our secret organization, the "Maffia," which was led at first by Beneš, Šámal and Rašin; and, after the arrest of Rašin and the departure of Beneš, by Šámal and others.

OUR TASK

To sum up. When war broke out we had to gauge the European situation, to estimate the strength of the two groups of belligerents, to judge, in the light of history, whither things were tending, to make up our minds and to act—above all, to act.

Inasmuch as my political outlook was derived from Palacký[1] and Havlíček, I, like our other political men, had sought for arguments to justify our connection with Austria; and, as may be seen from my studies on the evolution of Czech aspirations, I, like the leaders of our national revival, had been tormented by the problem of our being so small a nation. Attentive readers will, however, notice that, as in the case of our other political men, I began early to waver between loyalty and antagonism to Austria. Hence my constant pondering over the idea of revolution. In my study on Palacký's "Idea of the Czech People" I recognized the fundamental contradiction between the Czech idea and the Hapsburg Austrian idea. Unlike Palacký, I had already reached and expressed the conclusion that, if democratic and social movements should gain strength in Europe, we might hope to win independence. In later years, especially after 1907, the better I got to know Austria and the Hapsburg Dynasty, the more was I driven into opposition. This Dynasty which, in Vienna and in Austria, seemed so powerful, was morally and physically degenerate. Thus Austria became for me both a moral and a political problem.

In judging Austria morally as well as politically I differed

---

[1] Francis Palacky (1798-1876), the foremost historian of Bohemia and of the Czech people, and a leader in their national revival during the nineteenth century. So great was his influence that he is often styled "The Father of the Nation." He was the author of the much-quoted and misunderstood phrase that "If Austria did not exist she would have to be invented."

from the Young Czech Party and, subsequently, from the Czech Radicals. My view of what was called "positive politics" differed also from theirs. I thought we should take part in the Government not merely in order to reform the Constitution but also to infuse a Czech spirit into administrative practice. I used to speak of "unpolitical politics" and always insisted on the moral and educational side of public affairs. Seats in Parliament and strictly "political politics" did not seem to me to make up the whole of real democracy.

These views led to many a dispute. I do not now claim in self-defense that my opponents failed to understand me, for I confess that, at first, I was not clear or consistent and that I often made tactical mistakes. My opponents erred, however, and spurred me on by claiming that they were the better Czechs, by "patriotizing," as Havlíček use to say, whereas the real dispute was about the objects of patriotism and the substance of the Czech ideal. Love of country and of our people could be taken for granted. The question was how to apply this love. My opponents thought me too Socialist; and my religious ideas were repugnant to their Liberalism. For my part I could not agree with their German, Russian and Slav policies. My object was to de-Austrianize our people thoroughly while they were still in Austria. What our eventual form of government might be and to what foreign State we might ultimately be attached, seemed to me, as things then were, matters of secondary importance. I felt I was fighting against political and educational narrowness, backwardness and parochialism; and I fought simultaneously on two fronts—against "Vienna" and against "Prague." Czech Radicalism and its tactics seemed to me agitation rather than genuine warfare; and when the hour struck, when the situation of the world changed and fate compelled us to decide, it was not my opponents who took the decision and transformed it into action.

Having weighed Austria in the balance of my judgment and found her wanting, I had naturally been led on to the study and observation of Germany. As history shows, Austria, despite all differences, is bound up with Germany and with Germany alone. For the Germans, and especially the Prussians, I felt some respect, but I disagreed on principle with Bismarck and Bismarckianism. Under him, a blood-and-iron system had been established in home as well as in foreign affairs. I had been impressed by the cleverness of his moderation in 1866 when he merely excluded Austria from Germany and avoided humiliating "Vienna" in order to bind her all the more closely to Germany; yet he was dangerously mistaken in relying too much on Austria-Hungary, whom he despised—"Vienna" particularly—in his heart of hearts. In 1870-71 he had forsaken his tactics of 1866 and had blundered by annexing Alsace-Lorraine, however foolish the policy of Napoleon III may have been. Afterwards he had wavered between Russia and England. In this man of blood and iron there was too much of the old Machiavellian spirit.

After Bismarck's fall in 1890, the young Kaiser's "new course" had been worse than wavering. Politically and diplomatically it was short-sighted, indefinite, erratic and therefore untrustworthy. In colonial and maritime policy it overshot the mark. The young Emperor William disquieted not only the English but the Russians as well and, in general, showed an inadequate psychological perception of men and of peoples. Like Bismarck, he awaited from others obedience and submission rather than matter-of-fact agreement; and he also bound himself too tightly to Vienna. His rule was soon marked by the very opposite of the old Prussian simplicity. In alliance with the growing power of capitalism, the German Imperial dignity and German world-Imperialism took on an upstart, vulgar and morally dubious character—a tendency to which the universities succumbed. The philosophy and the policy of pan-Germanism ought to have been a warning to thoughtful public men; but they were not. The higher command of the army and the army at large, especially the officers, were pan-German. To the pan-German movement I constantly drew attention and urged our people to study modern world-politics so as to give a universal setting to our own policy. Indeed, it was opposition to pan-Germanism, to whose ends Vienna and Budapest were subservient, that caused me to take part in the Austro-Serbian conflict and, finally, in the World War.

I need hardly say that I did not look upon the Great War as a struggle between Germans and Slavs, although Austrian hatred of Serbia was the excuse for and, in part, the cause of it. The very fact that the German Imperial Chancellor, Herr von Bethmann-Hollweg, and the Emperor William as well as the Vienna and Budapest Governments, cast the blame for the war upon Russia and pan-Slavism, enjoined prudence in accepting so German a theory; nor could the arguments of German Professors like Lamprecht and Gothein convince me of its soundness. I saw more than this in the war. Viewed in historical perspective, pan-German Imperialism seemed to me a continuation of the age-long antagonism between Rome and Greece, West and East, Europe and Asia, and, later, between Rome and Byzance—an antagonism not merely between races but also between civilizations. Pan-Germanism and its Berlin-Baghdad scheme set a narrow nationalist and chauvinistic stamp upon the inherited Roman-German tradition; and two nationalist Empires, the German and the Austrian, which had emerged from the medieval Holy Roman Empire, joined hands for the conquest of the Old World. Not only were Germans and Slavs ranged against each other, but Germans against the West, the German against Western civilization, America being comprised in the West. On the German side stood the Magyars and the Turks (the Bulgarians were of less account), and the German aim was the subjugation of Europe, Asia, Africa and the Old World. The remainder of the world revolted and, for the first time, the New World—America—lent its aid to non-German Europe in repelling the German onslaught. Though America was neutral at first, her sympathies were with France and the Allies, whom she helped from the outset with raw materials and armaments. In the end, America joined in the war and contributed greatly to the final decision—though this could not be foreseen at the beginning. In this union of many nations under Western leadership lies proof that the war was not merely racial—that it was the first grand effort to give a unified organization to the whole world and to mankind. Racial aspirations were subordinated to the general cause of civilization and served its end. Naturally, interests overlapped in many places; but I need not repeat here what I have said on this subject in "The New Europe."

In virtue of our whole history our place was on the side of our Allies. Therefore, after analyzing the European situation and estimating the probable course of the war, I decided to oppose Austria actively, in the expectation that the Allies would win and that our espousal of their cause would bring us freedom.

The decision was not easy. I knew and felt how fateful it was; but one thing was clear—we could not be passive in so great an hour. No matter how good our right might be, it had to be upheld by deeds if it was to be real; and, since we could not withstand Austria at home, we must withstand her abroad. There our main task would be to win goodwill for ourselves and our national cause, to establish relations with the politicians, statesmen and Governments of the Allies, to organize united action among our people in Allied countries and, above all, to create an army from among Czech prisoners of war. My first message, taken to London by Mr. Voska, shows that I had thought out this military policy from the beginning. Very early in the war, from August 10 onwards, the Russians had captured a large number of Austrian soldiers—according to my reckoning some 80,000 men by the middle of September. Among them I concluded there would be from 12,000 to 15,000 Czechs who could be won over to our League in Russia, the "Družina"; and as the number of prisoners was constantly increasing, our future army would increase likewise. Indeed, the idea of forming an army abroad was so natural that Czechs outside Austria began everywhere to act spontaneously upon it.

Finally, it was necessary that our leadership abroad should

be in constant touch with home. The very existence of an organized struggle outside the country would naturally have a stimulating influence on home affairs. It might aggravate matters and demand sacrifices; but, without sacrifice, freedom and independence cannot be won.

Nor need I say that, in all this thinking and deciding upon the fight against Austria, there rang through the depths of my soul the questions: Are we ripe for the struggle, are we mature for freedom, can we administer and preserve an independent State made up of the Bohemian Lands, Slovakia and considerable non-Czech and non-Slovak minorities? Are there enough of us so trained politically as to understand the true meaning of the war and the task of our people in it? In this world-historic hour do we grasp its significance? Are we again fit to act, really to act? Shall we make good, once for all, the disaster that overwhelmed us as a nation in the Battle of the White Mountain three centuries ago? Can we vanquish in ourselves the influence of Austria and of the centuries of subjection to her? Is the hour of fulfilment of Comenius' Testament at hand: "I, too, believe before God that, when the storms of wrath have passed, to thee shall return the rule over thine own things, O Czech people!"

Before starting, I drafted for Dr. Beneš and his associates a scheme of anti-Austrian policy at home. Taking account of how the war might go, I set forth in detail what was to be done according to the turn of events. This draft was afterwards completed by correspondence and in conversation with Dr. Beneš, in Switzerland. In war—revolution, too, is war—courage and determination are not everything; there must be also a well-thought-out plan, the coordination of all forces and unified leadership.

CHAPTER II

ROMA AETERNA

(DECEMBER 1914–JANUARY 1915)

ON December 17, 1914, I left Prague for Italy by way of Vienna. I had decided to go first to Italy in order to find out what people were thinking in Rome and whether Italy would remain neutral. Then I meant to go to Switzerland.

I was not without fear that the police in Prague, or on the Austro-Italian frontier, would put obstacles in my way, though luckily their hands were tied to some extent by my possession of a passport, made out before the war, that was valid for three years and for all countries. There was also a report in the newspapers that my daughter Olga was ill; as I took her with me this was an explanation of my journey. So things went pretty smoothly. On the frontier an official did make some difficulty and inquired by telegram from Prague whether he should let me pass; but before he could have got an answer the train for Venice would have left. Therefore, claiming for the first time my rights as a Member of Parliament, I took my place in the train and left.

From Venice, where I met one of our newspaper men, M. Hlaváč—who was extraordinarily well informed on all Viennese and Austrian matters and especially on the activities of Count Czernin, the Austro-Hungarian Minister at Bucharest —I went on to Florence and reached Rome on December 22. During the journey I thought of my first visit to Italy in 1876 when I had seen all the larger Northern and Central cities and had been impressed by the many memorial inscriptions bearing witness to the tyranny of Austria. Italy had then been to me a museum and a school of art; I had lived in the Renaissance. Later on, I had lived in Classical Antiquity though I had been equally able to enter into early Christianity. The Italian Renaissance had attracted me by reason of the remarkable synthesis of Christianity and Classical Antiquity which it offered—a synthesis that really dates from the very beginnings of the Church. Though Christianity was antagonistic to the traditions of Antiquity it had to carry them on and to preserve them in spite of itself. I am more and more convinced that the Emperor Augustus was really the first Pope. Or think of Thomas Aquinas—Aristotle's Janus-like countenance. The "Reception of Roman Law," of which so much has been written and said, was preceded and accompanied by the reception of classical thought and culture. The strange transition from pagan Rome to Catholicism may be traced in the plastic arts, especially in architecture, e.g. in the Roman Pantheon. This ocular proof impressed me more deeply than the arguments of modern theologians who draw from literary sources their accounts of the Classical-Catholic synthesis.

And Catholicism itself, the Church and the Papacy, the grandiose continuation and culmination of the Roman Empire, is the work not of the Romans alone but also of their successors, the Italians. Catholicism is a product of the Roman spirit, though Jesuitism, the basis of neo-Catholicism, came from Spain. Italy has contributed, besides, notable moral and religious individualities standing more or less apart from the Church, like St. Francis of Assisi, Savonarola, Giordano Bruno and Galileo.

Nor do the later periods of Italian thought lack interest. I was attracted especially by the genius of Vico, his philosophy of society and of history, his psychological insight into the real social forces and their workings, his grasp of the spirit of Roman Law and of Roman civilization—again and always a synthesis of Catholicism and Classical Antiquity, for Vico was a priest as well as a philosopher of history and the first of modern sociologists. Indeed, Catholicism, with its long ecclesiastical tradition, led to the philosophical writing of history; and Vico's predecessor was Bossuet.

Politically, the rebirth and unfication of Italy commanded our sympathies; and, in point of time, the period of the Risorgimento coincided with that of our Czech national revival. In Italy likewise there arose the serious problem of the relationship between Church and State. Many a powerful Italian thinker racked his brains over the fate of the Papacy and the part it might play in relation to national unity. In this respect Rosmini and Gioberti, both priests and men of keen mind, interested me—as did their opponent, Mamiani, who ended by adapting himself to their ideas—far more than the Italian disciples of Kant and Hegel; and in all three of them can be felt the pulse of Italy and the nature of her problems after the French Revolution. At length Italy was unified, in despite of the Papacy. For her, and not for her alone, the year 1870 is memorable. In July the Vatican Council proclaimed the new dogma of Papal Infallibility; a few weeks later an Italian army occupied the Papal territory which, by a plebiscitary vote of 153,000 against 1,507, threw in its lot with Italy. No Catholic Government raised a finger on behalf of the Papal State—in such fashion fell the Temporal Power of the Church and of its theocratic Head, Pius IX. Nor could his successor, Leo XIII, save the Middle Ages, notwithstanding his revival of Scholasticism and of the study of Thomas Aquinas. My hope that other theocratic States might fall in their turn was naturally and logically linked with this world-historic event.

It is no accident that the most recent Italian philosophy should have turned so strongly towards sociology and the study of social phenomena. Apart from a philosophy of history based upon a long and rich tradition, the substance of modern Italian thought reflects the problem of a growing population—a problem which has necessitated a colonial policy and has stimulated the industrialization of the North, the intellectual awakening of the Center and the South, an increasing consciousness of national and political importance and the practical unification of the country. To me, moreover, Italy symbolized the question of revolution in various forms, particularly in those of secret societies and political outrages. On this subject Mazzini and his philosophy are a living storehouse of ideas.

Somewhat unsystematically, my study of modern Italian literature had begun with Leopardi—on account of his pessimism which had interested me from early youth as a psychological problem of the period. From Leopardi to Manzoni was but a little way, though Manzoni—a follower of Rosmini—preached Christianity and both Leopardi and Manzoni were Romanticists and parents of the newer tendencies in Italian poetry. Then, with a jump, I came to D'Annunzio, who revealed to me the decadent movement and its relationship to Catholicism; and, however anachronistic it may seem that I should have returned from D'Annunzio to Carducci, there is an organic link between them, for Carducci's blasphemous "Hymn to Satan" belongs naturally to what I call "decadence." On this matter I shall have more to say when I deal with France. Here I would only point out that D'Annunzio's political activity is in line with his literary work, for it is a vain attempt to fill his decadent spiritual emptiness. The transition from Romanticism to Realism and subsequently to Futurism and other phenomena of "revolt" are, on the other hand, characteristic of the spiritual crisis in the whole of Europe, not in Italy alone. In Italy, as elsewhere, physicians have arisen to offer remedies for this literary anarchy, some prescribing a return to Dante and others to Leopardi— physicians and patients alike obviously suffering from equal impotence.

All these things I pondered, in much fuller detail, as I was weighing in Rome the question whether Italy would or could join Austria and Germany against the Allies. My answer, dictated by my own philosophy of Italian history and civilization, was always: "It is not possible."

WORK IN ROME

In Rome there was a chance of getting news and of establishing political relationships. Diplomatic representatives of all countries were there, in many cases two from each country, one being accredited to the Vatican. First of all I approached the Serbian Minister, Lyuba Mihailovitch, and the Southern Slav politicians. Some Southern Slav members of the Austrian Parliament had already joined other well-known Southern Slavs abroad, and their numbers were constantly growing. I was the only Czech Member of Parliament outside the country —to my regret, because a Member of Parliament is thought, in the West, to be a more serious politician than a professor. Therefore I did a thing which I should never have dreamed of doing at home, or had there been no war. I had visiting cards printed as follows: "Professor T. G. Masaryk, Czech Member of Parliament, President of the Czech Progressive Group in the Austrian Reichsrat." Mestrovitch, the Southern Slav sculptor, who was then in Rome, was also a political asset. The Italians had recognized and esteemed him as. an artist since the Venice Exhibition in the spring of 1914. Working beside him were Dr. L. Voinovitch and Professor Popovitch. Among Southern Slav members of the Austrian or Hungarian Diets and Parliaments were Dr. Trumbitch and Dr. Nikola Stoyanovitch, while Supilo was in London. By a lucky chance he had been in Switzerland when war broke out and had stayed abroad. Of the Slovenes, Mr. Goritchar, a former Austro-Hungarian Consular official, was in Rome as well as Dr. Županitch of the Belgrade University Library. So as to elude the Austrian spies, we met late at night at the Serbian Legation, discussed the whole position and agreed to work closely together. The idea of a corridor between Slovakia and Croatia interested the Southern Slavs in Rome, though I thought that, at best, it should only be mooted as a tactical move. Several Southern Slavs took it up, but Trumbitch was reserved and wished it to be left to the Czechs.

At that time an agitation was beginning in Italy about Dalmatia, "Our Dalmatia," as it was called, though the Italians themselves, as distinguished from the Austrian Italians or Irredentists, paid little heed to it. They thought rather of Asia, the African Colonies, Trieste and Trent—and of Trieste more than of Trent. I advised the Southern Slavs to start careful counter-propaganda. Notwithstanding the difficulties, which were serious, they could probably have made headway among a section of the politicians and of the people; for I noticed that the people were influenced less by Imperialism than by hereditary dislike of Austria. Against the Germans of Germany their feeling was not so strong, though it was affected by the German violation of Belgium. Imperialism does not come from the people. Its vanguard and its main forces are everywhere monarchs, generals, bankers, merchants, professors, journalists and "intellectuals." Nor ought it to be forgotten that, in 1913, Italy twice resisted an Austrian temptation to assail Serbia. But many Italians looked upon the war as something that concerned the French, the Russians and Germany, not Italy; and I often heard the argument, which Nitti repeats, that the war was a struggle between Germanism and Slavdom. This argument could be used either in support of neutrality or in favor of joining the Germans against the Slavs in the cause of "Our Dalmatia."

Though, as I have said, I envied the Southern Slavs for having so many political men abroad, I saw even in Rome that dissensions might spring up among them. They all had one program—the unification of the Southern Slav, or Serb, Croat and Slovene race—but they had not worked it out in detail. This was clear from all they said, and the influence of the old quarrel between Serbs and Croats could be felt. The Serbian Minister strongly favored unity in good understanding with the Croats; yet it seemed to me that many Croats were over-insistent upon the superiority of their culture and forgot that what mattered chiefly then and in the whole war was military and political leadership. As my Southern Slav friends knew, I thought their unity should be achieved under the political leadership of Serbia, and imagined it as the result of a consistent and gradual unification of the Southern Slav Lands, each of which had its own culture and administrative peculiarities.

In December 1914 Count Tisza, the Hungarian Prime Minister, praised the Croat troops of Austria-Hungary for their "true-hearted bravery in the fight for the common Fatherland." Against him the Southern Slavs in Rome issued a protest, which was published in the "Corriere della Sera." It was signed by "The Croatian Committee," this collective name being used in order to preclude the reprisals which the authorities in Vienna and Budapest would have taken against the families of individual signatories. In those days the Southern Slavs also talked of an "Adriatic Legion" to act under the guidance of a "Southern Slav Committee." Indeed, in January 1915 a "Southern Slav Committee" issued a number of declarations. Thus, in organization at least, the Southern Slavs were ahead of us; and I used this circumstance to urge our people in Prague to send some of our journalists and Members of Parliament to join me abroad.

PERSONAL RELATIONSHIPS

Neither in Rome nor afterwards did I waste time on people who merely held official positions. Though at first our people at home took it amiss if I failed to visit this or that Minister or Member of Parliament, I knew the value of the men who were politically active in various countries and always sought to ascertain on the spot their real influence. In Rome I saw the Polish Professor Loret, and also the Germanophil Danish writer, Rasmussen, but I had little contact with the Russian Embassy except through some of its officials and the military attaché, for the Russian Ambassador had no influence either in Rome or in his own country. M. de Giers, the Montenegrin, was more interesting. M. Svatkovsky, with whom I had got into touch while still at Prague, I have already mentioned. Though I had known him for years I had not worked much with him as I did not wish to damage his official position as the representative of the Russian Official Telegraph Agency for Austria-Hungary and the Balkans. When I returned from

Germany in the autumn of 1914, he had sent me a trustworthy messenger through whom I let him know that I should be in Rome towards the middle of December; and he was waiting for me there when I arrived. As his name shows, his family was originally Czech. He was a descendant of the Svatkovskys of Dobrohosht who took part in the Bohemian insurrection of 1618. After the confiscation of their estates, his ancestors emigrated to Saxony and thence to Russia. Hence his sincere interest in our affairs. The Russians had been defeated in East Prussia, and there were rumors of treason in the army and in the Russian administration. Svatkovsky knew many details of this business (the notorious Masoyedoff affair) and his keen criticism of official Russia and of the army surprised me. He shared my views of Russia and also my fears. With the Russophilism of our people in Prague he did not agree; and he aptly remarked that a Russian Grand Duke, installed as ruler in the Royal Castle there, would mean champagne and French mistresses. Svatkovsky settled presently in Switzerland where we saw each other often; and he followed me to Paris afterwards.

We went quietly over the whole situation. I found that I could trust him and therefore I informed him of my plans. He reported to St. Petersburg not, or not exclusively, through the Russian Ambassador of whom he thought little. Finally he compiled a complete memorandum setting forth my views and plans and sent it to St. Petersburg. Thus the Russian Foreign Minister, Sazonof, received a second report from me (January 1915), the first having been sent through Seton-Watson in October 1914. In point of fact I kept in constant touch with representatives of Russia; and the closeness of my relations with them from the outset is one reason why I did not hasten to Russia, although our own people, there and elsewhere, who knew nothing of these relations, thought I kept away because I was a "Westerner" and anti-Russian. The truth was that the whole position obliged me to remain in the West, where we had no political relationships and had to make people understand our ideas. Before leaving home I had recognized that the fate of Europe would be decided in the West, not in Russia; and the longer I stayed in the West the clearer did this become.

With the French I did not establish permanent relations while in Rome. I thought I would leave that until I had studied the position in Paris, and I imagined that France had been better informed of our affairs in former years than proved to be the case. The British Ambassador, Sir James Rennell Rodd, I saw occasionally and he forwarded letters for me to London. Prince Bülow, the German Ambassador, I did not see though a meeting with him had previously been arranged. I should have been glad to talk to an official German public man, but Bülow begged to be excused, saying that he had no time. He was then trying to win Italy over to the side of Germany and Austria. He offered the Italians parts of Austria—and Vienna got angry. Indeed, Vienna was suspicious of the whole relationship between Italy and Germany.

Italians in official positions I did not approach. Italy was neutral and, as I was obliged to assume that the Austrian and perhaps also the German Embassies were watching me, I had no right to compromise anybody. One episode I remember. When I visited the Italian historian, Professor Lumbroso, who was publishing the "Rivista di Roma," he was taken aback, for he heard that I had been knocked on the head in Prague at the beginning of the war and, as a conscientious historian, he had published an article on my death. "You will live long," he said.

Rome gladdened me. The result of my observations and information was that, for the time being, the Italians would remain neutral, and that, if they should march, it would be rather against the Austrians than with them. Against England, Italy would not fight and with France she had a secret agreement, dating from November 1902, that pledged her to neutrality in case of war. In this war Germany had hardly acted according to the defensive spirit of the Triple Alliance since she had declared war upon France and Russia; and Austria had been positively disloyal towards Italy by ignoring Clause VII of the Triple Alliance which bound her to inform Italy of the action to be taken against Serbia—a characteristic display of Austrian contempt for the Italians.   Therefore Italy had declared her neutrality as early as July 31, 1914.   Moreover, her expedition to Valona had seemed to foreshadow active intervention on the side of the Entente, though it foreshadowed also a dispute about the Balkans, especially with the Southern Slavs.

By December 1914 and January 1915 a strong movement had begun for Italian participation in the war.   Giolitti, the former Prime Minister, was attacked for favoring Germany and Austria.   In reality he was opposed to war because he believed that Austria would make the necessary concessions without it; but he was not for peace at any price, particularly if Austria would not give way.   I thought it unlikely that Austria would give way—people in Vienna were too puffed up.   They felt no fear of Italy against whom the Austrian military clique, with General Conrad von Hoetzendorf, the Chief of General Staff, at its head, had long wanted war, regardless of the Triple Alliance. It had taken Aehrenthal all his time to defend himself against Conrad, as the Italians well knew.

THE POSITION OF THE VATICAN

The bearing of the Vatican had been at first decidedly pro-Austrian and pro-German.   Statements were circulated by the Austro-Hungarian Embassies to the Vatican and to the Quirinal that Pope Benedict XV personally favored Austria and Germany against Serbia.   Count Pálffy, the Austro-Hungarian Ambassador to the Vatican, of whom I had trustworthy information, gave it out that Austria, as a Catholic State *par excellence,* was the protectress of Catholicism against Orthodoxy and that both the Pope and the Cardinal Secretary of State approved unconditionally of Austrian action.   Austria-Hungary was, indeed, the only great Catholic State in Europe, and it was natural that the Vatican should side with her.   Besides, the close personal relationship between the Papacy and the Emperor Francis Joseph was a weighty factor.   True, the Vatican knew

that Austrian Catholicism was a "morass" (an opinion which
the chief Catholic authorities in Germany shared); but it put
its trust in German Catholicism whose vitality and political
power would, it hoped, control the Austrian and the Hungarian
Catholics. The German Center or Catholic Party and, in
particular, its principal leader, Erzberger, certainly played a
conspicuous part from the very beginning of the war by propaganda and political initiative.

Yet Vatican policy in the war could not be determined solely
by regard for Austria-Hungary and Germany. The Catholics
in other belligerent countries had to be taken into account.
Statistically there were more Catholics on the side of the Entente
than on that of the Central Powers. Therefore the conduct of
the Vatican was bound to be cautious, that is to say, indefinite.
Hence the continual disputes among Catholic politicians as to its
real opinion. For the same reason the Vatican press and even
Cardinal Gasparri, the Secretary of State, had constantly to
"explain" Papal utterances. Not that Vatican policy was decided
only by numbers. When the South American Republics turned
against the Central Powers, less weight was assigned to them than
to the Catholic nations and States of Europe. Especially delicate
was the position of the Vatican in relation to France. During
the war some French Bishops spoke out against the Vatican and
the Pope alike; nor was the position easier after Italy had joined
the Entente. By degrees the Vatican toned down its Austrophilism—a point on which Belgium and the influence of Cardinal
Mercier had some effect. In general, the Vatican may be said
to have specialized in attempts to make peace, and to have
directed Catholic propaganda in all belligerent countries towards
an early cessation of hostilities. As things then were, this
proved advantageous to the Germans, particularly in England and
America.

But, on both sides, the standpoints of political Catholic
leaders were national rather than religious. The German
Catholics sent a memorandum to Rome early in September
1914; the French Catholics answered it early in 1915, and the

Germans issued a rejoinder. Outwardly the Vatican kept up a certain degree of impartiality, chiefly by evading positive issues and contenting itself with general observations upon its divine mission. It is necessary to distinguish between the official policy of the Vatican and the personal opinions of this or that Pope or of the individual Cardinals and Prelates who work in its various departments. Throughout the whole war I watched the Vatican very keenly. Presently we established relations with it; and, in conducting them, I never forgot that "qui mange du Pape, en meurt."

In Rome I thought at times of returning for a while to Prague in order to put heart into our people and again to discuss with them our whole plan in the light of what I had learned in Italy. I wished also to store my most valuable books in a safe place, for I did not doubt that the police would ransack my home if I stayed abroad. To this end I drafted a letter assuring the police that they would find nothing political among my papers. At all events I made while in Rome provisional arrangements for an escape from Trieste into Italy. But I was not destined to go back. On January 11, 1915, I left Rome for Geneva after having visited my beloved Pantheon for a last time.

CHAPTER III

IN ROUSSEAU'S BIRTHPLACE

(GENEVA. JANUARY–SEPTEMBER 1915)

IN Rome I had still been getting my bearings. Now, in Switzerland, systematic work was to begin. Bordering on friendly and hostile countries, and especially on Austria, Switzerland suited my purpose well. Thence it was fairly easy to communicate with Prague. Political refugees from many countries sought asylum on Swiss soil and I could meet and confer with them. Enemy newspapers and the whole range of German and Austrian publications, political and military, were available; and, naturally, also our own press—a great advantage since it enabled us to follow the course of things at home and throughout Austria. This was invaluable in our fight against Austrian and Magyar propaganda. At Geneva and Zurich all the necessary books, reviews and maps were to be had; and I needed quantities of them for my friends as well as for myself. Later on, in London and even in America, I got what I wanted from Switzerland. For purposes of precise political observation, I was accustomed to supplement the reading of daily newspapers by the study of political and historical literature. In fact, I have always kept in touch with the literatures of the principal countries so as to comprehend their political development in the light of their material and mental life. At Geneva I soon collected quite a respectable war library.

In Switzerland, moreover, there were colonies of Czechs, whereas in Italy there had been none. We had to tell them of the situation at home, to bring together those scattered in various Swiss towns and to organize them systematically for joint action. At Geneva we soon found vigorous helpers and, among them,

Dr. Sychrava who took over a heavy journalistic task—all the heavier because no contributions came from Prague and he was almost single-handed.   In addition, he superintended communications with Prague.   From Count Lützow, the well-known Czech nobleman who was then living at Montreux, I held aloof so as not to compromise him.   But he knew what I was doing and agreed with it, as mutual friends afterwards told me in England. Especially did he agree with my Russian policy.

Hardly had I settled in Geneva when news of my son Herbert's illness came unexpectedly from my family in Prague; and, on March 15, a telegram announcing his death.   Thus, like thousands of families at home, we were stricken.   He was clean and honorable in rare degree, a poet-painter whose ideal of beauty was simplicity.   Healthy he was, too, and strong through physical exercise.   He had done all he could to avoid fighting for Austria and yet found death through the war.   Typhus, caught from some Galician refugees whom he was helping, killed him—a case for fatalists!   My old Clerical opponents did not fail to send me from Prague their coarse and malicious anonymous letters. "The finger of God!" they said.   To me it seemed rather an injunction not to abate or to grow weary in my efforts.

Our first and most urgent task was to organize "subterranean" work, the sending of messengers to and from Prague.   It went well, for we all worked with a will.   I threw myself heartily into it.   The task was at once technical and psychological. Very onerous was the work of composing ciphers and different keys to them so that they could be changed at intervals.   M. Baráček, an engineer who was with us at Geneva, invented a special ciphering machine.   We invented, too, or made up, all sorts of things in which letters, coded and otherwise, could be hidden.   For instance, a skilful joiner made chests and boxes with sides in which a good number of newspapers and letters could be stowed away; and the police never found us out, notwithstanding their vigilance.   Our rule was to do nothing usual —no false bottoms, nothing hidden in boots or clothes.   Every dodge had to be new.   It was harder to choose and train men.

Each messenger had to be instructed according to his talents and his degree of education, so that he might be equal to emergencies. In such matters trouble often arises because messengers do not stick to their instructions but improvise thoughtlessly or grow careless. It was through imprudence of this sort that Dr. Kramář [1] was compromised. He and, soon afterwards, Dr. Rašin [2] were arrested, together with members of the staff of my newspaper, the "Čas," Madame Beneš and my daughter Alice. I was particularly anxious about Dr. Beneš. It would never have done for him to be caught. He was a member of our subterranean organization, and a Social Democrat; and it irked him to see his Party taking so small a share in the work abroad. So, unknown to me, he took it into his head to send a messenger to its leader, Dr. Soukup, by way of stirring up the Party. The police caught the messenger. It was a bad business for us, as we had to begin all over again with new methods. The police, too, had become smarter, so that we were obliged to be more wide-awake than ever.

To some extent we communicated with Prague "legally," by post. In the early days, at least, non-political letters got through. Thus, in a form agreed upon, I was able to hint that, in certain circumstances, I should come home. True, Dr. Beneš had telegraphed at the end of January that this would be impossible, and Machar [3] sent me word that I should be executed on crossing the frontier. Friends in Prague got wind of a telegram sent from Rome by Baron Macchio, the Austro-Hungarian Ambassador to the Quirinal, charging me with treasonable activities in Rome. Macchio had disliked me ever since my fight against Aehrenthal in 1909–10, when he was a Permanent Under-Secretary at the Ministry for Foreign Affairs. To keep me

---

[1] The leader of the Young Czech Party and a strong Nationalist. He was condemned to death but not executed, and afterwards became the first Prime Minister of the Czechoslovak Republic.

[2] A prominent public man of outstanding financial ability. As Finance Minister he carried through the reform of Czechoslovak finance.

[3] J. S. Machar (born 1864), a realist Czech poet-philosopher of strong originality, whose writings have had marked influence upon the younger generation.

informed, our people at home made clever use of the advertisement columns of the newspapers, including the German newspapers. Dr. Beneš even managed to come twice to see me in Switzerland for a few days. Professor Hantich, M. Habrman (a Member of Parliament) and Dr. Třebický came also.

Another aspect of our task was to create a single organization for our people in all Allied countries. In this progress was slow, because correspondence was difficult. As time went on I managed to visit our principal centers myself or to send emissaries to confirm written instructions. We felt the need for a journal to guide and inform all our colonies as a substitute for voluminous correspondence. Friendly newspapers helped us to some extent by publishing news and interviews—as did hostile newspapers by their denunciations and indictments—and our people everywhere understood what was wanted. At Berne they formed a Central Executive Committee of Czech Societies in Switzerland (January 3, 1915). In Paris, the weekly papers "Na Zdar" and "L'Indépendance Tchèque" were published, and soon afterwards the "National Council of Czech Colonies" was formed. (It must, however, be confessed that these Paris undertakings did harm as well as good. They were short-lived and led to strife. There were, naturally, personal and party differences in all our colonies, in Paris more than elsewhere; but there was also abundant goodwill.)

In the United States a Congress of the "Czech National Association in America" met on January 13 at Cleveland, and formed a center for the efforts of our American colony. At Moscow the first Congress of the delegates of Czechoslovak Societies in Russia was held, and a General Association of those Societies founded. Our people organized themselves likewise in Serbia and Bulgaria. In Germany, where they were more numerous than elsewhere, they could not, of course, form a militant organization.

Everywhere, too, plans were approximately the same, opposition to Austria-Hungary taking the form of enlistment in the Allied armies, though the statements of our political aims were often very radical and ill-conceived. Some of them, for instance, claimed that not only should Vienna and Austria be included in Czechoslovak territory but also the whole of former Silesia and other regions which had once belonged for a time to the Bohemian Crown. It never seemed to occur to these enthusiastic politicians that a Czechoslovak State thus constituted would be mainly German. As long as these fantastic ideas were confined to our own people they did little harm, but harm was done when they were laid before Governments and statesmen.

Nevertheless, towards the summer of 1915 the process of creating a "single front" was practically completed. My authority was promptly recognized on every hand without much difficulty. We established, too, a press with a single policy. On May 1 our friend Professor Denis brought out in Paris his periodical "La Nation Tchèque." On June 15 Pavlu published the "Čechoslovák" in St. Petersburg, while Švihovsky issued the "Čechoslovan" at Kieff. Finally we had the "Československá Samostatnost" (Czechoslovak Independence), edited by Dr. Sychrava, which appeared, from August 22 onwards, in the little French town of Annemasse. This was the official organ of our whole movement abroad. In America the Czechs and Slovaks had their own separate journals; and, in Russia, a Slovak paper was published in May 1917. Later on, in Siberia, there were Czech as well as Slovak papers. In response to my constant demands that some Members of Parliament and journalists should come from Bohemia to help us, M. Dürich, a Member of Parliament, arrived at the end of May. I had met him in the Vienna Reichsrat. He was quite a good parliamentarian, speaking French and Russian but not strong enough politically for the situation now facing us. He came saying that Dr. Kramář had selected him specially to represent our nation in Russia. To this I had no objection as long as we were agreed upon a program. He was for the Tsar and even for the Orthodox Church, like so many of our Russophils who awaited salvation from Russia. But among our fellows at Geneva his inert pro-Russianism and his failure to take part in our work made bad blood. They

reproached him for not hastening to Russia and, in order to avoid
an open quarrel, I had more than once to act as peacemaker.   At
the Russian Legation in Berne I noticed that they were corresponding with St. Petersburg about his journey, though they said
nothing of it to me; and I was struck by the delay in arranging it.

SLAV DIFFERENCES

In Switzerland, ties with the Allies grew stronger.   Above
all we gained many new friends among the Swiss themselves,
the French Swiss in the first instance but among the Germans
too   I was soon in touch with the press and the universities
and, in this respect, my daughter Olga was very helpful.   Our
news from Prague contained valuable information, particularly
on military matters—a reason for establishing regular contact
with the Italian Legation.   Cooperation with the Southern Slavs
continued.   We let each other know what was being done, took
counsel and often acted together.   From all Yugoslav lands,
public men, political and other representatives, came to Geneva;
and in London a "Yugoslav Committee" was formed on May 1,
1915, as the organ of the Southern Slavs of Austria-Hungary.
This Committee published a "Bulletin Yugoslave" in Paris and
laid memoranda before the French Government and the British
Parliament.   The Serbians of Serbia produced their own journal,
"La Serbie," at Geneva, where there was also a Serbian Press
Bureau.   The progressive Montenegrins had an organ of their
own, while King Nicholas issued his "Glas Crnogorca" at Neuilly
near Paris.   When the Young Yugoslavs issued their national
program, I wrote a preface to it.

Old acquaintances, among them Professor Božo Markovitch
of Belgrade (who had been an important witness in the Friedjung
trial), were in Geneva, and Supilo himself came for a time on his
return from Petrograd, whither he had gone early in 1915 to
plead the Southern Slav cause with official Russia.   Of that
journey I shall have more to say.   Through these friends we got
news of our people in Serbia; and from Paunkovitch, the Com-

mander of the Serbian camp for prisoners of war, we heard what was going on and how many of our fellows had been taken prisoners by Serbia. I thought of going to see them, but circumstances kept me at Geneva. The Serbian Consul provided us all with the necessary passports and visas for France and elsewhere.

As Bulgarian propaganda was pretty strong in Switzerland, keen disputes soon arose between Bulgarians and Serbians, partly on account of the Russian "Cadet" leader, Milyukoff, who sided with Bulgaria where he had lived after his expulsion from pre-Duma Russia. Though I disapproved of Bulgarian policy (since the Bulgarians claimed not only the whole of Macedonia but Old Serbia and the territory of the so-called Bulgarian Morava) I took no part in this dispute; for it should not be forgotten that the Allies had promised those regions to the Bulgars when they wanted to win them over. This Allied policy, directed against a Serbia who was bleeding for the Allied cause, was much discussed by my Southern Slav and English friends.

Disputes arose too among individual Southern Slavs and their organizations, the Serbians holding fast to a Great Serbian centralized program, most of the Croats and Slovenes to a Federal program, and not a few Croats to a Great Croatian program. All alike proclaimed national unity in "Yugoslavia" as their object, but that comprehensive term covered very different and often hazy ideas. There were, besides, some special shades and tendencies of opinion, one of them being pro-Austrian, even in Serbia as well as in Croatia.

M. Svatkovsky, who was already in Switzerland, kept me in constant touch with Russia; and though I maintained relations with the Russian Legation in Berne they were unimportant. I corresponded, however, with the leaders of the Czech colony in Russia; and, at the beginning of February, one of them, M. Koniček, a member of the first Czech deputation to the Tsar, came to me by way of Paris ostensibly for the purpose of offering me the leadership in Russia. I "sized him up" at once. He was one of our many political tyros in Russia, a thoroughgoing partisan of the reactionary "Black Hundreds." Even in public meetings he began his speeches with the words, "Little Father, the Tsar, sends you his greetings." That put him out of court at once with all our colonies, in Paris, in Geneva, and afterwards in America. Many took him for a Russian official agent. He soon fell foul of me and began to intrigue in the grossest fashion. It was he who had dominated the "National Council of the Czechoslovak Colonies" in Paris, and had founded the "Indépendance Tchèque." He brought trouble enough upon us and aroused French ill-will by his reactionary pan-Slavism, though he gained several adherents, some of whom were guilty of conduct so excessive that they were taken for Austrian *agents provocateurs*.

Toward the middle of April 1915, when our organization was sufficiently advanced, I went for a short time to Paris and London. From our colonies in both cities I had received news of political and personal bickerings, and my friends, Seton-Watson and Steed, urged me to come for political reasons. In Paris I discussed everything with Professor Denis and saw many members of our colony. Peace was made. In London it was comparatively easy to settle the dissensions, but I stayed longer there so as to work out a memorandum for Sir Edward Grey and for political circles generally, defining more exactly what I had discussed with Seton-Watson in Holland. I laid stress upon our historical right to independence and vindicated our whole undertaking. This was the more necessary because a number of English political men were inclined to conceive the future settlement of Europe on racial lines rather than to take account of historical rights. I criticized also the allotment of a considerable part of Dalmatia to Italy. Of this I had heard something in London as well as in Geneva and Paris, for the negotiations between Italy, England, France and Russia had been long drawn out.

On the situation in Germany I got trustworthy information in London. There I saw the Russian Ambassador, Count Benckendorff, to whom I gave a number of documents and explained our position and that of Austria. He seemed to be under the influence of the Treaty with Italy; at any rate he could not trust himself to make any promise, and what he said showed that Russia had no definite Slav policy. This was no news to me, but Benckendorff's bearing confirmed it. He advised me to go as soon as possible to St. Petersburg in order to see Sazonof and, particularly, the Grand Duke Nicholas, who was apparently omnipotent.

On the way. back to Geneva I made another short stay in Paris and completed what I had begun there. With Professor Denis I considered the outlook in all Slav countries and the world situation on the basis of his book, "La Guerre," which I had sent to Prague as soon as it appeared. On the whole we were agreed, though Denis differed from me on the very important question of Constantinople.

In Paris, too, I met the Southern Slavs. Among them the most important was M. Vesnitch, the Serbian Minister, whom I had known as a student. He was our true and helpful ally throughout the war. We discussed of course the concessions in Dalmatia which the Allies, including Russia, had made to the Italians; for, even in Paris, Slav interests were long driven into the background by the desire to win over Italy. On this account I did not approach the French Foreign Minister, M. Delcassé, as I thought he might not like it; besides, I knew that he would not last long. He resigned, indeed, on October 13, 1915.

ITALIAN ACTION

Yet I was delighted when Italy cut loose from the Triple Alliance on May 4, 1915, and declared war against Austria on May 23. The moral, political and military significance of her action was all the greater because the Allied position in the field was then unfavorable. True—and this was characteristic of the Italian political standpoint—Italy did not declare war against Germany until August 28, 1916; and the Austro-Hungarian

Croats and Slovenes were sorely disquieted by the terms of the Treaty of London which brought Italy into the war.

Prince Bülow, as I have said, had tried to hold Italy back; and, under German pressure, Austria-Hungary had suggested terms for the maintenance of Italian neutrality. On March 27, 1915, the Austro-Hungarian Foreign Minister, Count Burián, had offered Italy the Italian-speaking part of Tyrol, but on April 9 the Italian Foreign Minister, Baron Sonnino, demanded much more and especially territory inhabited by Austrian Germans and Slavs. Before the Austro-Hungarian counter-proposals were made, on May 10, the Treaty of London had been signed on April 26. It promised, among other concessions, about half of Dalmatia to Italy. In quarters that were quite well informed it was said at the time that the German Emperor had compromised the position of Germany and Austria-Hungary by his unbridled personal criticism of the King of Italy; and I learned afterwards that he had in fact insulted the King by a curt peremptory telegram calling upon him to fulfil his obligations as an Ally.

In following the course of the war from Switzerland, the articles contributed to the "Journal de Genève" by the famous Swiss military writer, Colonel Feyler, were a great help. I was still tormented by the question that had worried me at the outset—whether the war would really last as long as I had reckoned. At the beginning of 1915 a number of French politicians and soldiers, e.g. Generals Duchesne and Zurlinden, still looked for an early triumph, thanks to Russia; and when, in the following summer, I got to know the position in the chief Allied countries and realized how little we were known and how scanty were our political relationships, I feared we might achieve nothing if the war ended quickly. If it were protracted we should have more time for propaganda. Meanwhile, there was much talk of a drawn war; and in 1915, as subsequently, the situation was not such as to put this contingency out of the question.

The battle of the Marne and its consequences I studied constantly and sought in all directions expert views upon them, though I only got them fully in England. After that battle the struggle in the West transformed itself more and more into a war of position—a circumstance which suggested that it would last long. In April 1915 the Germans, employing their usual tactics of intimidation, sprang a surprise on the Allies with gas attacks. But there were no decisive battles.

In the Eastern theater the Russians, who had been beaten in East Prussia in 1914, were again beaten on the Galician front at Gorlice and Przemsyl in 1915. Thus vanished the hopes of a Russian occupation of the Bohemian Lands. In the summer the Germans occupied Russian Poland. Warsaw and Vilna fell, and the Russian army, though not annihilated, was driven back into the interior. The position in Russia and the political and military incapacity of the Tsar and his advisers were revealed on September 6 by the Tsar's decision to take over the supreme command in person.

Elsewhere things dragged. The Italians advanced slowly, fighting a whole series of battles, twelve I believe, on the Isonzo; and the bold British attempt, begun in February, to capture the Dardanelles was soon seen to be fruitless.

So effectively did German propaganda in Switzerland turn to account the situation in the field that I went for some days to Lyons in order to watch French military arrangements and especially the recruits. Alarming accounts of their spirit and of anti-war feeling at Lyons and in Southern France were being disseminated by enemy agencies, just as unfavorable accounts were being spread of the state of mind in Northern Italy. In France I noticed how the Catholic movement affected the army and saw recruits wearing medals of the Virgin Mary. Here, as everywhere else during the war, I kept a careful eye on religious movements. But from France, as later from a short trip to Northern Italy (where I stayed with the Russian writer, Amfiteatroff), I returned with an easy mind.

ACTION AGAINST AUSTRIA

The time had come to take public action against Austria. All Czech colonies abroad expected and demanded it. In Russia a Czech Military Unit, or "Družina," had been formed in the autumn of 1914. In France our fellows had joined the army. In all Allied countries our people were vigorously opposing Austria and Germany, and our men were behaving well in the Austro-Hungarian army. We made this widely known with good effect. On April 3, 1915, when the Prague Regiment went over to the Russians at Dukla, even the Austrian newspapers announced that it had been disbanded, though they had until then said nothing of our movement. Political reprisals at home became more severe. As I have said, Dr. Kramář and Dr. Rašin were arrested. The Government at Vienna, yielding more and more to German influences, changed the State escutcheon and abbreviated the constitutional style of the country from that of "The Kingdoms and Lands represented in the Reichsrat" to that of "Austria."

In our propaganda we turned all these things to account, but we lacked, so to speak, an official designation. The Southern Slavs were ahead of us with their Central organization and their manifestos. The truth was that we needed funds. Money is the sinews of all war; and, for the moment, I had little. None came from Prague, and communications with America were slow. Without money I would not and could not begin to act officially; for action, once begun, must not slacken but must increase and be intensified. Therefore I began by educational propaganda. On July 4, 1915, I spoke of John Hus to our own people and to some Germans at Zurich; and, on July 6, the fourth centenary of his martyrdom, Professor Denis and I held a meeting in the Hall of the Reformation at Geneva. Denis gave an historical address to which I added political comment. Thanks to good publicity the celebration found a favorable echo in all Allied countries, while upon our own colonies and soldiers it had the educational effect of showing that, in the spirit of our Hussite ancestors, we were fighting for a moral as well as for a political purpose. In following years we organized successful Hus celebrations everywhere. On July 6, 1916, for example, references were made to Hus and the Czechs in all English churches. Even in Austria the Geneva celebration of 1915 hit the mark, the "Neue Freie Presse" denouncing it as "the first Czech declaration of war against Austria." From purely political declarations I still refrained, partly because I had been advised from Prague to wait a while. So I sent our people there a draft manifesto and awaited the arrival of Dr. Beneš. When he came for good on September 2 and our work abroad had been properly apportioned, we came out publicly against Austria on November 14, 1915. By that time I was in London.

The Meaning of the Fight

I have said that the resolve to fight Austria involved for me a moral as well as a political problem. I had long pondered over War and Revolution, for they are the main moral problem, and Humanity was more than a word to me. And the problem of humanity is a specifically Czech problem. Our writers and leaders, Kollár and Palacký, had decided in favor of Comenius the question whether our model should be Žižka, the Hussite soldier, or Comenius, the educator. In our own time Tolstoy had dealt with the problem on general grounds. Him I had often visited. With his doctrine of non-resistance I could not agree. I held that we must resist evil always and in everything, and maintained against him that the true humanitarian aim is to be ever on the alert, to overcome the old ideals of violence and heroic deeds and martyrdom, and to work with loving-kindness and wholeheartedly even in small things—to work and to live. In extreme cases, violence and assault must be met with steel and beaten off so as to defend others against violence.

Neither morally nor, I think, psychologically, did Tolstoy recognize the distinction between aggressive violence and self-defense. Here he was wrong; for the motives are different in the two cases and it is the motive which is ethically decisive. Two men may shoot, but it makes a difference whether they shoot in attack or in defense. Though both do the same thing the implications are not the same; the mechanical acts are identical but the two acts are dissimilar in intention, in object, in morality. Tolstoy once argued arithmetically that fewer people would be killed if attack were not resisted; that, in fighting, both sides get wilder and more are killed; whereas if the aggressor meets with no opposition he ceases to slay. But the practical standpoint is that, if anybody is to be killed, let it be the aggressor. Why should a peace-loving man, void of evil intent, be slain and not the man of evil purpose who kills? I know well that it is easy to pass from defense to attack and that it is difficult, when resisting attack, to remain strictly on the defensive; but against doctrines like those of Tolstoy no other ethical principle can be invoked than that of the right of self-defense. I know, too, that it is sometimes hard to say precisely who the aggressor is; yet it is not impossible. Thoughtful men of honest mind can distinguish impartially the quarter whence attack proceeds. In my work "The Czech Question" and elsewhere I dealt fully with the humanitarian problem of aggressive and defensive war and of Revolution; and, shortly before the Great War began, in "Russia and Europe."

At Geneva, Romain Rolland, who was working in the Office for Prisoners of War, represented Tolstoy's views. His hatred of war exposed him to much hostility and he was often accused of having sold himself to the Germans. This was thoroughly unjust, as discerning readers may see from his articles collected under the title: "Au-dessus de la mêlée." Tolstoy's doctrine was Rolland's starting point, and it was in the light of it that I judged his pacifism. It led me, indeed, to pass my own humanitarian ideas once more in review.

At that time pacifism was spreading everywhere. Against Rolland's pacifism I have nothing to say for he, who could not and would not fight, worked for the prisoners of war. But there are several sorts of pacifism—for instance, a pacifism of the naturally weak and timorous, a pacifism of the terrified and sentimental, and a pacifism of speculators. Yet another variety was that of the extreme International Socialists which found vent in their Conference at Zimmerwald on September 3, 1915. Very repugnant to me were the pacifists who defended the Germans as though they had been victims of aggression whereas they had long been and then were the bitterest foes of pacifism. I refer, of course, to official Germany which wanted the war and waged it. Among the German people themselves, as elsewhere, there always had been pacifist tendencies, some of which survived even during the war.

My point of departure is that war in the field is not the worst evil that can befall human society. But in war there is much besides the fighting of heroes. By the side of it there has hitherto been a whole system of abominations—lying, greed, baseness, vindictiveness, cruelty, sexual outrages and what not. People of romantic, too romantic, mind see in war only the Napoleons and the heroic leaders depicted by painters of the older school, and forget that even in the field Ulysses counts for more than Achilles. The social conditions out of which war arises have also to be taken into account, and the plight not only of the fallen but of those who are crippled or broken in health, and the way they are cared for. All this is war.

In my case the issue, Humanity *versus* Violence, came to a very practical head in the question whether Czechs and Slovaks, fighting as the soldiers of our revolution, ought to fire upon their Czech and Slovak brethren in the Austro-Hungarian army. This was no abstract casuistry, for our legionaries actually met their fellow-countrymen in battle. In some instances, brother fought against brother, father against son, though as a rule they recognized each other, those on the Austrian side coming over to our Legion. But there were also instances of very stubborn fratricidal strife when our men in Austrian regiments clung to Palacký's original view that "if Austria had not existed it would have been necessary to invent her."

Many a sleepless night did I pass in thinking of the fate of our volunteers and insurgents who fell into the hands of Austrian military justice. Reports of the execution of these young fellows grew more frequent—and I felt burning pain at the thought that I was preaching stern resistance and was urging them on to a life and death struggle. Often I yearned to go into the fighting line, since I was proclaiming war—yet I had to remember that, in the very interest of the fighters, the leader must not expose himself. This much I did resolve—that I would shirk no danger, or fear for my own life, that is to say, I would not give way to fear, for I think every man feels fear when his life is in danger and mine was certainly in constant danger everywhere.

Not less tormenting was the thought of what our people would say if we did not win. Into the details of that complicated question I cannot enter. I can only explain the reasons for my action against Austria and Germany, and why my humanitarian ideas drove me into the ranks of the belligerents; for that is what our work really meant, as I had gone abroad in the conviction that we must have an army of our own. In Switzerland, France and England our numbers were small. Few volunteers could therefore be enrolled. In America and in Russia our colonies were stronger; and in Russia there were our prisoners of war, many of whom had given themselves up to the Russians. Hence our army must be formed in Russia. America might provide a certain number of recruits, though her neutrality would be an obstacle. Unless we had a fighting force, our claim to freedom would hardly be heeded. In a world at war, mere tracts on "historical and natural rights" would be of little avail.

From Russia I often got scraps of news of what our people, and especially our "Družina," were doing there. Russia was practically cut off from the West and her propaganda was feeble. Russian papers came late and irregularly. I eked out what I got with my own knowledge of men and things, and to cover emergencies I sent a special messenger to Russia. Other messengers went into Austria and even to Prague. They were, of course, mostly neutrals, men and women of education and intelligence who went for the sake of the cause. I gave them careful instructions not to approach my acquaintances but to get all possible information about conditions and persons. Visitors from Russia, Austria and Germany often gave me news; and I met in Switzerland some well-informed men from Vienna, among them officials who disagreed with the policy of the Government and told me frankly what they knew. One Parisian banker, a Hungarian citizen thoroughly versed in the affairs of Vienna and Budapest, gave me many an interesting detail in the course of a walk by the lake.

The Question of War Guilt

From the humanitarian standpoint the question of war guilt was very weighty. Literature upon it grew mightily even during the war. To-day it forms a whole library. My own judgment was based upon long observation of Germany and of Austria, and especially upon the pan-German movement. In forming a right opinion, details alone are not decisive—whether this or that country mobilized a few hours or a few days sooner or later—but the question who did most to create the whole political atmosphere out of which, when opportunity offered, the war arose almost mechanically.

In the German Empire and in Austria-Hungary the guilt lies with Imperialism and Imperialistic militarism. German Imperialism, as defined and practised by the pan-Germans, was at the bottom prone to violence. In Germany and in Austria-Hungary violence was shamelessly done to non-German races, and violence characterized domestic policy as a whole; yet it must be admitted that Europe made no protest. A German philosopher, Eduard von Hartmann, advocated the extermination of the Poles, while the historian, Mommsen, taught that Czech skulls should be cracked. In German diplomacy, with its aggressive, ruthless, domineering and impatient character, a corresponding tendency prevailed. On the one hand, pan-German doctrine was the expression of actual practice; on the other, its teaching that the Germans were a "ruling race" fashioned the whole policy of Germany and Austria. In this spirit German philosophers and lawyers exalted violence into an ethical and juridical principle. It was the Germans who most zealously developed the theory that right proceeds from might and force, and it was they who, at the same time, practised it most effectually and ruthlessly. In lands where public opinion had thus been pervaded by aggressive militarism, where uncompromising pan-Germanism became the creed of civilians and officers alike, where the army was kept in constant readiness, the State and, with it, the people, rushed light-mindedly into war as soon as opportunity offered. The Sarajevo outrage offered it.

The thesis of Treitschke and, after him, of all the theorists of the German *Drang nach Osten* that it has ever been the task of Germany to colonize the East and, in particular, to subjugate the Slavs—may explain though it cannot justify this aggressive education of the German people. It is clear from the secret Austro-German Treaty of 1909, which made the true meaning of the Triple Alliance clear, that Austria and Prussia-Germany were always thinking of war. (The Viennese editor, Dr. Kanner, has rightly drawn attention to this Treaty.) But, in Allied countries, the whole onus of guilt. was somewhat one-sidedly thrown on to the Germans, less attention being paid to Austria because the conflict with her was indirect. Yet Austria bears a great part of the guilt, and her fate and her punishment have rightly been proportionate to it. Austria had a right to demand, as she did demand—though, oddly enough, rather late—satisfaction for the Sarajevo outrage. On this point all States were agreed. But Austria was to blame for having risked and pro-voked war with Russia by her exaggerated claims upon Serbia. After the Sarajevo outrage it was falsely declared in Vienna and Budapest that the Serbian Government had instigated it. The Serbian protest had no effect. A Serbian warning of the possibility of an outrage was given in Vienna, as is shown in Professor Denis's book on Serbia and as the recent Memoirs of Biliński, the former Austro-Hungarian Minister, confirm. Under Count Berchtold the Austro-Hungarian Foreign Office pursued against Serbia the same Machiavellian policy as it had followed under his predecessor when the anti-Serbian documents were forged. Vienna and Budapest literally raved against Serbia. She was to be annihilated. There was disagreement only upon the most effective means to this end.

In relating the Pashitch-Berchtold incident during the winter of 1912 I have already referred to the difference between the leading Ministers of Serbia and Austria-Hungary. During a victorious war the Serbian Prime Minister had been ready to rule out further conflicts with Austria-Hungary; and the Austro-Hungarian Minister had haughtily rejected the offer. Biliński rightly says in his Memoirs that the Great War might never have broken out but for Berchtold's inability to understand that offer —an inability that was, however, inherent in the Austrian and the German system.

The great guilt of Germany is that she gave her ally a free hand and allowed Austria-Hungary, in so far-reaching a matter, to take the decision; and that, under the pretext of allied loyalty, she used the declaration of war against Serbia as a long-expected opportunity. The Memoirs of General Conrad von Hoetzendorf now make it certain that Germany promised to support Austria even if the action against Serbia should bring on a big war. Conrad heard this from Berchtold as early as July 7, 1914. Germany was capable of greater wisdom than the superficial, good-for-nothing Austro-Hungarian Government and is therefore the more to blame. One strong, decided word from the Emperor William would have frightened Vienna. *Corruptio optimi pessima.* Further, Germany is guilty of not having utilized the English proposal for a Conference and of not having arranged a meeting of the Emperors, Kings and Presidents, or their Foreign Ministers, in order to deal with the dispute directly and face to face. The conduct of the war by Germany and Austria-Hungary, and especially the "frightfulness" of their methods, confirmed their guilt. The sinking of the "Lusitania," the shooting of Miss Cavell at Brussels, the bombing of London, and many other strategically superfluous raids, the use of poison gas and similar methods rightly inflamed feelings against Germany everywhere. Moreover, the advance of the Austro-Hungarian armies in Serbia and in Galicia was wholly barbarous—thousands and thousands of people were killed and tortured, often with a cruelty that was sickening. Karl Kraus's drama "The Last Days of Mankind" is based on authentic proofs of these things. It reveals at the same time the cruel degeneracy of the Hapsburgs. Nor must I forget Professor Reiss, a Swiss, who saw the cruelties perpetrated by the Austrians and the Magyars in Serbia, and spoke in public of them in Switzerland and in Paris and London. His addresses and writings helped us and the Southern Slavs greatly.

Of a piece with this policy of violence were the untruths and positive lies systematically circulated by German and Austro-Hungarian propaganda; for what I say of Germans and Austrians applies equally to the Magyars. For instance, the lie that the French opened hostilities by crossing the frontier and by bombing German territory from aeroplanes, whereas in reality the French withdrew their army six miles behind the frontier in order to avoid "incidents." I am persuaded that this action on the part of the French helped to win them sympathies and to overcome the reserve of England. I verified the untruth of this lying allegation; and though I admit that untruths about the Germans were spread by the Allies, it was done on a much smaller scale. English and American writers were besides, incomparably more decent and honorable than those of the enemy. For us, the character of German and Austrian propaganda was of especial importance because we were able to expose its methods in the United States. But of that I shall speak when I come to America.

The question of war guilt is being zealously debated everywhere, if only for the reason that at Versailles the Allies charged the Germans and their allies officially with aggression. I have gone through the whole literature of the question without finding any reason to change my view. In Germany and also in Austria it is now noticeable that their guilt begins to be more generally recognized than it was during the war and immediately after the peace; and I repeat that, while there may be differences of opinion upon all sorts of details, for example, whether the Russians or the Austrians mobilized a few hours sooner or later, the war of 1914 was a necessary consequence of the doctrines of militarism and of the right of the mailed fist which were most effectually formulated and propagated, philosophically and scientifically, in Prussia-Germany. Therefore the heaviest share of guilt for the war lies with Prussianism. It may be said that guilt should be ascribed in the first instance to States and to their Governments rather than to peoples. This I admit though I cannot deal here with the question how far a people is responsible for its State and, in this case, for Prussia, the leading German State. That is a problem to which I shall revert.

INTRIGUES IN SWITZERLAND

Even in free Switzerland Austria gave us a taste of her quality. Like Germany, she was officially represented there and used her advantage. The police searched the dwellings of our people, and the authorities of the Canton of Geneva forbade anti-Austrian propaganda. In practice, the prohibition was mildly applied. All the same, Dr. Sychrava transferred our Czech paper, the "Československá Samostatnost," to the French side of the frontier at Annemasse—to which a tramway runs from Geneva. Otherwise things went on as before, though we had to be very careful not to get the Government into difficulties. Later on, in February 1916, Sychrava was expelled from Switzerland; and a number of Czech students who returned home were imprisoned and condemned to death because they had listened to my address on John Hus and had talked to me.

In Switzerland, as elsewhere, German Austrian and Magyar propaganda was strong and there was a considerable current of pro-Austrian feeling. Professor Lammasch and other Austrians came personally from Vienna and established relations with many subjects of enemy countries. It was not only to us that Switzerland gave asylum but to all others, including pacifist Socialists; and it was thence that Lenin started for Russia with the help of Swiss Socialists. German Switzerland was strongly pro-German, as were the higher officers and heads of the Swiss army.

Austrian spies were always at our heels. One came from Prague straight to my hotel. I had, however, been warned of his coming—a proof that our subterranean communications and the "Maffia" in Prague were working well. I asked him to see me the very next day and put him all sorts of questions, in the most innocent fashion, about Prague and the police. My younger comrades had plenty of fun with him. Some of them won him over to our side and made a double traitor out of him. More interesting was an Austrian officer, a Moravian by birth, who pretended to be a deserter and offered me an invention to enable airmen to hit a given target. I put him into touch with the French at Annemasse, but in Paris they thought his invention worthless and kept him at a distance. He told me a long romantic story which I verified and found false. Then he evaporated. In the spring of 1915 one of my arms began to give trouble. Small abscesses began to appear on my shoulder. My doctor ascribed them to poisoning and our own people thought the Germans were trying to get at me through my laundry. The matter would not be worth mentioning but for the fact that the same thing happened to me in England, where the doctor also diagnosed poison. I put it down to lack of air and exercise, and took to riding; for on horseback one is supposed to pass twice as much air through the lungs as when walking.

Naturally our chief care was to counteract Austrian intrigues and propaganda, the stupidity of which often helped us. But we took into account the difficult position of Switzerland who was exposed to ruthless German and Austrian pressure. At the same time I studied with interest the racial and political institutions of the Swiss; for the relationship between the French, German and Italian Swiss resembled roughly what the relationship of Czechs, Germans and Magyars would be in the Czechoslovak State which we hoped to found. There are indeed many similarities between us and the Swiss. Switzerland, too, arose from a struggle against Austria and, like us, she has no access to the sea. Weightier seemed to me the fact that, despite the sharp antagonisms of racial feeling, the unity of the Helvetian Republic was not disturbed during the war. Many distinguished German Swiss, like the poet Spitteler, came out strongly against Prussianism. I had already known Swiss writers, e.g. Keller, C. F. Meyer, Spitteler, Amiel, Seippel, Rod and Ramuz; and after the war I made the acquaintance of the German Swiss writer, Roninger. The realism of these Swiss writers is, I believe, an effect of Swiss democracy. I have always taken the quality of Swiss literature as a proof that inter-racialism is not detrimental to racial character and that no harm is done when French and Germans live as friends side by side. Linguistically and racially, Switzerland is a classical example of strong racial originality combined with the closest inter-racial intercourse.

Small though she is, Switzerland gained her influence upon European civilization through her spirit. She has developed inter-racially as intensely as racially—witness the humanitarian international institutions, from the Red Cross to the League of Nations, which are established on her soil. True, Switzerland is democratic and free whereas, in Austria and in Hungary, races were held together by force under monarchical absolutism. For this very reason we Czechs may learn from the Swiss, though we must always remember the differences between us and them. Of these the most important is that Switzerland is a Federation of small independent State-Cantons all of whose citizens belong racially to great nations, organized as great independent States, and that from time immemorial there have been no racial conflicts in Switzerland.

Thanks to the Swiss mobilization, I saw something of the army and studied the militia system which the Socialists recommended and which I also adopted. The very fact that a militia is possible proves how firmly founded is Swiss democracy. But observant foreigners must study the democratic institutions and the freedom of a nation as a whole. Therefore I visited various Cantons and studied the relation between Federalism and democracy, comparing it with the arrangements in the United States and Germany.

The Swiss Cantons are small and the whole Federation is

thinly populated.   Hence many forms of direct Government by
the people, such as the Referendum and the Initiative.   The
smallest Cantons have no regular Parliament.   The people
meet and decide.   The election of the Government and of the
President, the nature and the duration of their functions, correspond to the peculiar simplicity of this State mechanism.   Switzerland has also proportional representation.

The tendency of Swiss democracy towards direct government
found expression in Rousseau, the leading theorist of modern
democratic philosophy, whose political and religious outlook was
influenced by his Swiss Fatherland.   Upon him and his theory of
democracy the Calvinism of Geneva also set its mark; and his
statue, which I saw several times a day, brought again to my
mind the whole problem of Rousseau and impelled me to study
it anew.

CHAPTER IV

IN THE WEST

IT was time to transfer the center of our work to the Allied capitals.   Even before leaving Prague I had urged that we should be represented in Paris, London and Petrograd, at least; and that, to this end, enough of us should go abroad. Beneš, whom I was expecting, was destined for Paris, while I was to be in London.   He reached Geneva on September 2, 1915. I left on September 5, and he followed me to Paris on September 16.

In 1915 Paris was the military and London the political headquarters of the Allies.   For France it was important to win and to hold British sympathies and, through them, to influence America also.   Besides, England stood closer than France to the Italians.   Therefore I decided to live in London, and to visit Paris occasionally. Despite the submarines, communications were quick and easy.   Now and then Beneš was to come to London.   That, in fact, is what we did.   Paris and London together formed an active political whole.   The Anglo-French Entente was of the utmost importance during the war and the making of the Peace; and it is important still.

London suited me, too, for purposes of communication with America—an increasingly weighty matter.   A very notable branch of our propaganda was being developed in America, as I shall presently show; and when mishap compelled us to alter our channels of underground communication with Prague, I used messengers from America and Holland.   From London it was easier to keep in touch with both of these countries.

But our political position in England and France was still precarious. Of our political leaders I alone was abroad, whereas a number of prominent Southern Slav members of the Austrian and Hungarian Parliaments, whose names had become known through the Agram High Treason trial of 1909 and through their anti-Austrian activities generally, had got away in time. In addition, the heroic struggle of Serbia created a living program for all the Southern Slavs and indeed for Europe—a program written in blood, for the savagery of the Austrians and Magyars in Serbia served the Southern Slav cause. Polish propaganda, too, was effective. The Poles had long been known abroad and their aspirations were everywhere recognized.

Of us, on the contrary, the French knew little, hardly more than we could tell them with our feeble means; and in Paris we were especially compromised by the conduct of the Mayor of Prague, Dr. Groš. The Vienna Parliament was not in session. Consequently no Czech voice could be heard there. Yet this was not altogether a misfortune, either for us abroad or for the development of things at home.

The Austrian, Hungarian and German press kept up a conspiracy of silence about us, and in the Paris "Temps" a statement unfavorable to us had already appeared. No wonder that friends like Professor Denis in Paris and Seton-Watson in London grew nervous. They urged me continually to come to Paris and London. Therefore I hastened thither as soon as Beneš, by a lucky chance—if chance it was—turned up in Geneva. In Switzerland the work was already organized, and to some extent in Paris. Denis's French review, "La Nation Tchèque," had been appearing since May 1; Dr. Sychrava's Czech paper came out on August 22, it having been much harder to establish than the French review, for we had no Czech contributors. All of us had our hands full of other work, my funds were still meager, and money was beginning to play a more and more important part. The failure of our people at Prague to find roundabout means of sending us money showed that they were not thinking of political propaganda of the kind that was necessary; hitherto, indeed, we had not undertaken it. Yet we lacked neither gladness in our work nor hope of victory. If we were few, all the more reason for intense and thoughtful effort.

PROFESSOR DENIS

Something should be said of Professor Denis and of the part he took in our campaign of liberation. The authority he had won among us by his historical work proved useful from the outset in our Paris colony, though it was beyond his power to settle the dissensions among its members. He was new to such things and they took him unawares. In French political quarters he was looked upon merely as a professor and man of letters, and he had not a few opponents even among people of his own kind —including the comparatively small circle of Slavonic specialists. Though his book on the war gained him a wider circle of friends, he had no influence with French political parties or in official circles. Nor could anyone conversant with French conditions be surprised that, as a Protestant, he should be politically at a disadvantage—exactly as he would have been in Bohemia! While the French Protestants showed their mettle publicly and stood firm in the national ranks, they were slightly suspected of pro-Germanism, even by French Liberals. Denis's book was enough to show thoughtful readers where he stood; but calm, clear thought was rare in those days. Thus I was by no means astonished to meet with certain difficulties on his account, difficulties that took us long to overcome. At last, Dr. Beneš succeeded in geting official quarters to understand the truth about Denis, and then no further exception was taken to him. Naturally we said nothing of this to anybody, least of all to our own people, some of whom official influence had prejudiced against Denis while others could not understand his horror of party squabbles within the colony. Yet, as a writer, he did great and good work for our cause and helped us also by his efforts to organize Slavonic studies in Paris. His book on the Slovaks was welcome indeed. With him I often discussed our affairs and Slav policy in particular. On the whole, we were agreed. He got on well with Beneš also, though his relations with Štefánik were chilly.

CZECH COLONIES ABROAD

To give a better idea of the nature of our work abroad it will be well, in this connection, to say something of our colonies. The largest of them, in Russia, America and Germany, I had known before the war, and also those in England and Serbia. I had often stayed among them, had watched their development and had known personally most of their leading people. It was only those in Switzerland and Paris that I met first in wartime.

The question was how to unite them all and to keep them informed—a hard matter on account of their geographical dispersion and of the derangement of communications by the war. All of them were split up into parties and groups, and each of them took on a special color from the country in which it lived. There was no regular tie between them, and, at first, no leading central journal. Hence the necessity of a Czech paper proclaiming our program and giving news. Immediately after reaching Geneva in March 1915 I had, indeed, given each colony instructions and sent it a statement of our aims.

Our colonies consisted mainly of workmen most of whom had left home in search of bread though many had gone to escape military service. In America and in Russia there were tradesmen, engineers and contractors among them, as well as agricultural laborers. Our more educated emigrants were not always of the best quality, and in our journalists the bulk of our people felt too little confidence. Yet in America and Russia an educated class grew up within the colonies. It included lawyers, doctors, merchants and bankers. To some extent this younger generation had found its way into American or Russian society, at the cost of becoming assimilated; but, on the whole, each colony was a little world by itself. Though its numbers grew with the coming of fresh emigrants from home, it remained unknown to the people among whom it lived. Even its knowledge of things at home—drawn from newspaper reading—was inadequate. Our work during the war did our colonies good, especially in America, inasmuch as it drew the attention of their countries of adoption to them.

We were chiefly concerned with three colonies, those in America, in Russia and in Paris. The Paris colony I have mentioned already. Its numbers were not large, but it was politically lively and excitable. In America, the tendencies of the leading section of our people were Radical—a Radicalism derived politically from the old Liberalism of the 'sixties which had survived in isolation and had been influenced by American democratic ideas and institutions. Here and there this Radicalism tended to become Socialism and even Anarchism, albeit a Socialism of the American sort. To the Radicals our Catholics and Protestants were opposed, the Catholics more sharply than the Protestants.

It is needless to refer ully to the dissensions in our various colonies. They were mai y local and personal; and, in America and Russia, centers like New York, Chicago and Cleveland, or St. Petersburg, Moscow and Kieff were so distant from each other that there could be no real unity. Nor, in the absence of instructions from Prague, could they possess, at first, a single plan of action. Instinctively they had all ranged themselves against Austria, but I found it necessary to remind their leaders more than once that the final political decision lay with Prague; for there was no lack of hot-headed fellows who claimed for themselves the right of decision and of leadership. There were also people "on the make." In many a Paris pothouse and elsewhere positions and offices in the future Czech Kingdom were distributed, from the kingship down to the lowest ranks of the official hierarchy. But these things were negligible. On every hand our people rallied to me. Subscriptions came from Canada and South Africa as soon as it was known that I was organizing our colonies, and many touching gifts from simple Czech mothers and grandmothers, accompanied by charming notes on which tears of hope and love were scarcely dry. In money our colonies were not rich. Subscriptions came slowly at first, even from America, though later on larger amounts flowed in.

Numerically, our American and Russian Colonies were the most important. The American Czechs could finance us, and in Russia an army could be formed out of our prisoners of war. Yet it was in Russia that we met with the greatest difficulties. As regards America, it was fortunate that Mr. Voska had brought news of me from Prague at the beginning of the war; and, in the autumn of 1915, Vojta Beneš (brother of Dr. Beneš) got away with fresh and fuller tidings. In all the branches of our American colony he organized collections, united the various parties and groups, and urged upon them the need for financial effort.

More serious in Russia than elsewhere was the political strife both between Czech Conservatives and Czech Radicals, and between Kieff and Petrograd. Some of our earlier emigrants to Russia held the political views that had been current when they left home, but the majority had come under the Conservative influence of their surroundings and of the Russian Government and were, in truth, very reactionary. They were entirely dependent upon the goodwill of Russian officials. With the progressive and radical educated class in Russia—Liberals and Socialists of all sorts—our people were hardly in touch at all, and were therefore almost unknown to that influential section of Russian society. Not until the Conservatives had been driven into the background by the Revolution of 1917 was it possible to unite the colony. After the arrival of Dürich in the summer of 1916 (the Czech Member of Parliament whom I have already mentioned as having been selected by Dr. Kramář for work in Russia) its dissensions had been especially acute, for Dürich joined the Conservatives and got caught in the toils of the reactionary pro-German Russian Government.

This Dürich affair, to which the Horký affair was presently added, was amply discussed at the time by our press in Russia and America. I wanted to stop bickerings among us and to prevent foreigners from being dragged into them. In this I succeeded, on the whole. Dürich was imprudent, and he had been exploited by dubious people in Paris who wished to use the Czech army for their own purposes. In Russia he succumbed to the pressure of the reactionaries and of foolish officials. As early as January 1917 I published a declaration that we were financially independent of the Allied Governments. That parried the attacks of the enemy press and dispelled whatever doubts were felt here and there. But Dürich's dependence upon the Russian Government made a bad impression in London and Paris where fear of a pan-Slav Russia was far too general. These matters I explained confidentially in the proper quarters, for the trouble with Dürich and about Dürich had arisen in Paris and had spread thence to Russia and even to America. It affected Beneš and Štefánik more than me. At last, there was nothing for it save to exclude Dürich from our National Council so as to silence all doubt in our colonies. Of course, we wrote as little as possible about it; and even if our very reserve enabled opponents to cast suspicion upon us until the Russian Revolution helped to clear things up, the affair did us little harm. The controversy compelled our people to reflect more seriously upon our aims and tactics. With the Allies, our vigorous suppression of Dürich did us good—as was recognized by the Southern Slavs and the Poles who found it less easy to settle their personal squabbles. Similar strife and personal animosities in Allied countries came to my knowledge, and I used them to silence references to our troubles, or to those of the Southern Slavs and other organizations of "small peoples."

One complication arose out of the unexpected influx of brand-new Czechs and Czechoslovaks into our colonies. Even Dürich fell into the hands of these "new Czechs." Since, in Paris and elsewhere, it was not pleasant to be classed as a German, all kinds of renegades who knew a few words of Czech claimed fellowship with us, especially when the Allied Governments granted privileges to our citizens and recognized us not only as a nation but as an Allied Nation.

THE NATIONAL COUNCIL

For our fight abroad we needed, above all, a leading central authority. At first, I was that authority, and the questions were: Where to find assistants and how to unite our colonies? The geographical dispersion of the colonies made this a long business. I did not wish to behave like an autocrat by proclaiming myself the national leader abroad, but acted constitutionally, by parliamentary methods. As I have said, the colonies had known me personally before the war, and my authority grew as the work went on. Our people saw what I was doing and understood my tactics. I explained to them why I had gone abroad, who and what parties had known and approved of my departure. Everywhere I was recognized as leader, my membership of Parliament carrying weight in this respect; it constituted my political title. But I was alone. My assistants were not members of Parliament, neither Beneš nor Štefánik. Because other members of Parliament were expected to come from Prague, the formal setting up of our central authority was long postponed, nor did I hurry matters even when several colonies got together and linked up with me. As a name "The National Council" suggested itself naturally on account of old traditions, but I feared to use it lest it compromise our National Council at home and expose its members to reprisals.

Yet, as things developed, we were obliged to set up our central authority formally. We had to make public declarations under a recognized name. We had also to deal with "personal affairs" like those of Koníček and Dürich. Of Dürich I have spoken; but, when Koníček came from Russia to proclaim the Russian Czech program which the Tsar and the Russian Government had ostensibly endorsed, the question of his credentials arose and also that of the right of final decision in case of dispute. We settled Koníček more easily than Dürich. Another urgent matter was our public declaration of hostility to Austria which, for reasons I have mentioned, had been put off long enough. When we issued it on November 14, 1915, I signed it as "The Czech

Committee Abroad." It was signed also by representatives of all our foreign colonies. This made it the proclamation not only of a provisional Government but of a Parliament abroad.

A Government was exactly what we needed. So, in the course of 1916, the National Council was constituted. When I was in Paris, I agreed with Beneš and Dürich (before the latter went to Russia) upon the name and the form of the organization. Beneš, who was appointed Secretary-General, carried the work through and used the name "The National Council of Czech Countries" in his official correspondence. Publicly the name was first used by Štefánik in drawing up the so-called Kieff Protocol on August 29, 1916; and on November 1, 1916, our Czech organ in France, "Československá Samostatnost," (Czechoslovak Independence) announced that the National Council consisted of me as President, of Dürich and Štefánik as vice-Presidents, and of Beneš as Secretary-General. Its headquarters were in Paris. In opposition to it Dürich afterwards set up a special "National Council" for Russia—though he had not then resigned his position as vice-President of the Paris National Council—but the Russian Revolution soon made an end of it. On March 20, 1917, our brigade in Russia proclaimed the Czechoslovak State with the Paris National Council as Provisional Government and me as Dictator; and, at a Congress in Kieff, a branch of our National Council for Russia was established on May 12, 1917.

Thus constituted, the National Council was recognized by our colonies and their elected representatives. In Switzerland, Holland and England there was no opposition; but in Paris the ambitions of sundry bibulous aspirants to high office in the future Russian Satrapy of Bohemia gave a little trouble. They were a small minority and soon offered me their services. One or two of them even offered their money—not going further than an offer, however. In America, recognition was spontaneous and determined, first by the Sokol organization on September 15, 1916, and by the Czechoslovak National Association on December 14. Even from Kimberley in South Africa recognition came on February 18, 1917.

THE ART OF PROPAGANDA

Lack of political relations between Prague and foreign countries had, as I have shown, obliged us to start the work abroad from the very foundations. Yet there was the compensating advantage that we could begin systematically and proceed circumspectly. Thanks to the duration of the war, the work succeeded. Of course, each of us linked up with our friends and acquaintances. Štefánik knew already a goodly number of influential men and politicians. Dr. Beneš and Dr. Sychrava, like Dr. Osuský later, made their own circles. Through my old friends in Allied countries the radius of my own action was constantly enlarged.

Our propaganda was democratic. We sought not only to work upon politicians and men in official positions but above all on the press and, through it, upon public opinion. It was precisely this that helped us in democratic States like France, England, America and Italy, where Parliament and public opinion were much more influential than in Austria, Germany and Russia. We followed the same method in Russia after the Revolution. Naturally I always tried to establish relations with Governments, and particularly with the Ministries of Foreign Affairs as well as with the Ambassadors of Allied countries. This also was done systematically. For instance, I have said that, in 1915, I made no attempt to see the French Foreign Minister, M. Delcassé, partly for reasons I have given and partly because I knew that he had long worked to promote agreement between England and France—a circumstance more helpful to us, as things then were, than a conversation would have been at a moment when the Anglo-Franco-Russian Treaty with Italy would have compelled him to show reserve. I made, however, the acquaintance of the principal French Foreign Office officials who knew the situation and were influential; and we were often helped by lawyers, bankers and others who, themselves outside politics, had friendly access to leading statesmen and politicians.

In the psychology of propaganda one point is important—not to imagine that people can be converted to a political idea merely by stating it vigorously and enthusiastically or by harping on its details; the chief thing is to rouse interest in your cause as best you can, indirectly no less than directly. Political agitation often frightens or alienates thoughtful people whom art and literature may attract. Sometimes a single phrase, well used at the right moment, is enough. Long-windedness is always to be avoided, especially in private talk. True, propaganda of this kind presupposes culture, political and social breadth of view, tact and knowledge of men on the part of those who undertake it. Paderewski and Sienkiewicz—a musician and a writer—had been the most successful propagandists for Poland from the very outbreak of the war. Those who had read Sienkiewicz's "Quo Vadis" were already as good as won for the Polish cause. In much the same way Mestrovitch, the sculptor, served the Southern Slavs. Our store of such helpers was small. In Paris we had the painter, Kupka, who joined the Legion; in Rome there was another painter, Brázda, though he was only a beginner; and I think Madame Destinn, the prima donna, lent a hand for a time.

Another weighty point is this—propaganda must be honest. Exaggeration is harmful and lies are worse. Some among us thought that the whole art of politics consists in gulling people. Until we stopped them they tried to disseminate "patriotic" untruths, forgetting that falsehoods can be exposed. Our enemies used these untruths against us as, for instance, in the case of the falsification of a speech which a Czech Member of Parliament, Stříbrný, had made.

A third rule is not to praise one's own goods, like inferior commercial travelers. Intelligent and honest policy must accompany intelligent and honest propaganda.

In the chief cities of Allied countries I spoke to big audiences and small. Opponents and pacifists I visited personally, and got into touch with the Universities, particularly with historians and economists. In England, as I have said, the name of Hus helped us. In a word, a policy of culture needs cultivated propaganda. ·Newspapers were influenced by discussions with their proprietors and editors, and also by writing for them. I wrote many articles and gave interviews myself. We established press bureaus to keep in touch with and inform newspapers and agencies, e.g. the Czech Press Bureau at the end of 1916 in London, and the Slav Press Bureau in America from May 1918 onwards. As early as possible I sought to promote the publication of periodicals which, while political in character, should be scientifically edited. Such an one was Denis's "La Nation Tchèque." Later on we had in Paris a strictly scientific review, "La Monde Slave." In Great Britain and elsewhere Seton-Watson's excellent weekly "The New Europe," which appeared from October 1916 onwards, was of the greatest assistance. I urged Seton-Watson to publish it because I recognized his uncommon capacity, political keenness and breadth of view. As regards Europe its standpoint was identical with ours though, in Italian policy, I was more moderate than its editor. The "New Europe" was eagerly read in France and Italy as well as in Great Britain, and it served as a guide for our organs abroad.

Nor was our propaganda solely literary. We took a shop in Piccadilly Circus, one of the busiest corners of London, fitted it up like a bookseller's window, showed maps of our country and of Central Europe, together with the latest news about ourselves and the enemy and denials of untrue rumors and reports. We founded an Anglo-Czech Society and used Chambers of Commerce for special purposes. In short, we left no stone unturned.

My whole past proved advantageous to me, especially my controversy with Aehrenthal over the "Friedjung" forgeries and my work for the Southern Slavs in general. My book "Russia and Europe" attracted attention in proportion as the Russian situation became acute. Many had read the German edition of it and, during the war, it was translated into English though the translation only appeared in 1919 under the title "The Spirit of Russia." The stand I had made in 1899 on behalf of the Jewish tramp, Leopold Hilsner, who had been falsely accused of ritual murder, was also accounted to me for righteousness. And, as my political authority increased, I was able to strengthen the spirit of concord and steadfastness among our colonies. In wartime, as the Romans knew, efforts must be concentrated; and, in our case, the distances between our colonies and between the Allied countries made concentration indispensable. There was not the slightest rivalry about the leadership. Beneš and Štefánik were loyal, true and devoted friends. We all said the same thing, we all had the same aim. In the Southern Slav and the Polish camps there were, on the contrary, sharp differences. A sort of dictatorship grew up spontaneously in our midst though its character was Parliamentary; and, as the Dürich and sundry minor cases showed, firm decisions had sometimes to be taken.

Towards the end of 1916, thanks to our work, people began to be interested in the Czechs and Slovaks, to know something of them and to talk about them. When I was "interviewed," a newspaper placard announced the fact. Vienna, too, helped us mightily. The Austrian news we proved to be false. The persecution of our people at home carried conviction that we were rebels in earnest. Martyrdom, and especially blood, win sympathies. The imprisonment, trial and condemnation of Dr. Kramář and Dr. Rašin brought grist to our mill, while the arrest of my daughter Alice was of great service to us in England and America. People argued that when even women were imprisoned the movement must be serious. Throughout America, women petitioned the President to intervene and appealed directly to the American Ambassador in Vienna. These movements in America and in England made our rebellion better known.

Counter-propaganda against Austrian, Magyar and German propaganda was, with us, a specialty and, as we knew the circumstances thoroughly, we soon made our mark. From the summer of 1916 onwards, the American Slovak, Dr. Osuský, who knew Magyar and Hungarian affairs well, did excellent service. We could see through the enemy announcements and interpret them; and, in addition to our own news from home, which we turned to good purpose, we read between the lines of the Prague newspapers. Our military information proved trustworthy and was gladly received. It won us many a friend, not least because we refused payment and gave it in the interest of the Allied cause. On this point I was adamant, though it was not easy to keep an eye on all our helpers when this branch of our propaganda grew into a regular system of espionage and counter-espionage. Yet, with insignificant exceptions, nothing went wrong.

Part of our work was to get Allied news into the German and Magyar press. In Austria and Hungary the progress of the Allies was being kept dark. Therefore we tried successfully to smuggle news of it into the Austro-Hungarian newspapers. Dr. Osuský could tell many a tale of the dodges by which he got into Budapest papers reports of the great help the Allies were receiving from America. He did it mostly in the form of attacks upon the Americans; and the news was reproduced by the Vienna and the Prague press.

In the United States Mr. Voska cleverly organized a very efficient system of counter-espionage, gaining thereby political prestige both for himself and for us, as I shall presently relate. In Russia the difficulties were more serious though, after the Revolution, we surmounted them. We never used money, that is to say, we never bribed. I helped some respectable people, Czechs and others, discreetly and without their asking, when I heard they were in need. In that stormy time not a few were in want through no fault of their own.

Beneš, Štefánik and I kept ourselves deliberately independent of the funds supplied by our people in America. My salary as a Professor at London University (its resources were limited during the war) was small, but I was well paid for my articles and was, besides, helped by personal gifts from American friends. As I have said, Dr. Beneš put money into our "enterprise" from the first and still had enough for himself. Štefánik, too, had an income of his own. This financial independence impressed our people favorably, and our frugality had a good effect. All sorts of stories were told about it, and many thought that the cause should be more smartly "represented." But we needed no such "representation." We were working. Later on, "representation" came by itself. When I reached America from the Far East our people took for me an apartment in a first-class hotel, as biggish permanent quarters were required for the reception of my numerous visitors. But in Europe we inverted the Czech proverb "Little money, little music" and got plenty of music for our little money. In other words, we were all working with a will and made our slender resources go a long way. We did more with a penny than the Austrian and German diplomatists could do with pounds. I doubt whether revolutionary propaganda abroad has ever been so cheaply carried on; nor does modesty prevent me from saying that few political campaigns have been so well thought out as ours was. Here is an account of the money I received from America for the cause:—

1914–1915	$37,871
1916	71,185
1917 (up to the end of April) . .	82,391
1918 (from May onwards) . .	483,438
	$674,885

While I was in Russia in 1917-1918 Dr. Beneš received about $300,000, so that the whole work cost less than $1,000,000. The subscriptions from America did not increase notably until after the United States had entered the war. Almost all of them came from Czechs. During the war the Slovaks gave little, though they sent $200,000, including some amounts from my American acquaintances, after I had become President. This money, and the balance of the Czech Revolutionary Fund, I spent, as President, in charitable gifts and subscriptions of which public account has been rendered.

THE WORK IN ENGLAND

I stayed more than eighteen months in London—from the end of September 1915 to the end of April 1917. Now, as before the war, I enjoyed the hospitality of that mighty City, more populous than the whole of Bohemia. In such a wilderness of people a man disappears unobserved, and can throw himself entirely into his work. I lived in Hampstead, on the edge of the country, and went into town on the top of an omnibus, making up for the loss of time by watching life in the streets. If it rained or snowed I went by underground. Taxis or a motor I could not afford.

Beneš stayed in Paris and, like Štefánik, went now and then to Italy, so that we were officially represented in the chief Allied countries (with the exception of Russia) and were able, besides, to negotiate in London and Paris with the Italian and other Ambassadors.

Once settled in London, I took up the work that had been begun by my earlier memorandum to the Foreign Secretary, Sir Edward Grey. The University (King's College) offered me a Slavonic professorship. Other Slavonic specialists were to be enrolled and a Slavonic department established. Seton-Watson pressed the professorship upon me again and again on behalf of Dr. Burrows, the Principal; and though I was reluctant to take it, because I am not a Slavonic specialist and feared that I should have no leisure for scientific work, I ended by accepting it—and did well to follow the advice of my friends. On October 2, 1915, I settled matters with Dr. Burrows whose manliness and devotion to his University I esteemed highly. In gratitude and friendship I record my relations with a man who was at once a distinguished Classical Hellenist and an authority on modern Greek culture and politics.

The subject of my inaugural lecture on October 19, 1915, was "The Problem of Small Nations in the European Crisis." It was our first big political success. Above all, the fact that the Prime Minister, Mr. Asquith, had agreed to take the chair accredited me to the broader political public in London; and, as Mr. Asquith fell ill, Lord Robert Cecil represented him—a political background that gave our cause a great lift. In itself, the lecture had a good and far-reaching effect, as had the French translation of it. It brought out for the first time the political significance of the zone of small peoples in Europe that lies between the Germans and the Russians; it enabled me to put both the German "Drang nach Osten" (The Urge towards the East) and Russian policy in a new light, and to show the essential characters of Austria-Hungary and Prussia. In this light, the breaking up of Austria-Hungary by the liberation of her peoples was revealed as the main requirement of the war. Finally, I argued strongly against the fear of the so-called Balkanization of Europe and urged, convincingly I think, that small nations are capable of and have a right to independent development as States, each according to its own culture. The lecture was widely reported and its effect noticeable. Henceforth the small peoples and the possibility of their independence were seriously talked and written about. The positive side of the war —reconstruction—came into the foreground, replacing the conception that its object was either defense against the Germanic Powers or their overthrow, and placing the war in its true light as the beginning of the great refashioning of Central and Eastern Europe and, indeed, of Europe as a whole.

I found in London my dear old friends, the trio Mr. Wickham Steed, Madame Rose and Dr. Seton-Watson. They were the friendly refuge and the center from which my political circle was daily enlarged. Steed had helped me in Vienna during the contest with Aehrenthal and in the Pashitch-Berchtold episode; Seton-Watson's interest in Slovakia had brought me near to him. All three knew Austria-Hungary and the whole of Central Europe. This made me feel all the more at home with them. Round Steed gathered not only the English political world but the French and, in fact, the whole of Allied and neutral Europe— men of manifold interests and spheres of activity, soldiers, bankers, journalists, Members of Parliament, diplomatists, in short the active political world. I remember also meeting at his house the author of the "Life of St. Francis of Assisi," Professor Paul Sabatier, and many others. Steed and Seton-Watson rendered great service to the cause of our liberation, not so much because

I was able through them to set forth our aims in the papers controlled by Lord Northcliffe or because the influence of these two friends gave me access to the most influential quarters in London, but especially because both Steed and Seton-Watson fought for our aims and, as British political men and writers, made the anti-Austrian policy their own.

Soon after I reached London, and almost simultaneously with my inaugural lecture at King's College, Steed published in the "Edinburgh Review" for October 1915 a program in which he postulated a radical transformation of Austria-Hungary as the condition of a lasting peace, and called for the unification of the Southern Slavs and for a "United Czech-Moravian-Slovak" State. While I was in Paris for a time in 1916, he published a "Programme for Peace" in the same review (April 1916). In it he foreshadowed a United States of Yugoslavia, an autonomous Poland under Russian suzerainty, an independent or, at least, an autonomous Bohemia with Moravia and Slovakia, and a united Roumania. On account of the military situation he framed the demand for our independence with a certain reserve; later on, the reserve disappeared. Dr. Seton-Watson did his part in defining our aims and spreading knowledge of them through his excellent weekly review "The New Europe" of which the influence was very considerable. It may, I think, be gauged by the fact that adversaries moved heaven and earth to get him conscripted into the Army Medical Service—since he was not fit for the fighting ranks. In this they succeeded, until he was released for special work by order of the Government, though even then he was forbidden to write.

Our friends' publications and utterances had an echo in France, Italy and America. Steed was in constant touch with France and Italy, and often went there during the war to lecture and to do other propaganda work. Through these activities, as well as by his personal influence in the most important political circles, his views gained currency and weight. He often found (temporary) difficulties in official quarters. Soon after the outbreak of war, Lord Northcliffe and "The Times" criticized some features of official foreign policy, and the Foreign Office broke off relations with "The Times" during the whole winter of 1914-1915. It was not until May 1915 that the breach was healed.

As soon as I had got my bearings in London I began to call on official personages. One of the first was Sir George Russell Clerk, of the Foreign Office, afterwards the British Minister in Prague; then Sir Maurice de Bunsen, the former British Ambassador in Vienna, and a number of secretaries and officials in the Foreign Office and other departments. Mr. Philip Kerr, the secretary of Mr. Lloyd George, I remember particularly and likewise the group of the "Round Table," with some members of which I had personal relations. This serious review published a number of instructive and pertinent articles upon our question and European problems generally. Among Members of Parliament I must name Sir Samuel Hoare and Mr. (now Sir) Frederick Whyte (afterwards the First Speaker of the Indian National Assembly). Whyte was a friend of Seton-Watson and a diligent contributor to the "New Europe" which he edited while Seton-Watson was under military discipline. I extended also my acquaintanceship with journalists, Mr. Steed and Madame Rose giving me good openings to this end—openings that enabled me not only to meet prominent newspaper proprietors and writers like Northcliffe, Mr. Garvin of the "Observer," Dr. Dillon and Dr. Harold Williams, but to "place" articles and interviews. With French, American and many other press representatives I was also in touch; and, from time to time, I approached eminent men in other spheres of life. Among these were Sir Arthur Evans, the famous authority on Cretan culture, who knew the Balkans well, the Southern Slav Lands in particular; and the Russian savant, Professor Paul Vinogradoff, of Oxford. Lord Bryce—whose works on the Holy Roman Empire and on America gave me occasion to discuss with him Germany and her war plans—I had often opportunity to see, and at his house I met Lord Morley, the biographer of Gladstone. We plunged forthwith into a discussion of Austria on the strength of Gladstone's famous saying: "Nowhere in the world has Austria ever done good." Soon after reaching London I looked up Mr. Maurice, the well-known writer on Czech history, and in his company I met a circle of interesting writers of somewhat pacifist tendencies. The historian, Professor Holland Rose, and Professor Sir Bernard Pares I remember well, while I formed a literary connection with Mr. Oscar Browning of Cambridge. And I must make special mention of Mr. Robert Fitzgibbon Young, a young and active supporter of our cause. The memory of Mr. Hyndman, the Nestor of English Socialism, whose knowledge of European affairs and of the Socialist movement was widely esteemed, is dear to me, as is that of his wife, who took a lively interest in the Ukraine. Mrs. and Miss Christabel Pankhurst I must mention, too. They supported our movement in their women's organizations. Nor can I forget Professor Charles Sarolea of Edinburgh, a Belgian by birth. I had long known him and his extensive literary work. Before 1914 he had written a book proving that Germany would soon provoke war. As long as he edited that excellent popular weekly "Everyman," he gave me ample space in it.

Needless to say, I did not avoid people of different or even of hostile views. I met Mr. Noel Buxton, the pro-Bulgar; and, at a lecture, Mrs. Green, the widow of the famous historian, who was active in the Irish movement. The pitiable Sir Roger Casement was, at that moment, about to meet his fate—an incident that reminds me how sharp an eye opponents kept on me and how they missed no chance of turning things against us. In several Irish papers the news suddenly appeared that I was going to Ireland to take part in the Irish agitation; but the Austrian and German agents who inspired these announcements overspiced them to such an extent that it was not even necessary to issue a denial. The facts were that Dr. Baudyš, a lecturer at the Czech University of Prague and a student of Erse and the Celtic languages of Great Britain, had got stranded in London and that, in his interest, I spoke to Mrs. Green about the publication of his work. Afterwards I met other Irishmen, in official positions and otherwise, for instance Mr. Gerald Fitzmaurice, the expert on Turkey and the Balkans. Had there been time I should have been glad to visit Ireland, for I knew the political and literary sides of the Irish movement and our people had long sympathized with the Irish. The question that interested me most was how and to what extent the Irish character expresses itself in Irishmen who no longer speak the Irish language. English writers often allude, in their portrayals of character, to the peculiarities of Celtic race and blood. Can a people live if its language is dead? The Irish writer, George Moore, once stated this problem very trenchantly as regards himself and the Irish—and it stuck in my mind.

Lectures and public meetings I attended pretty regularly, among others those at which Mr. and Mrs. Sidney Webb and Bernard Shaw spoke. I had, of course, long read Shaw's writings; but I got to know him as politician and pacifist propagandist. The level of these meetings and of the discussions that followed them was very high. Opponents listened calmly to arguments and sought calmly to refute them. In similar meetings I came across G. K. Chesterton and his brother, the anti-Semite, and I had a look even at Horatio Bottomley, the proprietor of "John Bull," a nationalist brawler and super-patriot. This gentleman had been involved in ugly financial affairs before the war, and similar affairs were afterwards to get him a seat in prison in exchange for his seat in Parliament. During the war he was the self-constituted mouthpiece of the John Bulls—undoubtedly a man of talent, a typical exploiter of patriotic feeling —and he actually contrived to get an invitation to visit the British Commander-in-Chief at Headquarters. As Dr. Johnson knew, "patriotism is the last refuge of a scoundrel."

If I add that I went to numbers of churches (the ritualistic movement had long interested me), that I heard sermons and watched the piety of the people in its relation to the war, I shall have given a sufficient account of my doings in London.

Meanwhile our propaganda was going well. The Press Bureau and the shop window in Piccadilly Circus had their effect. We searched the history of Anglo-Czech relations and turned it to account. Those relations began with the marriage of Anne of Bohemia to Richard II in 1382. We emphasized Wyclif's relationship to Hus and to our Reformation, and the interest taken by Comenius in English education; and we drew attention to the English and American disciples of the Moravian Brothers and of Hollar.[1] Nor did we forget the arms and the motto of the Princes of Wales that were taken from King John of Bohemia at the battle of Crécy. This and especially the fact that there had existed mutual relations—political, religious and educational —between Bohemia and England, had a beneficent influence. But, as I had accepted the Professorship at London University, I had to think of my lectures as well as of propaganda. At the time I thought this a bothersome interruption though to-day I understand that Seton-Watson and Dr. Burrows advised me well when they urged me so insistently to accept the appointment.

THE MILITARY OUTLOOK

As was natural, I heard much in London of the English army and of the situation on the various fronts. Indeed, I had now a chance to consult English and French experts on all military questions. I have repeatedly said that I had been worried by the problem of the war's duration. As late as the spring of 1915, taking account of every military opinion, I admitted at times that the war would be over by the end of the year. Yet the situation in the field foreshadowed a protracted struggle. The war of position dragged on. It enabled the belligerents to raise forces at home, to equip and train fresh divisions and re-serves, and to adapt industry to war purposes. People talked of the growing part that aircraft and submarines would play. To judge by the news, it seemed unlikely that the Allies would make peace without some big success at the front, even though influential people on both sides were working for peace. The victory on the Marne had not been decisive. True, there was

[1] Wenceslas Hollar, a Czech artist who came to England in 1637 as a refuge from Hapsburg persecution after the Battle of the White Mountain, and left engravings of great value.

some nervousness in Germany, at least among the Socialists, as was shown by the debate on peace terms in the Reichstag and by the attitude of Schiedemann at the beginning of December 1915. Everything I could learn from sound soldiers in all the armies, and occasionally from prisoners, led me to believe that the military operations would last long—a view which political considerations confirmed. What I heard in London of military plans—and I heard much—was not always pleasant. There were sharp differences of opinion even in responsible quarters, not only about the Dardanelles but also about the French and Russian plans of campaign. It was curious to see soldiers as well as politicians put forward ideas of strategy of which the impossible and fantastic character was clear even to laymen. Colonel Repington's articles in "The Times" showed distrust of British and Allied leadership on sea and land, and still more distrust of the Government and the politicians. His articles were cut by the censor, but I read them in the original and, in many respects, agreed with them.

As a result of discussing all these things with intimate friends I wrote for them at their request, towards the end of November 1915, a memorandum on the war strength of both sides. Starting with the assumption that Austria-Hungary and Germany had not recruited more than five or six per cent. of their populations while the French had recruited between two and three per cent. more, I concluded that England, with whose case I was principally concerned, would have to accelerate the mobilization and training of her man-power if the Allies were to withstand Austria-Hungary and Germany in case the latter should raise their percentage. My news from Bohemia showed that more Czechs than Germans were being called up and that, in the south (Bosnia-Herzegovina and elsewhere), more than eight per cent. were being called up as a punitive measure. My object was to show that the Central Powers had mobilized as many men as the Allies though, collectively, the latter had larger populations and had, at first, also had more men under arms. Now, the Russian factor was becoming more and more uncertain.

True, numbers and percentages were not alone decisive. Resources and relative ability to equip and to feed the forces raised also came into account. As early as March 15, 1915, Lord Kitchener had spoken doubtfully on this point in the House of Lords, though he seemed to be thinking rather of numbers than of modern equipment. Sharply, albeit indirectly, by laying stress on the superiority of the Germans, I criticized the policy of the Allies and their conduct of the war, and drew especial attention to the lack of unity in Allied military operations. That question had already been publicly raised though it was not recognized as an urgent problem of Allied strategy and policy until there had been further failures in the field.

My friends gave this memorandum to the military authorities, several of whom then discussed it with me. Some admitted the gravity of the situation but showed no fear, saying that the British forces would reach France in good time and that conscription, which had been introduced on October 28, would yield adequate results. Others openly demanded a larger army. Repington worked for it, and Major-General Sir William Robertson, who had been on the French front since the beginning of the war, publicly urged an increase in the strength of the army during the following autumn. Lloyd George also believed in the necessity of raising very considerably the strength of all the Allied armies if the German front was to be broken through.

Indeed, on all fronts the situation was getting unpleasant and increasingly complicated. Everywhere there was lively disappointment with Russia. In October 1915 Bulgaria joined the enemy, the conduct of negotiations with her being criticized in London, where the failure to win her over to the Allied side was thought a serious diplomatic reverse. Simultaneously a new Allied center was established at Salonica—after a long discussion which ended in the acceptance of the plan by England and France, thanks to the influence of Briand. The fighting, which began in November 1915 between the Bulgars and the Allied forces under General Sarrail, turned out badly, while the overthrow of Serbia by Mackensen's army, and the taking of Belgrade on October 8, made a deep impression of which the depressing effect was, however, neutralized by the heroic conduct of the Serbians in withdrawing the remainder of their army across Albania and in transferring their Government to Corfu. And, while the Turks were victorious in Mesopotamia, bloody and indecisive fighting continued on the Western front, where the Germans stood on the defensive because their main forces were opposing the Russians.

This was the position when I decided to issue our manifesto on November 14, 1915, and to declare open war against Austria. As I have said, the manifesto was signed by our "Committee Abroad" and by representatives of all our colonies. It was issued because of the excitement in our colonies and of their fears lest I fail to take a public stand, but especially in order to prevent our people at home from being tempted to give way. I was afraid, too, that the defeat of Russia might have an unfortunate effect at home and lead to reprisals; and I had received in advance the assent of our secret circle of public men, known as the "Maffia," which had approved of the general lines of the manifesto.

In view of the unfavorable situation, I hardly expected the manifesto to make much impression on the Allies. Yet its effect was considerable. In the French press it was widely reproduced; M. Gauvain wrote upon it a leading article in the "Journal des Débats"; and there was considerable comment in the English papers. At that moment we were better known in France than in England. Soon, however, people in England got to know us better, beginning with intellectual and political circles and with official quarters. We made headway, thanks to our work in London and throughout the country, and thanks also to Voska's doings in America which were highly appreciated in London.

THE WORK IN FRANCE

In agreement with Dr. Beneš, who had been in the habit of coming to London to report to me on our position, I went over to Paris at the beginning of February 1916. Briand had been Prime Minister since October 28, 1915, and Štefánik had prepared him for my visit. I saw him on February 3, and laid before him a small map of Europe and my view of the war—that the division of Austria into her historical and natural elements was a condition of the reconstruction of Europe and of the real enfeeblement of Germany, that is to say, of French security. I spoke tersely, almost epigrammatically, but Briand has a good French brain and grasped the heart of the matter at once. Above all, he accepted our policy and promised to carry it out. Štefánik told me that Briand was really convinced. My visit to him was announced in an official *communiqué;* and, as a public supplement to it, the kindness of M. Sauerwein enabled me to publish a brief statement of our anti-Austrian program in the "Matin." This statement hit the mark not only in Paris but in all Allied countries. It is no exaggeration to say that our policy of resolving Austria into her constituent parts gave the Allies a positive aim. They began to understand that it would not be enough to overthrow the Central Powers and to penalize them financially and otherwise, but that Eastern Europe and Europe as a whole must be reorganized. Briand's reception of me and my intercourse with him made an impression in London and strengthened our position there. Announcements favorable to us appeared not only in "The Times" but in other papers also —the "Matin" had a skilful correspondent in London! It goes without saying that we used this great success to the utmost throughout the press; and we soon had occasion to see that the fact of my having been received by Briand had a profound effect upon Slav politicians and especially upon Russian diplomatists.

I stayed about a month in Paris, paying visits that deepened and strengthened the influence of Briand's action. I cannot record them all. They included interviews with M. Pichon, afterwards Minister for Foreign Affairs; with M. Deschanel, President of the Chamber and afterwards President of the Republic; with M. Leygues, afterwards Minister of Marine and Prime Minister; with the philosopher, M. Boutroux; and with well-known writers like MM. Gauvain, Fournol, de Quirielle and Chéradame. I was kindly received also in the family of Mlle. Weiss (who now edits "L'Europe Nouvelle") and in the hospitable salon of Madame de Jouvenel. Štefánik's physician, Dr. Hartmann, brought me into touch with a select society; and, naturally, my intercourse with Professors Denis and Eisenmann was constant.

These visits and relationships were valuable both in themselves and because our opponents, the partisans of Austria-Hungary, got frightened and began to work harder. In London, as in Paris and elsewhere, there was a strong pro-Austrian and pro-Magyar tendency which we could not hope to overcome at one stroke. The decisive battle with it was still before us. The strength of the pro-Austrians in Europe and America lay in the belief of Allied politicians that Austria was the safeguard against the "Balkanization" of Europe—"Now we have to deal with one Power; it would be impossible to deal with ten!" they were wont to exclaim—and a bulwark against Germany. This, if you please, at a time when Austria was fighting alongside of Germany!

ISVOLSKY AND THE SLAVS

In Paris I often saw the Serbian Minister, Vesnitch, and exchanged news and views with him upon the whole outlook and the questions that concerned us most nearly. Some of the younger Serbs in Paris were against him—for personal reasons, I felt—and were unjust to him politically. Isvolsky, the Russian Ambassador, I found interesting. When he was Russian Foreign Minister before the war, the contest with Aehrenthal had brought us together. I expected therefore that he would pay some heed to our cause. In talking of Aehrenthal he seemed reserved, perhaps because he had lost interest in him, as I had, and other and weightier matters were then uppermost. What he told me confirmed my opinion that, during their famous meeting at Buchlau at the beginning of September 1908, just before the annexation of Bosnia-Herzegovina by Austria-Hungary, neither he nor Aehrenthal had agreed distinctly enough upon their respective claims. This business is not yet sufficiently cleared up nor, despite the recent statement of Professor Pokrovsky of Moscow, is it certain whether a record of it was kept. I have never heard that a record has been found. Upon things in Russia and at the Court, Isvolsky spoke fully, not disguising his fears of Russia's future. I could see that he knew the Court well, its practical personages and especially the Tsar. Though he was absolutely devoted to his Sovereign and to the Court, his criticism of them was sharp in substance if moderate in words. In this he was a type of those decent and reasonable Russian officials of high rank who saw through the situation and condemned it, but did little or nothing to improve it. I told him what I thought of Russia. He did not and could not challenge my views. And, like so many Russian officials, even Isvolsky had no clear idea of us and of the non-Russian Slavs. Obviously, he thought only of the Orthodox Slavs, or "Brothers." The unification of the Southern Slavs was no part of his policy; the Catholic Croats were to be left out, even if they got independence. This he often said to many people who told me of it in detail; and it was quite clear that his Government had not told him of any official Slav policy. Briand's action in our favor impressed him deeply, and he promised to support us in Paris and London. As I found afterwards, he kept his word. Svatkovsky, who joined me in Paris, kept in constant touch with him. Yet it was pitiful to see how unorganized and incapable of organization were the Russians of all parties who were then in the French capital. I conferred with them all. In the hope of organizing them we even got up a meeting at which Beneš and I demanded that there should be a better service of news from Russia and that Russian politicians abroad should get together—but all to no purpose.

At that moment the relationship of all Western Allied countries to Russia was growing troubled. Though France had binding Treaty engagements with her and an official friendship of long standing, a considerable part of the French political public had always shown reserve, while another part was actually hostile. The French Liberals, to say nothing of the Radicals and Socialists, had little love for Tsarism which, even during the war, they continued to oppose theoretically and practically, in the press and otherwise. British relations to Russia had become more friendly in recent years, though in England, too, the Russian system was still regarded unfavorably by a wide public. Italian views of Russia and the Slavs were vague and, at the beginning of the war, somewhat unfavorable. These anti-Russian feelings were strengthened by the reverses of the Russian army. I learned from a number of French and English public men that Russia had assured France and England of the excellent state of the Russian army and had declared that Russia would have no fear of war if France were well prepared. Many an Englishman and Frenchman took the Rusian defeats as a failure to fulfil a pledge and, indeed, as deceit. It should, I think, have been the duty of those Westerners who knew Russia to take her assurances less uncritically, for while the war with Japan had obliged the Russian military administration to undertake a more vigorous reorganization of the army, the work had been done on a much smaller scale than was necessary.

In view of this state of mind in Paris, Professor Denis repeated to me a request he had made before—that I should give a lecture on the Slavs at the Sorbonne. It was to be the first of a series of lectures on Slavonic affairs, like those that were already being given at King's College, London; and he thought that, if I could speak in Paris, my standpoint might reassure the political public about our own endeavors, and those of the Slav peoples generally, by showing that they were not pan-Slav in any aggressive Russian Imperialist sense. In support of his proposal, Denis mentioned the misplaced declarations of Koniček and others, including Dürich, whose zeal for the Russian dynasty, and assurances that the Czech people would embrace Orthodoxy, had made things worse. These views were hawked round Paris as representing the policy of Dr. Kramář; and the pro-Austrians and our opponents in general fastened on them eagerly and turned them to account. Indeed, Austrian and Magyar agents found it easy to approach our ingenuous people from whom they extracted all sorts of sense and nonsense. I believe, too, that in France and England some impression had been made by the assertions of the German Emperor and of Bethmann-Hollweg that Russian pan-Slavism had caused the war. Sympathy with Russia had, moreover, been deadened by the behavior of Russians, of various party allegiance, in Paris and the West; and when finally a small Russian force came to France, its lack of discipline upset the French, and French military men in particular.

Therefore I gave my lecture on the Slavs and pan-Slavism at the Sorbonne on February 22, 1916. In it I proved that among the Slavs and in Russia there was no Imperialism of the pan-German sort. True, I did not defend Tsarism—but that was no abandonment of the Slav cause. I advocated the creation of an Institute for Slavonic Studies at the Sorbonne, and we founded the scientific Slavonic review, "Le Monde Slave." My relations with the Russians were excellent in all Western countries; and with the Southern Slavs and Poles, as later with the Ukrainians, I worked openly everywhere. We are and mean to be Slavs, albeit European Slavs and citizens of the world.

ŠTEFÁNIK

During this visit to Paris I was constantly with Štefánik. I had known him, years before, when he was a student at Prague. He was poor, and I had found means of making life easier for him. From Prague he had gone to Paris, in 1904 I believe, where he had become Secretary to the Astronomical Observatory. In this capacity he was sent on scientific and astronomical missions to various parts of the world, near and far, such as Mont Blanc, Spain, Oxford, Turkestan, Algiers, South America and Tahiti. Before going to Paris this time I had not, if I remember rightly, had any written correspondence with Štefánik since the outbreak of war, nor had I met him though we had been in touch from time to time through mutual acquaintances. I wish, however, to indicate what he did during the war. I cannot give a full account, and this or that detail may even be wrong; but, as a whole, it will place upon record what I know.

Štefánik began, as soon as war broke out, by persuading a friend who was a French police official, that the Czechs, Slovaks and other Slavs, though officially classed as Austrians, should be given the same privileges as Allied citizens. Then he started propaganda, resolving to gain at least one supporter daily for our cause. He volunteered for service in the French Air Force and, in July 1915, took part in the battles on the Aisne and near Ypres. Afterwards he was sent as an airman to Serbia; but, during the Serbian retreat, his machine "crashed" in Albania and he reached Rome at the end of November on a special torpedo boat from Vallona. In Rome he got to know the French Ambassador, M. Barrère, and Sonnino, the Italian Foreign Minister. Two months later, in February 1916, I found him lying in a Paris hospital after a severe operation. As an astronomer he had a good knowledge of meteorology, and distinguished himself during the war by establishing meteorological stations on the French front. Before the war he had acquired French citizenship and thus had access to places from which non-Frenchmen were excluded.

After his recovery he went to work for us in Italy; and in July-August 1916 he traveled to Russia, where he found means to confer with all the military authorities and even with the Tsar. As a curious detail I may mention that the Tsar sent me, through Štefánik, very friendly greetings and urged me to go on with my policy—this at a time when the Russian Ministry of the Interior was playing off Dürich against me! Part of Štefánik's work in Russia was to neutralize the exaggerations of Dürich and some of Dürich's friends. For this work he had also the authorization of the French Government. With Dürich he sought to reach an agreement by the so-called Protocol of Kieff.

From Russia, Štefánik went at the end of 1916 to the Roumanian front, where he organized many hundreds of our prisoners of war for service in France. There they arrived in the summer of 1917. He himself returned in January 1917 to Russia and thence to Paris, staying with me in London on the way. In Paris he kept in constant touch with Southern Slavs and Italians; and from Paris went again to Rome. The summer (June-October) of 1917 found him in America for the purpose of enrolling Czech and Slovak volunteers. He hoped to get a lot of them but was disappointed. On the other hand, he won Roosevelt for our cause. His strength of character may be judged from the fact that when, on the day of his departure from New York for Europe, he was taken seriously ill after a big meeting in the Carnegie Hall, he had himself carried to the ship on a stretcher. He was then hurrying back to Italy, as far as I remember.

From April 1918 onward he was again in Italy, where he took part in the Congress of Oppressed Austro-Hungarian Races; and, after effective propaganda, he concluded with the Italian Prime Minister, Orlando, the Conventions of April 21 and June 30 of that year. On September 6 he came to me in Washington on his way to join our army in Siberia with the French officer, General Janin, who was to command it. His original intention was to bring our army back from Siberia to Europe by way of Turkestan, the Black Sea and the Mediterranean—the existence of a Russian railway through Central Asia, and the Allied operations against the Turks in Asia Minor evidently suggested this idea to him—but he recognized that the plan was impracticable and, in February 1919, he returned from Russia to Paris, where he secured the support of Marshal Foch for the transport of our army to Europe by way of Vladivostok. In Paris, too, he convinced many people that the Russians were incapable of an offensive against the Bolsheviks. Then, in the spring of 1919, he prepared to fly home from Italy. In the hope of seeing D'Annunzio, he went from Rome to Venice, but missed him. On May 4 he started from Udine—and on the same day his machine crashed near Bratislava, where he found death on his native soil.

This, in the briefest compass, is Stefánik's record. As I have said, I saw him daily in Paris at the beginning of 1916, often together with Beneš. All circumstances and persons of importance for our movement in Allied countries we passed in review, and worked out in detail a plan for our future action. At that time negotiations were going on in Paris for the transfer of a Russian army to France. The Russians made big promises—40,000 men a month—but ultimately an insignificant number came and, indeed, it would have been better had none come at all. The Russian troops were already demoralized, and their demoralization helped to lower the prestige of Russia in France and among the Allies generally. We had thought that our prisoners of war could be brought to France from Russia together with the Russian troops—a plan of which the French Government approved. Štefánik went to Russia to further it. News from several quarters and from my own trustworthy messengers had shown clearly that the Russian Government did not desire our army to be formed and transferred to France, and that our own people were weak politically and in organization. That is why one of us had to go to Russia.

According to our general plan, Štefánik was also to work in Italy, organizing our prisoners of war behind the Italian front so that they, as well as our prisoners from Russia, might possibly be brought to France. We wished to assemble as large a military unit as possible on one front, and we had, besides, an ulterior project—that our army should march with the Allied armies to Berlin at the end of the war and go home by way of Dresden.

In Italy Štefánik made many friends, especially in the army when, in the spring of 1916, he flew over a part of the front and detected the presence of some strong Austrian divisions of which the Italian Commander-in-Chief, General Cadorna, knew nothing. But for Štefánik's discovery, these divisions would have surprised the Italian forces. As it was, his information enabled Cadorna to check the Austrian offensive in the nick of time, and afterwards to employ the Italian reenforcements that had been concentrated on the Trentino front for the remarkable maneuver by which Cadorna won the battle of the Isonzo in August 1916 and captured Gorizia.

In Italy, too, Štefánik established with the Vatican relations which he developed throughout the remainder of the war. He, a Protestant, the son of a Slovak pastor, saw clearly how important the Vatican was for us. Indeed, his propaganda was of the greatest value. His methods were those of an apostle rather than of a diplomatist and soldier. In Paris, where he had gradually made a circle of friends and admirers, he smoothed the way for me and for Dr. Beneš in many an influential quarter and he did the same in Rome. When I think of him I always remember the picture of our little Slovak tinkers who wander through the world; but this Slovak wandered through all the Allied fronts, through all Government Departments, political drawing-rooms and Courts. From him Marshal Foch heard for the first time about us and our work against Austria. In the French army, as I have said, he made influential friends, though he had some opponents in the Government and among the officials.

His political views were more conservative than mine. When, in October 1918, I issued our Declaration of Independence at Washington, he dissented from the terse program I had drawn up. He feared that we might not be able successfully to organize and build up a consistently democratic Republic. But, after a time, he recognized that I had done right and withdrew his protest. He was hampered by inadequate knowledge of conditions and persons at Prague; and politically he was not always quite on his guard. For instance, the Kieff Protocol which he drew up with Dürich was so drafted that it might have been interpreted as a program based merely on the principle of nationality, whereas we had constantly insisted upon our historical rights. But then Dürich, who ought to have known better, was guilty of the same mistake. Similarly, Štefánik's political foresight was defective in Siberia, as is shown by his misreading of the true situation in the army, and of our own people as well as the Russians, especially Koltchak.

For me, personally, his affection was almost touching. I reciprocated it and was grateful for his help. He deserves the gratitude of us all.

VIEWS ON FRANCE

While living in London I was in constant touch with France not only through Beneš but through Frenchmen who either lived in London or came there. Thus I experienced the Anglo-French Alliance in my own person—an alliance organic in me for family and personal reasons. My wife's family is of Southern French Huguenot stock (their name, Garrigue, is that of a mountain range in the South of France), and her ancestors went to America by way of Denmark. Besides Czech and Slovak, English and French are currently spoken by the younger members of my own family; and it is no accident that my first Czech work at Prague was an essay on Hume and Pascal. Since childhood I had grown up in spiritual association with France, beginning to learn French at the age of thirteen; and though I had little actual intercourse with French people before the war, I kept so closely in touch with their whole literature that it became to me a living thing. So thoroughly had I studied France, her literature and her culture, that I felt no need actually to visit the country. Indeed, save for one or two landings at Havre, I had not been there before the war. It is sometimes said that Comte influenced me most. This is perhaps true of his sociology, but, as a theory of knowledge, or epistemology, I thought his Positivism too naïve. Comte sets out from Hume, from whose skepticism he escapes by appealing to tradition and to a so-called general opinion. In France, where science and scientific methods are always highly esteemed—of this Henri Poincaré was a recent example—Comte's Positivism had a powerful influence; but the Positivist yearning for clearness and precision may easily lead to a one-sided intellectualism. At bottom, the French cult of reason (from Descartes to the Revolution and to Comte's Positivism after the Revolution) is what Kant means by "mathematical prejudice" and "pure reason"; and in France as in Germany it ended in a fiasco. Comte himself became a fetish-worshiper and went off, here and there, into a wild Romanticism. One has to be careful about the famous clarity of French thought!

Very early in my intellectual life, the great problem of the French Revolution and Restoration began to persecute me. It was as a link between the Revolution and the Restoration that Comte interested me, for the founder of Positivism and of the Positivist Religion of Humanity carried out the policy of de Maistre. I read Rousseau, Diderot, Voltaire (who, somehow, I did not like) on the one hand, and de Maistre and de Tocqueville on the other. I mention only the most important, though I was acquainted with all the rest, great and small.

I had a pretty severe attack of French Romanticism. Even as a boy I took delight in Chateaubriand and the whole Romantic school. Kollár's strictures upon Romanticism displeased me, and it was comparatively late before I became aware of the unhealthy element in it. This may be seen from many of my criticisms of what I have often called "Decadence," though that is not quite the right term for it. I was struck by the peculiarly morbid and even perverse sexualism in the French Romantics, a trend of feeling of which I believe de Musset has hitherto been the most typical exponent. In this element of Romanticism I sought—rightly, I think—the influence of Catholicism on quasi-Catholic people; for Catholicism, with its asceticism and ideal of celibacy, turns the mind too much towards sex and magnifies its importance even in tender youth. The sexualism of French literature—and, in this respect, France is truly representative —I attribute especially to this Catholic education. The pro-Catholic poet, Charles Guérin, expressed it as the "eternal duel between the fire of the Pagan body and the celestial yearning of the Catholic soul." It is not asceticism alone but exaggerated transcendentalism as a whole that leads skeptics and unbelievers of Catholic origin to the extremes of extreme naturalism. I compared the French and the Italians with the English, the Americans and the Germans. Among Protestant (and Orthodox) peoples and writers there is neither this sexual romanticism nor the peculiar kind of blasphemy that arises from the constant and obvious contrast between the transcendental religious world and the ascetic ideal, on the one hand, and the real world of experience on the other. This contrast disturbs and excites. Protestantism is less transcendental; it is realistic. In Baudelaire the romantic association of the ideal of a Catholic Madonna with a naturalistic Venus finds graphic and typical expression— the same somersault is turned as when Comte surrenders Positivist science to fetishism. Zola threw this somersault in his naturalistic novels, which are strange mixtures of unpositivist Positivism and of gross Romanticism.

Carrère's literary studies on Romanticism, which I had not seen before, were a pleasant surprise. He says many things that I had already said in my essays. One of the chief tasks in French spiritual development has hitherto been to analyze and to criticize Romanticism. De Tocqueville, as afterwards Taine and Brunetière, condemned it. To-day its adversaries are numerous, for instance, Seillière, in his "Away from Rousseau," and his pupils, Lasserre, Faguet, Gillouin and also Maurras—names which show that opposition to Romanticism may spring from divergent views and aims. It is, above all, a moral problem. The Revolution against the old Régime— in the last resort, against Catholicism—degenerated in France into an exaggerated naturalism and into a sexualism that was unhealthy and therefore decadent. In this tendency I see a grave question not only for France but for the other Catholic nations and, indeed, for the whole modern era; and its gravity is not lessened by the fact that the tendency has prevailed in so marked a degree over the more powerful French women writers like Rachilde, Colette and Madeleine Marx.

Since this literary and moral problem bore directly on the war, it is natural that I should have given it attention in Paris and London. I felt it important to ascertain how France and, particularly, her intellectual class would stand the hardships of war. True, I did not accept the arguments on which pan-Germans based prophecies of the final decadence of France and of the Latin peoples. But even temporary decadence has its dangers; and, in the case of France, they were the more threatening because the de-population which alarms the French themselves is certainly connected with moral decadence. And this danger, it seemed to me, would not be wholly averted even by an Allied victory though, at that time, everything depended on victory.

I thought over the stories of disorder in the French army— disorder not explicable solcly by pacifist resistance to bloodshed —in connection with this problem of decadence. General Joffre, it was said, had only restored order by extreme severity. These stories were exaggerated, as I discovered; and it must be frankly acknowledged that, against decadence and its tendency toward passivity among the intellectual classes and especially in Paris, there were in France strong activist movements. The nationalism of Barrès proved itself in the war; and, alongside of Barrès, Bourget and Maurras exhorted the youth of France vigorously to withstand the pan-Germans. The names of Bourget and Maurras are associated with the younger Catholic movement, of which the best and most influential section, and its organ, the "Sillon," were democratic. Since the Revolution, and particularly since de Maistre, the Catholic movement and the religious question have been foremost issues in France. Everywhere and always the fight for control of the schools and for the separation of Church from State has been on the order of the day. In thought, the French Catholic movement is not uniform; and in its chief literary exponents, as, for instance, in Claudel and Péguy, it is by no means orthodox. Maurras combines a national Classicism with his Catholicism, and others attempt in other ways to reach a synthesis between Catholicism and various factors of modern life. The influence which these tendencies exerted and exert is considerable and, on the whole, beneficent. Péguy's death in battle was characteristic. Eloquent witness for modern France in all her intellectual manifestations was, indeed, borne by the large number of young writers who, like him, fell in the war.

By the side of this mainly political Nationalism there arose, out of the older humanitarian and international movements, a realist European movement, activist, energetic and propagandist. It included, on the one hand, writers like Romain Rolland, Suarès, Claudel and Péguy, to whom, in this respect, the poet Jules Romains may be added: and, on the other, Jaurès, who strove in the same way for a more concrete internationalism on the basis of a new patriotism, not a patriotism inspired by a spirit of revenge but by the ideal of a positive association of all nations in an harmonious whole. Most of these various personalities and leaders in French thought had one thing in common— a yearning for activity that was, in effect, a more or less definite protest against the abstract intellectualism of the Positivist heritage and against the skepticism which found its most artificial expression in Anatole France. To this protest Bergson's attitude, in his "Intuition and Philosophy," is akin. In him, as in Gide, Claudel and Jaurès, the watchwords are *"élan vital —ferveur—ardente sérénité—effort."* Sorel raised the note to "violence." In this I see more than the French were conscious of—the influence of German psychology with its "Activism" and "Emotionalism," from Kant to Nietzsche and after.

I descried in the Entente, in the effective alliance of France with England and Russia, and subsequently with America, a practical expression of this European tendency of French minds. Strong Russian influences were at work in it as well as German, Scandinavian, English and American; and the question arises whether the unhealthy element in Romantic decadence will be overcome by this active striving for comprehension and by the effects of the war.

The best and precisely the most modern minds are well aware of the problem of decadence and regeneration. They are constantly examining it. The compound novel, or series of novels, is therefore characteristic of French literature. In this form, and by means of analyzing a whole epoch, an effort is made to present a picture of modern France. After Balzac we had the novels of Zola, of Romain Rolland and, latterly, of Martin du Gard and others.

VIEWS OF ENGLAND

I returned to London from Paris on February 26, 1916. My stay in the French capital had brought home to me the great difference between the two cities in war-time. Paris gave the impression of being a city of mourning—Victor Hugo's Capital of the Universe had become the necropolis of our civilization. More than once I imagined that I could hear the guns of Verdun. Fort Douaumont fell on the day of my departure.

In London there was hardly a trace of the war. Everything was calm, "business as usual." Not until later did the war spirit get a hold—slowly, but in grim earnest. Troops came and went. The wounded soon returned; and, presently, German shortsightedness made a point of rousing the country by bombing, with Zeppelins and aircraft, cities like London and other towns strategically unimportant.

Naturally, my stay in London and visit to Paris, as well as constant intercourse with Englishmen and Frenchmen and the observation of French and English soldiers, Anglo-French agreement and disagreement, stimulated me to compare French with English literature and culture. Among British philosophers Hume had attracted me most, for he stated most forcibly the great problem of modern skepticism in its relation to the theory of knowledge; and since Comte, like Kant, took Hume as a starting point, I compared Comte with Hume. How different they are! The Frenchman returns to fetishism and seeks salvation in a neo-antique religion, whereas the Briton or, rather, the Scot, escapes from his own skepticism through a human ethic, not, like Comte, through a Religion of Humanity. Again, the Catholic and the Protestant! Among the more modern philosophers John Stuart Mill—who was also to some extent a follower of Comte—appealed to me as a representative of English empiricism. From Buckle, whom I can only mention, I got a clear notion of the meaning of history. Darwin I had found a knotty problem. I rejected and still reject Darwin-ism, though not the theory of evolution. Spencer interested me much as a philosopher of evolution and as a sociologist.

Yet, to be quite frank, I paid more heed to English and American literature than to English philosophy. I soon got to know it pretty thoroughly and could compare it with the French in its bearing upon Romantic decadence. Rossetti and Oscar Wilde I had examined already; and now, in London, I deepened my acquaintance with the Celtic renascence and, in this connection, verified my analysis of French Romantic sexualism. W. L. George among the younger, and George Moore among the older writers, seemed good subjects for this inquiry; but, since the war I have found in Joyce the most instructive case of Catholic-Romantic decadence. In him there is a really palpable transition from metaphysical and religious transcendentalism and asceticism to naturalistic and sexual worldliness in practice.

This element of decadence, so strong among French writers, is not to be found among the English. Not that it is confined to the French; it exists also in Italian and Spanish and, to a marked degree, in German-Austrian literature as well as in that of Poland and in our own. This peculiarity perplexes the historians of English literature. Some speak, very superficially, of English prudery and cant; others simply cannot explain a difference that is undeniable. In reality, the difference between France and England is the difference between Catholicism and Protestantism, between the morality of religious transcendentalism and a morality more human and natural. Hence there is not in England and in English literature the same crisis that exists in French literature and in France; there is not the same dualism, the same conflict between body and soul. A writer like Lawrence is an exception. He seems to have got his decadence from reading Freud. On the other hand, the Irish, as Catholics, certainly go with the French. I look upon English literature as the healthier; yet, if I ask, with Taine: "Musset or Tennyson?" I answer, "Musset *and* Tennyson, the French *and* the English (with the Americans), but be critical of both." And, while interpreting decadent eroticism in this way, I ask myself whether it can rightly be ascribed to temperament and race, for such an explanation of it is assuredly wrong and based on superficial observation of peoples.

The centenary of Charlotte Brontë, my favorite authoress, was celebrated soon after my return from Paris to London. In her there is Romanticism, if you will, but pure and strong withal, love potent yet by no means material, utterly different from the French. I read her again, and Elizabeth Browning, too. In London it dawned upon me that England has, proportionately, the largest number of powerful women writers. With Mrs. Humphry Ward and May Sinclair, and many a novel by Marie Corelli, by ingenious "Ouida," and other authoresses whose books were published in the Tauchnitz edition, I was already familiar. Now I came across a series of them—Reeves, Ethel Sidgwick, Kaye-Smith, Richardson, Delafield, Clemence Dane, Woolf. This is by no means the whole list; for, from Jane Austen to Charlotte (and Emily) Brontë, George Eliot and Elizabeth Browning, the number and the power of English women writers are extraordinary, higher proportionately than those of other countries, though I am not quite sure about America. This shows the penetration of women into public life; they are freeing themselves from the harem-kitchen domain. During the war one could see in London, as indeed in other countries, how women were taking up callings formerly reserved for men. After the return of the men from the war there would doubtless be a change, but, meanwhile, women had extended their rights and also their responsibilities. In the daily press and privately one heard of a strikingly high number of suicides among women —as statistics now confirm. They suggest that women were bearing burdens too heavy for them, and that loneliness had its effect.

The knowledge I had acquired from the history of literature and from literary criticism was thus supplemented in London by reading the authors themselves; for even in the best of our libraries at home there was many a gap. Samuel Butler and his humor did not enthral me. Of Thomas Hardy I had known only the more sensational novels; now I read him right through, and likewise George Meredith, whom I came to like better than before. I extended, too, my acquaintance with George Gissing, Galsworthy, Walpole, Arnold Bennett and Conrad, among the later writers. Wells I knew already. From them I went on to one of the youngest, Swinnerton; and Hutchinson, Lawrence and others likewise cast their spell over me.

English culture I hold to be the most progressive and, as I was able to see during the war, the most humane. Not that I think all the English are angels. But in their civilization the Anglo-Saxons—and this is true of America, too—have expressed humanitarian ideals the most carefully in theory, and have practised them in a higher degree than other nations. In English views of the war and in its conduct this was evident. The English soldiers were better looked after and better treated than those of other armies. The sanitary service and military hygiene were particularly good. The claims of "conscientious objectors," opponents of war on religious and ethical grounds, were very liberally admitted. Besides, the English published trustworthy news of the war and did not suppress enemy opinions.

Is all this bound up with England's wealth? No European city seems so rich as London. I walked and rode through its length and breadth, in all directions. Almost everywhere the door handles were in good order, the many brass plates of business houses were polished, garden fences well kept—these things showed me the wealth of England more clearly than any statistical figures.

THE CINEMA SPIRIT

In London, as elsewhere, I went to the cinema to see war films. They showed every side of war technique, from the initial stages in factories and dockyards up to the life in the trenches. The French pictures were mostly political; and though the French and the English public both liked appeals to sentiment, the English and the American films were less mournful than those of France. I noticed, too, in London, and later on in America, that when portraits of political and military personages were thrown on the screen, the loudest applause was always given to the King of the Belgians, louder, in fact, than to Joffre and Foch. In England, as in America, it was for Belgium that the people had gone into the war. In the cinemas I realized, moreover, that in modern English literature all novels, even those of Hardy and Meredith, have a strong strain of the cinematograph spirit, a preference for mysteries and complicated plots of the detective story type. True, in the older French literature, in Balzac, for example, the novel is already a detective story. While the Germans and we ourselves, led nd perverted by the Russians, analyze the soul and dig out ot it what is weird and morbid, the English and the Americans are always simpler. Puzzles of a more mechanical sort interest them, though they also have managed to spoil their minds with modern theories, problems and super-problems, and even with Freud's ridiculous psychology. Take, for instance, Mr. Lawrence, who sometimes seems like Barbusse and Jaeger!

The trenches and trench warfare could be seen comfortably enough in the cinema—but at Verdun, from February 1916 onward, month after month the fighting was terribly bloody and grim. Yet the Germans failed, a failure characteristic of the military situation. On the Somme, the war of position was likewise long and bloody. If the Eastern front had been the more generally important in 1915, the center of gravity shifted again to the French front in 1916. In Russia, the Germans were carrying out their pan-German plan; and, at the beginning of 1917, Mitau fell. Hindenburg and Ludendorff had been placed at the head of the German army in August 1916; and, in the following December, General Nivelle in France took over the chief command from Joffre—on whom the dignity of Marshal was bestowed—while Foch became Chief of Staff. In April 1917

Nivelle sought in vain to break through the German front; his losses were too heavy. The Germans for their part, began unrestricted submarine warfare on February 1, 1917, and shortened their land front in the West by taking up the Siegfried line in March.

Since the beginning of 1916, large British reenforcements had been reaching the front. Though, at first, they were kept in Belgium and the North, their presence was felt along the whole French line. By 1916, too, the Allies had evidently become preponderant in munitions and war material; the German army began to grow nervous and to lose confidence.

I watched the growth of the British army, saw the recruiting and the life in camp and barracks. For the "Tommies" I felt a hearty liking. The Canadians also came through London; and, as the French Canadians and their language interested me, I went to see them. A Continental observer could not fail to be struck by the superiority of British military equipment and general arrangements; and in this respect the Americans outdid even the English. In them both one must recognize the good, nay, the great qualities of steadfastness and tenacity. Mr. Steed always used to console us—and our English friends—by saying that Englishmen take time to get going, but when they start they keep it up; and in 1916 Mrs. Humphry Ward wrote much the same thing of the British war spirit. It turned out to be literally true.

The unexpected death of Kitchener on June 5 seemed a bad omen to many people in England, though the evacuation of the Dardanelles (January 18, 1916) and the capitulation of Kut-el-Amara in Mesopotamia (April 28) had already taken place. A German mine, not a submarine, is said to have sunk the cruiser "Hampshire"; yet, as Kitchener's departure was a dead secret, treason was suspected and it was feared that he might have been the victim of a submarine. If treason there was, we thought that it must have come from St. Petersburg, for it was on the Tsar's invitation that Kitchener was going to Russia to work out a strategical plan against Austria.

Even after his death, the Dardanelles episode continued to be hotly debated in London. The venture may have been a mistake but its boldness was encouraging. England had, however, troubles nearer home. In April the Irish rebellion broke out. Lloyd George took Kitchener's place at the War Office in July, and became Prime Minister in December 1916. The battle of Jutland (May 31–June 1, 1916) was at first reported in London as a British defeat and the truth was not known till later. In point of fact, the German fleet never again dared take the offensive.

Then the British wiped out their defeats in Mesopotamia and took Baghdad—to my eyes, a very welcome breach in the pan-German Berlin-Baghdad line. (An entry in my diary on January 15, 1916, runs *ad* Berlin–Baghdad: First Balkan train Berlin–Vienna–Budapest–Belgrade–Sofia–Constantinople.) Jerusalem, too, was taken; and, in the Balkans, General Sarrail began successful operations from Salonica which allowed the remnant of the Serbian army to come into play, a matter of considerable political importance for Serbia. In the Tyrol the Italians were hard pressed, but on the Isonzo they advanced in August 1916 and occupied Gorizia; and at the end of the same month Italy declared war on Germany.

On the Russian front Brusiloff took the offensive against the Germans and Austrians between June and November 1916. He triumphed at Lutsk, and made hundreds of thousands of Austrian prisoners, among them many future Czech legionaries. Though he was checked, his advance relieved the pressure on France, several German divisions having to be transferred from the Western to the Eastern front. Likewise Brusiloff relieved the Italians by compelling the Austrians to stop the offensive they had successfully begun in the Tyrolese Alps towards the middle of May, and to withdraw troops thence for the Russian front. The Russian advance also helped to bring Roumania into the war after protracted negotiations with Russia and the Entente. Roumania declared war on August 27 and pressed rapidly forward into Transylvania—though, by the end of the year, Mackensen was master of Bucharest.

Yet, despite Brusiloff's fleeting success, the year 1916 saw the total elimination and retreat of the Slav armies—Russia was definitely defeated. The overthrow of Serbia at the end of 1915 had reached its climax in January 1916 by the downfall and occupation of Montenegro. The Germans of Austria had followed the Magyar example and, on October 11, 1915, "Austria" arose—to vegetate for three years—in the place of the old "Kingdoms and Lands represented in the Reichsrat." The assassination of the Prime Minister, Count Stürgkh, on October 21, 1916, and the death of Francis Joseph on November 11 were omens of impending collapse.

The next year, 1917, was fateful for all the belligerent nations and above all for Russia. It had long been whispered that in Russia a storm was brewing. The characteristic premiership of Stürmer, whom Benckendorff regarded as a dangerous pro-German, had lasted from February 9 till November 23, and had been generally condemned; and though the rigorous Russian censorship prevented news of the extraordinary excitement from reaching Europe, there were too many Englishmen and Frenchmen in Russia for alarming accounts not to be sent or brought to the West. Attention had been drawn to the situation at Petrograd and in the army by the members of the Duma who visited Paris and London; and, later on, Milyukoff's speech against Stürmer in the Duma of November 14, 1916, which culminated in the question "Madness or Treason?" illumined the position for the public at large. The original British view of the Russian Revolution was that the fall of the pro-German régime would enable Russia to wage war more efficiently and successfully.

THE AMERICAN DECLARATION OF WAR

Hard upon the Russian Revolution of March 1917 followed a second far-reaching event on April 6—the decision of the United States to declare war upon Germany and to join the

Allies in the fight against the Central Powers. Less attention is usually paid to the naval war between England and Germany than to the fighting on land, though, in reality, this aspect of the struggle was extremely stubborn and of great importance in deciding the issue. Germany had challenged England by the undue expansion of the German navy and by the endeavor to show the German flag on every sea. Immediately after the outbreak of war, England and her Allies began by blockading Germany in order to prevent the importation of foodstuffs and raw materials. The French fleet lent its aid. Germany replied by submarine warfare. Without dilating upon this contest I must point out that America saw in it a danger to her own shipping and to her trade. As early as August 5, 1915, she tried, unsuccessfully, to mediate between the belligerents; and when, in February 1915, Germany declared British waters a war zone, America immediately protested, her protests being renewed whenever German submarines endangered the lives of American citizens. In February 1916 the Germans intensified their submarine campaign until, on February 1, 1917, they passed to unrestricted submarine warfare. America was incensed, her aversion from Germany having been increased by German and Austrian propaganda in America and by attacks upon American trade and industry in the United States itself. Of this I shall give some account when I tell of the part we took in opposing this phase of German action.

At first the German submarines were very successful. By the spring of 1917, despondent voices were increasingly to be heard in England, foretelling starvation and surrender. Lloyd George himself was seriously alarmed. As I had been living in England since the autumn of 1915, I followed with the utmost attention the course of the naval struggle. One was continually reminded of it in London, even in the daily details of domestic life. There was much talk of a German invasion—a possibility officially admitted as late as the spring of 1918. The question was very important because it affected the estimates of the number of troops that ought to be held in readiness at home and therefore withheld from France. Hence I took comprehensible interest in American protests against Germany. Even before the sinking of the "Lusitania," on May 7, 1915, their tone was sharp, and it became still sharper in the Notes dealing with the "Lusitania." In December 1915 an American Note was also addressed to Austria on the sinking of the "Ancona" by an Austrian submarine. In 1916 came the Notes on the sinking of the cross-channel steamer "Sussex" until, finally, war was declared on April 6, 1917. The declaration of war counterbalanced not only the successes of the German submarines but those of the German armies. Such, at least, was my firm belief when I decided, In the spring of 1917, to go for a time to Russia.

About Russia and her fate I had worried continually. Now and again I had gone to see the Russian Ambassador, Count Benckendorff. The Russian journalist, M. de Wesselitsky, known to readers of the "Novoe Vremya" as "Argus," lived also in London; and I made the acquaintnace of Dioneo, a Russian emigrant, and of Prince Kropotkin, besides Professor Vinogradoff, whom I have already mentioned. Milyukoff and other members of the Duma came over from Russia in April 1916 with Protopopoff, and we agreed with Milyukoff upon our anti-Austrian program. He issued a declaration upon it in Paris after discussing it with Beneš. Presently he came back to lecture at Oxford, where we had an opportunity of going more fully into political and military details. The Russian writer, Amfiteatroff, who went from Italy by way of London to Petrograd at the end of November 1916, should also be mentioned. He was to edit Protopopoff's daily newspaper, and he promised me to conduct it on liberal lines. I gave him an article in which I explained to the Russians the necessity of destroying Austria—a doctrine that needed to be preached as much in Russia as in the West, because many Russians held to a vague idea of a diminished Austria in which we Czechs should play the leading part.

Thanks to the Russian visitors, to my own messengers and to a number of our own people who came from Russia to

London, I was able to keep an eye upon Russian conditions, our colonies there and their leaders. Dr. Pučálka was one of the first to come; and he worked also for our men in Serbia. Then Pavlu, a journalist, turned up, got to know the state of affairs in England and France and saw for himself the relationship of the West to Russia. Messrs. Reiman, Vaněk and Professor Písecký should also be mentioned. Stephen Osuský, the young Slovak lawyer to whom I have already referred, came from America in June 1916. After a time he went on to Beneš in France, and, learning French quickly, became a valuable helper.

The Russian Polish leader, Roman Dmowski, who came to London in 1916, understood that the preservation of Austria was and would be a continual danger to the Poles. On many points we agreed. Little was then said of the Silesian question, which was very subordinate in comparison with our common aims. I negotiated with Dmowski about it afterwards in Washington.

THE SOUTHERN SLAVS AND ITALY

I have already said that in London, where they were numerous, the Southern Slavs had organized their Yugoslav Committee. They, especially the Croats and Slovenes, made their political headquarters in the English capital. Among them were Supilo, Hinkovitch, Vosnyak, Potochnyak and Mestrovitch, the sculptor. The Serbian Minister was M. Jovanovitch, whom I had known in Vienna, and until he came the Legation was in charge of M. Antonievitch, whom I also knew well. Professors Savitch and Popovitch, and Father Nicolai Velimirovitch, who carried on skilful ecclesiastical propaganda, were prominent among the Serbs; and when, in April 1916, the Serbian Crown Prince arrived with the Prime Minister, Pashitch, I had conversations and entered into friendly agreements with both.

In view of the Treaty of London, relations with Italy always formed a delicate point, not only for the Southern Slavs but for me too; and, as I was working steadily in concert with them, the Italo-Yugoslav problem was always with me. My former championship of the Yugoslav cause—on behalf of Bosnia-Herzegovina in 1891–93, in the Agram and Friedjung trials of 1909 and in the struggle against Aehrenthal and in the Vashitch trial at Belgrade—gave me an exceptional position among them. In the present case, their conflict with Italy became especially acute because the Italians in London were diligent in defending the Treaty. My opinion was that Italy would give way in the final peace negotiations. She could not have taken part in the war without some recompense, and the question was whether we did not all need her help to ensure an Allied victory What if the Austrians and Germans should win? In that event the situation would have been very much worse for the Yugoslavs also, and for a very long time. With insignificant exceptions, our Yugloslav friends were sharply antagonistic to Italy, though some of them held more moderate views and kept in touch with the Italians—which was tactically advantageous. The official Serbian attitude was calm, but it had the effect of exciting distrust among the Croats and Slovenes who often complained that, like Russia, Serbia was betraying the Yugoslavs and Slav interests in general. Our views differed from those of the Croats and Slovenes on yet another feature of the London Treaty —the provision by which the Allies, in deference to Italian wishes, undertook to exclude the Vatican from the Peace Conference.

To us, the relationship to Italy was important for an additional reason. In fighting against Austria, the Italians soon made prisoners of a large number of our men and, as in Russia, we were able to organize them into a Legion. As I have said, our National Council entrusted Štefánik with this work. Beneš also went to Italy and was always in contact with the Italian Embassy in Paris. But our colonies acted in unison with the Southern Slavs.

In England our colony was not numerous. Some personal antagonism among its members had been removed during my first visit to London. I usually met my fellow-countrymen at a restaurant kept by Mr. Sykora. He and Mr. Francis Kopecký found much difficulty in getting English officials to safeguard the interests of our people, whom Kopecký urged to join the British army, he himself setting a good example. In August 1916 we organized jointly with the Southern Slavs a demonstration against Austria, at which Viscount Templetown presided and Seton-Watson spoke. In Seton-Watson and Steed the Southern Slavs had ardent supporters. Both of them favored openly the standpoint of the Southern Slav Committee in regard to the Treaty of London. Seton-Watson helped to organize the Serbian Relief Fund and the important Serbian Society of Great Britain. On the latter model an Anglo-Czech Society was afterwards formed. In the spring of 1917 a Montenegrin Committee was constituted in Paris. Its tendency was antagonistic to King Nicholas; and in March it issued a program of Montenegrin-Yugoslav union.

The controversy about Italy and the Treaty of London revived, as I noticed, the old dissensions between Croats and Serbs; and the personal quarrels which also arose among them became so hot as to damage the Yugoslav name. Supilo, who had helped me against Aehrenthal after the Bosnian annexation crisis of 1908–9 and during the affair of the Friedjung forgeries, was often with me. He had been in Russia at the beginning of 1915 and had returned indignant because the Russians had accepted the Treaty of London. To this I shall refer when I come to Russia. After the outbreak of war, my intercourse with him began at Geneva. Before long, however, he fell out not only with the Russians and Serbia but with the Southern Slav Committee as well. I did my utmost to put matters right; and the day before I left for Russia, Supilo promised me to bury the hatchet. He kept his word—but I did not dream when I left him that we had seen each other for the last time. He died in the following September.

One incident of the more private side of my life in London recurs to me. As in Geneva, I had blood-poisoning. The doctors could not explain it. On their advice I went for a time to the seaside at Bournemouth, where I was operated upon. The surgeon affirmed that I had been poisoned through my laundry; and it was not unnatural to suppose that my Austrian enemies were looking after me in this way. Both at Geneva and in London I had proofs that they were watching me. So I kept up my revolver practice—as I might have done in any case, for I was always fond of target shooting—and it was just as well for those who were shadowing me to see that I was on my guard. One day, indeed, thieves broke into my house—probably secret agents who wanted to get at my papers. By a lucky accident they were scared away; but, on the advice of the police, I had electric alarm bells fixed at every point where the house could be broken into.

PEACE FEELERS

Meanwhile our systematic propaganda was bearing fruit in all directions. Seton-Watson's "New Europe" was remarkably helpful in political quarters. The Allied press proclaimed more and more definitely our anti-Austrian program and the right of small peoples to self-determination; and, in England, the cause of Belgium had drawn attention to the small nations from the very beginning of the war.

Yet the tense situation on all fronts continued to be disquieting. The Germans shouted "victory," but began to put out peace feelers; they no longer felt sure of victory. We know now that, by the end of 1916, Ludendorff and others were apprehensive about the position in the field, though their "fears" may have been meant to bring on unrestricted submarine warfare. The idea of withdrawing from France in the West and of holding on to Russia in the East was obvious in the German peace feelers. On October 31, 1916, the German Emperor ordered Bethmann-Hollweg to draft peace proposals; and on December 12 the German Chancellor handed them to the American, Swiss and Spanish representatives. Briand was the first to answer and to reject them. The other Allied statesmen followed suit and, on December 30, the Allied Governments sent a collective reply.

At this juncture a new and weighty political factor came into play in the person of President Wilson. On November 7, 1916, he had been reelected to the Presidency of the United States and thus acquired great weight. On December 21, in a Message emphasizing the right of small peoples to self-determination and proposing a League of Nations, he asked the belligerents to state their war aims. A striking passage in this Message insisted that his action had not been prompted by the peace feelers of the Central Powers; and it transpired subsequently that Berlin had been pressing him since the summer to make a peace move and that he had been unpleasantly surprised by German and Austrian action.

The Allies answered Wilson on January 12, 1917, in a joint Note that was a brilliant success for our cause, inasmuch as it included among the Allied conditions of peace "the liberation of Italians, Slavs, Roumanes and Czechoslovaks from foreign rule." This answer made a stir in all our colonies and strengthened us greatly; and not only in our colonies but in the press and political circles of Allied countries, because we Czechs and Slovaks were especially mentioned by name. This, however, caused some discontent in the Southern Slav and Polish colonies, who thought our success disproportionately great.

I could see at once from the text of the Allied reply that the word "Czechoslovaks" had been inserted into a completed draft which had demanded only the liberation of the "Slavs" in general; and this turned out to have been the case. Dr. Beneš heard that the Allied reply had been drawn up. He conferred with M. Philippe Berthelot and others, but met with great difficulties because the Allies hesitated to bind themselves to break up Austria-Hungary entirely or to promise freedom to the Austro-Hungarian peoples. Verbally and in writing Beneš insisted that this promise should be given to strengthen the resistance of the oppressed Hapsburg races, and asked in particular that the Czechs and Slovaks should be expressly mentioned. Influential persons like M. Leygues, the chairman of the Foreign Affairs Committee of the French Chamber, supported him. M. André Tardieu, in the "Temps," and M. Jules Sauerwein, in the "Matin," wrote in our favor on January 3; and the "Matin" reminded M. Briand of the promise he had given me a year before. The Allies had decided, after discussions between Paris, Rome and London, to speak only of "Slavs" in general so as not to give umbrage either to the Italians or to the Southern Slavs; but the French Foreign Office succeeded in fulfilling the desire of Beneš. There is an interesting point of inner history in the use of the word "Czechoslovaks." Three proposals were made—the liberation of "Bohemia," of "the "Czech People" and of "the Czechoslovaks." The third was accepted after consultation between Beneš, Štefánik and Osuský.

Despite the Allied reply, President Wilson did not lose hope of a comparatively early peace. The German Ambassador at Washington, Count Bernstorff, invoking the authority of Colonel House, asked the German Government for its peace terms on January 28, 1917. Thereupon Germany sent, on January 29, a list of her demands in which she made the most of the military *status quo*, foreshadowing, in particular, a frontier rectification at the expense of Russia, and pleading for Poland as a country under German control. Washington found this answer unsatisfactory.

It is characteristic of German diplomacy that, simultaneously with the peace terms, it should have notified Wilson of the beginning of unrestricted submarine warfare. This notification was published on January 31, 1917; and, on February 5, the United States broke off diplomatic relations with Germany. Next day President Wilson called upon the neutrals to do the same. Their answers were interesting. As far as I could find out, ten of them replied, some in the negative, others evasively. Austria, for her part, made a parallel peace move when feeling against Germany began to rise in America. Through his brother-in-law, Prince Sixtus of Parma, the Emperor Charles secretly approached Poincaré and other Western statesmen.   To this I shall refer more fully later on.

All these peace moves I watched very carefully.   No less than the operations in the field, they indicated the general situation.   Hopes of peace, and pacifism, had everywhere been stimulated by the downfall of Tsardom and by the Russian Revolution.   On April 10 a declaration of the Russian Provisional Government promised self-determination to all Russian nationalities. This was followed on April 15 by a manifesto of the Russian Workmen's and Soldiers' representatives demanding peace without annexations or indemnities and, on April 19, by a manifesto of German, Austrian and Hungarian Social Democrats supporting that of the Russian Workmen and Soldiers—pronouncements of which the effect was weakened by the American declaration of war.   From Wilson's utterances and those of the Allies it was obvious that America had declared war in earnest, not as a momentary means of pressure.   All doubt on that score was set at rest by the rapidity of American armament for which, indeed, some preparation had already been made.

A Disavowal

I did not and could not expect that our success in the Allied reply to President Wilson, a success won by intense effort on our part and by the exceptional friendliness of France, would bring about what I so greatly feared—that our members of Parliament at home might disavow us.   The course of home affairs I had naturally followed with keen attention.   Not only did we get the Austrian and Czech papers, and news by messenger from Prague and Vienna, but, as far as I could manage it, the principal reports made to the Allied Governments.   I have already mentioned that people in Allied countries taxed us with supineness.   Enemy propaganda constantly harped on the same string, not without effect.   We made the most of the persecution of our people by the Austrians, though it is comprehensible that the arrest and condemnation of men like Dr. Kramář and Dr. Rašín could not have the same effect abroad as at home. The Allied peoples had their own losses and sufferings, especially in France, where nearly every family was mourning the death of one of its members. We utilized everything that we decently could, and there was no lack of material. For instance, the summing up of the Court against Dr. Kramář contained an eloquent description of our anti-Austrian work, and we took advantage of it. Thus the folly of Vienna and of the Austro-Hungarian Commander-in-Chief recoiled upon itself.

After I had left Prague there had been no great improvement in the political situation. Parties and persons were as divided as ever a matter of less moment because there could be no public political life under the prevailing military pressure. Therefore I welcomed the attempt that was made toward the end of 1916 to unite Czech parties and Members of Parliament in a Czech Association and in an (incomplete) National Committee. When the Emperor Charles succeeded to Francis Joseph on November 21, 1916, this union was judicious and certainly necessary. Indeed, Francis Joseph's death strengthened our position, for the opinion had long been prevalent that, on the death of the old Emperor, Austria would break up. I had often heard this opinion before the war, in America and elsewhere; and the death of the popular old Emperor was taken as an omen of the beginning of the end. The new Emperor was unknown, and what was said of him inspired few hopes. The assassination of Count Stürgkh, the Prime Minister, which had preceded the Emperor's death, had revealed Austria's weakness; and Dr. Adler's defense, an indictment in which he emphasized effectively her responsibility for the war, damaged her anew. We made it our care to spread documents like these far and wide in foreign countries.

Then came the Allied answer to Wilson, with its special mention of "the Czechoslovaks." It was not surprising that the Catholic Party in Bohemia should hasten to reject it (as early as January 14); nor was it astonishing that the German and Austrian press should hail this rejection as an act of loyalty.

But the Czech Association also repudiated it. I understood the difficult predicament in which our members of Parliament had been placed, and expected that they would be compelled to say something, particularly after the Clerical declaration. The only question was, How? I imagined what they might have said—but it turned out otherwise. True, the omission of my name weakened the effect of the disavowal, and this vagueness caused the press and the political public to take less notice of it; but Count Czernin, the Austro-Hungarian Foreign Minister, did us the best service in publishing only a short letter from three Members of Parliament whose names were unknown abroad. Nevertheless, the pro-Austrians abroad used the disavowal to the full, and it gave us not a little to do.

Our opponents rubbed their hands over a first manifesto in which the Czech Association and the National Committee had proclaimed, on November 19, 1916, their attachment to the dynasty and to its historic mission. The fact that both of these organizations took part in the coronation of the Emperor at Budapest on December 30, 1916, was likewise turned against us; and when the disavowal followed, it was skilfully linked up with the two other episodes. I explained the disavowal as an acknowledgment of the pardon granted to Dr. Kramář and his comrades, but it was unnecessary to have paid so high a price for it. As we heard abroad, Francis Joseph had thought the indictment of Kramář for high treason an act of weakness; and, by pardoning him, the Emperor Charles confirmed this view. Vienna would not have dared to take the lives of our public men whom she had imprisoned, and it seemed to us that our policy at home was concentrated too anxiously upon having them set free. I thought also that the disavowal might have been secured by the influence of the young Emperor, who was preparing for separate peace negotiations with France and the Entente, and held out to our people the prospect of an early peace. That was certainly a serious consideration. But a telegram of congratulation that was sent to the Austro-Hungarian General, Boroevitch, made a far worse impression on me. He had only been successful in a minor action on the Italian front, and it was all the more striking that our people should have congratulated him especially upon it.

Yet the disavowal was soon forgotten. The Russian Revolution and the entry of the United States into the War filled men's minds and strengthened hopes of an Allied victory; and its influence at home was evident in the manifesto which our Members of Parliament issued on April 14, 1917. This manifesto helped us because it contained, albeit indirectly, a criticism of Austria. And when, in view of this situation, the Austrian Parliament was convened, my fears began to diminish.

CHAPTER V

PAN-SLAVISM AND OUR REVOLUTIONARY ARMY

(PETROGRAD-MOSCOW-KIEFF-VLADIVOSTOK. MAY 1917-APRIL 1, 1918)

THE RUSSIAN REVOLUTION

ALL along I had feared a revolution in Russia; yet when it came, I was—unpleasantly—surprised. What would be its effect on the Allies and on the waging of the war? The first report was indefinite and hardly credible. After getting further information and beginning to find my bearings, I sent Milyukoff and Rodzianko, on March 18, 1917, a telegram in which I laid stress on the Slav program—emphasis by no means superfluous either in Russia or in the West. Since, to my knowledge, one of the Allies, Tsarist Russia, cared nothing for democracy or freedom, it had not been easy for me to say that the objects of Allied policy were the liberation of small peoples and the strengthening of democracy. But now, after the Russian Revolution, I could say unreservedly that a free Russia had a full right to proclaim the freedom of the Slavs. The Slav program I stated briefly as follows: The unification of the Poles in close association with Russia; the unification of the Serbs, Croats and Slovenes; and, equally, the unification and liberation of us Czechs and Slovaks. I added that it was a question not only of Slav but also of Latin nations, the French, the Italians and the Roumanians, and of their rightful national ideals. This program was in harmony with the recent Allied reply to President Wilson and with the views of the Allied political circles which were in sympathy with us. I had also to take into account the position of the post-revolutionary Russian Government and especially of Milyukoff as Foreign Minister. He sent at once a friendly answer.

I have said that the news of the Revolution, and of its rapid course in particular, disquieted me. At that juncture, despite my knowledge of Russia, many of the revolutionary leaders and what they stood for were unknown to me. One may feel fears, have intuitions, imagine a general situation and guess how it will develop, yet not possess, at a given moment, concrete knowledge of realities, of the chief persons at work and of their motives and intentions. This knowledge I lacked. As I knew that the middle-class and the Socialists (the Democrats and the Revolutionaries) were unprepared, I had expected a demonstrative outbreak, not a revolution, to follow the reverses in the field. The meeting of the Duma, notwithstanding its dissolution by the Tsar, had been such a demonstration. What surprised me was that the army and the whole machinery of State, together with the Tsarist system itself, should be so deeply shaken, however clearly I had long seen through and condemned Tsardom and its incapacity.

With official Russia my relations had not been pleasant. For years I had been on the Index; but, on the other hand, I had friends in the progressive parties. Though the Russian translation of my first book "On Suicide" had been destroyed, it had aroused the interest of Tolstoy. The censorship passed my "Critique of Marxism," which was widely read in Russian and made my name known. The Marxists disagreed with it but it did not estrange even them. Then, once again, my "Russian Studies" were banned. Nevertheless, in the German edition, they attracted attention. In the autumn of 1914 Trotsky wrote disparagingly of my "Russia and Europe," from a one-sided Marxist standpoint, in the Viennese Social Democratic Review, "Der Kampf."

Knowing that the Russian reactionaries liked neither me nor the Allies, I did not hasten to Russia during the Tsarist régime. A conflict which might have arisen with the Russian Government, would have encouraged our enemies. For this reason I had always tried to influence official Russia through Russian and Allied diplomatic channels and by means of Svatkovsky and other Russians who came often to the West, and to keep in touch with our own people in Russia by letters and messengers and through members of our colony who came to see me. But when the Revolution had put my personal friends and acquaintances in power, some of them being members of the Government, I decided to go to Russia and to carry through the creation of an army among our prisoners of war. Upon Milyukoff as Foreign Minister I counted especially. We had long known each other and, as I have said, we had met in England during the war and had agreed upon the chief points of a war and peace program.

Another reason for going to Russia, where I expected to stay a few weeks, was the serious position that had grown up on the Western front at the beginning of 1917. So, having made the necessary arrangements in London and discussed conditions in Russia with Lord Milner, who had just returned from his official mission there, I set out on April 16, 1917, with an English passport. The German submarines had begun a pitiless campaign against North Sea traffic, and the boat on which I was to have sailed from the little port of Amble on April 17 was sunk. I waited a day or two, when there came suddenly a telegram from London to say that Štefánik had returned from Russia, and a messenger calling me back to London. Thus the mishap to the boat had the advantage of enabling me to get a detailed report from Štefánik. He informed me of the development of our Legion; and he shared the view of leading Russian soldiers that the Revolution would enable the Russian army henceforth to operate more vigorously and effectively against the Germans, thanks to the removal of pro-German influences. Many leading men in the Russian army had favored the Revolution and hoped that its achievements would be consolidated by military victory. Beneš joined Štefánik and me in London and we were able again thoroughly to discuss our future work in Europe in the light of Štefánik's news of the work in Russia.

On May 5 I found another boat and started from Aberdeen. This time we went to sea escorted by two destroyers, and reached

Bergen safely. During the night we nearly struck an enemy mine which the captain only avoided at the last moment by a smart maneuver. This I learned next morning. From Bergen, where it was evident that Norwegian feeling was pro-Ally, I went by way of Oslo to Stockholm, spending a day there but not the night, so as to escape passport formalities. Though my passport was made out in another name, I had been warned in London that, under Austrian pressure, the Swedish authorities might interpret their neutrality in such fashion as to have me interned as an avowed enemy of Austria; and the precedent in Switzerland made prudence advisable.

Pavlu, who had been to see me in London, awaited me in Stockholm. Preparations were being made there for a conference of the International, especially of Scandinavian and Dutch Socialists. The International was in ebullition. In April the German Social Democrats had split into two camps at Gotha, and the Independent Socialist Party had been formed. The influence of the Russian Leninites was already perceptible—Lenin had reached Russia on April 4—pacifism was spreading and, with it, a certain pro-Germanism. I, however, went on by way of Haparanda to Petrograd. On entering the city I noticed a black cloud of ravens; evidently, it had not struck me in the same way during my previous visits. . . .

I called at once on Milyukoff, whom I found on the point of resignation—an unpleasant surprise. However, I established relations little by little with the other members of the Provisional Government, including the Prime Minister, Prince Lvoff, and with Milyukoff's successor, Tereshtchenko. At the Foreign Office and War Office, with which I was chiefly concerned, I met, here and there, a few intelligent people who were open to reason and had retained pro-Ally feelings. Especially useful, in view of the obvious unpreparedness and weakness of the Government, were my relations with the Allied representatives, particularly General Niessel and Colonel Lavergne, of the French Military Mission at Petrograd; Major Buchsenschutz and General Janin (who was afterwards Commander-in-Chief of our army) at headquarters; General Tabouis at Kieff, and General Berthelot at Jassy—all good friends and helpful. In the place of the French Ambassador, M. Paléologue, who had just left Petrograd—my train must have crossed his on the way—I found M. Albert Thomas, well disposed towards us, whereas Paléologue had been pro-Austrian. M. Thomas's secretary was Pierre Comert, a good friend of Steed's.

The British Ambassador, Sir George Buchanan, was very obliging. As a loyal friend of the Provisional Government and of Liberal circles generally, he had remarkable influence in the Petrograd of that time. Against him the Conservatives and Reactionaries spread all sorts of obviously slanderous gossip, accusing him of having caused the Revolution. With the Italian Ambassador, Marquis Carlotti, my relations were very intimate. He urged his own Government to form a Czechoslovak Legion in Italy out of our prisoners of war. Finally, I was in constant touch with the Serbian Minister, Dr. Spalaikovitch—whom I had known when he gave evidence in the Friedjung trial—and with the Roumanian Minister, M. Diamandy.

An American Mission, led by Senator Root, came to Petrograd just then. Among its members were my old friend Mr. Charles R. Crane, Dr. John R. Mott and others. The Slavonic expert, Professor Harper, whose father had been Rector of Chicago University when I was lecturing there, was attached to it. Voska also turned up from America to organize a Slav Press Bureau for the American Government, and with him were our fellow-countrymen Koukol, Martinek and Švarc. Mr. Arthur Henderson, the English Labor leader, was likewise sent by the British Government to report upon the position, while Vandervelde came from Belgium. With Vandervelde I had already corresponded, and I had met him personally during the crossing from Aberdeen.

Besides Milyukoff, I was in touch with Peter Struve and other Cadets; with Plekhanoff, the Socialist, whom I had last seen at Geneva; and with Gorky, who was then publishing his daily newspaper. I made the acquaintance of several Social

Revolutionaries, and of Sorokin, the editor of one of their chief journals. Savinkoff I saw afterwards at Moscow. With academic and University circles I renewed old relations; and when Kerensky's Government came into power, I had to negotiate with its members. Kerensky himself I did not meet as he spent so much of his time away from Petrograd, especially at the front; but I often saw his uncle, Professor Vasilyeff, to whom I gave my messages and requests. I, too, traveled constantly between Petrograd, Moscow and Kieff.

As in London and in Paris, I gave public addresses in all these cities or arranged meetings with leading and influential persons. I kept the newspapers informed and wrote a number of articles. The refrain of my propaganda was "Break up Austria!" —propaganda not less necessary in Russia than it had been in the West, since the Russians had no definite anti-Austrian policy but accepted rather the idea of making Austria smaller. With the leading Russian Poles whom I met in all the chief towns —their center was at Moscow—I made acquaintance immediately after my arrival, and we agreed upon joint or, at least, parallel action in the army question. The Poles were forming their future army out of their men in the Russian ranks, and their difficulties were naturally the same as ours.

THE RUSSIAN ANARCHY

Before leaving London I had promised my friends to send them as soon as possible a report on the position in Russia. The question was whether and to what extent the Allies could still rely upon Russian help in the war. Upon military Russia, I soon discovered, the Allies could not and ought no longer to reckon. In a telegram to "The Times" on or about May 25, I expressed this conviction; though, as telegrams were censored, I cannot say whether the text as printed was what I actually wrote and what the Petrograd correspondent of "The Times" had agreed upon. I could do no other than dispel, once for all, the hope of Russian military help, for it was in the interest of us all not to cherish illusions. In England, as in other Allied countries, many people looked upon the Revolution as a protest against the feebleness of Russian military leadership; but, in Russia, the utter breakdown of the army, of officers and men alike, was evident everywhere and in everything. I will not describe its daily progress, but I remember the painful impression presently made upon me by the women's battalion, in which not a few ingenuous Europeans and Russians failed to see a symptom of military decline and general demoralization.

A pertinent example of the state of official Russia and of the Court was the Rasputin affair. I had heard of it in London, but in Petrograd I learned the whole story. Just imagine that the Tsarist Court and, with it, the Government of Stürmer and Trepoff, had lain under the influence of a fellow like Rasputin, coarse and almost illiterate, albeit gifted and astute, and that this had lasted six years! If religious mania is pleaded as an extenuating circumstance, the answer must be that such religion was gross and repulsive superstition. Moreover, Rasputin was not the first adventurer to whom the credulous Court had succumbed, nor did the moral plague infect only the Court. The fact is that neither official, political nor ecclesiastical society withstood Rasputin's influence sufficiently or was capable of protecting the Tsar and Russia against it. What must the position have been, morally and legally, if murder alone could get rid of Rasputin—murder committed by a great noble, by a Conservative Member of Parliament and by a member of the Imperial Family who knew what was afoot and witnessed the deed! In reading the detailed account of the murder (by Purishkievitch himself) I can see how shallow and incompetent these people were, even in crime, and, by reason of their shallowness, needlessly brutal. The very way the deed was done reveals the decline and the demoralization of official Russia—it may sound cynical, but it is true: these people were incapable even as criminals, and were therefore the more criminal.

And what of the Imperial Family, with its swarm of Grand Dukes who wielded decisive influence in the army and in the civil administration? I admit that, *mutatis mutandis*, things were much the same in Austria and, to a lesser extent, in Prussian Germany. But, in Russia, the stench of the moral and political morass at Court spread also to the nobility—and to the ecclesiastical hierarchy as well. The spirit of caste, not ethical or religious motives, turned the nobles against Rasputin; and therefore they hatched a plan to get rid of the Tsar, in the worst event, as the Emperor Paul was got rid of. Extremes of this kind are always the last resort of passive folk unable to overcome evil by systematic work. I learned of the plot for a Palace revolution from several trustworthy quarters, and the news of it has since leaked out, here and there, in the press.

My chief task was, however, to reconnoiter the military and political situation. Clearly, I could reach no other conclusion than that which I stated in "The Times." To such a Russia neither we nor the Allies could look for help. The decisive cause of disaster in the field had been the moral depravity of the upper classes of Russian society and of no small part of the whole Russian people. The trial of Masoyedoff (who had been in touch with Rasputin and was hanged in March 1915) and that of Sukhomlinoff (who was arrested in May 1916) revealed the demoralization among military leaders. Such trials sufficed to condemn the army administration, even if there were no treason in favor of Germany—though this was widely alleged. To my mind it matters little whether or not a separate peace with Germany was discussed when Protopopoff met Wahrburg in the German Legation at Stockholm during the former's journey abroad with the members of the Duma. It seems that it was not discussed but, in any case, the meeting was out of place and politically indiscreet. The real guilt of Tsardom seems to me to lie in the fact that it went to war unprepared, rashly and without conscientious consideration even of its own interests; for this reason, after the first defeats, it was driven towards Germany. As early as March 1916 there were reports that Stinnes was seeking an arrangement with Russia; and it was on account of Germany that Stürmer, like his successor, Trepoff, was appointed Prime Minister. No wonder the Allies lost faith in Russia. For a time they even hesitated to provide her with arms and war material lest these be turned against themselves.

Naturally, too, the military insufficiency of Russia compelled the Allies to change their strategy. Distrust of the Russians spread in France because the army they had promised was not sent. Yet, after every reverse, the Russian Command kept the Allies quiet by saying that there were millions and millions of Russian soldiers; and General Alexeieff is stated really to have wished to call up millions of men, without thinking that there would be no means of feeding, arming or managing them. I felt sick when, after the Brusiloff offensive, Russian generals boasted that they had still more than 15 million men at their disposal. They promised to send at least half a million men to France— and actually sent, in 1916, an insignificant 16,000 who were so undisciplined that they had to be interned. Neither then nor later had Russians any right to reproach the West with ingratitude. Rather would the Allies be entitled to reproach Russia for having failed to keep her promises. In the West, soon after the Russian defeats in 1914, this view was certainly expressed. It was recognized that Russia had gone into the war unprepared and as a gamble. This I heard more than once in Paris, London and Washington. Nevertheless, I admit that the goodwill of Russia cannot be gainsaid. At the beginning her promise to help Serbia was sincere. She invaded Prussia when Paris was threatened. Brusiloff began his offensive in order to relieve Italy; and Kerensky also wanted to help.

Russians often put forward the excuse that only the German clique at Court, led by the Tsaritsa, was guilty of treason. This is wrong. The Tsaritsa committted no treason. I have verified the stories told even by members of the Duma, and have come to the conclusion that she was no less loyal to Russia than were the Russians themselves. I do not say that there was no treason in her entourage, for she put blind trust in Rasputin who was in the hands of people cunning enough to take advantage of his relationship to the Empress—a fatal mistake. The Tsaritsa's shortcomings lay in her lack of education, in her gross and morbid superstition and in the political incapacity which she combined with a domineering temperament. And her greatest shortcoming lay in her complete influence over the weakling Tsar, who believed in her as in a prophetess. Thus she became the strongest political power in Russia. She was a sworn foe of constitutionalism and of the Duma; and the Tsar shared her feelings. Not until February, 1916, in the midst of the war, did he pay his first visit to the Duma! General Alexeieff wished to place her under arrest—but then it was too late.

The Tsar himself was loyal to the Allies. When Count Eulenburg, the Marshal of the German Court, put out peace feelers through Count Fredericks in December 1915, the Tsar would have nothing to do with them, just as he rejected the attempts made at the end of March 1916 by the Grand Duke of Hesse, the Tsaritsa's brother. Not less was he against Witte's pro-German agitation. In words, he wished the war to be vigorously waged, but he knew not how to wage it vigorously in deed. As they said in Petrograd, he was "wooden"; and, even when he saw the unhappy state of things, he did nothing. Equally weak was he when a section of the Court clique hatched a plan to let the Germans through to Petrograd in order that they might save Tsardom. The news I had received in London about Goremykin proved that this plan did not stand alone. Though, in comparison with his successor, Goremykin was a Russian Minister of the better sort, he did not shrink from the idea of courting defeat and of letting the Germans march into the Russian capital so that they might put things in order.

To the Tsar's weakness and untrustworthiness the history of his reign bears frequent witness. In the Björkö affair of 1905, for instance, he heeded the whisperings of the Emperor William —whose plan showed a remarkable degree of political shortsightedness—and promised that Russia would be a party to a Franco-German alliance against England. Witte and the Foreign Minister, Count Lamsdorff, had to prevent the ratification of the Treaty at the last moment. The Tsar was just as foolish during the war. At the wish of the Tsaritsa he took over the Chief Command himself and did nothing but harm; he dismissed good men like Sazonof and accepted creatures like Stürmer. In our case, as we shall see, he broke his promise in the same way as, in the Björkö affair, he had gone back on his signed word.

Witte, in his Memoirs, says that the Tsar was a very well-bred man but, as regards education, on a level with a Colonel of the Guards of good family—a judgment terribly borne out by the published extracts from the Tsar's private diary at the time of the Revolution and of his abdication. He was a pure nonenity. In distrusting his whole policy and character I see that I was not unfair to him. The Tsarist Sodom and Gomorrah had to be destroyed with fire and brimstone—not only the Court and Court society—for the demoralization had spread to all social strata, including the so-called "intelligentsia" and even the peasantry. Tsarism, the whole political and ecclesiastical system, had demoralized Russia.

In insisting upon the moral defects of Tsarism I am well aware that the morality and immorality of a community naturally show themselves throughout the official and military administration. Of this moral deficiency the inadequate provisioning of the Army and of the civil population was one result, a result, moreover, which revenged itself upon the Government and the system. Practically, the Revolution in Petrograd was brought about by hunger, and the commissariat troops were the first to revolt. The lack of weapons for the army, the senseless recruiting of masses of men which, in the autumn of 1916, swept the laborers from the soil, were symptoms and effects of a moribund administration. I am entitled thus to judge Russia during the war because I had judged and condemned her before the war. My judgment is not founded only upon her failures in the war, since these were but the outcome of the severe moral disease of the whole Tsarist system and, therewith, of the Russian people.

On this point, study of pre-revolutionary Russia and especially of her literature leaves no room for doubt. Her greatest writers show us the sickness and enfeeblement of the Russian soul, yet also its elemental yearning for truth. Tolstoy did but bring this yearning into high relief when he descried the foundations of art in truth and truthfulness. Tsarism was untrue; and the war brought out its untruthfulness no whit more clearly or fully than it had been revealed by Pushkin, Gogol, Lermontoff, Goncharoff, Turgenieff, Dostoievsky, Tolstoy and Gorky. The Russians now call Dostoievsky the Prophet of the Revolution—in the war and the Revolution, Russian literature found bloody confirmation.

Russia fell, had to fall, as Kirieyevsky would say, through her own inner falsehood. This inner falsehood merely found in the war a great opportunity to stand forth in all its nakedness, and Tsarism collapsed in and through itself. It had contrived to civilize Russia crudely, to lend some European quality to the nobles, the officials and the officers; but the peasantry and the peasant soldier—who were Russia—lived outside this Tsarist civilization. Hence they gave it no protection when, in the war, it failed through its own insufficiency and inward poverty.

As to the Russian Church, to whose inertia much of the blame is assigned, its sin was a sin of omission. It cared too little for the moral education of the people. What the Slavophils, and especially Kirieyevsky, praised in the Russian Church was, as Chaadaieff saw, precisely its chief shortcoming.

Russia and the Slavs

This conviction as to the moral basis of Tsarism I had reached long before the war; and, in my book on Russia which appeared before the war, I had analyzed and described Russia's unhappy state. Thus, when war broke out, I could not agree with our uncritical pro-Russians at home or in Russia, where our people expected the Tsar to set Bohemia free. Their standpoint was the more comprehensible in view of the political upbringing of our colony in Russia, especially as the Tsar himself treated its members well. As early as August 20, 1914, he received a Czech deputation. To the hopes which this reception aroused at home I have already referred. On September 27, 1914, he gave audience to another Czech deputation, and showed his interest in Slovakia by asking for a memorandum upon it. In 1915 he sent decorations to our Legionaries in France, and in 1916 he discussed the Czech question with Štefánik whom General Janin had strongly recommended to Russian military circles and to the Court. In June of the same year he agreed to the release of the Slav prisoners of war in Russia; and in the following December received yet another Czechoslovak deputation.

All the greater therefore was the difference between the Tsar's personal behavior and the working of the Tsarist system. What he said to our people may not have been binding, but they grew enthusiastic whenever the "Slav Brethren" of Russia were mentioned. By "Slav Brethren," official Russia meant primarily the Orthodox Slavs, as I had pointed out from the first. It is true that Russia, and the Tsar particularly, supported Serbia from the outset—as did the other Allied Powers. None of them would allow Vienna to touch Serbian independence. But, like England, Russia would have agreed to an Austrian "punitive expedition."

On careful perusal, the report of the audience of September 17, 1914, which our people in Russia thought especially significant, makes a disappointing impression. Political children can be put off with words, especially by the words of a political child like the Tsar. He expressed his interest but promised nothing definite. The deputation showed him a map of our future State —which included Vienna and Upper Austria! Of this fantastic product the Tsar said nothing beyond: "I thank you, gentlemen, for what you have told me. I trust that God will help us and that your wishes will be realized." I, too, believe in God but not in a Rasputinian God—and things turned out as I expected.

At his father's Court the Tsar had heard all sorts of things about the Slavs, and is said to have taken interest in the Wends of Lusatia; but neither he nor his Ministers had a comprehensive Slav policy. Otherwise he would never have given office to a fellow like Stürmer, whom he knew to be a strong pro-German, nor would he have agreed, in March 1916, with Baron Rosen—an anti-Slav and pro-German—that Russia and the Allies must make peace without delay, if possible under American leadership.

To the substance of Sazonof's speech in the Duma on August 8, 1914, I have already alluded. Even Sazonof had no positive Slav and Czech policy in the war. I knew his past and his views. He certainly disliked the Rasputin business, for he was a good type of man; and at last the Tsar dismissed him because of his alleged liberalism. In the West, Sazonof was known to have been against the war and to have striven to avoid the conflict with Germany. For this very reason he cherished no such Slav policy as that which our people ingenuously attributed to him. When he spoke of the Slavs, Sazonof, like all high Russian dignitaries, meant chiefly the Orthodox Slavs. This is clear from his talk with the second Czech deputation in September 1914, though our people thought it very important. Sazonof asked the Czechs for their ideas of the relationship between an Orthodox dynasty and a Catholic people, and expressed doubts about it. The deputation referred him to our principle of toleration. According to the notes taken by our people, Sazonof spoke of us very kindly and also appealed to God, saying: "Should God grant decisive victory to Russian arms, the reestablishment of an entirely independent Czech Kingdom would be in accordance with the intentions of the Russian Government; this question was considered before the beginning of the war and decided in principle in favor of the Czechs." I have no quarrel with Sazonof for having spoken thus cautiously. As a Russian and as a responsible Minister it was his right, nay, his duty. My only object was to rid our people of pan-Slav and pro-Russian illusions.

What I have said of Isvolsky applies also to Sazonof's interest in the Orthodox Slavs. Paléologue, the former French Ambassador to the Russian Court, relates in his Memoirs that, on January 1, 1915, he suggested to Sazonof that the Entente should turn Austria against Germany; Austria might perhaps cede Galicia to Russia, and Bosnia-Herzegovina to Serbia, and thus settle the matter. Sazonof asked him what was to happen to Bohemia and Croatia, and Paléologue answered that the Czech and the Southern Slav questions were of secondary importance to France and that it would be enough if the Czechs and the Croats were given a large measure of autonomy. According to Paléologue this argument made an impression on Sazonof, who admitted that the idea was worth considering. If Paléologue's account is accurate, it would follow that, in the first period of the war, Sazonof had no general Slav policy; otherwise he must have put forward his own counter-arguments. It is noteworthy, too, that Sazonof spoke only of Bohemia and Croatia but said nothing of the provinces appertaining to them.

Similarly, the conquest of Slovakia or, at any rate, of Central and Eastern Slovakia, had been contemplated in many unofficial Slavophil Russian circles, the Bohemian Lands being left out of account. These, and particularly Bohemia, were to be given up to the West, though, according to some of these Slavophils, Moravia was graciously to be received into the Russian bosom. Some of our Slovaks remembered this idea during the Russian advance in the winter of 1914 and the offensive of Brusiloff in the summer of 1916. The fact is that Tsarist Russia had not thought out any Czechoslovak policy. On the contrary, official Russia was in so far anti-Slav as it desired to round off the Russian Empire on strategic principles and to reach Constantinople without troubling about individual Slav peoples. Its readiness to sacrifice considerable portions of those peoples was not due to ill-will but rather to weakness and ineptitude.

As the war went on, bringing defeat after defeat, Russian declarations in regard to the Slavs became more and more reserved. The high-sounding proclamations at the beginning of the war I have already mentioned. On May 29, 1916, Sazonof still spoke in the Duma of Russia's "Slav Brethren," though he referred only to their "future organization" and promised far-reaching autonomy to the Poles. But, in Trepoff's speech on War Aims, in December 1916, nothing more was said of the Slavs; and, in an Order to the Army and Navy, the Tsar repeated what Trepoff and, before him, Stürmer had said—that the aims of Russia were Constantinople, and a free Poland inseparably joined to Russia.

The real war aims of Russia were revealed in the secret agreements which she concluded. Of these the weightiest was the Secret Treaty made with France and England on March 18, 1915, of which the chief feature was the conquest of Constantinople. This Treaty is certainly important, particularly as regards England. The second (provisional) Treaty was Doumergue's convention with Pokrovsky on February 12, 1917, by which France claimed a frontier on the Rhine and Russia a new frontier on the West. According to the situation, and under the Secret Treaty with Roumania (August 17, 1916) to whom the whole Bukovina (including the Ruthenes) Transylvania and the Banat were promised, this new Western frontier would, in harmony with Russian policy towards the Poles, have included Galicia, Poznania and perhaps a part of Prussian Silesia; though, as far as I can discover, the project was not worked out in detail.

An indication of the way official Russia looked upon Slav questions was also given by General Alexeieff. With him I had a conversation or, rather, a controversy upon Russia and the world situation. He was a cautious man of critical mind who, though Conservative and narrowly Russian in his views, would not have hesitated even to sacrifice the Tsar for the sake of saving Russia. He was one of the first to realize, as early as 1915, that the Russian army could not stand up to the Germans; and, therefore, at the time when I met him, there could be no question of his entertaining any serious Slav policy. Upon our people in Russia he looked with a critical eye, and the confusion about them in Petrograd displeased him. On Europe, on us and the Austro-Hungarian people, his views were hazy. At the beginning of the war he had imagined that Austria-Hungary could be divided into States serviceable to Russia. The Czechs were to extend to Trieste and Fiume on the Adriatic, and thus to take over a large part of German Austria, including Vienna, but were only to get a bit of Slovakia, as far as Kosice, while being presented with a lot of Magyars—that is to say, according to the Russian plan, the Czech State was to have a non-Czech majority. Serbia was to extend northwards to the Russian frontier as far as Uzhorod. Since the Tsar had promised to help Serbia, her northern frontier must march with that of Russia! Of the Magyars, Alexeieff took no account, though at first even he had reckoned upon their detaching themselves from Austria, in which case he would have felt no compunction in sacrificing to them his "Slav Brethren." The Russians had long had a chance—indeed, it should have been their duty—to pursue a Slav policy towards the Poles and the Little Russians; but the policy they actually followed forms at once a sorry chapter in Russian history and a proof of how un-Slav Russia really was. Tsarist Russia was not Slav but Byzantine, and perverted by Byzantine decadence.

SUPILO

Supilo and his visit to Russia I have mentioned more than once. According to his own report, he left London in January 1915 and went by way of Rome to Nish—then the seat of the Serbian Government—to consult Pashitch; and thence through Southern Russia to Petrograd in the hope of persuading Sazonof and Russia to oppose the reported negotiations with Italy which afterwards took shape in the Treaty of London. He was in Petrograd at the end of March; and, at the beginning of June 1915, in Geneva, he gave me a full account of his visit.

Supilo found that official Russia understood nothing whatever of Slavonic matters and was interested in the Serbs only because they were Orthodox. Sazonof demonstrated to him (a Dalmatian!) that Spalato was entirely Italian, drew a distinction between Catholic and Orthodox Dalmatia, and believed that the Orthodox Serbs lived in the South. He was extremely surprised when Supilo explained that the Orthodox Serbs lived not in the

South but chiefly in Central Dalmatia, the very part which Russia was handing over to Italy. Thus Sazonof revealed to Supilo the negotiations with Italy, and said that the Southern Slavs would get Spalato and the supposedly Orthodox South. Supilo guessed that Sazonof was not expecting Northern Dalmatia to go to the Yugoslavs, and asked him pointedly what would happen to Sebenico. From this question the Russian Foreign Minister concluded that Supilo was aware of the negotiations and told him further details. Thus Supilo heard of the Treaty of London before it was actually concluded. He telegraphed the information to Pashitch and Trumbitch, and wrote a lengthy memorandum to the French Foreign Minister, Delcassé, in Paris.

Supilo was interested not only in the extent of the territorial concessions to Italy but in the question whether the Southern Slavs would in future be united or still be divided into three parts—Serbia, Croatia and Montenegro. Undoubtedly, the Treaty of London was inimical to the unification of the Southern Slav Lands and corresponded rather to the Great Serbia program. In the West it was said that Sazonof was for a long time decidedly opposed to Italy. Others asserted that he opposed her only in so far as he did not want her to have Southern Dalmatia which he erroneously assumed to be Orthodox. This point is not yet quite clear.

Besides Sazonof, Supilo saw the Grand Duke Nicholas. His report of his long conversations with the Russian Commander-in-Chief and those about him, gave an uncanny picture of the political ingenuousness of the Russian leaders and of their ignorance of other things besides Slav questions.

Though Supilo was right, I did not agree with the agitation by which he set Petrograd not only against himself but against the Croats, while intensifying the antagonism between them and Serbia. He did not realize the difficulty of the position in which defeat had placed Russia, nor did he see that necessity had driven her and her Allies to make the Treaty with Italy. It had also to be remembered that the dynasty and the foreign policy of Serbia were Conservative and Tsarophil. Pashitch, the Prime

Minister, wished to go to Petrograd himself after the conclusion of the Treaty of London, but Sazonof thought it neither opportune nor necessary. In the whole Slav policy of Tsardom nothing was realized save that St. Petersburg became Petrograd.

As regards us Czechs, Petrograd feared our Liberalism and our Catholicism. In the Russian Foreign Office, where there was many a decent, honest man, I learned that they did not take us seriously until Paris and London began to recognize us. Briand's reception of me, in January 1916, which, as I have said, impressed the Russian diplomatists abroad, had also its effect at Petrograd, where my opposition to the German Berlin–Baghdad scheme attracted attention. But Petrograd was displeased at my acceptance of a Professorship in London. It was taken as showing the intention of England to gain control of our movement; and the story passed round that I was working in London to secure an English Prince as our future King. At any rate, London and Paris caused Tsarist Russia to pay heed to our revolutionary movement, and Bohemia came to be thought important as a barrier against German pressure on the Balkans and on the East generally. In the autumn of 1916 these considerations inspired the policy that ended in the creation of Dürich's pro-Russian "National Council."

Yet, as I have said, official Russia had received our National and Slav program very early in the day. I sent it repeatedly and I presume that the Russian Ambassadors in London and Paris had reported upon it. But, beyond insignificant correspondence, neither of them, nor the Ambassador in Rome, received political instructions about it. No single act of the Tsar's Government can be compared with Briand's intervention on our behalf, or with the Allies' mention of us in the definition of their war aims to President Wilson. The first Allied pronouncement in favor of our liberation was not—as we might have expected—attributable to Russian initiative or cooperation (for Isvolsky merely signed it) but to the understanding and the help of the Western Allies, and especially of France. The quality of Tsarist care for the Slavs is, moreover, most strikingly illustrated in the history of our army.

OUR ARMY IN RUSSIA

Like all the others, our colony in Russia declared itself for the freedom and independence of our people on the outbreak of war, and it took steps to form an army of Russian Czechs and Slovaks. These manifestations were spontaneous, and a logical consequence of our national program. After the Paris colony, which was the first to take action, the Czechs of Moscow laid before the Government a scheme for a Czechoslovak Legion on August 4, 1914, a day before the Austrian declaration of war against Russia. At the end of August, organization began; and by the end of October, the Družina, as our legion in Russia was called, left for the front.

Permission to form this legion, as a part of the Russian army, was given to the Russian Czechs as Russian subjects. But when the prisoners of war began to volunteer for service in it, political inequality became apparent between the Russian subjects belonging to it and our own men. Many of the Russian officers were against the non-Russians; though, after the official difficulties had been overcome and recruiting among "trustworthy prisoners" was sanctioned, the non-Russians soon formed a majority. At Tarnopol, when the prisoners entered the Družina at the beginning of 1915, the name "New Družina" was used, but it was not applied to those who joined it later. The Government demanded that the prisoners should apply for Russian nationality and that at least a third of the officers should be Russians. It wanted to make of our people a reliable Russian army. Moreover, the military authorities, and particularly the General Staff, assigned to it from the first a political rather than a military task. When Austria should be occupied, the Družina was to be a corps of propagandists who were to facilitate the occupation by winning the goodwill of the inhabitants. Its non-military character was officially accentuated by demanding of it a discipline less stringent than that required of the rest of the army;

it was supposed only to need just enough discipline to enable it to reach, in tolerably good order, the sphere of its propagandist work. As time went on, it was used for scouting purposes, thanks to our lads' skill, intelligence and knowledge of languages; and, despite the opposition of the military authorities and of many Russian officers, they gained the favor of Radko Dmitrieff, Brusiloff and other commanders, and thus got a hold upon the scouting service. Yet, as a result, the Družina became scattered over a long front and could not bring itself to bear as a unit.

I will not describe the tribulations of these first Czech soldiers, the rebuffs and the disappointments they had to endure from Russians and even from Czechs—but they held out and lost neither their feelings as Slavs nor their liking for the Russians, albeit chiefly for the Russian peasant soldiers. Upon the Russian officers they soon came to look with a skeptical eye.

Though everything showed that the Government and the military authorities did not want a Czechoslovak army of any size, a regiment of Czechoslovak riflemen was formed out of the Družina in January 1916; and, in May, the creation of a brigade was permitted. It was more or less a nominal affair, for its strength was small; but it was a beginning. Štefánik was then in Russia and used his influence to this end. In October 1916 authority to form a Division was even given—but soon withdrawn.

Very early in the war—from March 11, 1915, onwards—our colony, organized as a "League," entered enthusiastically into the establishment of the Družina. There was great devotion on every hand and, after the battle of Zboroff, the colony at Kieff looked after the sick and wounded in every possible way. Gladly do I recall the work of the Červený family; while Dr. Girsa, Dr. Haerink and others gave our men first-rate medical attention.

Personally, I was able to overlook differences of political opinion and to keep in touch with the Conservative members of our colony, though I could not fail to see that many of them lacked both political vision and military sense. The "League" was a Russian organization composed of Czech subjects of Russia and loyal to the Government. Hence it adopted the official view of the Družina's propagandist task. Besides, fear lest our nation lose its future citizens in battle reconciled the "League" leaders to the idea of keeping our army small. Many were satisfied with military symbolism, such as the consecration of colors, or worked to convert our men to the Orthodox Church, and behaved in very unmilitary fashion. Even the prisoners started an agitation in favor of Orthodoxy as, for instance, when a number of officer-prisoners were solemnly converted at Murom. Some drew up incredible definitions of what a Czech soldier ought to be, and other puerilities of a like description.

Misunderstandings, too, arose between the Petrograd and the Kieff Czechs, and then misunderstandings at Kieff itself, where a singular "Czechoslovak Association" was set up which attacked the "League" and denounced everybody, especially me and my alleged Westernism. It addressed its complaints and denunciations, misstatements and lies, to the Russian military authorities and Departments of State. The better Russian soldiers, like Alexeieff, were disgusted by them, but they found a hearing in other quarters and even in the Ministry for Foreign Affairs. I need not describe all the fantastic and impossible things that were done, and were brought to my notice by the Russian authorities themselves. The name of Slavdom was used to cover orgies of reaction and of political shortsightedness. The circumstance that our prisoners came to be more and more the decisive factor in our army and, finally, the Revolution, prevailed over these effects of a Russian education; for the corruptibility of Tsardom and its political illiteracy had spoiled not only Russian society but many of our own people as well.

When I reached Petrograd in May 1917, the antagonism between the progressive Czechs of the capital and the more Conservative Czechs of Kieff, and between the "League" and the "Association," had been formally set aside. Like the members of the "League" and the great majority of our prisoners, our people in Petrograd had always recognized our Paris National Council. At any rate, our brigade had recognized it as the supreme political authority and had proclaimed me Dictator on March 20, 1917; and the "League" followed suit, on March 23, by recognizing me as the sole representative of the Czechoslovak nation. Finally, the third Congress of the "League," held in Kieff at the beginning of May, adopted by a large majority the program of the National Council which Štefánik expounded. The effect of the so-called Kieff Pact, or Protocol, which was signed by Štefánik, Dürich, Delegates of the "League" and the delegation of American Czechs, was to compose, at least outwardly, dissensions that had lasted since the beginning of the war; though, as I found, there remained quite enough personal bitterness and ill-humor.

In fairness to the politicians among the Czech and Slovak colony, it should be said that, at first, our prisoners, as well as our people from Bohemia and Slovakia who had been in Russia when the war broke out, put all their hopes in official Russia. Not until they had got to know what official Russia really was, and after the Revolution had opened their eyes, did they change their views. All the greater is the merit of the Petrograd colony whose members kept an open mind throughout, particularly during Stürmer's administration, and were steadfast in the conviction that our struggle for independence must bear a uniform character. Three names deserve special mention—those of Pavlu, Čermák and Klecanda. To this policy our prisoners rallied; and, at the end of 1916 and the beginning of 1917, even before the Revolution, voices from our camps called for uniformity of action under the Paris National Council. The way our prisoners organized themselves politically in the various camps, and gave expression to their views in all kinds of memoranda which they addressed both to the "League" and to the Russian Government, is the more significant because the camps were isolated and the action they took was, I believe, taken independently.

MILITARY DIFFICULTIES

In Petrograd my first care was to get my bearings and to learn in detail what had happened since 1914 in relation to our military affairs. True, I had received, from time to time, written and oral reports besides the news from Štefánik; but now I was in a position to go more closely into things. What I knew of official Russia had never led me to expect any great readiness on its part in helping to create our army; and, naturally, the reverses of 1914 and 1915 had not increased Russian eagerness to trouble about any non-Russian formations. Yet, in 1916, with Brusiloff's offensive, hope had revived, and France had supported our movement in Russia through Štefánik. When Brusiloff failed, pessimism set in again and, with it, indifference towards any new undertaking. The Russians were estranged, moreover, by the haziness of our own people as to what they really wanted and by the unsavory quarrels between them. Frankly, I often wondered that the Russians had so much patience with us.

On behalf of the Czechs at Kieff, Dr. Vondrák had laid before the Russian Ministry for Foreign Affairs and the War Office a scheme for a Czech army. This scheme asked the Russian Government to recognize the "League" as the representative of the Czech people, for its authors never seem to have thought that they needed some credentials from the Czech nation itself if they were to possess authority in Russia. Nor did it occur to them that the Russian Government was not entitled to decide who was to represent our nation. As Russian subjects, they could only represent those members of our colonies who were likewise Russian subjects. They did not want a big army—not more than a division at most—and it was only to come into action after the occupation of Slovakia, which was to form part of the future Czech State. The Kieff Czechs feared that the Austrians would execute Czech soldiers who might be taken prisoners. This they hoped to obviate by an occupation of Slovakia, a proclamation of Czech independence, and the deposition of the Hapsburg dynasty. In addition, Russia was in some way to guarantee the future of the Czechs—perhaps, like that of the Poles, by a manifesto of the Commander-in-Chief! Should the Austrians nevertheless execute Czech prisoners, reprisals were to be taken upon Austrian prisoners.

Neither the Russian Departments of State nor Russian military men heeded witlessness of this sort, and Maklakoff, the Minister of the Interior, rejected the Kieff scheme categorically in May 1915. It was, indeed, an idle project, for it actually announced that, in the Czech army, officers would not be accepted, even if they were Czechs. Notions like these were hotly discussed in our colony; and not a few officers who joined the Družina and afterwards, the Czech brigade, were very badly treated by these civilian wiseacres. The effort to create an ideally Slav, democratic and brotherly army, degenerated into fruitless hairsplitting about the "ideal qualities" of the Czech soldier—and, truth to tell, well-meant nonsense of the same kind cropped up even in the New Družina and among our prisoners of war.

The second Congress of Czechoslovak Societies, which met at Kieff from April 25 to May 1, 1916, resolved, in accordance with the plan we had worked out in Paris and had sent to Russia, to form an army out of our brigade and to set about getting our prisoners released. But in June 1916, the "League" (now established at Kieff) presented to Russian Headquarters a fresh scheme for a Czech army. General Alexeieff recommended the General Staff to work it out—which the General Staff did, after its own fashion—but still Headquarters would not sanction it. The Russian Foreign Office also raised objections, and General Alexeieff, hearing from General Červinka accounts of indiscipline in the brigade and of the complaints of the Czech "Association," turned against it. Thus, early in August, it fell through.

Despite this failure, several influential people spoke for our prisoners, among them Brusiloff who made a full report to Alexeieff on January 6, 1917; but even he had no success. Our people had put great hopes in the Tsar's own wish for the release of Slav prisoners, for he had agreed to it in principle on April 21,

1916, and had sanctioned, on July 10, the report of General Shuvayeff which urged strongly that they should be better treated. This, however, only authorized their release. Their formation into an army was still a long way off, as our people at Kieff realized. Hence, while invoking what the Tsar had said when he gave them audience, they asked for a decision by the responsible Government, remembering that Russia, albeit incompletely, was now bound to be constitutional.

In the autumn of 1916, as I have said, the Russian Foreign Office began to pay more attention to the Czechoslovak movement which it decided to direct and control. In this it was inspired by a spirit of opposition to the West and by dislike of the favor shown to us in England and France. Consequently, at the beginning of December, civil and military reactionaries got to work on their scheme of setting up a special Czechoslovak National Council for Russia. On December 17 they proposed to the War Office that Dürich should be placed at the head of this Russian semi-official National Council. On January 18, 1917, the Council of Ministers and, on February 2, Bielyaieff, the War Minister, gave their assent. Yet, while supporting Dürich, official Petrograd did not altogether agree with his policy in regard to Russia. He described himself as a supporter of Dr. Kramář, advocated the incorporation of Czechoslovakia in Russia and even the adoption by us of the Orthodox Faith. But the Russian Foreign Office, aware of French and British dislike of pan-Slavism and pan-Russianism, rejected or toned down Dürich's scheme of annexation and local self-government. As I have said, our Liberalism and our Catholicism were not liked. Therefore, while seeking to control us, the Russians found my program of complete independence more acceptable.

Into particulars of the change that occurred between the Tsar's approval of the release of our prisoners and the hostile acts of Stürmer and Trepoff towards us, I will not enter, for I had neither the time nor the inclination to go fully into it. Our people naturally suspected Stürmer's pro-German guile; and, though I cannot say what part pro-Germanism actually played, it certainly had some effect. To my mind, one of the most practical explanations is that Stürmer opposed the liberation of Slav prisoners of war in deference to capitalist wishes, since the Czech prisoners in particular were well qualified for work in factories and mines. This was also to the liking of some of our manufacturers at Kieff, who consequently wished our legion to be kept small and non-military. In support of this explanation stands the fact that, after the Revolution, even the Provisional Government had an eye on our skilled workmen and would not let them join the army. Under Stürmer's pressure, the Tsar himself agreed that his assent to the release of the prisoners should not take effect. My information was derived from a trustworthy informant, and it is confirmed by one of the Tsaritsa's letters (which have been printed) to the Tsar on August 17, 1916, asking, in the name of Rasputin, that the Slav prisoners should not be released. Another letter from the Tsaritsa, dated August 27, also gives color to what I learned—that it was intended to honor the Tsar's word by admitting gradually a small number of prisoners to our brigade so that its strength would have been slightly increased without making an army of it.

UPS AND DOWNS

So things went on until the Revolution broke out in March 1917. Štefánik and the French military mission had been urging the military and civil authorities in 1916 and 1917 to permit the formation of our army. The General Staff at Petrograd had set up a Commission to work out Regulations for it. Like so many others, this Commission served to delay matters. When the Regulations were ready, in October 1916, they were at variance with our program. The Družina was to be slightly enlarged but it was not to be ours. It was to be entirely Russian, with a Russian Commander and Russian superior officers. General Červinka gave the Regulations to Headquarters. Then our "League" stepped in and rightly demanded that our army should be at least partly Czech, not wholly Russian. Headquarters instructed the General Staff to revise the Regulations. Their final text was still being drafted in February 1917 when the Revolution broke out, and they were confirmed only by the new revolutionary Government.

Like the Russians, our people changed front after the Revolution. On April 3, 1917, the "League" presented to the Prime Minister of the Provisional Government a declaration against Dürich's National Council and in favor of my leadership; and, in a lengthy document addressed to the Provisional Government, it proposed that I should represent the Czechoslovak nation in international affairs while the "League" would represent the Czechs and Slovaks in Russia. This was a repetition of the constitutional error into which the Czechs of Kieff had originally fallen. The "Association" also hastened to present to the President of the Duma a memorandum hotly attacking Stürmer and Dürich—a right-about-turn that did not astonish me on the part of this section of our people. Had not Priklonsky, of the Russian Foreign Office, who had been a warm supporter of Dürich not so long before, threatened immediately after the Revolution to have him locked up!

Nevertheless, Gutchkoff, Minister for War in the Provisional Government, upheld the old decisions against us, refused the "League's" application for a Czechoslovak army and ordered that our skilled workmen should be drafted into the factories which were working for the defense of Russia. On the other hand, Milyukoff, the Foreign Minister, supported our cause. On March 20 he asked Gutchkoff to assent to the "League's" application; the question of unitary leadership could stand over until I came. He demanded further, on March 22, that Dürich's National Council should be dissolved. Four days later Gutchkoff agreed. Finally, on April 24, the Military Council of the Provisional Government confirmed the "Regulations for the Organization of the Czechoslovak Army." On the basis of these Regulations, General Červinka, as President of a Commission *ad hoc*, began to form the army in May, after the General Staff had instructed the Military Districts to permit recruiting among our prisoners.   Thus I reached Petrograd in May at exactly the right time.

RUSSIAN ANOMALIES

In the West we had long been recognized.   In agreement with the Russian Ambassador in Paris, the Entente had declared our liberation to be one of its chief war aims; yet, in Russia itself, we only received recognition—and then indirectly—at the twelfth hour, thanks to the Revolution.   Why this crying anomaly?

The sober account I have given—in broad outline, omitting details—shows that the Russian civil and military authorities, beginning with the Tsar, failed to carry out their promises that our army should be formed.   When a scheme had been sanctioned, its application was everywhere resisted, even at Headquarters.   It was held up and fresh obstacles were continually created.   This was a consequence of the very nature of official Russia and of its fundamental ideas—Absolutism, Orthodoxy, Nationality, that is to say official Russian Nationality.   In the eyes of Tsarist Russia, we were not first-class Slavs and Brothers.

Day by day, in my countless dealings with military and civil authorities of all sorts, I felt the weight of Tsarist Absolutism even after its formal disappearance.   The Regulations for the formation of our army, duly sanctioned, were in my possession. Assurances and orders were given, yet nothing was done, and there was open opposition at Headquarters.   Individuals always made promises, and broke them.   I dealt with the highest and most influential persons, with Korniloff, with Brusiloff, who promised and promised; but, month after month, the creation of the army was put off.   On all sides I was aware of distrust and incomprehension.   True, their own army gave the Russian military authorities enough cause for anxiety at that moment.   They had more men than they could deal with and saw little use in a Czech army.   The officials were obviously tired.   Russia was losing, her army disintegrating—why make such an effort? That, at least, was a pertinent argument.   But many, confounding two different conceptions, feared our Liberalism and our

Catholicism. And—in keeping with the third term in the Russian absolutist trinity of ideas—the apprehension was expressed that, if a Czech National Army was set up, national armies would have to be granted to the Poles and others. For this reason our small brigade was kept as a part of the Russian army and our men had to swear allegiance to Russia, though not a few Russian Generals understood that, if only for military reasons, our men ought above all to swear allegiance to their own nation. Often, too, I heard complaints of Bulgarian ingratitude —doubtless the Czechs would be just as ungrateful!

In the eyes of many Russian administrative officers, our prisoners were still simply "Austrians." Legitimist even in regard to Austria, they could not comprehend that our men should be Czechs and Slovaks. Hating the Russian Revolution, they would not recognize the Czech Revolution. In the prisoners' camps our lads had constantly to turn a deaf ear to the reproach that they had sworn allegiance to Francis Joseph and that, were they to betray him, they would likewise betray the Tsar. It is some excuse for these Russians that, albeit only at first, the same argument was used against us in Italy, England, America and occasionally in France. Only by explaining our position over and over again could we manage to de-Austrianize ourselves. Even Alexeieff must be reckoned to some extent among the Russian Generals and officials who were so steeped in legitimism that they could not sympathize with our Revolution. Our people thought him their best friend. He was; but he could not free himself from his inveterate Russian views.

The legitimist argument took more practical shape in the contention that, if the Czechs were used against Austria, the Germans and the Austrians might use their Russian prisoners against Russia—the very contention which Sonnino adopted on behalf of Italy. It was the less justified in the Russian case because the Germans were already carrying on systematic propaganda for Germany among the Russian prisoners. But the Russian reactionaries who, in their heart of hearts, disliked the Entente and the West, made yet another point against the formation of a big

Czech army—it must not be sent to France! In support of this plea they could appeal to some of our own people, for General Červinka did not favor the transfer of our men to France. One very influential reactionary explained to me his dislike of the West by saying that Brusiloff's offensive in 1916 had brought no gain to Russia though, in the course of it, her troops had taken half a million prisoners and nearly a million guns! In reality, the number of prisoners was about 150,000 and that of the guns proportionately very much lower. He claimed that, under pressure from the Tsar, whom the King of Italy had influenced, Brusiloff had been obliged to strike before he was ready—proof that Russia was not working for the King of Prussia but for the Kings and Presidents in the West!

At last the Revolution gave things a turn for the better. It was fortunate that Milyukoff, whose support for our policy I had secured in England, should have become Foreign Minister. Yielding to the new spirit, General Dukhonin, who was then Quartermaster-General, ordered, on June 13, 1917, that our brigade should be raised to four regiments and that the battalions of the reserve should also be strengthened in view of a further increase. Militarily, also, things grew better after the battle of Zboroff,[1] where our brigade showed both bravery and strategical skill. Our lads were officially commended, the name of the Czech Brigade became known throughout Russia and, as a recompense, the Supreme Command ordered the formation of a second division.

Its actual formation was, however, put off more and more. There was a fundamental difference between the Revolutionary Government at Petrograd and the Army and its command. Though Liberals and Socialists held political power, the superior military authorities were either monarchists or men of purely military mind, and the whole military machine was unchanged. Milyukoff and the Liberals recognized me, the Paris National Council and our policy, but the soldiers continued to tread their

---

[1] In Eastern Galicia. The battle was fought on July 3, 1917, the heights of Zboroff being gallantly stormed by the Czech and Russian troops.

wonted path. Indeed, before the battle of Zboroff, we were opposed even by Socialists and Liberals of all shades, who thought us Chauvinists. The Liberal and Progressive Russians had always been in opposition to the Government and to its official Nationalism. Therefore they were likewise against our national aims, especially when the antagonism between the Right and Left wings of our movement showed that many of our people were reactionary, either tactically or on principle. For this reason Kerensky, as War Minister, ordered that our brigade should be disbanded; and the new Commanding Officer of the Kieff district, a Social Revolutionary named Oberutcheff, did the same. To Kerensky I explained the position in a memorandum on May 22, and I persuaded Colonel Oberutcheff also to be more moderate. But the change was wrought chiefly by the battle of Zboroff.

In explanation of Russian distrust, it should be said that, after the Revolution, all official archives fell into the hands of the new Government, and that in them were found a number of reports, official and unofficial, which compromised several of our people. Moreover, from liberal officials whose lips were now unsealed, I heard what had happened in the Russian Foreign Office and elsewhere under the Tsarist Government. An influential member of our "League" was alleged to have been in direct contact with the Okhrana, or secret political police, and with Protopopoff. Hence, our army had been disliked in military as well as in official quarters, for even the decent Russian Conservatives objected to Protopopoff and the Okhrana.

Our position emerges the more clearly if the lot of our brigade be compared with that of the Serbian Legion. Permission to form a Serbian Legion out of the Austro-Serbian prisoners of war had been easily obtained by Spalaikovitch, the Serbian Minister at Petrograd. Serbia was Orthodox, an independent State, an ally of Russia and was officially represented at Petrograd. Therefore the Russian authorities allowed her forthwith to recruit "Austrian" prisoners, despite the legitimist arguments that were brought forward against us. Several detachments were sent to Serbia as early as 1915. The Serbian General Živkovitch, was at Odessa, and to him the Austrian-Serb officers and non-commissioned officers were despatched. Thus the first Serbian division in Russia was formed in 1916. Many of our officers and men, tired of waiting for a Czech army, joined it, the Serbians promising to organize a special Czech contingent; but Kieff opposed the scheme and it was dropped. Consequently, a number of our men left the Serbian division. Sad was the fate of those who remained in it, and of the Division itself. Strategically, its gallant struggle in the Do-brudja against Mackensen's advance was bootless, yet it strengthened the ties between us and the Serbs and enhanced the closeness of our cooperation. I need not tell how the forma-tion of a second Serbian Division was begun or how dissensions caused it to be disbanded, for I wish only to show the difference between the bearing of official Russia towards the Serbians and towards us. But I remember with gratitude our officers and men who gave their lives on the Dobrudja plains for Serbia and for our common freedom. In April 1917 the Serbian command released our men, who returned to join our own army at Kieff.

Our treatment by the Russian authorities reminds me of a story that is told of the Commander of an Austrian fortress who once gave the Emperor Francis Joseph a hundred reasons why a salute had not been fired in honor of his Majesty's arrival, the final reason being that there was no powder. In dealing with me, the Russian military officials were in an analogous position. They gave me all sorts of explanations, reasons and excuses which I have faithfully set forth; but they did not tell me what I learned only after the Bolshevist Revolution—that, from 1915 onward, the supreme military and political authorities had definitely decided not to create a Czech army. The Serbian military attaché, Lontkevitch, told me of this decision and promised to send me, to Paris or America, copies of the official minutes recording it. Unfortunately, he died; and, if he sent them, I never received them.

In the light of this information, I understood that Russian

soldiers, trained in obedience, should have felt themselves bound by the decision and by official secrecy in regard to it; but I was surprised that neither Korniloff nor Brusiloff, despite their admiration for our lads, dared to change a resolution taken in wholly different circumstances. It became clear to me why the Tsar's promises had not been kept and why, when the Regulations for our army were finally sanctioned, they had been at variance with our political program. From Vienna I received trustworthy information that people there knew of and rejoiced over the resistance of the Russian authorities, and over the way in which things were being put off. Our lads attributed to Austrian bribery this systematic obstruction on the part of the Russian civil and military authorities; and the possibility that Austro-Hungarian influences were at work was often discussed in the Russian branch of our National Council. The presence of the same influences was suspected in the dissensions between our parties in Russia, and in the formation of Dürich's National Council—unknown to Dürich himself—for its organizer, Priklonsky, was publicly accused, even by Russians, of being in Hungarian pay. He had been Consul at Budapest before the war and was seen there again after the Revolution. Štefánik mentioned to me what he thought well-founded suspicions of one of our people at Kieff—the one and only case of alleged treason. I doubted it, and Štefánik promised me written proof. This proof was probably burned when his aeroplane crashed near Bratislava after the war, though I am still unconvinced that it was conclusive.

ORGANIZATION

When I had got to know the situation and the principal people I drew up a plan of my own. Our task was to build up the army or, as we called it in Russia, the "Corpus," out of the original Družina, which had been transformed, first into a brigade and then into a division with the nucleus of a second division in it. My plan foreshadowed the creation of a

"Corpus" and preparation for a second "Corpus," since plenty of prisoners volunteered for service. I took up the work where Štefánik had left it. Against the Russian idea of making a political, propagandist army, he had upheld our view that we needed a real army, as big as possible, and that it must be sent to France. Upon this we had agreed as soon as Briand had recognized us and our anti-Austrian program at the beginning of 1916.

But the work was greatly impeded by the variety and number of authorities with which we had to deal. At Petrograd there were the War Office, the General Staff, the Foreign Office and the Council of Ministers; at Moghileff there was General Headquarters; at Kieff, the chief of the Military District; and, finally, the Commander-in-Chief had a word to say, as well as the Commander and the Staff of the Army Corps to which our units were attached. There were continuous pilgrimages from Pontius to Pilate, and long journeys from town to town. Everywhere and from everybody we had to get a *Bumaga,* a "paper" of some sort, which took long to make out; for in Russia the army, like everything else, was bureaucratized. The Allied representatives helped us generously and, in a number of minor matters, backed us up in our dealings with the Russian authorities. The military attachés, who were generally stationed at Moghileff, helped us too.

The work was simplified by the setting up in Russia of the "Branch" of our Paris National Council. Both the "League" and the "Association" had taken a hand in the military business; and, alongside of the "League," there had been Dürich's pro-Russian "National Council." Our "Branch" simplified all that. In accordance with its statutes, I became its head on reaching Russia; things grew more orderly; the work was more unified; and thus we gained the confidence of the Russians and of the Allied representatives alike.

We extended the "Branch" and divided up the work. Most of it, of course, had to do with the army and its development. The correspondence with our prisoners, singly and with whole camps, was immense. Members of the "Branch" and many officers and men had to visit the camps and direct the recruiting. Money troubles soon arose, but we amended an old scheme and issued a national loan. I simplified things as much as possible, even in the arrangements made by the Russians. Klecanda, the "Branch" secretary, whose premature death was a great loss, was of the utmost assistance to me. He was a dear fellow, devoted to the cause, and a tireless worker. My private secretary was the young historian Papoušek. The Russian Government had entrusted General Červinka, a Czech by birth, with the technical organization of our army. He was a Russian soldier and, if only on that account, had some trouble with the "League" and with the "Association"; but he labored devotedly for the Czech cause. If, as a Conservative, he was not altogether in agreement with me, that did not prevent our working together. In fact he had been a good intermediary between the Russian Government, the "League" and, afterwards, Dürich's "National Council." He had been put in charge of Czech military affairs in the Kieff Military District, to which he was attached soon after the outbreak of war; and, when the General Staff issued the order for the formation of our army in the autumn of 1916, the execution of it was entrusted to him.

My Own Plan

My own plan differed from those of the Russian Government and of the "League" in that my aim was to have an independent army at our own disposal. It was not enough that it should be a part of the Russian army since, in this case, it might be dispersed along a huge front without coming into play as a unit. Besides, I wanted as large an army as possible, an army really military, not political. Its spirit had to be Czech, not Russian, albeit pro-Russian. To me it mattered little whether the command were Russian or Czech, the main points were what its commanders would be like, what its spirit and what purpose it would serve. A Czech army must know clearly what political aims it was fighting for, and why; it must swear allegiance to our nation; in a word, it must be our own army.

Secondly, the army must be transferred to France. This had been agreed upon in Paris a year before, and to this end Štefánik had worked in Russia before I came. The anti-French and the anti-Western Russians had all along opposed the transfer which had been discussed in various Departments of State and in the Council of Ministers before the Revolution. On reaching Petrograd after the Revolution, M. Albert Thomas renewed, on behalf of the French Government, the request for the transfer; and, on May 14, 1917, the Russian General Staff granted it, on good grounds. The Revolution had broken the ice. I arranged with the French Military Mission that, as a first instalment, 30,000 prisoners should be sent to France, including some thousands of Southern Slavs. M. Thomas agreed and helped in every way to hurry things on. This Agreement with him was the first Treaty to be concluded by our National Council with a State; and, once again, France was the first to recognize our National Council as a contracting Power. It was understood that some of these prisoners would work in French factories. The Russian Foreign Office and General Staff promised to get the convoy off as quickly as possible by way of Archangel; but, in consequence of delays, the first contingent started only in November 1917, and its numbers were much smaller than we anticipated. At that time we hoped, however, that before long we should all be able to get to France by way of Siberia.

The prospects of service in France naturally affected the organization of our troops. To make things easier, we introduced French discipline and appointed French liaison officers. My whole care was to keep the army together and to prevent it from being drawn into the Russian military chaos. In this I succeeded to some extent, thanks to the collapse of the Russian army and to the demoralization of the country. The collapse taught our men a lesson; and, on the other hand, it helped us to get, from the Russian military magazines, material that would otherwise have been merely looted. We had to take what we wanted, for it was out of the question to make arrangements with the authorities, so great was the prevailing uncertainty and so rapidly did the authorities change. No sooner had I settled something with Korniloff than, on the morrow, Brusiloff was in his place. In short, there was utter confusion.

The official permission to form an army was merely a framework. Details had to be filled and, particularly, the final dimensions of our force had still to be determined. At first I asked only for one Corps, to which a second could be added according to circumstances. General Dukhonin, the new Chief of General Staff at Headquarters, made me this important concession on October 9, 1917. Unlike Brusiloff, Korniloff and Alexeieff, Dukhonin, who knew and appreciated our lads, their work as scouts and their gallantry at Zboroff, had the pluck to set aside the obsolete decision of the Tsarist Government. Thus we got our Corps which, by definite agreement, was to be independent of the Russians. Furthermore, it was expressly stipulated with Dukhonin that it should only take action against the foreign enemy—an acceptance and confirmation by the Russians themselves of my main principle of neutrality in regard to Russian internal affairs. This safeguarded us against the danger of being dragged into Russian party quarrels, to-day on one side, to-morrow on another; and it reassured the Conservatives and Reactionaries in the Russian army who feared and resisted to the last the establishment of an independent Czech force.

Dukhonin was a young, vigorous and capable officer and a very honorable man. He understood our position and helped us. He withstood Lenin's orders to conclude an Armistice with the Central Powers. Unhappily, he was killed by the Bolshevists on December 2 when, under Krylenko, he took possession of Russian Headquarters. For days his dead body was barbarously profaned at the Moghileff railway station before it could be taken to Kieff for burial. We assembled to pay our last respects to him, but the funeral was forbidden; and permission to bury the body at night could only be obtained by requests and pressure from all quarters. A few days later I visited his widow and learned, to my horror, that Dukhonin would gladly have accepted the command of our Corps. Indeed, Madame Dukhonin hinted that he had expected it to be offered to him. This had not crossed my mind when I discussed with him the choice of a Commander, since, in view of his high rank, I supposed he would look upon the command of a Corps as a degradation. Certainly, he would not have lost his life had he left his position at Moghileff to become our Commander. We shall ever hold him in grateful remembrance, for he gave body to the decision of the Provisional Government, and made a living thing out of what had been mere words and paper.

Soon after getting Dukhonin's consent, I had chosen the Russian General Shokoroff to command our Corps and appointed the former General Dieterichs to be its Chief of Staff. I had known of Dieterichs earlier, at Headquarters; and, when I heard that he was working as a laborer at the Kieff railway station, I was all the more disposed to take him for our Staff. With these two appointments, the formation of our Corps was practically assured. For the other superior commands we had to take Russians since we had only subalterns among our prisoners, and most of them were inexperienced and young. It was the same everywhere; and, just as the higher officers were Russian in Russia, they were French in France and Italian in Italy. In Russia, moreover, the tendency had prevailed from the beginning to make the leadership of our army Russian, inasmuch as the army was to be Russian, not Czech. It naturally caused difficulties, principally because most of the Russian officers did not understand their work. Many, too, were obviously affected by the general military and administrative demoralization of the Tsarist system. I had not a few worries on this account. Nor, for instance, did all our own officers and men forthwith understand why, soon after reaching Russia, I had removed Mamontoff from the command of our brigade, despite his popularity and the confidence he inspired. He was undoubtedly an able man, but more journalist and tribune than soldier.

In the Družina, the language of command had been Russian. In the second Division it was Czech; and, in the Corps, Czech was introduced though, in some respects, only nominally, because our men had neither the time nor the capacity to translate the Russian words of command quickly and to adapt them to our needs. This was one of the difficulties inherent in the very character of our military organization.

THE MATERIALS OF AN ARMY

Some effort of imagination is needed to understand how troublesome the work of organization really was. It was not merely a question of the language of command and of army signals, but of the whole military administration. Our men were volunteers. They had joined of their own free will, and this gave them a certain liberty. Our ideal was to make a democratic army; and it is comprehensible that, in the Russian chaos, the notions of liberty, equality and fraternity were, at times, somewhat anarchically interpreted. Especially after the Bolshevist Revolution, when Bolshevist ideas began to spread even in our ranks, it was a heavy task promptly to work out a democratic system of discipline and obedience such as is indispensable to an army in the field. As I have said, we adopted the French disciplinary system, with some necessary and provisional alterations.

Among our volunteers there were, of course, members of all our parties and factions at home—another source of trouble, because the men, and particularly the officers, could not always distinguish between politics and strategy. Yet antagonisms were not so sharp as they would have been at home. Nevertheless, in such circumstances, it was by no means easy to put the army on a purely military basis and to make it efficient. It was not, I repeat, merely a question whether the command should be Russian or Czech (though this was long debated) but of settling a far wider problem—what strategy and tactics would best express the spirit of our nation? In any event, we had to make our volunteer army fit to face a first-class foe; and, despite all our care, some degree of amateurishness remained in the organization and command both of the whole and of the various parts. The solution of many a puzzle cost me, a civilian, much hard thought. Our soldiers naturally compared themselves with the Russians around them, but we had to judge by the standard of the Germans and the Prussians whom we wished to fight. In battle, discipline and technical knowledge save lives. Not only military but humanitarian considerations demand good equipment and sound soldierly training.

Circumstances themselves required independence of thought and action on the part of individuals; and, in this respect, our Corps came out well on the whole. In big things and small, talent and a gift of improvisation were shown. It was not possible simply to order our men to ignore Bolshevist examples. Soldiers' committees had, for instance, to be set up, but, as early as the Kerensky period, they were limited to economic and educational work. The democratic administration of a— volunteer—army demanded that the men themselves should have some voice in decisions. And, in a democratic army, the privileges of officers are hard to determine—ought they, for example, to have their own mess? Such matters could not be dealt with at one stroke and in the lump, for conditions did not permit of strict uniformity. Therefore the various detachments did more or less as they liked. The principles and ideas of the Sokol organization served as a standard; and though I was well aware of the difference between a soldier and a "Sokol," the influence of the Sokol idea was great and good. We made mistakes but, on the whole, we succeeded. Before long we numbered more than 40,000 men for whom arms, clothing, boots, bread and meat had to be provided—the commissariat question was difficult indeed. To some extent, as I have said, the breakdown of the Russian army helped us; but it was not easy to get corn and flour from the Ukrainian peasants—they demanded tools and nails, not money, in return—and the constant changes in the political situation hampered us. At first we had been dependent on the Russian military authorities; but, by the time we had mustered in the Ukraine, the Russian authorities were giving place to Ukrainian in proportion as the Ukraine gained independence. Yet we could not avoid dealing also with the new Bolshevist authorities who were coming into power. Then the grave problem of transport arose. How was our army to get to the East—for we held firmly to the plan of reaching France by way of Siberia and the sea—when the management and the rolling stock of the Russian railways were deteriorating daily?

Even had our men been veterans of uniform quality, things would thus have been hard enough; but, naturally, not all of our 40,000 volunteers were of equal character and worth. Naturally, too, not all of them had been prompted to join us by patriotic enthusiasm. Upon them the effect of life in most of the Russian prisoners' camps had been very harmful, especially on account of the constant and bureaucratic pressure which the uneducated Camp Commanders had exercised. Thus, to many of our men, service in our Legion meant release. This was certainly the case in the post-revolutionary period of 1917 and particularly in 1918. The Legion offered greater personal safety and better treatment, especially for the sick; it offered, too, protection against Austria; for, had they gone home, they would have been put into the Austrian army and would have fared worse. More lives would have been lost.

The men themselves kept a sharp eye upon the various forms of malingering. About a hundred members of the original Družina—born and bred in Russia—made themselves scarce before the battle of Zboroff; but the great majority of our men were good, trustworthy fellows who did their hard job honorably and well. I had many an opportunity to watch them and to study in them the Czech character. As I do not know how many Czech and Slovak prisoners there were in Russia, I cannot say what proportion they bore to the total number of our Legionaries. My impression was that a fairly large number did not join us. Had exact figures been obtainable they would have formed a good measure of the general degree of enlightenment and political determination.

With the men my own relations were those of a friend and comrade, though my rulings were severe and, in case of need, very severe. In a commander of high rank or low, I think sincerity is the best quality. Next to it, consistency and, above all, justice are requisite. An army is unconditionally based upon authority. In war, commanders and officers discharge the same functions as leaders in political life. But a military leader must not be a demagogue. If he is, he soon pays for it, even in person, for war is a matter of life and death and, in the moment of danger, men stand no nonsense but judge their superiors pitilessly. Misconceived democratism leads officers into demagogic insincerity and falsehood.

Soldiers are franker than civilians. The relations of superiors to inferiors, and *vice versa,* are free from the formalities of civil life. They become, as it were, laconic, corresponding to the precision, definiteness and efficacy of the whole military mechanism. A comparatively high degree of equality, and the circumstance that soldiers have not to think of bread, clothing and quarters, that they are free from the economic struggle for existence, tend to make them open and straightforward. Living constantly in the society of his comrades and, so to speak, in public, a soldier becomes more objective, less subjective. In essence, his calling does not foster skepticism. He is ingenuous, childlike and has childish weaknesses. The fact that an army is a hierarchy of duties and obligations gives rise to not a few jealousies; and men who are heroes when facing the foe may be childish and petty in the mass. Nearly every man in our Legion ran the gauntlet of censure and envy. Between the members of the original Družina and the later Legionaries there was often some degree of friction, the newcomers from the Serbian Legion being sharply criticized, and the shortcomings of which officers had been guilty in the Austrian army being remembered against them. Besides, the men from the various prisoners' camps in Russia were jealous of each other—another instance of the abnormal conditions in which our army was formed.

My intercourse with the men proved that they trusted me. They knew that at home I had advocated a sober and discriminating policy. Hence they expected that what I undertook and demanded of them in Russia would be well considered. I offered them a well-grounded program which they accepted. They were educated enough to understand, judge and adopt historical and political arguments. I appealed to reason, sought to convince and, by conviction, to engender a spirit of self-sacrifice. Our chief difficulties I discussed with them quite openly. They saw and learned by daily experience that I cared for their welfare; and I think that the simplicity of my own life and my fearlessness or, rather, my show of fearlessness, made a good impression on them. During the Bolshevist Revolution at Petrograd, Moscow and Kieff, as they knew, I had never avoided danger in the fulfilment of duty. Thus I earned the right to ask sacrifices of them, even the sacrifice of their lives.

I know well that the quality of an army cannot be assured by personal gallantry and individual efficiency. Efficiency must be upheld by general discipline. It is not only a question of courage under fire but of endurance in wearisome and exhausting service in the field. And soldiers do not live by discipline alone. They need bread. A good commissariat is a fundamental condition of success. A man, a regiment and a whole army may be valiant to-day, panic-stricken to-morrow. An army needs the right organization and management, and continual leadership. Individual courage is only one factor in victory. Hence the great importance attaching to officers and non-commissioned officers in a democratic army.

Our Czech soldiers are good fighters, brave to the point of heroism; but they must know wherefore they fight. The Slovaks are likewise good soldiers but accustomed rather to obey than to command or to lead. Our men are quick in action and in observation. They take their bearings rapidly. Though failure discourages them, they know how to cut their way out of a dangerous fix. I have already said that, in the battle of Zboroff, they showed a notable tactical skill as well as personal bravery. Sacrifice out of blind obedience, such as had been demanded and encouraged in the Austrian army, soon disappeared; and the revival of the Hussite spirit among us was no mere catchword but the outcome of sincere feeling and resolve. Nor was it simply an historical embellishment that, after the battle of Zboroff, our regiments should have borne the names of Hus, Žižka and others. As a characteristic detail I may mention that, as badges, our lads wore Hussite chalices and Bohemian lions. The Russian peasants nicknamed them "rjumotshky" and "sobatshky" ("liqueur glasses" and "puppies")—one of the reasons, I imagine, why the badges were not generally worn. The Hussite idea would have been expressed consistently in the whole of our military organization had there been time to eliminate the Austrian and the Russian traditions and to harmonize our ideal with modern conditions; for when, in Switzerland, I first came out against Austria on the day of the Hus Centenary, it was an organic consequence of our history, just as the revival of our Hussite and Taborite military traditions was organic and, at the same time, national in the best sense of the word.

THE BOLSHEVIST REVOLUTION

The Bolshevist Revolution of November 7, 1917, was a source of further difficulties. I had been an eye-witness of the Bolshevist movement at Petrograd and had seen it spread to Moscow and Kieff. By some strange chance I found myself, in each of those cities, in the thick of the Bolshevist fighting. At Petrograd I lived in the Morskaya, near the Castle, opposite the Telegraph and Telephone office, all of which were fought for. The rooms of our Branch National Council were at first in Basejnaya and afterwards on the Znamenskaya. I used to go through every day from the Morskaya and had to cross the

Litejni Prospect, where street fighting was often going on. My colleagues in the National Council grew anxious. One of them —I think it was our present Minister, Šeba—accused me of a physiological lack of the sense of danger. It was agreed that I should have an escort, and the prisoner Huza was attached to me. Then, under pressure from the Branch, I had to go to Moscow, lest evil befall me, the Branch itself meaning to come afterwards. So I went to Moscow; but, on the very morning of my arrival, the fight began between the Bolshevists and Kerensky's troops, and I suddenly found myself in the famous Hotel Métropole which Kerensky's cadets rapidly transformed into a fortress. There I spent six days, hotly besieged by the Bolshevists. When, at last, the Kerensky cadets withdrew unobserved in the night, and the Bolshevists captured the fortress next morning—the Hotel was very solidly built, with massive walls—I was chosen as spokesman for the foreigners; the Russians, who feared to speak for themselves, choosing a Pole to represent them.

Later on, when I left Moscow for Kieff, I found myself in the French Hotel on the Krescatik during the Bolshevist siege of Kieff—a dangerous place on account of its position. While we were conferring there, a huge shell fell into an adjoining room but, luckily, did not explode. Friends then insisted that I should move to a sanatorium, where the danger was certainly not less, because bullets found their way even into my room there, and I had to go regularly to the sittings of the Branch. One afternoon, Huza and I walked and ran through a hail of Bolshevist projectiles. Even now, years afterwards, when I think of what I went through during the Bolshevist occupation of the chief cities of Russia, it seems to me like a nightmare. By a singular association of ideas, the word "Bolshevism" recalls to my mind one scene among the many horrible and inhuman sights I saw during the Bolshevist Revolution. After the street fighting, at Petrograd and elsewhere, the bodies of the fallen were sent to their families, usually in the well-known Russian *izvostchiks*. The stiffened bodies were thrown like logs into the little vehicles, the legs sticking out on one side and the head or, sometimes, a hand on the other. Often the corpse was placed on its feet and bound fast with a piece of rope or a rag. I even saw one standing head downwards with the legs sticking up in the air. When I think of those gruesome sights, the unnecessary, senseless, barbaric killing of human beings by the Bolshevists always returns to my mind.

But it was from the standpoint of our army and of our military plans that I was chiefly interested in the Bolshevist Revolution. It soon became clear that, willingly or unwillingly, the Bolshevists would make peace with the Germans. Even in this they followed the example of the Tsar and of their predecessors. Fate is strangely capricious—Milyukoff left the Provisional Government before Kerensky, because Kerensky wished to amend its program in a pacifist sense; afterwards, when Kerensky attempted to fight, Milyukoff was ready to negotiate with the Germans for peace!

My own conviction was firm—not to meddle in the internal revolutionary affairs of Russia and to get away from Russia to France as had been agreed. Therefore, when the Bolshevists under Muravieff marched against the bourgeois National Council of the Ukraine and took Kieff, we made a Treaty with them. They guaranteed our armed neutrality and our freedom to leave for France. Thus we were recognized as a regular and independent army and Government; and, in order to strengthen our position, I declared—in agreement with the French Military Mission—that our army was a part of the French army. This was on February 7, 1918, a day before the Bolshevists captured Kieff.

Muravieff himself tried to keep his pledges; but, whether he knew it or not, the Kieff Bolshevist Soviet sent Czech agitators to persuade our troops to join the Red Army. This was one of the many critical moments we went through. After careful reflection I decided to let the Bolshevist agitators talk to our fellows. As a result, only 218 men out of our whole army joined the Reds, and several of them came back next day, for, naturally, they were not slow to see the defects of the Bolshevist forces. An episode which opened the eyes of the better sort more thoroughly than I could have done by any prohibition of Bolshevist propaganda, was that, on the morrow, one of our Reds boasted that he had a pocket full of watches. Not a few Russian and French officers were very skeptical about my decision to allow Bolshevist propaganda, but its upshot went in my favor and against military red tape.

I do not deny that there were decent and honest fellows among those who went over to the Bolshevists. Some of them afterwards rendered us good service as members of the Bolshevist army. But Bolshevist excesses at Kieff and in the neighborhood tried our patience sorely. We were especially upset by the news that, despite the Agreement, some of our sentries guarding military stores near the city had been killed; for the Bolshevists, in their brutal arrogance, had not only killed our men but had profaned their bodies after stealing their clothing and boots. It was hard to resist the natural impulse to chastise them; but, taking all circumstances into account, I confined myself to a strong protest and to the exaction of a promise that the culprits would be punished and the Treaty would be loyally observed.

We had signed the treaty with Muravieff before the fall of Kieff. Two days after the fall, on February 10, 1918, I negotiated with him in his railway saloon car, in the presence of the Allied representatives who chose me as their spokesman because they did not themselves know Russian. On February 16, Muravieff sent me a written guarantee that our armed troops might leave for France freely and unmolested.

My relations to Muravieff were the subject of much reactionary gossip in Kieff. His attentions to me were said to be "marked." He told me once that he had long known me by report and through my writings, and that he wished therefore to oblige me. I heard that he had been a police officer and had become a Bolshevist under compulsion. Later on, he was shot by order of Moscow for alleged embezzlement.

As I have said, Bolshevism was for me, at that time, a military problem first and foremost. How would it affect our army? Yet, naturally, I watched the Bolshevist movement with sociological interest. I had long been an observer of the Labor and Socialist movement at home and throughout Europe. This was the origin of my "Critique of Marxism." In studying Russia I had from the first kept an eye on Lenin's tendencies; and when I reached Petrograd I had seen the beginning of his revolutionary propaganda. Then, for nearly six months, I had lived under the Bolshevist régime and had noted its growth and evolution.

This is not the place to discuss Bolshevism itself; I will deal with it only in so far as it bears upon my narrative. But, as my standpoint in regard to Bolshevism puzzled a number of people, I propose to explain it.

If Communism is taken to mean absolute economic and social equality, I do not look upon it, in principle, as a social or socialist ideal. Without strong individualism, that is to say, without free initiative on the part of individuals, society cannot attain a normal political and social condition. In practice, this means a system under which many individualities, unequally endowed by nature, physically and mentally, may unfold. No two individuals in society are in equal positions or have the same social surroundings; each knows best how to utilize his own powers and his environment. If one man decides for another and directs him, the danger arises that not all his abilities will find full scope. This is everywhere to be seen.

Politically, it finds expression in all strongly centralized forms of Government. Now, Communism is centralistic. Bolshevist centralism, in particular, is very rigid. It is an abstract system deduced from a thesis and applied by force. Bolshevism is the absolute dictatorship of a man and his helpers. It is infallible and inquisitorial. Thus it has nothing in common with science and scientific philosophy; for, without freedom, science, like democracy, is impossible.

Democracy, consistently and rightly applied, I hold to be the state of society most desirable and suitable for our own time and for a long time to come, not only politically but also economically and socially. The capitalist system is imperfect by reason of its onesidedness. True, it gives to some, not to all, openings for individual initiative, spirit of enterprise and productivity; but the values thus created are not distributed or appropriated according to productive efficiency but according to rules for the appropriation of others' work and what it yields. In practice, democracy signifies a tolerable inequality, a least— and progressively lessening—common multiple of inequality. Doubtless, this is easy to say; but there are many ways of applying it, just as there are and may be many sorts of Communism—witness the Russian experiment, its rapid development and its great transformations.

In 1917, Lenin's object was not so much to put Communist principles and ideals into practice in Russia as to use Russia for the purpose of applying them, or, at least, of hastening their application, in Europe. On this point he often spoke his mind; but he erred because his view alike of the condition of Europe and of the condition of Russia was mistaken. His philosophy of history was unsound. Both Marx and Engels had been wrong in expecting and foretelling the "final revolution"; but this did not deter Lenin and his followers who, in their turn, looked for the "social revolution." When? Where?

What Marx, following Feuerbach, says about religious anthropomorphism is also true socially and politically. Not only do men make heaven after their own image but the earthly future as well. The Russians are incapable of carrying out Marxist Communism. Taken as a whole, they are still too uncultured, too perverted by Tsarism to understand and apply the Marxist views of Communism as the final stage of a long historical process. What Lenin and his fellows practised could not be Communism. It was, at most, a thing of Communist shreds and patches. As a system, it was a primitive (agrarian) capitalism and a primitive socialism under the control of a primitive State which arose out of anarchical elements that had broken away from a likewise primitive Tsarist centralism. Only the primitive condition of Russia—the mass of illiterate peasants isolated in their villages, the lack of communications, the decay of the army and the bureaucracy in consequence of the loss of the war, the collapse of Tsarism and of Caesaro-papism, the bewilderment of political parties and classes—made it possible for a vigorous usurper to bring about the Bolshevist revolution in the chief towns and to establish the rule of a small but organized minority.

On all hands the defects and inadequacies of social and political anthropomorphism were to be seen in Russia. Responsible administrative and military functions were mostly entrusted to young, inexperienced and technically untrained men. The best of them did what they could. They sought and found things long known and already existing. But many of them merely abused their positions and turned them to selfish ends. The integral calculus is beyond beginners in arithmetic. In Lenin's frequent admissions that mistakes had been made and that there was much to learn, lie something of Russian honesty and also an indictment. Neither in administration nor in politics is it necessary nowadays to invent the alphabet anew. Lack of system and countless improvisations produced the Bolshevist system. Bolshevist semi-culture is worse than no culture at all; its insufficiency and its strange primitivism are revealed in its official adoption of all the monstrosities of so-called "modern art." Uncritical, wholly unscientific infallibility is the basis of the Bolshevist dictatorship; and a régime that quails before criticism and fears to recognize thinking men stands self-condemned.

Even the mistaken Marxist conception of the State took its revenge upon the Bolshevist administration; for the Marxists never paid sufficient heed to the organization and administration of the State. Anarchism, in the proper sense of the word, or

Statelessness, seemed enough for them, and they insisted on the absolute pre-eminence of economic conditions, which they called economic or historical materialism. This Marxist materialism was well suited to the passive Russian character—why bother about anything save bread! But the State, Literature, Science, Philosophy, the Schools and Education, the health and morality of the nation, in a word, the whole civilization of the spirit, are not products of economic conditions but must be won alongside of them; and it is civilization that makes possible and ensures economic development—and bread. The Russians, even the Bolshevists, are children of the Tsarism in which they were brought up and fashioned for centuries. They managed to get rid of the Tsar but not of Tsarism. They still wear the Tsarist uniform, albeit inside out; a Russian, as is known, can even wear his boots with the soles inside.

The Bolshevists continued to employ the underground tactics which they had long practised. They were not prepared for positive administration but were fit only for a negative revolution, negative in the sense that, in their uncultivated one-sidedness and narrow-mindedness, they were guilty of much superfluous destruction. Particularly do I blame them for having reveled, after a truly Tsarist fashion, in the destruction of human life. Degrees of barbarism are always expressed in the way men deal with their own lives and those of others. In their extermination of the Russian intellectual class, the Bolshevists overlooked the warning example set by Severus when he killed off the old Roman families and especially the families of Senators. Thus Severus barbarized the State and the administration—and hastened the decline of the Empire. Historians may find more recent Russian precedents—in Ivan the Terrible or, apter still, in Stenka Razin.

In point of fact, the Bolshevists stand nearer to Bakunin than to Marx, or follow Marx in his first revolutionary period—1848—before his Socialist doctrine had been worked out. To Bakunin they could appeal in justification of their avowed Jesuitism and Machiavellism. To him they were drawn by their secrecy—which had become to them, as conspirators, a second nature—and by their striving for power, for dictatorship. To seize power and to hold it was their first aim. People who believe that they have reached the highest and ultimate degree of development, who think they have gained infallible knowledge of the whole organization of society, cease to trouble about progress and perfectibility and have one chief and only care— how to keep their power and position. Thus it was during the Catholic Reformation, when the Inquisition and the Counter-Reformation arose. So it is in Russia.

Of Russia, the Bolshevists know little. Tsarism forced them to live abroad. Thus they lost touch with their own country. Nor can I say that they got to know the West better. Since they lived in groups of their own, they did not know even the West. They knew enough of it to take an interest in it and to make of it a standard for Russia; and, as they believed that the social revolution would break out in the West sooner than in Russia, they devoted so much attention to propaganda in the West that their minds were diverted from Russian conditions. On this propaganda they spent, moreover, comparatively large sums. In short, Bolshevist policy is extensive, not intensive; broad, not deep, inwardly and outwardly. In a word, it is primitive.

Russian Bolshevism which is, at best, a form of State Socialism and State Capitalism, is by no means identical with Communism. Experience shows that real, lasting Communism is possible only on a moral or a religious basis—among friends— but we have all far to go before we attain a state of society founded on friendship and sympathy. At the beginning of a revolution, in the moment of enthusiasm, Communistic experiments may succeed, but they decline and degenerate when enthusiasm has to stand the test of daily life.

The way for Lenin's régime had been prepared by the Provisional Government and by Kerensky, both of whom showed administrative incapacity and entrusted wide spheres of action to bad and incompetent men. Lenin did likewise. The anarchical proceedings of the Russian intelligentsia, from 1906 onwards, had smoothed his path. Even the non-Socialist parties then failed to comprehend that, after a Revolution and the attainment of (no matter how imperfect) a Constitution, political action needed to become more positive. Lenin was a logical consequence of Russian illogicality. The sealed German railway carriages played a very minor part. Like many a usurper before him, Lenin took possession of Russia—usurpation fills a long chapter in Russian history. As means of agitation he utilized war-weariness, the disintegration of the army and the peasant yearning for land, a yearning stimulated by all the Socialist and Liberal tendencies after the liberation of the serfs in 1862. The peasants seized the land—there was no Communism about *them*—and the peasants are Russia. It is wrong to charge Lenin and his experiment with not being Russian. They are entirely Russian; and the Soviet system itself is an extension of the primitive Russian *Mir* and *Artel*.

This does not mean that, if Lenin's system did not establish Communism and if it was guilty of many sins of omission and commission, it has brought no good to Russia or to the peasant masses in particular. Bolshevism awakened their sense of freedom and the consciousness of their own strength. They learned the power of organization. They became convinced of the need for hard work, Lenin himself and not a few leaders setting, in this respect, a good example. A certain Rousseau-like simplicity came to prevail in the towns and among the more educated. These and other relatively good qualities of Bolshevism must be recognized by just and sober observers of Russian evolution; but they are offset by the moral degeneration, the decline of the schools and of education, the anarchy in morals and culture which make up a great and, to my mind, the greatest deficit. Besides, the question arises why there had to be in Russia so violent an awakening from Tsarist slumber—a question to be pondered by all who love Russia; not least by the adherents of Tsarism and of the Church.

What I have said applies especially to the first period of

Bolshevism. Subsequently, Communism developed or, rather, attempts were made to apply it, albeit at the cost of public welfare. As to foreign intervention in or against Russia, I am still a non-interventionist. Bolshevism is an internal Russian crisis which cannot be overcome by action from without; though the Bolshevist yearning for *de jure* recognition by bourgeois governments encourages interventionist tendencies.

THE UKRAINE

From the moment that the Bolshevists opened peace negotiations—they did so formally on December 3, 1917, by asking for an armistice, the Peace of Brest-Litovsk being signed on March 3, 1918—it was clear to us that our army had nothing more to do in Russian. Therefore we began as early as possible to march out of the Ukraine into Russia on the way to Vladivostok and France.

As long as Russia ruled in the Ukraine, our position was simple. Russia gave us the opportunity to organize and arm our Corps and to provide it with the necessary stores. In return we mounted guard over military material of all sorts, particularly in Kieff, and kept order.

But, soon after the Bolshevist revolution, the Ukraine began to grow independent. On November 20, 1917, the third "Universal" was proclaimed, declaring the Ukraine a Republic and an autonomous part of the Russian Federation. Hence the necessity of negotiating with the Ukrainian Government; and we made with it, on January 15, 1918, the same terms as we had made with Russia. At first, the relationship between the Ukraine and Russia was vague, and our relations to the Ukraine were therefore vague. But, on the whole, there were no unpleasant incidents, though difficulties arose on account of party quarrels and of the disturbed conditions in the Ukraine.

The detachment of the Ukraine from Russia began in January 1918. On January 13, the Ukraine was recognized by the Central Powers. I was well informed of what was happening and made arrangements accordingly. In a Ukraine completely separated from Russia I felt it would be impossible to stay, not only by reason of our earlier promises and obligations to Russia but out of consideration for our fellow-countrymen and especially for our prisoners in Bolshevist Russia who might otherwise have been persecuted. Without Russia, moreover, we could not reach Siberia on our way to France. When the Fourth "Universal" was issued on January 25, declaring the Ukraine a completely independent State, I informed the Ukrainian Foreign Minister, A. J. Shulgin (not to be confounded with the Russian V. V. Shulgin at Kieff) that the Fourth "Universal" had annulled our treaty and that our troops would therefore leave the Ukraine as soon as possible. Our army had been formed in agreement with Russia; our soldiers had sworn allegiance to Russia; we were devoted to Russia; and, though we did not wish to oppose the Ukraine or its policy in any way, we could not simply transfer our allegiance to it. Russia herself would also deal with the Ukrainian question and, on principle, we did not meddle in her internal affairs. I told Shulgin that, in the circumstances, I thought the detachment of the Ukraine from Russia a mistake, particularly because the Ukraine, in its disturbed and administratively immature condition, would be subject to excessive Austrian and German influences. I had serious reason to take this view; and a formal reason was that we could not remain in the territory of a State which had made peace with the Germans and the Austrians. This affected also our relations with the Bolshevists. The Ukraine had made peace with the Germans and the Austrians at Brest-Litovsk on February 9, a day after the Bolshevists had taken Kieff; and it is pertinent to remember that our non-recognition of the fourth "Universal" soon facilitated our negotiations with the Bolshevist Commander, Muravieff.

IN ROUMANIA

To go from Kieff to France by way of Siberia—a fantastical plan, I sometimes said to myself. Yet, as often as I weighed all the circumstances, I concluded that it was the most practical, notwithstanding the distance to be covered. Naturally we worked out all sorts of schemes. Some of our own people and the Allies proposed that we should go to the Cossacks in the Caucasus, and over the Caucasus to the British army in Asia. But France was the magnetic pole to which the needle of our compass pointed.

There had been a possibility of our fighting on Roumanian soil against Austria and Germany alongside of the Roumanians and the Russians. Before our Corps was formed we had gone into this possibility carefully at Petrograd with the French Military Mission and the Roumanian Minister, Diamandy. With the Roumanians we were always in friendly touch. In the prisoners' camps, our lads helped to enrol Roumanian volunteers for the Roumanian army. In Paris, too, it was desired that our army should go to the Roumanian front. Consequently, I negotiated with General Berthelot, the head of the French Military Mission in Roumania, where the Russians were under the command of General Shtcherbatcheff. Štefánik had informed me a year before of conditions in Roumania and the plight of the prisoners there, and from this information I concluded that, even in 1916, the Roumanians were in difficulties with their commissariat. Before making up my mind I had wished, however, to see things in Roumania for myself and therefore I had gone to Jassy at the end of October 1917, for Moldavia was not occupied by the enemy.

At Jassy I saw the Roumanian politicians and military leaders as well as the French Mission and the Russian Commander. I had interviews with the King and the Prime Minister, Bratianu. Take Jonescu I knew well, and he had been recommended to me by English friends, but I met for the first time the Ministers Duca and Marcescu. Among the foreign diplomatists, all of whom I visited, I remember particularly the Serbian Minister Marinkovitch and his military attaché, Hadžitch. With the Italian Minister, Baron Fasciotti, I had important talks upon a detailed plan for the organization of our Legion in Italy, continuing thus the negotiations I had begun with the Italian Ambassador in Petrograd. Nor should our fellow countryman, Vopička, who was the United States Minister, be forgotten. Among the Roumanian Generals whom I saw were Averescu and Grigorescu. At the front, where I went to observe the state of the army and its supplies, I watched the soldiers in action during an artillery duel. They made a good impression, and I noted especially how the victory of Marasesti had encouraged them and had strengthened their spirit of initiative and endurance.

From what I saw and heard I concluded that our army could not go to the Roumanian front. Commissariat difficulties were, I thought, already so great that it was doubtful whether Roumania could provide for an increase of 50,000 men; and, above all, I felt that Roumania would not be able to prolong her resistance. The troops and the officers made a very good impression and, as I have said, their spirit was excellent. The French officers in the Roumanian army did their work most honorably, but the situation as a whole seemed to be drifting towards peace, and it struck me that the Russian forces in Roumania were no longer trustworthy. It was clear that Bolshevist Russia would soon make peace with Germany. How would Roumania then be able to hold out? And what should we do on Roumanian soil when peace had been made? Events soon bore out my decision. News of the Caporetto disaster, which reached Jassy while I was there, only confirmed my estimate of the Roumanian position. In fact, the Roumanian peace negotiations began soon after those of Russia—armistice negotiations on December 9, 1917, provisional peace on March 5, 1918, definite peace on May 7. The comparison between Roumania, the Ukraine and Russia is interesting. With the two latter, negotiations went more quickly, whereas the Roumanian negotiations lasted six months.

People in Paris were dissatisfied with my decision. They could not judge accurately at that distance, though they soon saw that I was right. Politically, moreover, my stay at Jassy bore good fruit. Our personal acquaintance and cooperation

with the Roumanians in Russia were the germ of the Little
Entente. When Roumania decided to make war, Beneš, Štefánik
and I had sent Bratianu a telegram saying that Roumania was
fighting for the liberation of our people; and, after the war,
our common interests brought us together. The same is true of
the Southern Slavs though, at that time, the ideas of the Serbians
and Roumanians were not clear enough about the delimitation of
the Banat. I discussed this matter with both parties and advised
them to seek a peaceful agreement.

Why We Were Neutral in Russia

Our rule in Bolshevist Russia, as well as in the Ukraine and
in regard to all new political formations, was to avoid intervention in party disputes and conflicts. Since we were armed
neutrals, we had weapons for self-defense in case of need; and,
as a part of the French army, we should naturally have used
them to defend the French and all other Allies had we been
attacked.

From the first we had declared that our enemies were
Austria and Germany and that we wished to fight them even
in Russia. At Zboroff we did so, very honorably. But when
Russia could fight no longer, when both Bolshevist Russia and
the Ukraine began peace negotiations with the Austrians and
the Germans and we saw that peace was being made, we could
no longer fight our enemies in Russia. Therefore our whole
endeavor was to get to France where our army could be of use.
Early in November 1917 we sent a first detachment to France
under Husák; and, in February 1918, two members of the
Russian Branch of our National Council, Šeba and Chalupa,
started for Italy to organize our Legion there on the model of
our Russian Corps. A subsidiary yet not unimportant consideration influenced our efforts to reach France—there was no
connection between Russia and the West. News passed very
slowly and incompletely. The Germans and the Austrians controlled such communications as there were, and everything we

did was distorted or ignored. If we were in France, friend and foe would get a better idea of our army. The politicians and military leaders of Tsarist and pre-Bolshevist Russia had opposed our departure. Generals Korniloff and Alexeieff, as well as Milyukoff, urged me to make common cause with them against the Bolshevists; and even the Bolshevists and the Ukrainers were against our going, in the sense that both tried to get hold of our army for themselves. Muravieff was, as I have said, particularly friendly and persuasive.

I declined all these suggestions. I was convinced that the Russian Commanders and politicians misjudged the general situation in Russia, and I had no faith in their leadership or in their power of organization. The impromptu undertakings of Korniloff and Alexeieff only strengthened my opinion. Besides, these gentlemen forgot that we had negotiated with them and with their successor, General Dukhonin, a treaty to the effect that we would only fight against the enemy and that this treaty had been signed after the establishment of Bolshevist rule. Moreover, our Corps was unprepared and lacked arms and munitions. We had no heavy artillery and, without it, regular fighting was inconceivable. Nor had we aeroplanes, and our general equipment was inadequate. We should have had to fight the Germans and the Austrians who would have advanced against us. Muravieff and his army before Kieff we could have smashed, but we should not have been strong enough to deal with the Bolshevists of Moscow and Petrograd. And were we to run the risk of seeing the Germans and the Austrians defend them against us? Of the impossibility of regular transport, on outworn railways beset by the enemy, I need not speak. The fate of the Polish Legions as early as 1917 and their subsequent disarmament under Pilsudski, Musnicki and Haller, warned us not to try conclusions prematurely with the Germans and the Austrians; and, in the fighting near Kieff and Bachmatch, we had already found that, in comparison with the Germans, we were weak. Besides—and this was a weighty consideration—the Russian people would not have understood us. They, who were strongly opposed to war, would have looked upon us as foreign intruders and would have cut off supplies. The reactionary "Black Hundreds" would have attached themselves to us and would thus have given a large proportion of the people reason to turn against us. Finally, the Russian people then wanted one thing and one thing only besides peace—land, and this we could not give them.

Therefore the revolutionary conditions in Russia dictated categorically the principle of non-interference—conditions the more complicated because districts and towns as well as races made themselves more or less independent. It was no longer merely a question of dealing with Central Russia and her Government, or even with the Ukraine, but with other autonomous groups, like the Cossacks, for example. Nor was it possible to occupy and hold the immense territory of European Russia with 50,000 men. We should have had to occupy Kieff and a number of towns and villages in the direction of Moscow, leaving garrisons everywhere—an enterprise entirely beyond our strength. In Russia, though not yet in Siberia, the Bolshevists were beginning to organize an army. To the East and in Siberia there were fewer troops, and therefore the Siberian route was the surest way to France.

It must unfortunately be recognized that the Allies had no Russian policy and that their action against the Bolshevists was not united. Immediately after the Bolshevist Revolution the Allies had no objection to recognizing or, at least to negotiating with them. I knew that the French Ambassador, M. Noulens, had negotiated with Trotsky in December 1917. A little later, at the beginning of January 1918, the American Ambassador promised them help and formal recognition if they would take action against Germany. The French General Tabouis joined me in negotiating with them at Kieff. But the Allies soon turned against them. I thought the Allied support of anti-Bolshevist movements a mistake, especially when it was given to out-and-out adventurers like Semyenoff and others. The Allies were not strong enough for a real anti-Bolshevist campaign, and sporadic fighting was meaningless. Not until the autumn of 1918 was the idea entertained of sending six divisions of the Salonica army against the Bolshevists, but neither Clemenceau or Lloyd George supported it lest the Salonica troops prove insubordinate.

In regard to the Allies our position was difficult. We were autonomous, yet a part of the French army; on France and the Entente we depended for financial support. True, it had been agreed that the funds we received should be only a loan which our State would repay; but, in practice, we were not at that time independent. Nevertheless I went my own way and we set off for France.

Nor were the Allies agreed upon what our army should do. Paris wanted it to be brought to France, London would rather have seen us stay in Russia or in Siberia, possibly for reasons connected with the Bolshevist agitation in India. The details of our relations with the Allies in Russia I must leave to Dr. Beneš who will presently describe them. The fact that we had an army and that, in Russia, it was the only political and military organization of any size, gave us importance; and, in the negotiations for our recognition, respect for our army was a weighty factor.

In considering the question of intervention or non-intervention in Russia, a distinction must be made between meddling in Russian affairs under the Bolshevist Government and war against the Bolshevists themselves. Clearly, according to international usage, the Allies ought not to have interfered in Russian internal affairs; but the Bolshevists ought not to have interfered in Allied internal affairs. The Bolshevist doctrine of a proletarian International was naturally a serious matter; but, in any case, to fight the Bolshevists was, at that moment, to fight official Russia. If war was necessary against Russia—Bolshevist Russia, for there was no other—war, and the reasons for it, should have been formally declared. This was not done. I admit quite frankly that I did not approve of the way the Allies rode roughshod over political formality in their dealings with the Bolshevists—all the less because I was a much more radical opponent of Bolshevism, as far as principles went, than many gentlemen in Paris and London. I had thought much on the subject of a war against the Bolshevists and Russia, and I would have attached our Corps to any army strong enough to fight the Bolshevists and the Germans in the name of democracy. There was only one way to fight the Bolshevists—to mobilize the Japanese. This, neither America nor Paris nor London was prepared to do—as became apparent when, as I shall tell, our men came into conflict with the Bolshevists in the summer of 1918.

For us, in our isolation, neutrality was the more necessary on account of the political conditions in our army. A serious reverse would have imperilled its unity, since we should have been fighting for too negative an aim—an aim all the more negative because the Russian anti-Bolshevists were disunited, uncertain of the future of Russia and incapable of organization. And the Bolshevists, too, were Russians. In my eyes, Lenin was no less Russian than the Tsar Nicholas; nay, despite his Mongolian descent, there was more Russian blood in his veins than in those of the Tsar.

The Russian Bolshevists, and some of our own, have often sought to use against me an incident that occurred on October 29, 1917, during my absence from Kieff. In the fighting with the local Bolshevists, the Russian Commander led a section of our second regiment against them—treacherously—with the help of Colonel Mamontoff, who falsely alleged that he was acting under my orders. Maxa soon cleared up this ill-considered episode, though Dürich appeared on the scene with a number of lunatics. On the other hand, the Bolshevists fought side by side with our men against the Germans at Bachmatch. True, they were Ukrainian Bolshevists whose subordinate part in the affair was fortuitous, not inspired by a definite anti-German policy.

In the interest of historical truth it should be recorded that, even after the conclusion of the armistice on December 6 and 15, 1917, and during the negotiations at Brest-Litovsk, the Bolshevists thought of reorganizing the Russian army to fight Germany. At the beginning of the war, Trotsky had written a sharp little pamphlet against the Germans and the Austrians. In February 1918 he proposed to the Central Committee at Petrograd that they should get France and England to help in the reorganization of the army. Lenin approved of the plan. This I learned on the spot from trustworthy witnesses, though I cannot give details; but it is known that, in January and February 1918, Captain Sadoul informed the French Government that the Bolshevists wished the Entente to help in reorganizing the army. It is known also that the Bolshevists only accepted the Brest-Litovsk peace terms under strong pressure from Lenin and in the absence of Trotsky. Further, I am able to state as a fact that, after the conclusion of peace in March 1918, Trotsky negotiated with several representatives of the Entente in the hope of securing the services of General Berthelot who was about to leave Russia with his Military Mission; but the French Ambassador, M. Noulens, who was then at Vologda, opposed the idea. This I learned after I had left Russia, and I cannot say how Lenin then behaved. I knew the Soviet state of mind in regard to the Germans, watched it constantly and was well-informed about it. Naturally I took it into account and was anxious, for this reason also, not to drive the Bolshevists into the arms of Germany by attacking them. Moreover, the anti-German mood among the Bolshevists led me to hope that they would not put obstacles in the way of our march through Russia and Siberia.

I know that the Bolshevists are accused of one-sided pro-Germanism because they made peace with the Germans; but that is not my view. What were they to do? There was no other way out. All the negotiations at Brest-Litovsk, particularly the so-called Supplementary Treaty and the way in which the Germans forced peace upon them, show how unwillingly the Bolshevists made it. They followed the example of their predecessors during the Tsarist and post-Tsarist régimes. I have already said that Milyukoff would likewise have been ready to make peace with the Germans; and Tereshtchenko carried on peace negotiations with Austria though, in principle, he wished to continue the war. To this I shall refer later. The Bolshevists can rightly be charged with having foolishly accelerated the decomposition of the army (it had begun under the Tsar and was deliberately continued during the Provisional Government and under Kerensky) and with having exploited pacifist tendencies for purposes of agitation; though they soon found military reorganization indispensable. It may also be admitted that there were one-sided pro-Germans among them. But the chief errors of the Bolshevists lie in their home policy, not in their foreign; and, in so far as they were pro-German, they were the children of Tsarism.

The ignorance of Russia—and therefore also of the Bolshevists—which prevailed among the Western Allies was largely responsible for their mistaken relationship to Russia, both under the Tsar and during the Revolution. The anti-Bolshevist documents which have been published show how uncritically and ignorantly the Bolshevists were judged. What the Americans, English and French paid for those documents I do not know; but an expert eye could see from their very contents that our friends have bought forgeries—as was very clearly proved. The alleged documents, coming ostensibly from different countries, were all written with the same typewriter! It is true that, in these matters, the Bolshevists were no better. After the Revolution they began to publish the secret archives of the Russian Foreign Office and announced the publication as a great event. In point of fact, nothing came out that was not already known; and Trotsky's offensive against Tsarist secret diplomacy was somewhat childish.

My dealings with Russia, in all the phases through which she passed, were governed by our national policy and by my knowledge of Russian conditions. Though it was unpleasant not to be understood immediately in the West, the general result proved me not to have been wrong. The Russian situation, and the way Bolshevism necessarily grew out of it, were not known in Paris and London, though many Frenchmen and Englishmen who were in Russia and observed the position there, took less inaccurate views.

Finally, as regards the relationship of the Germans to the Bolshevists, it is wrong to say that the Bolshevists enjoyed German support from the outset and unconditionally. It is true that the Germans turned the Bolshevist Revolution to account, just as they had done with the agitation and the struggle against the Tsarist and the Provisional Governments. But their tactics were short-sighted; and not all German statesmen and military authorities were of one mind. The German middle-class parties, the Monarchists and the Social Democrats were anti-Bolshevist. Nor could the Bolshevists, at first, go hand in hand with the German Monarchists, politically or militarily. The Germans distrusted the Bolshevists and feared them to some extent, as may be seen from the Brest-Litovsk negotiations and from the fact that, in the spring of 1918, the Germans kept in Russia considerable forces which they could have put to more profitable use in France. In order to discover what the German-Bolshevist relations really were, I did my utmost to find out the real strength of the Austrian and German armies in Russia. Several Russian officers at headquarters estimated it at a million; my own estimate was about half a million—surely enough to make one wonder why the Germans kept up so strong a front in the East. I thought it was not merely as a precaution against the Bolshevists, for, at that time, the Germans reckoned with the possibility that the Bolshevist régime might fall and that, under another Russian system, especially if it were monarchical, the Russian army would certainly be resuscitated. To this conclusion I was led by General Hoffmann's threat to the Bolshevists that he would march on Petrograd and proclaim a Monarchy. There was reason to expect that the Germans would march on Petrograd. If they did not, it was because they were uncertain and wished not to spoil their relations with a new Russia.

A detailed examination of the Bolshevist relationship to the Germans would require a more careful analysis than is necessary here. Most of the theorists of Bolshevism were educated in Germany and Austria, and thus acquired to some extent a German basis; but on the other hand they found in the Germans, and even among the German Marxists, their most obstinate opponents —a circumstance which their affinity to the German Independent Socialists and to the followers of Karl Liebknecht did nothing to mitigate. Nor could the Bolshevists understand the German advance into Finland, or the policy of Berlin towards the Border States and the Ukraine.

If I review the whole course of affairs after the defeat of the Tsarist army, it seems to me that, as regards us and our liberation, the Russian Revolution of 1917 brought us more gain than loss. In saying this I take into account not only our forces in Russia but the influence of the Russian Revolution upon our people at home and upon Austria and Europe generally. Even the Bolshevist Revolution failed to harm us.

ACROSS SIBERIA

I had gone to Russia hoping that, in the course of a few weeks, I should be able to return to the West. Circumstances kept me there little less than a year. Serious difficulties both with the Tsarist and the post-Tsarist régimes had to be overcome; yet we carried out the chief point in the foreign policy on which I had insisted from the first—to make an army, and an independent army.

I have explained why it was important to transfer our army to France, and why the way through Siberia was safest. When the peace negotiations at Brest-Litovsk and the whole position on the various fronts suggested that the war would end in 1918, I felt bound—as I told our lads in my capacity of Quartermaster-General—to go to Europe. On February 2, 1918, I went from Kieff to Moscow for the purpose of making final arrangements. There I learned that the French and British Missions were likewise starting for Europe, and I decided to go with them. Lady Paget and Mr. Bagge, the British Consul, willingly gave me a place in one of their railway cars.

At Moscow we explained our position to the Bolshevists and set forth clearly the meaning of our Agreement with them. There had been reason to fear misunderstandings. Klecanda had many interviews with Fritch, the Bolshevist Commissar at Moscow. The Russian Branch of our National Council was determined on one point—that non-interference in Russian affairs did not mean that our army would not defend itself against attack. Self-defense and the defense of Allies who might be attacked, were natural implications of our independence. On this basis we dealt with the Bolshevists and again received recognition of our armed neutrality, though we handed over to them a proportion of our weapons which they claimed as Russian property. This demand was significant of their military position.

As we had agreed that our army should be allowed to go to France, it was obvious that, in France, it would be equipped by the French; and with the French representatives I had to settle also the financial question at Moscow. We needed money, enough money and in time, since we had to pay for everything we needed. Payment was strictly insisted upon. The British at Kieff had been the first to supply me with money because the French Mission was not then in a position to advance funds. The British gave me £80,000 which, as I heard afterwards, there was great difficulty in changing. At Moscow, all matters relating to finance and supplies were quickly and satisfactorily arranged with the French Mission, of which General Rampont was a member. On our side, Legionary Šíp was in charge of military finance.

On March 6, 1918, I took leave of my Czech fellow-countrymen in special proclamation, and said farewell to the army next day. It was hard to leave it and the Branch National Council alone in Russia, but I felt I must go to the West. Among the Czechs in Russia concord had been established. The army was harmonious and its spirit good. True, I expected that it would meet with many a difficulty on its long journey, though I was convinced that, by avoiding interference in Russian affairs, it would end by reaching its transports safely. One of my chief reasons for going to the West was to prepare shipping for it. Before starting, I gave Secretary Klecanda full powers to conduct political negotiations. I had worked with him for a considerable time and had discussed all contingencies, so that he was alive to all the problems of our work abroad.

The bad state of the Russian railways was likely to complicate arrangements for quartering and feeding our men; and, as I had seen at Moscow that Russia was daily disintegrating into more or less autonomous units, I anticipated trouble and misunderstandings with local Soviets. Strife among the Russian parties was a further cause of anxiety. Just before I left, there was talk of an offensive on the part of the Social Revolutionary elements in the Moscow Bolshevist administration. I thought it unlikely to succeed but, in any case, Klecanda was determined to hold strictly to our principle of non-interference. In the Bolshevist Peace Treaties with the Germans and the Austrians it had been stipulated that no agitation should be tolerated in Russia against the German Government, the State or the army. With this leverage the Germans might compel the Bolshevists to make our position unpleasant; and the lack of any concerted Allied policy or, indeed, of any policy in regard to Russia, might complicate the position still further. With Klecanda all these possibilities were considered at Moscow; and my written instructions were that the army should defend itself vigorously in case it were attacked in Russia, or in Siberia, by any Russian party. We agreed also upon the tasks to be assigned to a number of our people in the army and in the Branch of the National Council. It is sad that we should have lost Klecanda so unexpectedly. He died at Omsk on April 28.

Savinkoff, the Social Revolutionary leader, was then at Moscow. An acquaintance inquired whether I should like to see him. I had dealt with his philosophical novels in a section of my book on Russia and was therefore interested to meet the author of "The Pale Horse." I was disappointed in him. Politically, his view of Russia's position was wrong, and he underestimated the strength of Bolshevism; philosophically and morally, he failed to realize the difference between a revolution and individual acts of terrorism. Nor did he comprehend the distinction between offense and defense in war and revolution. Morally, he did not rise above the elementary notions of the blood feud. His subsequent career (he helped even Koltchak) revealed his weakness—the weakness of a Terrorist Titan transformed into a Hamlet.

VLADIVOSTOK

I started from Moscow at 8 p.m. on March 7, 1918, and reached Vladivostok by the Trans-Siberian railway through Saratof and Samara. I traveled in a third-class ambulance car, sleeping on a sort of mattress which I had bought at Moscow. The carriage was full of English people who were going to Europe. The time passed in observing Siberia, in reading, in finishing my little book, "The New Europe," and especially in procuring daily bread. We had to buy our food wherever we stopped. Nevertheless, traveling in Siberia was better than in European Russia. We often waited long in railway stations and between stations. The carriages, as well as the engines and the permanent way, were out of order. There was, for instance, a long wait at Amazar, for we had been warned in time that two trains ahead of us had collided and that the line was damaged. At Irkutsk we stayed a whole day and were able to look at the town and buy things. I collected whatever current literature and older publications I could get, as well as local newspapers and pamphlets. Klecanda sent me several telegrams, in cipher and otherwise.

The British Mission was accompanied from Kieff to Vladivostok by a Bolshevik guard of four soldiers. With their leader I had daily discussions on Socialism and the social question. They were curious Socialists and still more curious Communists.

At Vladivostok I spent a day seeing my fellow-countrymen, visiting the Czech "Palacký" Club and, above all, at the Post and Telegraph Office. Fellow-travelers took a number of letters to Europe for me and I sent telegrams to Paris, London and

America.   At Vladivostok I received news of the Allies which supplemented what I had learned during the journey by telegram and from Siberian newspapers.   It was an anxious moment. The great German offensive in the West had begun on March 21, 1918, while I was traveling, and the Bolshevist papers in Siberia had naturally made the most of the French and, especially, of the British reverse.   As far as our own army was concerned, the chief thing in my eyes was that the fighting with the Germans near Bachmatch was finished and that, after the march of our divisions from the Ukraine into Russia they had, on March 16, voluntarily handed over a portion of their arms.   On March 26 a treaty was signed with the Bolshevists guaranteeing our men an unmolested passage to Siberia and Vladivostok.   True, this had been already agreed upon with Muravieff after the Bolshevist troops had reached the Ukraine; but, to make assurance doubly sure, we negotiated also with the Moscow Soviet.   On March 26, indeed, the Moscow Commissar, Stalin, telegraphed to the local Soviets that the Czechoslovaks were not going through as an armed unit but as free citizens, and that they carried a certain number of weapons as protection against the counter-revolutionaries.   He added: "The Soviet of the People's Commissars wishes every assistance to be given them on Russian soil."

CHAPTER VI

IN THE FAR EAST

(Tokio. April 6–20, 1918)

INSTEAD of going to America by sea direct from Vladivostok, as I wished, I was compelled by a number of obstacles to take the Manchurian railway and to travel right through Korea as far as Fusan and to sail thence for Japan. Therefore, on April 1, 1918, I started by way of Kharbin and Mukden, reaching Shimonoseki on the 6th and Tokio on the 8th. In Tokio I was almost in Europe again, thanks to the foreign Embassies. Mr. R. S. Morris was the American and Sir Conyngham Greene the British Ambassador. Mr. Morris asked me for a memorandum—destined for President Wilson—on the state of Russia and Bolshevism, and submitted a number of questions to me. I answered them with the following short statement upon the need for a well-considered policy in Russia on the part of European Powers. After what I have said about Russia, it calls for no remark except that its date and the position at the moment should be remembered.

PRIVATE AND CONFIDENTIAL.

Written April 10, 1918, in Tokio.

(1) The Allies should recognize the Bolshevist Government (*de facto*—the *de jure* recognition need not be discussed); President Wilson's message to the Moscow Assembly was a step in this direction. If the Allies are on good terms with the Bolshevists they can influence them. The Germans recognized them by concluding peace with them. (I know the weak points of the Bolshevists, but I know also the weak points of the other parties; they are neither better nor abler.)

(2) The Monarchical movement is weak; the Allies must not support it. The Cadets and the Social Revolutionaries are organizing

themselves against the Bolshevists; I do not expect any considerable success from either of these parties. The Allies thought that Alexeieff and Korniloff would win a big success on the Don; I did not believe it and refused to join them, though I was invited to do so by the leaders. The same applies to Semyenoff and others.

(3) The Bolshevists will hold power longer than their adversaries suppose. Like all the other parties, they will die of political dilettantism. It is the curse of Tsarism that it did not teach the people to work or to administer; and the Bolshevists have been weakened by their failure in the peace negotiations and in the land question. On the other hand, they are gaining sympathies because they are learning to work, and because the other parties are weak.

(4) I am inclined to think, after a time, a Coalition Government (the Socialist Parties and the Cadet Left) might meet with general approval, though there would have to be also Bolshevists in the Government.

(5) A lasting Democratic and Republican Government in Russia will exercise great pressure on Prussia and Austria through the Socialists and Democrats. This is one reason why the Germans and the Austrians are anti-Bolshevist.

(6) All the small peoples in the East of Europe (Finns, Poles, Esthonians, Letts, Lithuanians, Czechs and Slovaks, and Roumanians) need a strong Russia lest they be at the mercy of the Germans and the Austrians. The Allies must support Russia at all costs and by all possible means. If the Germans subdue the East they will then subdue the West.

(7) A capable Government could induce the Ukrainians to be satisfied with an autonomous Republic forming part of Russia. This was the original idea of the Ukrainians themselves. Not until later did they proclaim their independence, though, in reality, an independent Ukraine will be an Austrian or a German province. The Germans and the Austrians are pursuing the same policy in regard to the Ukraine as towards Poland.

(8) It must be remembered that the South of Russia is the rich part of the country, with fertile soil, the Donetz Basin and the Black Sea. The North is poor. Russian policy will gravitate towards the South.

(9) The Allies must have a common policy upon the best way of supporting Russia.

(10) The Allied Governments must not leave their representatives in Russia without instructions. In other words, they must have a clear Russian policy.

(11) I hope the Japanese will not oppose Russia; that would suit the Germans and the Austrians. On the contrary, the Japanese should fight alongside of the Allies; the gap between Japan and Germany would thus be widened.

(12) Nowhere in Siberia did I see, between March 15 and April 2, armed German or Austrian prisoners. The anarchy in Siberia is not greater than in Russia.

(13) The Allies must oppose the Germans and Austrians in Russia:—

(a) By organizing a company to buy up corn and sell it where it is needed. Thus they will prevent the Germans from getting it. But the Russian and Ukrainian peasants will not sell their corn for money, which is useless to them. They need goods, such as boots, clothes, soap and tools. Since the Germans have no manufactured goods, the Allies have an excellent opportunity to get hold of the Russian market. The scheme only needs energy and organization. The capital that may be invested in it will repay itself.

(b) German and Austrian agents will flock into Russia. Counter-measures are necessary and must be organized. American and other agents should bring samples and, perhaps, a small traveling exhibition of selected goods, together with illustrated catalogues.

(c) The Germans influence the Russian press less through special journalistic agents than through the German prisoners of war who write for all kinds of papers throughout the country, especially in the smaller towns. Our Czech prisoners are counteracting their influence to some extent, but the whole thing needs organization.

(d) The Russian railways must be kept up. Without railways, there will be no army and no industry.

(e) The Germans have bought up Russian securities so as to control industry in future.

(f) The Germans are known to have influenced prisoners of war, for instance, by training Ukrainian prisoners for the Ukrainian army. The Allies might influence the German and Austrian prisoners who remain in Russia by means of the press and special agents.

(g) I succeeded in organizing a corps of 50,000 men out of Czech and Slovak prisoners. I have agreed with the French Government to send it to France; the Allies can help to transport it. They are excellent soldiers, as they showed in the offensive last June. We can organize a second corps of the same size. This must be done to prevent our prisoners from returning to Austria, where they would be sent to oppose the Allies on the Italian or the French front.

The Allies have agreed to provide us with the necessary means. In France we have also a small army, partly sent from Russia and partly composed of our refugees; and I hope that we shall likewise be able to form an army in Italy.

The significance of having the whole Czech army in France is obvious; and I must acknowledge that France understood the political importance of the matter from the outset and has supported our national movement in every way. M. Briand was the first states-man openly to promise our people the help of the French Republic. He it was who succeeded in putting into the Allied reply to President Wilson the explicit demand that the Czechoslovaks should be liberated. The Czechoslovaks are the most westerly Slav barrier against Germany and Austria. In present circumstances 100,000, nay, even 50,000 trained soldiers may be very important.

(14) My answer to the oft-repeated question, whether an army could be formed in Russia, is that a million men could be raised in from six to nine months. The Red Guard is unimportant and the Bolshevists have called upon the officers of the old Tsarist army to join their army as instructors. For the army, railways are needed.

Note.—To-day's "Japan Advertiser" (April 11) publishes the following news:—

VOLUNTEERS LAY DOWN THEIR ARMS
THE CZECHOSLOVAK CORPS ON ITS WAY TO FRANCE IS INTERCEPTED BY TROTSKY.

Moscow, *April 5.*

As a result of an understanding between Trotsky and the French Ambassador, the army of Czechoslovak volunteers which was going to France surrendered its weapons to the Soviet authorities. With the exception of General Dieterichs, who was accompanying the Corps to France, the officers have been dismissed.

This news is good. The corps going to France needs no weapons, as it will be armed again in France. The officers in question are Russian officers who had joined our army.

To the French Ambassador, M. Regnault, I expressed verbally the same views. At the English Embassy I heard what was happening in Europe. I called also upon the Japanese Foreign Minister. At that time the Japanese, naturally, knew little about us, and I gave the Secretary of the provisional Shidehara Cabinet a memorandum in Russian, and asked the British and the American Ambassadors to use their influence on our behalf with the Japanese Government. We needed Japanese help for the transport of our men from Vladivostok onwards, eventually across Japan, and for supplies of clothing, boots and other things that were unobtainable in Russia and Siberia. Everywhere I raised the question of getting ships.

In Japan, as elsewhere, I was in touch with the press—and had for some days, trouble with the Tokio police, whom my English passport perplexed. The newspapers called me by my name, whereas the passport was made out in another name. It was not surprising that it took the Japanese police a few days to clear up the discrepancy, for in London the same thing happened to me. There, my passport bore my own name but had been issued by Serbia, and the police could not understand how this fitted in with the facts of the case. I had already lectured at London University; the Prime Minister, Mr. Asquith, had sent one of his colleagues to introduce me to my audience; but the police of my quarter were uneasy for days. St. Bureaucras is the same everywhere—though the officials were quite right to do their duty.

While in Japan I read the well-known speech of the Austro-Hungarian Foreign Minister, Count Czernin, of April 2. His personal attack did not surprise me. The important point was that the former French Prime Minister, Painlevé, and especially Clemenceau, should have answered so categorically the Austrian falsehoods about Austria's peace proposals, and that the letter written by Prince Sixtus of Bourbon on March 31, 1917, should be published. Austria lied, the behavior of the Emperor Charles himself was unseemly and pusillanimous, and the affair ended with Czernin's resignation on April 15th. As I shall show, this episode was particularly important for us because it gave the Allies incisive proof of Austria's untrustworthiness and insincerity. In Tokio, too, I heard some account of the Rome Congress of oppressed Hapsburg peoples on April 8, 1918; of this, and of the important Declaration of Corfu which had been signed by the Serbian Prime Minister, Pashitch, and Dr. Trumbitch on July 20, 1917, I shall have more to say when I deal comprehensively with our relationship to the Southern Slavs.

My fortnight in Japan added little to my knowledge of the country, for my whole attention was given to the fate of our Legions, to the war and to the prospective peace. I visited various temples in Tokio, saw what was accessible, but cannot say that I studied Japan. I sought, indeed, to learn something of her economic condition and to see what the economic effect of the war would be upon so active a country. The circumstance that England and, to a certain extent, France, were prevented from exporting their goods to the Far East, naturally gave the Japanese an opportunity to extend their business in Asia and even as far as Egypt. I kept an eye on bookshops and art dealers, bought a few woodcuts and not a few European books. The influence of German (particularly German medical) literature was obvious, and I found a second-hand bookseller who dealt chiefly in German books.

On April 19th I went on to Yokohoma. By a lucky chance, a big boat, the "Empress of Asia," was starting for Canada. She was intended to transport troops from America to Europe. Thus I reached the American continent quickly. We sailed on April 20, 1918, at noon, and reached Victoria and Vancouver only nine days later.

CHAPTER VII

AMERICAN DEMOCRACY

FINIS AUSTRIAE

(WASHINGTON. APRIL 29-NOV. 20, 1918)

ONCE on a British boat I felt I was again in Europe and in America, not merely by force of international law but because all the surroundings were European or American. I am a good sailor, and the fine, calm weather restored me. Part of the restful effect of a sea voyage comes from watching the waves, the currents, the weather, the color of the water, and the skies. I noted that on April 24 we crossed the so-called date line, 181 degrees East Longitude. I thought of Jules Verne's "Round the World in Eighty Days" and how his hero unexpectedly gained twenty-four hours by going from West to East.

Among the passengers was Mr. Wright of the American Embassy at Petrograd with whom I discussed once more the Russian situation; and in the ship's library I found a number of English novels. I read, too, with interest the centenary work on Charlotte Brontë by Miss May Sinclair, an authoress with whom I am well acquainted. But much of my time was spent in reviewing the international situation as it had developed since I left England. Russia, I reflected, was out of the war and bound down by a forced peace. Kerensky's offensive in 1917 had come too late. Ludendorff and the Germans had feared it might come sooner and be dangerous. Since defeat and revolution had cost the Tsar his throne, failure in the war might be expected likewise to sweep away the Emperors William and Charles and their systems. Europe would thus be freed from absolutism, democracy would win and the freedom of small nations would be more fully assured. On the other hand it was a drawback that Russia could

207

fight no longer and that her internal development was uncertain, perhaps actually endangered.

After occupying Poland, the Germans had gone forward and had occupied the Border States. In September and October 1917 they had taken Riga and the islands of Oesel, Dagö and Moon. Then they had entered Finland on April 2, 1918, and had there beaten the Bolshevists who had failed to recognize the Finnish declaration of independence of July 19, 1917. (This, too, is proof that the Germans were not unreservedly pro-Bolshevist.) Ever since the battle of Gorlice in May 1915, they had gone on step by step till the pan-German "Urge towards the East" seemed to be satisfied in that part of Europe. They had recognized the small States which arose under their patronage—Courland, on March 15, 1918, Lithuania on March 23rd, Lettland or Latvia on April 9th, and Esthonia on April 10th. The two last-named declared forthwith (April 13) their adhesion to Germany. The Ukraine, yielding to *force majeure,* had made peace, Roumania likewise. The Germans and the Austrians were masters of Poland. The country had been occupied in the summer of 1915 and was administered by Germany and Austria-Hungary. Under the Governor of Warsaw, General von Beseler, a German scheme to raise a Polish army half a million strong had suddenly been formed. To this end the Kingdom of Poland was set up (November 5, 1916); but the scheme fell through and, despite the appearance of Austro-German concord, Germany wrestled long with Austria for mastery in the new Kingdom of Poland, as, indeed, in regard to Roumania. Russia, it should be said, had blundered badly from the beginning in her handling of the Polish question. The promises she made at first were whittled down—the censorship would not even allow "autonomy" to be mentioned—and the proclamation of an independent Polish State by the Russian Provisional Government, on March 30, 1917, came too late.

On the other hand, Greece had joined the Allies on June 27, 1917, after the expulsion of King Constantine; and, in Asia, England had continued her victorious course, the Turks losing many men in winter from hunger and disease. Moreover, England had made a wise move in November 1917 by pledging herself to support the establishment of a Jewish National Home in Palestine. Thus she gained the goodwill of Zionist as well as of non-Zionist Jews the world over. But German submarine warfare caused her serious anxiety until, towards the end of 1917, the Germans themselves began to doubt its efficacy and expediency.

In France, the increase of the American army had made itself felt from June 1917 onwards, though German pressure remained dangerous. In the spring of 1917 General Nivelle had failed to break through the German front; and, at the end of May, it had been necessary to suppress outbreaks of dissatisfaction with the leadership of the French army. Changes had again been made in the high command, General Pétain, the opponent of Nivelle's strategic plan, becoming Commander-in-Chief; while, after the great German offensive in March 1918, General Foch had been placed in command of the Allied armies on the Western front. Unitary leadership had long been necessary. An earlier attempt to secure it had come to nothing, though the Supreme Military Council of the Allies had been set up in November 1917. Now, after the German offensive of March 21, 1918, unity of command was indispensable. The offensive seemed at first so successful that the French thought once more of removing the Government from Paris; but the Germans failed to take Amiens, their chief immediate objective—a failure which convinced them that they or, at least, their strategic plan had not succeeded and that the "great battle" in France was still undecided.

Politically, France was winning. Clemenceau, who became Prime Minister and Minister for War, had established his vigorous rule from November 16, 1917, onwards. The internal situation was characterized by the expulsion of M. Malvy, the former Minister of the Interior, by the arrest of M. Caillaux, the former Prime Minister and Minister of Finance, on January 14, 1918, and by the execution of Bolo Pasha on February 5. It should be remembered, however, that the law against defeatism and pacifist propaganda had been passed on June 26, 1917, nearly five months before Clemenceau took office.

After the Caporetto disaster in October 1917 Italy had pulled herself together and had reorganized her army with the help of British and French divisions. Austria had won her victory with German aid; by herself, she was, obviously, no longer equal to her task, strategically or militarily. We know now that the object of the Caporetto offensive was so to crush the Italians that the enemy could cross the Alps into Southern France. I had all along expected an attempt of this sort.

The Peace Treaties which Germany had concluded with her Eastern adversaries, especially with Russia, were an index to the whole military and political situation. To me they seemed likewise to foreshadow peace in the West. In fact, a number of peace feelers were put out by both sides during 1917 and the early months of 1918, principally by the Central Powers. As early as December 1916 Germany and her Allies had made an official offer of peace to the Western Allies; and there were afterwards a whole series of secret offers, how many cannot exactly be said, emanating either from authoritative quarters or from influential persons acting on their behalf. After the death of the Emperor Francis Joseph at the beginning of December 1916 Austria opened with the Entente secret negotiations which were protracted until the spring of 1918. Of them I shall have more to say. It was significant that they should have been undertaken by the young Emperor Charles through his brother-in-law, Prince Sixtus of Parma. A year later, they were publicly revealed by Clemenceau. They bore witness both to the weakening of the Central Powers and to a decrease of the harmony that had existed between Austria and Germany under Francis Joseph. On April 12, 1917, Count Czernin, the Austro-Hungarian Foreign Minister, dilated officially on the weakness of Austria in a confidential report to the Emperor Charles. This report came to the knowledge of the Allies—through an indiscretion on the part of Erzberger, it is said, though Erzberger himself denied it. Czernin's report would certainly account for the young Emperor's peace negotiations; and, as we shall see, they were not an isolated effort.   Throughout the whole of 1917 Austria sought to approach all the Allies.

On July 19, 1917, the German Reichstag had adopted, by 214 votes against 116 and with 17 abstentions, a peace resolution demanding, after the Russian fashion, peace without annexations or political or economic indemnities; and secret overtures were also made to the Allies by official Germany. The German Chancellor, Bethmann-Hollweg, was prepared to treat for peace with France on the basis of ceding Alsace-Lorraine in whole or in part —so, at least, it was said in Vienna and stated by Austrian agents. Of one Franco-German peace overture details are known. Baron von der Lancken, the former Counsellor of the German Embassy in Paris, who was then in Belgium, got into touch with M. Briand through a number of intermediaries. Matters went so far that he was to have met Briand in Switzerland on September 27, 1917, but Briand did not go. There was a sequel to this episode in a controversy between Clemenceau and Briand. Next month (October) the Germans approached England through Spain, and still other threads were spun from Germany to England by way of The Hague.

Between Germany and Russia there had been several attempts to negotiate. I have mentioned two German offers to the Tsar. In October 1916 Russia apparently approached Germany, and in December Germany approached Russia. In February 1917 Bethmann-Hollweg tried to treat for peace during the last days of the Tsarist régime, and another attempt was made with Milyukoff under the Provisional Government. Other negotiations were carried on in Scandinavian countries by Rizoff, the Bulgarian Minister in Berlin, though I am not sure whether the German Chancellor went as far as he. During the Russo-German armistice Germany again sounded Russia through Erzberger, also in Stockholm; and Kerensky made peace proposals through a Polish intermediary, Ledwinski, the President of the Polish Liquidation Commission.

The German Emperor is known to have favored, in the autumn of 1917, milder terms of peace than those which had been offered in December 1916. Early in July he conferred with the Papal Nuncio, Mgr. Pacelli, and asked for vigorous peace propaganda by the Pope. During the following month, Vatican action, and the diplomatic correspondence to which it gave rise, were alike weighty, though the Vatican entirely failed to gain the ear of the Allied Governments. Besides issuing its public Peace Note, which was too vague to be taken by the leading Allied Governments as a basis for negotiations, the Vatican approached them and Germany very emphatically in secret. Through the British Government it made soundings for peace terms and, by means of Mgr. Pacelli, the Nuncio in Munich, it informed the new German Chancellor, Dr. Michaelis, that England wished to know the real intentions of Germany, particularly in regard to Belgium. The German reply was indefinite and therefore not acceptable. Bethmann-Hollweg had resigned the Imperial Chancellorship on July 13, 1917, because Hindenburg and Ludendorff opposed him—on the ground that the peace resolution of the Reichstag had been a sign of weakness. But at the end of July, mutinies broke out in the German navy, and Ludendorff himself soon began to waver. The year 1917 was marked, moreover, by developments in the German Social Democratic Party which gradually split into two groups and tendencies; and at the beginning of 1918, the first political strikes took place—in Vienna on January 16 and in Berlin on January 28—while, in Germany, workmen's councils were organized.

During this period—from the summer of 1917 to the summer of 1918—the situation at the front, and especially the German submarine campaign, disquieted the British Prime Minister, Mr. Lloyd George. He feared that England would not be able to raise enough men. Therefore he favored vigorous action against Turkey—which was taken—and defensive tactics in France. I do not know whose idea this was but I heard that outstanding Allied Commanders, even Foch, shared it. Pacifist tendencies showed themselves in England by the action of Lord Lansdowne and others; and the speech in which Lloyd George outlined his peace terms, on January 5, 1918, will be remembered. He, too, had taken part, albeit very prudently, in Prince Sixtus of Parma's secret negotiations with Austria; and in the spring of 1917 I heard in well-informed quarters in London that he was thinking of peace and was prepared to make notable concessions to Germany. How keenly I watched the maneuvers of Prince Sixtus may be seen by the following telegram which I sent from London on April 20, 1917, to our people in Paris: "Dear friends, be on your guard. Serious negotiations are alleged again to be going on for a separate peace with Austria. For this reason the Head of the Government has returned. Everybody seems to have had enough of the war. We are to get an autonomous administration, etc., in a slightly diminished Austria."

Still more important was President Wilson's message to the United States Senate on January 8, 1918, in which he laid down his well-known Fourteen Points. They were rejected by Count Hertling, on behalf of Germany, and by Count Czernin, on behalf of Austria, in a fashion that proved Berlin and Vienna to have been smitten with lasting blindness. I shall have more to say on the subject of Wilson's message.

Meanwhile, in June 1917, the Socialist International had held a Conference in Stockholm at which the Czech Social Democratic parties were represented by Habrman, Němec and Šmeral. Dr. Šmeral stuck to his pro-Austrian standpoint but confessed that 95 per cent. of our working-class, and of the Czech people as a whole, were on my side, not on his—an admission which we published everywhere with excellent effect. Moreover, the demand—publicly put forward by all three Czech Social Democrats—for an independent Czech State within a federated Austria-Hungary, was meant to counter the Austrian Social Democratic idea of restricting the autonomy of the Hapsburg peoples to educational matters. This Czech Social Democratic demand was the first authorized voice from within Bohemia to be raised abroad. Professor Maxa, whom I sent from Russia to Stockholm, told our members of Parliament there how well our cause was going in Russia and in Europe. Habrman was then preparing to stay abroad for good; but, as it seemed to me that he would do better work at home, I sent him word to go back and to insist that no compromises or concessions should be made and that we should not be disavowed again.

This review of the situation as a whole forced me to conclude that the hour of decision was drawing near. The elimination of Russia as a belligerent; Bolshevist influence upon the Socialist parties in Europe; the spread of pacifism; the war-weariness of the armies in the field, and their obvious discontent; the difficulty of winning a decisive victory; and the peace negotiations, secret and open, all compelled me to recognize that the war could not last much longer. I concluded, too, that the decision would be in our favor. This was no mere hope. It was a conviction formed after more than three years of critical observation. True, there were not a few shortcomings on the side of the Allies, whose political and strategical mistakes had been many and serious; but the Germans and the Austrians had blundered as often and as badly. The only doubt was whether American troops would reach France fast enough to bring the war to an end before 1919.

In the opinion of some political and military experts it would last until 1919. Even in the autumn of 1918, after his first victories over the Germans, Marshal Foch did not look for a decision until the spring of 1919. But, taking the situation as a whole, I judged that 1918 would see the end of the war, and therefore I hastened from Russia to the West.

We, for our part, had been ready for peace as early as the end of 1917 and the beginning of 1918. Our Legions were our greatest asset. Their success in Russia gave the final fillip to the organization of the Legion in France, and hastened it in Italy. No sooner had we begun seriously to make an army in Russia than I asked Beneš to negotiate with the French Government about it and to conclude a Treaty. Simultaneously I had sent contingents of our prisoners from Russia to France, including some from Roumania. Another volunteer contingent reached

France from America, where Štefánik had organized recruiting in 1917. So successful were Dr. Beneš's negotiations that, by August 1917, an Agreement was made; and eventually a decree, establishing a Czechoslovak army in France, was issued on December 16th. A few weeks later (January-February 1918) the French Prime Minister, M. Clemenceau, and Dr. Beneš concluded a final Convention. Thus we were, in any case, sure of important advantages in the peace negotiations.

In Italy, our difficulties were somewhat greater. We Czechs were little known to the Italians, and the Italian propaganda against the Yugoslavs was steadily gaining ground. Štefánik and Beneš worked hard in Italy and I dealt with the Italian Ambassadors abroad, especially in Russia. In January 1917 we obtained permission to concentrate the Czech and Slovak prisoners in one camp, and we continued our efforts to form an army. In this we were helped by an incident on the Tyrolese front at Carzano in September 1917 when a Slovene officer named Pivko secretly encouraged his men, among whom were a good number of Czechs, to go over to the Italians. His action made a great impression in Italy and awakened sympathies for the Austrian Slavs, all the more because the Viennese papers denounced the Carzano "treason" and the Austrian Germans raised the question in Parliament. Next month (October 1917) Italy recognized our National Council and allowed us to form Labor contingents. Most of the men who had gone over at Carzano remained on the Italian front and fought in October 1917 at Monte Zebio and Asiago. From February 1918 onwards, recruiting—conducted by Sychrava and Osuský—began among prisoners in Italy. Thus our Legion came into being there also. Its establishment was recognized in a first Treaty between the Italian Government and our National Council, signed on April 21, 1918, by Štefánik and the Italian Prime Minister, Orlando. Meanwhile the Congress of oppressed Austro-Hungarian peoples was held in Rome, on April 8, 1918, the day of my arrival at Tokio. The political importance of this Congress will soon appear.

My news from Bohemia and Vienna was also satisfactory. Upon the disavowal in January 1917 had followed, in April, the first declaration of our members of Parliament (to which I have already referred) and, above all, the manifesto of our writers in May. This manifesto, I felt, had been meant to encourage our Parliamentary politicians; and I ascribed the political liveliness in the spring of 1917 to the influence of the Russian Revolution which was bound to weaken Monarchism and to strengthen Republicanism. Indeed, the effect upon our people of the Russian Revolution of 1905, after the Russo-Japanese War, had been very similar. It is true that the Constitutional Declaration made by our members of Parliament on May 30, 1917, when the Austrian Reichsrat met for the first time since the beginning of the war, still referred to the Hapsburgs and to Austria and put forward the idea of a Confederation of States on a racial basis; but this did us no harm abroad because the Declaration demanded a Czech State, including Slovakia, notwithstanding its (obviously platonic) recognition of the dynasty. In any case, I thought, the meeting of Parliament could no longer do harm and might do good—as soon appeared from the interpellation brought forward by our Social Democratic members upon the suppression of their Stockholm demand. Very weighty, and very useful to us abroad, was the step taken by our members of Parliament in Vienna on July 23 when they decided (albeit by the small majority of three votes) to take no part in the proceedings for a revision of the Austrian Constitution. Unless I am mistaken, this decision was influenced by the news which Habrman brought home from Stockholm. Dr. Rašín and Dr. Kramář were released from prison; and though they were not allowed to return to Parliamentary life, Dr. Rašín was able to devote himself entirely to Prague and to the work in general, which was even better. The Austrian German interpellation of December 5, 1917, upon our disloyalty, was the very thing I wanted, for I knew that, from the end of September 1917 onwards, all the Czech members of Parliament had joined our

Parliamentary Association—a unanimity which I took as a proof that they too felt the decisive moment to be at hand.

Then came the Declaration of January 6, 1918. I thought it satisfactory despite its reference to earlier pronouncements which, by implication, had ratified the Constitutional Declaration made on the first meeting of Parliament in May 1917. Indeed, in its vagueness, this portion of the January Declaration was the less understood abroad because the rest of it was in harmony with my own program. I took this very vagueness to mean that some, perhaps a majority, of our members of Parliament would resist any definite pro-Hapsburg or pro-Austrian policy—a view apparently shared by the Austrian Prime Minister and the Austro-Hungarian Foreign Minister, both of whom denounced the January Declaration as "high treason." The Foreign Minister, Count Czernin, followed this up with a personal attack upon me. It did him harm in England and America, where personal vilification has long been discredited. In his rage, Czernin actually helped us by accusing our whole people of agreeing with me and by saying, "There are such fellows as Masaryk even within the frontiers of the Empire."

Our people at home were no longer unaware of our doings abroad. They had heard about the battle of Zboroff; and Habrman, Pšenička and others had brought back full reports. Despite the unpleasant position on the Western front, I had thus no reason to fear any further disavowal. Of this the solemn oath taken on April 13, 1918, by the gathering of Popular Representatives at Prague was an earnest; and I was delighted to get the news of the first Slovak act of revolt at Liptovsky St. Nicholas under the leadership of Šrobař.

IN AMERICA

At Vancouver, where alas! a cable from Vladivostok informed me of Klecanda's death, I was met by Mr. Schelking, a former official of the Russian Foreign Office whose advice had been very helpful to our people at Petrograd when they were working against the policy of Stürmer and Protopopoff. Once again we talked of Russia, the causes of her fall and of her prospects. Representatives of Czech and Slovak organizations in America met me also—Mr. Bosák for the Slovaks and Mr. Pergler whom my fellow-countrymen in America had chosen to be my secretary. I had cabled him from Tokio to meet me so that we might take advantage of the long journey from Vancouver to begin work at once. During my whole stay in America he was with me, working indefatigably. We left Vancouver on April 30, traveling through Western Canada to Chicago and breaking the journey at St. Paul so that I might see my fellow-countrymen, many of whom I had met there before. Chicago was reached on May 5. Here a new phase of activity began—and on a big scale from the start.

After the American fashion, our people in Chicago had arranged a spectacular reception for me. Next to Prague, Chicago was the largest Czech city in the world and it was also the center of our financial organization. It was the home of Mr. Štěpina whom I had begun to bombard with appeals for money as soon as I got to Venice at the end of 1914; of Dr. Fisher, the head of the Czech Alliance; and of Vojta Beneš (a brother of Dr. Beneš) who had gone the round of our colonies in America to collect the funds for our liberation. Our people had managed to win the goodwill of practically the whole of Chicago, the Americans as well as the Slavs. From the railway station to the hotel there was a huge procession; the city was beflagged with Czech and Slav colors; and during the procession English and Czech speeches were made in the streets. The reception was splendid and served as an example for other cities with Czech and Slovak colonies. It was followed by a number of meetings, great and small, Czech and Czecho-American. Towards the end of May, I had to return to Chicago in order to hold meetings of our various organizations. Then I spoke at the University, in the Press Club and elsewhere. At Chicago University I had already lectured in 1902, when I had made many friends among the Czechs and Americans; and Mr. Judson, now President of the University, had helped me very liberally.

Receptions and meetings like those at Chicago took place later on in New York, Boston, Baltimore, Cleveland, Pittsburgh and Washington. Everywhere things were so organized as to arouse American interest. Our national costumes, colors and emblems and the artistic arrangement of the processions were pleasing and drew the attention of the masses to our movement for independence. Before the war I used to denounce "flag-wagging"; but, in America, I realized that in so doing I had overshot the mark. Professor as I then was, I had failed to see that a well-organized procession may be worth quite as much as an ostensibly world-shaking political article or a speech in Parliament. During the Chicago procession I well remember thinking of the well-known British preacher, Spurgeon, who said he would be willing to stand on his head if, by so doing, he could call attention to a good cause—this in a church, then why not in the street?

At first there had been personal and political dissensions in our American colonies as elsewhere. America was then neutral; and German, Austrian and Magyar influences were strong. Some of our people distrusted the revolutionary character of our movement and among them were quite a number of pro-Austrians. But our movement made headway, the leadership of the National Council was recognized, the pro-Austrians no longer carried weight, and though the Dürich affair caused some excitement no political damage was done. Naturally our colonies were greatly and, in many cases, decisively influenced by the American declaration of war on Germany on April 6, 1917. Then doubts disappeared and unanimity prevailed, as the collections for our funds testified.

Two consequences deserve special mention. The first was that our Catholics went hand in hand with our "Freethinkers" and Socialists—so strong was the unifying force of the movement for liberation, as those will appreciate who know what the relations between the Catholics and the non-Catholics had been before. On November 18, 1916, the Czech Catholic Congress at

Chicago had agreed upon a memorandum to Pope Benedict XV which was entrusted to the Papal Delegate. He approved of it and promised to lay it before the Pope. It demanded Czechoslovak independence, the liberation of the Historical Lands of the Bohemian Crown and of Slovakia. I myself attended the Catholic Congress in Washington on June 20, 1918, where I defined my religious standpoint and explained why I had become a decided opponent of the political Catholicism which had been fostered in Austria and Hungary under Hapsburg influence. I advocated the separation of Church from State on the American principle; and the American Catholics understood that to be independent of the State is by no means harmful to the Church I promised to work for a peaceful separation; and, as regards Church lands, I repudiated confiscation. When the Executive Committee of the National Alliance of Czech Catholics in America resolved, on October 25, 1918, to send its representatives to the Czechoslovak Republic in order to enlighten the priesthood and the Catholics on the subject of separation, I welcomed the proposal in a letter dated November 15. I may add that on November 27 the "Association of Slovak Catholics" in America also recommended that the relations between Church and State should be settled in accordance with the principle of separation, due account being taken of conditions in Slovakia.

The other weighty consequence lay in the negotiations at Pittsburgh between Czechs and Slovaks. There, on June 30, 1918, I signed the Convention (the "Czechoslovak Convention" —not Treaty) between the Slovaks and the Czechs of America. It was concluded in order to appease a small Slovak faction which was dreaming of God knows what sort of independence for Slovakia, since the ideas of some Russian Slavophils, and of Štúr[1] and Hurban-Vajanský,[2] had taken root even among the Ameri-

---

[1] Ludevit Štúr (1815-1856), a Slovak Protestant leader and writer who organized the Slovak Protestants as a party in 1844, and helped to establish Slovak as a literary language.

[2] Svetozar Hurban-Vajanský (1847-1916), a Russophil Slovak poet and writer who had been influenced by the works of Štúr.

can Slovaks. Therefore Czechs and Slovaks agreed upon the Convention which demanded for Slovakia an autonomous administration, a Diet and Courts of Law. I signed the Convention unhesitatingly as a local understanding between American Czechs and Slovaks upon the policy they were prepared to advocate. The other signatories were mainly American citizens, only two of them being non-Americans, though further signatures were afterwards added without authorization. In the Convention it was laid down that the details of the Slovak political problem would be settled by the legal representatives of the Slovak people themselves, just as I subsequently made it clear that our Declaration of Independence was only a sketch of the future Constitution, and that the Constitution itself would be finally determined by the legal representatives of the people. And so it was. The Constitution was adopted by the Slovaks as well as by the Czechs. The legal representatives of Slovakia thus expressed themselves in favor of complete union, and the oath sworn upon the Constitution binds the Slovaks, the Czechs and me too. Even before the Pittsburgh Agreement, on May 1, 1918, the representatives of the Slovaks had declared themselves in favor of union at Liptovsky St. Nicholas, and they renewed the declaration on October 30, 1918, at Turčansky St. Martin. Union is the main thing. A demand for autonomy is as justifiable as a demand for centralism, and the problem is to find the right relationship between the two.

Among the Slovaks and Czechs in America it was rumored that, at the beginning of 1918, Count Károlyi [1] had come to the United States in the hope of inducing the American Government to recognize the indivisibility of Hungary; he was alleged to desire freedom for the Czechs but wished Hungary to retain the Slovaks. Colonel House informed the Czechs, who agreed with the Slovaks to stand together for a united State. Indeed, the more thoughtful Slovak leaders saw that the Slovaks would derive no benefit from territorial autonomy and that an independent Slovak

---

[1] A prominent Hungarian nobleman of Socialist views. He became Prime Minister of Hungary after the fall of the Hapsburgs.

movement for the liberation of Slovakia must end in a fiasco. This was fully discussed at the Pittsburgh Conference. I was able to show the Slovaks how little they were known in the political world and how serious a failure we should have courted had they acted independently. The idea of an independent Slovakia could not be taken seriously though there might be a theoretical possibility of Slovak autonomy under Hungary. But since this possibility as not practical in the circumstances, there remained nothing save union. During the war, all the small peoples were demanding freedom and unity. Both Slovaks and Czechs knew that I had always stood for Slovakia; that, as a Slovak by origin and tradition, my feelings are Slovak, and that I have always worked, not merely talked, for Slovakia. In Bohemia, sympathy for Slovakia has ever been lively. The Czechs —Havlíček, for instance—recognized the racial individuality of the Slovaks and Moravians. I know Slovakia and the Slovak people pretty well, being in touch with the older and the younger generations and having worked with both for the rebirth of the country. I know, too, that even the Russophil Slovak, Hurban-Vajanský, favored union with the Czechs when the question became serious, as his father had done, and Kollár before him. But I am quite aware that many Slovaks, in their racial and political humiliation, sought consolation in visions and dreams rather than in action or work. And when some Russians—Lamansky for example—took delight in Slovak racial originality, such Slovaks thought this originality sufficient and did little to resist Magyar pressure.

This state of mind persisted among some of the Slovaks in the United States; and, when America entered the war, the "Slovak League" published a memorandum—prepared in advance —in which the autonomy of Slovakia within the Hungarian State was demanded as it had been in the old memorandum of St. Martin. In reality, this "Slovak League" was not recognized by the authorities until May 17, 1919, and until then existed only in name. Yet, for a time, individuals and small local groups repeated the cry for an independent Slovakia linked, somehow or other, to Russia; and Koníček, to whom I have referred in earlier chapters, carried on an agitation to this end both in Russia and in America. The war brought about a Romantic revival among the Slovaks in Russia, whom the first Russian official proclamations filled with enthusiasm. They dwelt upon the interest which the Tsar had shown in the Slovaks during the audience he had granted to a Czech deputation, and upon the fact that the Grand Duke Nicholas had mentioned them by name in his manifesto to the Austrian peoples. The idea of Lamansky and others affected them, and many a Slovak workman dreamed of a Slovakia either independent or associated with Russia, just as other Slovaks maintained that Slovakia should join Poland, while yet others believed in joining Hungary. In 1915 the "Russo-Slovak Štúr Commemoration Society" was formed at Moscow where, under the influence of politically ingenuous Russians, all sorts of anti-Czech illusions were cherished in a vague and jejune pan-Slav and pan-Russian spirit which many a Czech shared. The Memorandum presented to the Tsar of September 1914 referred to a "Dual Kingdom"; and the "National Council" formed by Koníček among the Czechoslovak Communities in Paris sent a message to Slovakia on February 15, 1915, in which independence was promised to the "Slovak Regions" with a Diet of their own at Nitra. On May 31, 1915, the League of Czechoslovak Societies in Russia also declared that Slovakia would have a Diet and political and linguistic autonomy.

Nevertheless, the great majority of Slovaks and of their leaders in Russia and in America supported the only reasonable and practicable plan—a united Czechoslovak State. At a Congress held at Cleveland, Ohio, in October 1915, the Slovaks and Czechs agreed upon unity and coöperation; and the American Slovak leaders were among the signatories of the first anti-Austrian manifesto of November 14, 1915. The Czechoslovak agreement at Pittsburgh in 1918 was only one of a series of programs and, it may be noted, not the most radical of them.

But the activities of our Czech and Slovak colonies in America were by no means confined to this sort of thing. From the beginning of the war they engaged in political propaganda and, through their organizations, exercised considerable influence upon the American public—an influence the more important because America remained neutral for two and a half years. In 1916 our "National Alliance" in America issued a manifesto explanatory of our struggle for freedom. In May 1917 it and the "Slovak League" presented to President Wilson, through the intermediary of Colonel House, a memorandum setting forth our political aspirations; and in February 1918 a further memorandum put the Foreign Relations Committee of the Senate on its guard against Austrian promises of autonomy. On May 25, 1917, Mr. Kenyon, the Senator of Iowa, whose goodwill our people had won, moved a resolution demanding the liberation of the Czechs and Slovaks as a condition of peace; and a year later (May 31, 1918) Mr. King, Senator for Utah, put forward the same demand. In this way and by organizing numerous public lectures and meetings, our American colonies contributed politically as well as financially to our conquest of freedom—politically, perhaps, even more than financially. After I reached Washington our "National Alliance" induced Congress, on June 29, so to amend the Immigration Law that, like the American volunteers who had joined the Allied armies, our Legionaries should be allowed to return unhindered to the United States.

AMERICAN DEMOCRACY

When I reached Washington on May 9, work began at once in the form of giving interviews and in resuming close touch with Mr. Charles R. Crane whom I had last seen at Kieff. With him my relations had been intimate since 1901. At that time he had established a Slavonic Foundation at Chicago University where I lectured in 1902. Thereafter he had devoted himself with quiet intensity to Slavonic affairs; and his position in American industry had brought him into political life. An excursion with him and his friend, Mr. Houston, the Secretary for Agriculture (who enjoyed the goodwill of President Eliot of Harvard), and

with a British officer, Major Innes, to the battlefield of Gettysburg—where, on July 3, 1863, Meade defeated Lee—served to
inaugurate my American work in 1918.

As a memorial to the American War for national unity, Gettysburg impresses Europeans deeply. Many monuments are there,
great and small, but by no means monuments in honor only of
one military commander, or even of several. In this, too, the
spirit of democracy finds expression. Lincoln's Gettysburg
speech cannot be read without emotion—the speech which sums
up American democracy in the well-known words "Government
of the People, by the People, for the People." As a souvenir of
my visit, the local minister of religion gave me a bullet which he
had found in a grave and had kept as a warning symbol against
the spirit of war; and, as such, it lies on my desk to-day.

I cherished the hope that in America, and with President Wilson particularly, good fortune would attend me. My personal
and family ties with America were close. I had been there repeatedly, from 1878 onwards; and American democracy and the
development of American civilization had aroused my lively interest from the beginning of my scientific and political career.

There is democracy and democracy. As the latest historical
studies of the development of the American Republic clearly
show, democracy in the United States was built on religious
foundations. The importance of the moral influence of religion
upon the American Republic is rightly indicated by de Tocqueville. Nor has the splitting up of America into the most diversi-
fied sects weakened either the Republic or democracy, for sec-
tarianism is a sign of religious vigor, and equally of modern individualization. In America, as in England, even the Catholics
are more firmly rooted religiously than in the Catholic States of
Europe—an effect of a Protestant environment.

In the early days of the American Republic this religious
factor was of especial significance. Inadequate means of communication, in a huge, sparsely peopled territory, precluded effective control from one administrative center. Hence, through
their organizations, the various religious communities and

Churches acquired great importance as elements of cohesion.

The American Republic is the work of pioneers, energetic men who had shown their energy in breaking away from their home surroundings and who had only been able to keep foot in America by yet greater vigor and industry. The pioneers sought freedom and well-being—even to-day, the American Republic serves chiefly an economic purpose and ideal, all the more because it is free from political and racial problems like those of Europe. Independence and Puritanism made up the real religion of the pioneers. The Constitution, framed in the spirit of the Rationalist philosophy of law that was prevalent in France and England towards the end of the eighteenth century, is a veritable code of pioneer economics. Estranged by emigration from the English dynasty, the American colonies had no dynasty and therefore no aristocracy, no army and no militarism. The Republic was founded upon communities religiously organized, and its founders were not soldiers on expansion bent but pioneers, farmers mainly, then traders and the inevitable lawyers. Thus the American State differed from European States, particularly from Prussia, Austria and Russia. Even the French Republic inherited from the old régime institutions like the aristocracy and the army which, in America, did not and do not exist. In the course of its development the American State has grown to the size of a continent. Yet, in the process, it has but accentuated its original characteristics; for, by reasons of the gradual conquest of the West and the South, the pioneer spirit remained a constant moral and political factor.

In the cemetery on the Gettysburg battlefield and in other places my mind often dwelt on the idea that our Czechoslovak State would resemble America in that we have no dynasty of our own and no liking for a foreign dynasty; that we have no aristocracy, no army and no military tradition. The traditions of our Reformation, on the other hand, preclude intimacy with the Church—a point of weakness unless we can realize that a democracy and a Republic must rest upon moral foundations. Our reborn State, our democratic Republic would have to be based upon an idea, it must have a reason for existence which the world at large would recognize.

Some special features of the American Constitution are noteworthy—the Presidency, in particular. To the President the Constitution entrusts great power. He himself selects the Government, not among Members of Parliament—the American President is, after the English fashion, *de facto* an elective constitutional King. The American example might serve in some degree to correct those shortcomings of Parliamentarism against which protests are now to be heard on all hands—the disunion entailed by the growth and the splitting up of parties. Significant, too, is the principle that the constitutional validity of laws is subject to the judgment of the Supreme Court. In the federal character of her Republic and her Democracy, America gives us, moreover, a political lesson—the very reverse of European centralism which has nowhere made good. Even the small Swiss Republic points to autonomy and federalism. American federalism and autonomy must, however, defend themselves against the centralization which is developing strongly at the cost of autonomy. No inner harmony has yet been attained between the self-government of the various States and the Central Government, nor have the technical consequences of this lack of harmony, such as redundancies and lack of uniformity in legislation, yet been overcome.[1]

---

[1] Here I may cite the "American Creed" which won a public competition in 1916-1917. President Wilson and a number of prominent politicians and writers supported the competition of which the winner was Mr. William Tyler Page, a descendant of President Tyler. Its text is made up of various apt phrases taken from the Constitution, the Declaration of Independence and speeches of prominent statesmen. It runs:—

"AMERICAN CREDO."

I believe in the United States of America as a government of the people by the people for the people; whose real power derives from the assent of the governed; in democracy within the Republic; in the nation sovereign among many sovereign States; in a unity complete, single and indivisible; founded on the principles of freedom, equality, justice and humanity for which American patriots have sacrificed their lives and their possessions.

Therefore I believe it my duty to love my country; to uphold its Constitution; to obey its laws; to honor its flag; and to defend it against all foes.

In Europe, particularly in Germany and Austria, "Americanism" is often condemned as a one-sidedly mechanical and materialistic outlook on life, pointed reference being made to the almighty dollar, to the lack of political sense among Americans and to the inadequacy of their science and culture.   These strictures are themselves one-sided, exaggerated and, especially from a German standpoint, unwarrantable.   As though Germany herself had not been dominated by a machine—a military, milItarist, State machine!   In Germany, materialism triumphed alike in philosophy and in practical life, while German science and thought subordinated themselves to Prussian and pan-German domineering.   True, some members of European reigning families, and of the aristocracy of all countries, have been wont to woo American dollar princesses—as the Gotha Almanac bears witness—and it is comprehensible that such people can feel but little liking for the entirely non-military humanism of America. But if this is evidence against American democracy, it tells equally against European aristocracy.   American civilization appeals to me, and I believe it appeals also to our emigrants who form a notable section of our race.   In America we can and should learn not merely the mechanical side of things, but love of freedom and individual independence.   Political freedom in a Republic is the mother of the peculiarly American simplicity and openness, in social as well as in political and economic matters.   The American humanitarian ideal has been practically realized in exemplary hospitals and in welfare work.   In America, a philanthropic and generous use of money has been developed, and in not a few respects America is creating fine precedents for the civilization of the future.

AMERICAN LITERATURE

I do not and cannot assert that there is no dark side to American life, or that it presents no hard problems.   Antiquated forms of Puritanism and its narrow-minded rigor have long been censured in American literature (Hawthorne's "Scarlet Letter" ap-

peared as early as 1850 and he was by no means their first as-
sailant) in the same way as the parochialism of cities great and
small and of country districts is being attacked to-day. The
younger generation of critics tilts at the lack of artistic sense,
at the failure to understand social and socialistic thought, and at
the stereotyping and standardization of culture and intellectual
life. If the American philosopher, Baldwin, insists so emphatically upon æsthetic sensibility as the primary need, the conclusion may be drawn that American life is devoid of it.

In American literature, moreover, the beginnings and the
growth of decadence may be studied. A number of authors treat
of it, among them the well-known Mrs. Wharton. From time to
time our newspapers report that, in America, abortion has become a business and that the number of divorces is legion.
Whence does decadence spring? In France its source is said to
have lain chiefly in militarism, because the French were bled
white and enfeebled by wars and revolutions; yet America, a
wealthy land without army or militarism, is alleged to be de-
generating by reason of peace and wealth! If America is called
a young country, one must say that she is not young but new—
her inhabitants left Europe already old, and spent their strength
in pioneering. In Europe, decadence is attributed to over-popu-
lation and its consequences; yet America shows signs of decadence despite the comparative sparseness of her population. Who
can tell how the blending of races, the "great melting-pot," as
the Americans say, is working out morally and biologically?
Nervousness and neurasthenia are widespread, and the number
of suicides is increasing, just as in Europe; and there is constant
talk of the nervousness—I would rather say the "nerviness"—
of American women.

These and other American problems have always interested
me both in themselves and as reflected in literature. In 1877,
when I first came into close touch with America, a peculiar realism and, with it, new tendencies were making themselves felt.
The cleavage wrought by the Civil War was healed and the unity
and the power of the nation were expressing themselves in a

realist and critical consciousness of the special character of America and of Americanism. From the beginning my attention was fixed on Howells and his realism, for in him the thesis can be proved that realism is the method of democracy—the observation and artistic treatment of what is called "everyday," that is to say, non-aristocratic life. Just when I was beginning to pay more heed to American writings, the notorious case of Comstock and his campaign against literature, native and foreign, made a stir; and, through my personal associations, I was brought into lively intercourse with the great American writers then living—for, between 1877 and 1897, representatives of the elder generation like W. C. Bryant, Longfellow, Whittier, Lowell, Whitman, Holmes and Emerson, were still alive. My relations led me also to study older writers such as Thomas Paine, Theodore Parker, the two Danas and Daniel Webster. Hawthorne I have already mentioned; in substance and in artistic value he is akin to Edgar Allan Poe whose grave I often visited when in Baltimore. Poe was a decadent. Between him and Baudelaire the comparison is obvious, though there is a clear difference since Poe does not show the same degree of nervous sexualism. The name of Dostoyevsky came also into my mind for he, too, was certainly decadent; and I reflected that one finds in the "new" and "fresh" American and Russian world what "old" France also offers. The wonted classification of nations will have to be thoroughly revised.

In Europe, and especially in our country, we have but a fragmentary knowledge of American literature. This is a mistake. I admit that I took no pleasure in the American philosophers, neither in the school of Edwards nor in that of Franklin, nor even in the newer tendencies. The epistemology, or theory of knowledge, of William James's Pragmatism I found as impossible to accept as that of Positivism; though his brother, Henry James, was more interesting, particularly in his attempt (in "Daisy Miller") to analyze the characters of Americans and of Europeans. Indeed, I have always followed the spiritual development of America rather in her imaginative literature than otherwise. For instance, in the struggle against Puritanism and Calvinism a modern and humane standpoint is especially conspicuous; and the fight against slavery was waged with the pen long before the Civil War began. Throughout American writings a strong progressive element is to be observed. Knowing that their State and nationality were born of revolution, Americans feel no fear of what is new, and sympathize genuinely with nations that have won freedom. Thus, in our rebellion against Austria, we, like other races before us, found well-wishers in America.

American literature, not unnaturally, reflects mainly the external side of life—the life of the East, the West, the Center and the South, the social conditions of the various strata of the people and especially of the negroes and of the multifarious immigrants. The principal phases of American history, with their heroes, are—somewhat inartistically—portrayed; and, little by little, American writers are seen to have grown conscious of their specifically American speech, manners and outlook, and of the difference between them and Europe, even Anglo-Saxon Europe.

The growth of American realism is noticeable, too, in the treatment of women and of love—important themes with novelists—though this realism has developed side by side with the realism of European literature and, to some extent, under its influence. And in America, as in Europe, the short story is characteristic, albeit not wholly new, as Poe proves. Indeed, in the age of the telegraph and of the telephone, brevity and terseness are attained even in literary style and in scientific writing.

In 1914, when the war was coming on in Europe, an American periodical began to publish satirical poems, ostensibly written by the dead in protest against the lying eulogies upon their tombstones; and in 1915 they were collected under the title of "The Spoon River Anthology," by Edgar Lee Masters. The very title is a satire upon America and her intellectual and moral provincialism. There were 250 such poems with an epilogue. They interested me not on account of their poetry, which was poor, but because of their revolt against current American culture and civilization. They contained philosophical arguments which Voltaire, and others before him, had used in Europe, and echoes from Browning and parts of "Faust"; they formed, indeed, a compendium of the ideas of young or, rather, youngest America. Their author, who lives in Chicago, denounces Chicago and the big American cities in general. In his eyes Jesus, for instance, is a peasant farmer who is slain in the city by the city, that is to say, by bankers, lawyers and judges.

In the footsteps of Masters, a series of writers continued this literary revolution. Dreiser describes Chicago, Titan among cities, and shows us the titanic multi milliardaire. His strictures make Sodom and Gomorrah seem homes of virtue by comparison; for the moral decay of the Roman Cæsars, of Renaissance Italy, of Paris, of Moscow, of Berlin, falls short of the decadent perversity which he attributes to Chicago and New York. Nor does Dreiser's indictment stand alone. Anderson and many others write in the same strain.

In calling themselves realists, these critics of America imitate the Russians and the French. On principle they are opposed to Romanticism and Idealism and to modern English Transcendentalism. They wage war against the Churches, against machinery, with its moral and material effects, and therefore against industrialism, capitalism and mammonism. They assail narrow-mindedness, Pragmatism in philosophy, and the tendency to exaggerate the value of science. They stand up for complete freedom of conscience and for the emancipation of women, just as we do in Europe—and they make the same mistakes as we. In opposing one-sidedness they are radically one-sided. Their aims are hazy and negative, superficial with a typically American superficiality; and, here and there, they grow rhapsodical over "free love" and fall into excessive sexuality. It is one-sided to upbraid Puritanism for its lack of poetic and artistic sense and disdain for intellectual progress. There are more poetry and romanticism in the Old and New Testaments, which the Puritans never tired of reading, than in their ultra-realist opponents;

and a pretty thesis for a literary degree could be written on the way in which the highly imaginative, journalistic sensationalism of Poe grew out of the estrangement from nature and humanity with Puritanism, and Transcendentalism after it, fostered by their fantastic imaginings.

Alongside of the so-called American Realists there is a long list of modern poets, both realist and idealist, many more of the latter than of the former. Machinery and capitalism have by no means uprooted Romanticism in America—on the contrary, they may even have strengthened it, for the real miracles of modern mechanics have fostered the belief in the marvelous which is the main element in Romanticism. Witness the works of H. G. Wells and their influence on American literature.

There are, too, numbers of women writers though proportionately fewer than in England. This disproportion interests me, for I cannot quite account for it. Two of the newer American authoresses, Miss Cather and Miss Canfield, describe the West or, rather, the Middle West where—not in the East—many American sociologists now tend to place the modern center of American culture. Both of them analyze Puritanism, albeit less one-sidedly and negatively than the male writers. Miss Canfield makes a frankly critical effort to formulate a truer and purer view of men and women, and of their relationship to each other, than that of the American decadents who have followed in the train of European decadence; but she simplifies her problem by painting her Mephistopheles so black that the American Marguerite can hardly fail to withstand him. In Miss Cather's work there is a description of the Czech immigrants; and, notwithstanding her affection for them, her account is realistically accurate.

The influence of Europe upon American literature is interesting to trace. Besides the English influence, which was formerly decisive, that of French, Russian and Scandinavian writers is particularly evident in the more recent American work, whereas German influence expresses itself rather in science. America is being Europeanized just as Europe is being Americanized. Of her own accord America tends towards an increasing intellectual activity and condemns the narrowness of one-sided economic interests, while Europe is likewise Americanizing herself spontaneously. Politically, this drawing together of modern America and Europe is noteworthy; and, in it, immigrant influences are traceable, especially those of the Germans and the Jews. On the other hand, the interest which Young England takes in Young America should not be overlooked, although, or perhaps because, Young America deliberately takes its stand against Anglo-Saxondom and claims that America is no longer Anglo-Saxon. And it is only in the nature of things that Bennett, Cannan, Walpole and Lawrence should be widely read in America alongside of Wells. The American decision to join the Allies, and thus to evince a lively interest in Europe, was not wholly unconnected with this intellectual development and with the change in modern America which is reflected in her literature.

I hasten to add that my own interest in American literature was political rather than literary. As in the cases of France and England, I sought in literature an answer to the question what part the Americans would play in the war, with what spirit and with what success. Nothing evil was prophesied even by the most trenchant critics and malcontents; and what I saw and heard strengthened my conviction that the American contribution to victory would be weighty. To the numbers and equipment of the troops sent to Europe I paid special heed. The way the troops were looked after—not only the officers but the men —impressed me greatly. Europeans, accustomed to aristocratic armies in which the officers are chiefly cared for, would have called it downright luxurious.

I was glad to find that the transport arrangements worked faultlessly and that the German submarines were powerless. In America, too, I realized from direct experience how huge is the share of industry in modern warfare—the quantities of food, arms and munitions were astounding. It was a mass war waged in the mass. The manufacture of artillery and rifles, machine-guns and other weapons grew in bewildering proportions. Ships were built in the twinkling of an eye. True, the hopes first placed in the production of innumerable aircraft were not fulfilled; and, like other countries, America had her "war rich" and her profiteers. But, as American soldiers told me gleefully, the French were astonished at their technical skill and at the rapidity with which railways were laid from harbor to battlefield.

THE POLITICAL ASPECT

Naturally, I sought to get a grasp of the American political situation without delay. This meant, in practice, making the acquaintance of the most influential people in the Government, in Congress and in society. Mr. Charles R. Crane was an admirable auxiliary, for he knew nearly everybody whom I wanted to meet and was "close to" President Wilson. His son, Mr. Richard Crane, afterwards the first American Minister to Czechoslovakia, was a Secretary of Mr. Lansing, the Head of the State Department. Besides Mr. Lansing I must mention Mr. Phillips, the first Assistant-Secretary of State; Mr. Polk, a Counsellor of the State Department; Mr. Long, Assistant-Secretary of State; Mr. Baker, Secretary for War; and Mr. Lane, Secretary for the Interior. Finally, through the good offices of Mr. Crane, I came into touch with Colonel House and President Wilson.

Our task was to gain the favor of the public, and in this we succeeded. Before long I was able to place interviews and articles in the largest and most influential daily papers, weeklies and reviews, and to establish personal relations with prominent writers of all opinions. Mr. William Hard, whom I saw frequently, Mr. Ira Bennett, Mr. Dixon of Boston and Mr. Martin of Cleveland I mention by way of example, for from a fuller list I might inadvertently omit some deserving names. To them all, and to American journalism in general, I owe a debt of gratitude.

My work obliged me to visit the principal cities, to get into personal touch with people and to look up old acquaintances; and, in Washington, to cultivate the society of the Senators and Congressmen of the two chief parties and of all shades of political opinion—including, of course, Mr. Hitchcock, Chairman of the Foreign Relations Committee of the Senate—and Republicans like Senator Lodge whom I sought to inform. Senator Root I had already met in Russia. I had, too, the advantage of knowing the Preparatory Committee which, under the Chairmanship of Professor Mezes, was working upon material and memoranda in view of the peace negotiations and for the President. On behalf of the Czechs, Professor Kerner worked with him. Later on, the journalistic staff which Mr. Creel got together for the Peace Conference acquired great importance. I was in touch with him and, in fact, with all the principal organizations and institutions. But I had little leisure to visit the Universities or to see men of learning, though I went to the Universities of Chicago and Harvard. To the President of Chicago University I have already referred; and in Cambridge (Mass.) I must recall especially President Eliot who, as ever, took a truly scientific interest in the political problems of Europe. Among the historians I remember Professor Coolidge; Professor Wiener, the Slavonic Scholar who has long been well known; while President Butler of Columbia University supported me with his goodwill and his understanding of world affairs. The French philosopher, Bergson, and the French author, Chéradame whom I had known in Paris, were among the prominent Europeans whom I met.

In America, as elsewhere, the Jews stood by me; and particularly in America my former defense of Hilsner, the Austrian Jew who had been falsely accused of ritual murder in 1899, did me a good turn. As early as 1907 the New York Jews had given me a gigantic reception. Now I had many personal meetings with representatives of Orthodox Jewry as well as with Zionists. Among the latter I must mention Mr. Brandeis, a Judge of the Supreme Court, who came originally from Bohemia and enjoyed President Wilson's confidence. In New York Mr. Mack was a leading Zionist and I met Nahum Sokoloff, the influential Zionist leader. In America, as in Europe, Jewish influence is strong in the press, and it was good that it was not against us. Even those who did not agree with my policy were reserved and impartial.

Especially did I make a point of cultivating the pacifists and the pro-Germans. In their camp were some of my former acquaintances, and I was therefore the more eager to vindicate our national cause in their eyes—an important matter, because pacifism was widespread and inadvertently supported the Germans, in America as everywhere. On account of the high percentage of Americans who had either been born in Germany or of German parents in America, German influence was, directly and indirectly, a very serious factor. And, last not least, I sought out the men I knew in financial circles, not so much in the official world where President Wilson's son-in-law, Mr. McAdoo, was Secretary of the Treasury, as among bankers and in the Bankers' Club of New York.

To ex-President Roosevelt, whose goodwill Štefánik had gained for us, I must make special reference. Before the war I had opposed and had written against him; but, during the war, he took a decided anti-German stand and, in speeches and statements, came out strongly for the Czechs. I met him only once, on Lafayette Day in New York, where I heard him speak for the first time. There was little chance of personal intercourse, though we had a number of mutual friends. After the war, not long before his death, he sent me the full program of a lecturing tour which he intended to carry out in Europe, and it was his intention to deliver a whole series of political addresses in Bohemia.

In my work I had, as personal assistants, Mr. Pergler who had met me at Vancouver; and, as I soon needed a literary secretary, Mr. Cisař who had received mathematical, scientific and literary training. Together with Pergler he did much useful propaganda. Everywhere in the vast country we made friends and gained well-wishers of whom I must mention, at least, one— Mr. Townsend, a young naval officer and son of a former First Secretary of the American Embassy in Paris. Notwithstanding fatal illness—influenza killed him—he worked for us to the last.

DIPLOMATIC RELATIONS

The democratic character of our propaganda did not by any means exclude active relations with Ambassadors and Ministers. Through them I had to second the work of Beneš and Štefánik in Europe, and all of them rendered me valuable service. It is fitting to give the first place to the French Ambassador, M. Jusserand, who had been many years at Washington, knew everybody, was known to everybody and, of all the Ambassadors, had the greatest influence on American statesmen and President Wilson. Both by reason of his political experience and literary culture—he wrote in English as well as in French—he had become a recognized authority in diplomatic circles and in Washington society. We had besides to negotiate with the French Military Mission and with Frenchmen who came to America on special service.

With the British I had frequent and very pleasant intercourse. At that time Mr. Hohler, the Counsellor of Embassy, who knew Constantinople and Petrograd, was representing the Ambassador; and when Lord Reading came to Washington he gave us generous support. Sir William Wiseman, whom I had known in England, was also helpful in many matters as head of the British Intelligence Service. Count Cellere, the Italian Ambassador, understood our position, realized the moral and political significance of our endeavor to form a Legion among our prisoners in Italy for the fight against Austria, and therefore did all he could for us. In Baron Cartier, Belgium had a good and experienced Minister. The Japanese Ambassador, Count Ishii, acted as intermediary in the difficult relations with Japan and Siberia; while Russia was represented, even during the Bolshevik period, by the former Ambassador, M. Bakhmetieff. And, as a matter of course, I got into permanent touch with the Serbian Legation and with all Yugoslav representatives and workers immediately after reaching the United States.

COOPERATION WITH THE YUGOSLAVS

Cooperation with the representatives of the other races which were striving for freedom, formed, indeed, part of the propaganda by which we secured recognition in America and among the Allies in general. All along, my object was to show the Allies by practical demonstration, as it were, that the object of the war was and must be the political transformation of Central and Eastern Europe in particular, and the liberation of a whole series of peoples whom the Central Powers oppressed. Hence I appeared in public as often as possible with the leaders of those peoples' organizations which were working for the same end. My relations with the Southern Slavs before the war, particularly during the Balkan Wars of 1912-13, made intimate cooperation with them natural during the Great War itself. I have already said how it began in Prague and developed in Rome, Geneva, Paris, London and in Russia. In America, it was the more effective because, like us, the Yugoslavs possessed in the United States colonies of considerable size, among whose members were men well known to the Americans, such as Professor Pupin and Dr. Bianchini (the brother of the Austrian member of Parliament from Dalmatia), whom I had long known, and who worked at Washington as President of the Yugoslav National Council. As early as 1915 the Southern Slavs had sent envoys to their fellow-countrymen in America—Dr. Pototchnyak, Marianovitch, Milan Pribitchevitch and, in 1917, Dr. Hinkovitch. Not only did we leaders work together, but our people held joint meetings; and in our own meetings we advocated freedom for the Southern Slavs and they advocated our freedom in theirs.

At this point it is expedient that I should, with due discretion, complete what I have already said and should speak my mind on Southern Slav conditions and political problems; though, as I am not writing the history of the movement for Yugoslav freedom, I shall refer only to matters which affected us directly and in which circumstances involved us. But I had watched, in our own interest and with the closest attention, the development of Southern Slav political affairs of which I had known much beforehand and learned more during the war.

Despite the temporary reverses suffered by Serbia in the field, I looked upon her as the center of the Southern Slav world and, what counted most, as its political and military center. The Croats had assuredly their own special rights. It was just that they should invoke them and should appeal to the maturity of their culture. This, however, did not preclude the recognition of Serbia as the political point of crystallization. The lessons of history, an accurate valuation of the guiding ideas and forces, and a right estimate of Austria and of Hungary, all pointed in this direction.

It was on account of Serbia that Austria had provoked the war. Serbia, then a small country, based her hopes chiefly upon the solemn promises of the Tsar, of the great brotherly Slavonic Empire. But, from the spring of 1915 onward, the defeat of Russia had shifted towards the West the center of gravity in the Serbian and Yugoslav question, and the Treaty of London (April 26, 1915) had made of the relationship between Italy, Serbia and the Southern Slavs a big problem which determined in a high degree the subsequent development of the war and of war aims.

I did not like the terms of the Treaty of London, though the military situation in 1915 made it a question whether the entry of Italy into the war was not a necessity for the Southern Slavs themselves, lest Austria triumph. Italy had her irredentist aspirations, and it was natural that she should invoke her historical rights and should claim union with the minorities of Italians beyond her borders. At first, this point of view was not understood. Many a Croat and Slovene looked upon me as excessively pro-Italian and pro-Serb. The more gladly do I therefore recognize that, as time went on, the leading Croats, Dr. Trumbitch in particular, appreciated the importance of Italy for the Allied and particularly for the Southern Slav cause. After the conclusion of the Treaty of London, Russia, for her part, sided with the Italians and the Allies in the Yugoslav question.

Many Serbians, among them people in official positions, were, I admit, prejudiced against the Croats. But the Croats were also prejudiced against the Serbians though the common interest should have commanded them not to show hostility towards Serbia. The absurd lengths to which some people went may be seen from their allegations that the Serbian Government was financing our movement, Štefánik especially being made an object of direct suspicion. To dispel this distrust I had from time to time to issue statements, even in writing.

Yet it was not distrust alone that played a part; there was a kind of friendly jealousy, for our Yugoslav friends made no secret of their astonishment that we Czechs should make such rapid headway in the political world, and they envied us for having been expressly mentioned in the Allied reply to President Wilson. Much the same thing could be seen among the Poles who, like the Southern Slavs, forgot our Legions and our united and consistent action on the basis of our program, whereas they had long wavered in regard to their own program. Nor were there among us the same dissensions and internal struggles as among our friends—it was only in Russia that, at first, our house was not quite in order. We gained the ear of the Allies precisely by our discipline and precision, while the Yugoslavs and the Poles complained to them about their own people.

Even Dr. Trumbitch came under the influence of unjustified suspicions, and taxed us with selfishness during the discussions on the Declaration of Corfu, as I heard from people who took part in them. But the main thing was that he, as President of the Southern Slav Committee abroad, should have come to an understanding at Corfu with Pashitch on July 20, 1917, and that both of them should have signed the Declaration in which the Serbian Government and the Southern Slav Committee agreed that the Serbo-Croat-Slovene nation would be united in one State under the Karageorgevitch dynasty, and that the Constituent Assembly, to be elected by universal suffrage after the

Peace, should draft the Constitution. This Corfu agreement gladdened me the more because there had been serious instability in the Southern Slav Committee since 1916. In America I learned that Trumbitch and Supilo had previously settled the lines of the Corfu Declaration with Steed and Seton-Watson in London. It was a notable political success that, after the Declaration had been issued, the British Prime Minister, Lloyd George, should have had both Sonnino and Pashitch beside him on the platform when he made his Queen's Hall speech in London at the end of July 1917.

Important and helpful, too, was the Rome Congress of April 8, 1918, at which all the oppressed peoples of Austria-Hungary agreed upon common action against their oppressor, even the Italians and the Southern Slavs making friends with each other. Thus they toned down the effects of the Treaty of London which, by lapse of time, had already lost the keenness of its edge. Though many Italian politicians still invoked it, neither the public opinion of Europe and America nor President Wilson himself accepted it. Once again, the credit for the agreement in Rome belonged mainly to Steed and Seton-Watson.

After the Caporetto disaster the Italians and the Southern Slavs had begun to come together, both sides acknowledging that they stood nearer to each other than to Austria-Hungary, and the Southern Slavs realizing that the defeat of Italy would be a defeat for them too. Towards the middle of December 1917 Steed invited Italians and Southern Slavs in London to a joint meeting at his house, where they found a basis of agreement against Austria-Hungary. Then Steed persuaded the Italian Prime Minister, Orlando, to negotiate with Trumbitch. This was done in Steed's presence in January 1918. In February, an Italian and a French Parliamentary Committee made preparations for a Congress of oppressed Austro-Hungarian peoples; but the negotiations were by no means easy. They began in Paris with Beneš. On the French side, MM. Franklin-Bouillon and Fournol took part in them and, on the Italian, two members of Parliament, Torre and Gallenga, with Amendola, Borgese and

Lazarini, who possessed the confidence of the Italian Vice-Premier Bissolati. Florescu represented the Roumanians and Dmowski the Poles, though the Poles showed some reserve. The task of Dr. Beneš was to keep the Yugoslavs in line—a difficult matter, for our Southern Slav friends made very drastic demands upon the Italians. Torre and Borgese went to London and negotiated with Steed and Seton-Watson amid constant difficulties. Trumbitch was recalcitrant until the sharp language of Steed and Seton-Watson finally led to the adoption of a common formula. Nevertheless, in Paris, Dr. Beneš had still to persuade Dr. Trumbitch not to hold aloof. In the end, the Congress, at which our representatives were Beneš and Štefánik, went well. Its proceedings were solemn and their high political significance and influence were enhanced by the circumstance that, under Lord Northcliffe, England began vigorous anti-Austrian propaganda on the Italian front, Steed having drafted the policy on which it was based. He proposed to the Allies that they should proclaim forthwith the freedom of the Austrian peoples and should make the fact known to the Slav regiments in the Austro-Hungarian army by means of leaflets. Though the Italian Prime Minister, Orlando, and the Commander-in-Chief, General Diaz, were in agreement with Steed, Sonnino made objections as usual; but the British and the French Governments gave their assent. The leaflets bearing this Allied proclamation undoubtedly had a strong anti-Austrian effect upon our own and the other Slav troops in the Austro-Hungarian army on the Italian front. Moreover, the importance of the Rome Congress may be judged by the fact that, on May 29, 1918, America accepted its resolutions, and that the American acceptance was adopted by the Allied Conference on June 3.

Before referring to the final phase of our relations with the Southern Slavs, I must revert for a moment to Russia and to her attitude towards them and Serbia. By official Russia the Southern Slavs were ignored; she took cognizance only of Serbia and Montenegro. The Southern Slav question was treated as a dynastic and family affair in which Montenegrin as well as

Serbian influences made themselves felt. Therefore, after the Treaty of London, the Russian Government acted in accordance with it and prohibited, for instance, the demonstrations on behalf of Dalmatia which, probably at Supilo's suggestion, had been started by Professor Yastreboff; and in the Italian semi-official "Messaggero" the Russian Government actually made a declaration in favor of Italy.

After Supilo—whose doings I have already described—had left Petrograd, Dr. Manditch went there in the summer of 1915 on behalf of the Southern Slav Committee. He soon found that, in the eyes of official Russia, the Southern Slav question simply did not exist. According to Russian ideas, Serbia was to get Bosnia and Herzegovina, that is to say, their occupation by Austria-Hungary was to cease; and Serbia was, besides, to obtain access to the sea. As for Montenegro, nobody at Petrograd dreamt that she might disappear. Like the other Allies, Russia still took Bulgaria into account at that time, and when, in the autumn of 1915, Serbia was overrun by the Austrians, and Bulgaria sided against the Allies, official Russia was painfully affected by the "treachery" of the Bulgarians—but threw the blame for it on Serbia. Sazonof thought Serbia responsible for not having given Macedonia back to Bulgaria in time. But Russian official opinion changed at the beginning of 1916, when the overthrow of Serbia and Montenegro was complete. Then some members of the Duma, Milyukoff especially, began to take an interest in the Southern Slav question. Yet there was still a total absence of any clear and definite Southern Slav program, or of a policy in favor of a united Yugoslavia.

Simultaneously, an experiment analogous to that made in regard to us by official Russia in the Dürich affair was undertaken in regard to the Southern Slavs. It failed; but, on the other hand, the Serbian Government put forward a scheme for a united Yugoslavia under the leadership of Orthodox Serbia—the emphasis was on the "Orthodox"—and Spalaikovitch, the Serbian Minister at Petrograd, supported it. Milyukoff, on the contrary, opposed it, and advocated the unification of the

Southern Slavs irrespective of their ecclesiastical allegiances; but the "Novoe Vremya" characteristically sought to prove that the idea of unity was absurd and impossible. Even as late as February 1917 Professor Sobolevsky insisted upon this Russian official standpoint. Then came the Revolution; and, just as revolutionary Russia declared in favor of us and our program, so it supported the idea of Yugoslav union. Notwithstanding the difficulties and wranglings among the Yugoslavs themselves and in the Southern Slav Committee, the Declaration of Corfu and the Rome Congress were, as I have said, finally brought about with the help of Steed and Seton-Watson.

When I reached Russia in May 1917 the dissensions between the Serbs, Croats and Slovenes were very acute and their respective programs diverged considerably. The Slovenes published a periodical called "Yugoslavia" and demanded a Great Slavonia which would join Serbia and Croatia in a federation—a program of which the vagueness and exaggeration were by no means diminished by the verbal explanations which Slovenes gave me.

One effect of these dissensions was to smash the Yugoslav Legion in Russia. The Croat and Slovene section of it, to which some of our volunteers belonged, broke away from the Serbian section and vegetated at Kieff; and the Yugoslavs in Russia suffered still further from the consequences of the unhappy episode at Salonika, where the secret society of Serbian officers known as the "Black Hand," otherwise "Union or Death," had begun its revolutionary activity. An attempt was alleged to have been made upon the life of the Prince Regent. On this account the former Chief of the Serbian General Staff, Dimitriyevitch, was shot in June 1917, and some of his associates were deported to North Africa. Serbians assured me that the French command on the Salonika front had insisted on the punishment of the offenders; but, in Russia, the partisans of Dimitriyevitch appealed for Russian sympathy and approached me also with a memorandum. Naturally, I held aloof, for I had heard something of the "Black Hand" in Belgrade before the war. But, again and again, I reconciled the warring factions and calmed their excitement. Though I recognized that the Serbians had made mistakes, the situation demanded discipline and quieter tactics.

Later on, towards the end of the war, the Italian occupation of Croat and Slovene territory led to further differences with the Serbians. The Diet of Zagreb addressed to President Wilson, on November 4, 1918, a protest against the Italian occupation, and further protests followed from Dalmatia and Bosnia. Among the Croats the rumor spread that Dr. Vesnitch, the Serbian Minister in Paris, had assented to the Italian occupation. Dr. Trumbitch, on the other hand, maintained that it ought not to be carried out either by Italian or by Serbian but by American troops—a standpoint which gave displeasure in Serbia.

Before I had been long in America I saw that the Yugoslavs were at sixes and sevens. Among the Croat colonies in the United States—and in South America too—local views and influences were making themselves felt just as they had done at first in our own case. Bad blood was caused also by the action of Pashitch, the Serbian Prime Minister, in pensioning off the Serbian Minister at Washington, Mihailovitch, in July 1918, for having, it was said, consistently supported the Declaration of Corfu and the unification of the Southern Slavs. Therefore he lost the favor of Pashitch who, according to serious Croat information, had been convinced by the pro-Austrian war aims speeches of Wilson and Lloyd George in January 1918 that Yugoslav unity would be unattainable and that Serbia must secure for herself at least Bosnia-Herzegovina and access to the sea. It should, however, be said that the Declaration of Corfu had been expounded in America one-sidedly and in a manner suggestive rather of a "Great Croatian" and republican program than of Yugoslav unity.

For the sake of completeness I ought to say that a representatives of Montenegro, or rather of the King of Montenegro, came also to see me. King Nicholas had looked upon me with disfavor since the days when I had criticized Montenegrin policy in the Vienna Parliament. I admit that I handled him somewhat severely in that speech, and he let me feel it when I went later on to Cettinye, though I went with his permission. But the war effaced these memories, and he sent to me one of his Generals who wore rather too much gold braid, and made, in consequence, a doubtful impression upon the Americans. I advocated the union of Montenegro with Serbia, whereas the Montenegro representative was working in the interest of the King. I reminded him that, in the spring of 1914, King Nicholas himself had proposed to the King of Serbia a union between the two countries, and I argued that, after the war, their relationship would have to be more intimate. The Montenegrins in America, for their part, addressed to President Wilson a vigorous protest against the policy of King Nicholas.

After we had been granted recognition by the United States on September 3, 1918, the Yugoslav leaders wished likewise to be recognized and asked me to approach the American Government to that end. Towards the middle of October Dr. Trumbitch sent me the same request from Paris. It was natural that I should do all I could for the Yugoslavs; and the Corfu Declaration and the Rome Congress made things easier for me. But, just as our adversaries were on the alert, so were those of the Southern Slavs. They kept the Allied Governments and influential people informed of all the Southern Slav dissensions, and stirred them up against us. The mood which prevailed in many quarters towards the end of the war may be judged from the fact that, even at the Peace Conference, Clemenceau said France would not forget that the Croats had fought for the enemy. Moreover, to some extent, the attitude of the old official Orthodox Russia, which had favored Croat separatism, still made itself felt; and the adversaries of the Southern Slavs drew the attention of the American authorities to the various pro-Austrian declarations which had been made by Slovene members of Parliament on September 15, and by the Catholics of Bosnia-Herzegovina on November 17, 1917.

All along, the circumstance that they were officially represented by Serbia hampered the Yugoslavs; and, at the beginning of the war, Serbia had put forward a strong claim for union with them. Serbia commanded lively sympathies everywhere; but the Yugoslav emigrants from Austria-Hungary, who were still nominally Austro-Hungarian subjects, had to organize themselves in some way since neither the Serbian Government nor its diplomatic representatives abroad could really take charge of their interests. Thus the Southern Slav Committee arose. I know that Pashitch himself originally favored it and recommended it to the Allied Governments. But it was not long before the views of the Committee diverged from those of the Serbian Government. Supilo's action in the spring of 1915 caused anxiety in Western Allied circles as well as in Russia; and it was noticeable that, under the influence of the military reverses of Serbia and Montenegro, "Great Croatian" tendencies presently grew stronger among the Croats and Slovenes, in whose eyes the ultimate fate of Serbia seemed uncertain. Even Serbia was obliged to contemplate a future less brilliant than she had dreamed of. I have no wish to dwell upon this point, for I was often caught between two or more fires. Nevertheless I worked steadily in the Yugoslav interest; and when I met Dr. Trumbitch in Paris in December 1918 we found ourselves in excellent agreement. It is true that, at a Conference held in Geneva at the beginning of November, Pashitch had agreed with Dr. Trumbitch, Dr. Koroshetz and the representatives of the various parties upon racial and territorial unity and also upon the recognition of the Southern Slav National Council which had been constituted at Zagreb on October 6 as a representative Government for the Southern Slavs of Austria-Hungary. They had agreed further that a unitary Government for Serbia and the Southern Slavs should be elected alongside of the individual Serbian and Southern Slav Governments. Consequently, I looked upon the anti-Serbian proclamation in favor of a Southern Slav Republic, which the Southern Slavs in America had issued at Washington on November 1, as having been disposed of by the Geneva agreement. (The proclamation had been the work of Dr. Hinkovitch who, together with a large number of the American Southern Slavs, had abandoned the Southern Slav Committee.) But undoubtedly the Geneva agreement accentuated dualist tendencies among the Southern Slavs, despite its non-ratification by the King and Government of Serbia.

If I refer thus to the history of the Southern Slav movement it is, I must repeat, solely in order to deal with those aspects of it which affected us and to insist that complaints against us were and are unjustified. There was no dispute between us as to principles. The Southern Slavs, not we, decided upon their program, though I always advised them to formulate it more concretely. I was often in disagreement with them about tactics, as, for instance, about Supilo's action in regard to Russia. Neither did I approve of the Southern Slav Committee's protest in "The Times" against Lloyd George's war aims speech of January 5, 1918, in which he demanded only autonomy, not independence, for the oppressed Austro-Hungarian peoples, nor of the impossible plan which the Committee originally cherished for a convention of all Southern Slavs, with the King and the Serbian Skupshtina at their head, to decide upon the future organization of the Southern Slav lands. One of their leading men in America rebuked me for not having taken action against Lloyd George. True, I did nothing publicly; but I drew the attention of President Wilson—whose demands, at that time, were the same as those of Lloyd George—to the inadequacy of mere autonomy for the Hapsburg peoples. Besides, my views were well known in England and we had vigilant friends there. President Wilson had also communicated confidentially to the Allies the memorandum which I addressed to him from Tokio. I was continually conferring with Allied Governments and statesmen, but kept the fact out of the press.

Upon my Yugoslav friends I had always urged the necessity of solving the urgent problem of centralization and self-government, that is to say, the question whether the Southern Slav provinces of Austria-Hungary should enjoy some degree of autonomy or should be united to Serbia under one central Government. Unification, I pointed out, would naturally be the chief thing in the eyes of all the liberated Slav peoples and States.

Hence the need to think of it betimes, and carefully, and to prepare both for the peace negotiations and for the early years of their new State. In giving this advice I assumed that the Southern Slav Committee abroad, or a considerable part of it, would go to Belgrade as early as practicable in order to come to an understanding with the Serbian political leaders.

THE POLES

With the Poles our relations were not less constant than with the Southern Slavs. In America I continued the work begun in Russia, where we had held joint Czech and Polish meetings and I had maintained lively intercourse with the Polish leaders, especially with Grabski. Paderewski and Dmowski were in the United States; and among the American Poles I remembered the writer Czarnecki. Paderewski I had not seen personally before, though I had met Dmowski in England.

On September 15, 1918, we organized a gathering of the oppressed peoples of Austria-Hungary after the model of the Rome Congress. Paderewski represented the Poles, Dr. Hinkovitch the Southern Slavs, and Stoica the Roumanians. It was an immense gathering. The Carnegie Hall was crowded, not only with Slavs and Roumanians but also with Americans. Paderewski was well known in the United States, and, doubtless, many who had heard him as a pianist came also to hear him make a political speech. I had prepared a terse statement of our national and political program; but Paderewski, to whom I gave precedence, put me out of my intended stride. Of the Polish national program he said little, but of me much. He gave a sketch of my life and praised me to the skies. This surprised me the more because Paderewski was a Conservative by conviction and I should therefore have expected him to treat me with some reserve. He had nearly finished before I could think how to answer him. At the last moment, however, I decided that, like him, I would say little of my program but would speak for Paderewski by explaining the relationship of politics to art. Incidentally I wished also to defend him against those of his fellow-countrymen who opposed his political leadership because he could "only play the piano." Polish literature, particularly the writings of Mickiewicz and Krasiński, helped me to illustrate the bearing of poetry upon politics, and to reveal the artist Paderewski as a true political awakener of his people. Though non-political or, at least, not directly political, my speech made a considerable impression, as newspaper comment showed and as American politicians and journalists told me after the meeting. They had been curious to see how I should answer Paderewski and were greatly pleased. The incident helped to show that the most effective propaganda is not to be always harping upon one's own program, but to arouse and hold public interest. This, at any rate, was my main method, especially in society and in private talk.

With the Poles, and notably with Dmowski, we frequently discussed in detail the post-war relationship of our peoples. Dmowski himself favored the closest relations and often advocated federation. We considered, too, the question of Silesia, for the incorporation of Polish Silesia in Poland was claimed even then in Polish circles, and Dmowski spoke of it, albeit with moderation. I proposed that, as a first step, we should agree upon the text of a Czech-Polish agreement or declaration which would help us to prove to the Allies and, above all, to the Americans, that we were friends, and would permit us at the same time to cope with extremists on both sides. I suggested to Dmowski that he himself should draft the declaration, while I drew up economic stipulations such as the railway through Teschen and a sufficient supply of coal. I pointed out that, against us, the Poles ought not to insist upon a purely racial and linguistic policy, seeing that they laid so much emphasis upon their historical, over and above their ethnographical, claims. In this overlapping of claims I descried a certain danger for the Poles. Both of us saw that, between us, the matter in dispute was comparatively insignificant, and that we must settle it without ill-feeling. But Dmowski did not draft the declaration I had suggested. Dissensions were caused by individuals among our own people, as well as among the Poles, and I had often to take action to prevent public controversy. The Poles complained of oppression in Austrian Silesia and cited the poet Bezruč in proof of it, while our people taxed the Poles with pro-Austrian and pro-German tendencies; and I stopped in the nick of time the publication of an attack upon Brückner, the Slavonic scholar of Berlin University who had shown pro-German leanings.

In Allied circles some degree of nervous irritation against the Poles was noticeable from time to time, and I was more than once obliged to give explanations of Polish policy. The Poles were accused of working with Germany as well as with Austria. From October 14, 1917, onwards, Germany and Austria had set up a Regency Council in Russian Poland. Between the two "liberators" this Regency Council was, one must admit, in a very tight place, for each "liberator" had its own Polish policy and, among the Poles, there were alleged to be pro-Austrian and pro-German tendencies. Austria and Germany had, indeed, one and the same purpose—to use Poland for their own ends. What those ends were can be seen from the fact that the protracted disputes which arose out of the occupation of Poland in 1915 were only settled on August 12, 1916, by an agreement that Poland should belong neither to Austria nor to Germany. But, being stronger than Austria, Germany secured the supreme control of Poland and the command of the Polish army. The Warsaw Government, or Regency Council, recognized this Austro-German agreement more or less officially; and thus a third tendency arose —that of the Regency, which sought to obtain compensation for Galicia and Poznania at the expense of Russia. This tendency derived strength from the anti-Russian feeling of the Poles. At the end of April 1918, the Regency submitted a more definite scheme to Austria and Germany. It was discussed long and fruitlessly because neither Germany nor Austria would say the final word. Thus it came about that, toward the end of September 1918, representatives of the Warsaw Regency visited the Emperor William at Spa and then went to Vienna. Of these, as of the earlier negotiations, I soon heard details; and, at the moment, the important thing was that Warsaw had taken up a position hostile to the Allies—a hostility expressed, moreover, in Polish disagreement with the Allied policy of intervention in Russia. The strengthening of Russia would have impeded the Warsaw policy of compensation which aimed at securing possession of Lithuania, White Russia and parts of the Ukraine.

Though this Warsaw policy was psychologically and historically comprehensible to me, my own view, as expressed in my general program, was that Warsaw had been too hasty in giving up Galicia and Poznania to Austria and to Germany (as early as the summer of 1918 the Austrian Emperor had thought he would lose Galicia) and I descried a danger for Poland in the acquisition of so much Russian territory. These circumstances led to constant discussion of the Polish question with Allied politicians and statesmen, for the representatives of Russia repeatedly raised it. We had relations, too, with the Little Russians of the Ukraine, Hungary and Galicia, including Sitchinsky who, some years earlier, had shot Count Andrew Potocki, the Lord-Lieutenant of Galicia. Sitchinsky lived in America and was an unexpectedly pleasant and sensible man. The Poles in America treated him very decently, albeit with comprehensible reserve; and I had to be extremely careful not to annoy them by my intercourse with him and the Little Russians.

Cordial, though less frequent, was our intercourse with the Russians. Since the Bolshevist Revolution, the position of M. Bakhmetieff, the Russian Ambassador, had been peculiar. The American Government recognized him, though not unreservedly, possibly because not a few influential American journalists and politicians were, in theory, favorably disposed towards Lenin and the Bolshevists. Their sympathies went out to the adversaries of Tsarism, but they were sympathies nevertheless. The peculiar relationship of the American Government to the Bolshevists was illustrated by the case of Professor Lomonosoff who had been sent to the United States by the Kerensky Government in 1917. After the Bolshevist Revolution he joined

Lenin's party and attempted to open relations with the American Government as an official representative of the Soviets. Towards the middle of June 1919, in a big meeting at New York, he declared himself a Bolshevist and ceased to be a member of the Russian Mission. Thereupon the American Government interned him.

Baron Korff and Prince Lvoff were also among the Russians then living in America. I had met the latter in Petrograd; and shortly before leaving America I discussed with him the necessity of uniting Russians abroad on the basis of, at least, an outline of a common political program. It was really painful to see how incapable of organizing themselves the Russians in foreign countries were. To me this incapacity seemed part and parcel of the general incompetence of the Russian intellectuals.

THE MID-EUROPEAN PEOPLES

Cooperation with the Roumanians, which I had begun in Russia, was continued in America where, however, there were fewer Roumanian representatives. Dr. Lupu, a Roumanian member of Parliament, came, however, for a time. But I often met the representatives of the Lithuanians, the Letts and the Esthonians. All these peoples had colonies of their own in America, the Lithuanians especially. With them and with the Greeks, Armenians, Albanians and others I had conversations out of which a unifying organization arose—"The Mid-European Democratic Union." I thought originally of founding a society of Americans to work for the small oppressed peoples. But, in this form, it could not be done, and the Mid-European Democratic Union was established instead. Against my wish, it chose me to be its President, an American Professor, Herbert A. Miller of Oberlin, being associated with me. The Union met pretty often to discuss all the ethnographical and political problems of the smaller mid-European peoples. As an instance of our method I may say that I used to bring the Poles and the

Lithuanians or the Greeks and the Albanians, together so that they might clear up their ideas beforehand and avoid serious disputes in the plenary sittings of the Union. The Italian Irredentists attended our meetings assiduously. One of my objects was to make the Union an agency for working out a plan for the Peace on lines which I had laid down in "The New Europe." So well did the Union consolidate itself that President Wilson received a deputation of which I was the spokesman. It was a happy thought—whose, I forget—that a public conference should have been arranged at Philadelphia where the various peoples put forward their programs. On October 23, 1918, the conclusions of the Conference were signed in the memorable Independence Hall; and then, in the courtyard, I read out a joint declaration while the Bell of Independence was rung in accordance with historical precedent. The proceedings were thoroughly "American," but they were sincerely meant and were successful.

The Union was an excellent means of propaganda, with the practical object of giving the public and the press information upon some or all of the peoples belonging to it. Eleven of them were represented at Philadelphia. Our object was also to put before the Americans a concrete idea of the zone of small nations in Central Europe upon the importance of which in the war and, indeed, in European history, I constantly insisted. By getting to know and informing each other reciprocally the representatives of the various peoples were to prepare themselves for the Peace Conference and, if possible, to enter it with a concerted plan. This was the ideal. In reality, there were not a few antagonisms and disagreements as when, for instance, the Poles seceded from the Union, alleging that they could not sit side by side with the Little Russians after the latter had taken action against them in Eastern Galicia, though some of the Poles assured us that this was not the real reason. Despite dissensions, the representatives of the other peoples stayed in the Union. For a time it was feared that the State Department might turn against Professor Miller, some of whose utterances had given offense. But I averted this danger and, even after my departure, the Union worked on for some time.

As I had always reckoned with the dismemberment of Austria-Hungary, I had not forgotten the Ruthene, or Little Russian territory in Hungary and what its fate might be when Hungary should collapse. The importance of this region is obvious on account of its proximity to the other Little Russian lands and to territories inhabited by Roumanians, Magyars and Czechoslovaks. Slovak writers, in particular, had long paid keen attention to the Little Russian part of Slovakia. As long as Russia was victorious it was a question whether she would not lay claim to Hungarian Ruthenia, especially as Eastern Galicia had been immediately occupied by Russian forces. At that time, however, Russia had no definite ideas on the subject since she thought that the Magyars might turn against Austria—a singular pro-Magyarism to which I have already referred. The Allies, on the other hand, did not wish the Russians to extend south of the Carpathians. (On this point Dr. Beneš will have something interesting to say when he describes the negotiations at the Peace Conference.) But, after the defeat of Russia, there arose the possibility that sub-Carpathian Ruthenia might wish to join our Republic. At first this was little more than a pious aspiration. In Russia and particularly in the Ukraine I had, however, been obliged to take account of it since the Ukrainian leaders had discussed with me the future of all the Little Russian regions outside Russia, and had raised no objection to the incorporation of sub-Carpathian Ruthenia in our State.

In America the Little Russian emigrants from sub-Carpathian Ruthenia are numerous; and, as they were acquainted with the Slovaks and the Czechs, I was soon in touch with them. They joined the Mid-European Union and were represented in it by Dr. Žatkovič, but it was Dr. Pačuta who first approached me on their behalf. He belonged to the pro-Russian school which was, to some extent, Orthodox. Dr. Žatkovič, on the other hand, spoke for the great majority of the Ruthenes who were devout, ecclesiastically organized Uniates, that is to say, Roman Catholics with an Orthodox rite. Politically, few of them had any definite views. Their intellectuals had received a Magyar education; and, even among those who recognized themselves as Ruthene, or Little Russian, few could speak the language. Each spoke his own local dialect, and even the better educated of them found difficulty in expressing themselves grammatically, for they had no schools under the Magyar Government. They called themselves "Hungarian Ruthenes" or, in English, "Uhro-Russins" referred to their Church as the "Russin-Greek Catholic Church" and to their country as "Rusinia," whereas Pačuta's pro-Russian followers were known as "Carpatho-Russians." The Ruthene Uniates, as Catholics, repudiated the Great Russian and Orthodox ideas, as well as those of the Ukrainians which they likewise regarded as Orthodox; and they were also opposed to the Little Russians of Galicia. Linguistically, as I have said, and as their newspapers showed, they were in the earliest stage of forming a written language, adhering to their dialect or, rather, dialects of which the spelling, unlike that of the Ukrainians, was more historical than phonetic.

In the debates of the Mid-European Union the Hungarian Ruthenes learned something of the political situation and of their eventual relationships to neighboring peoples. They came into contact with Poles, Ukrainians, and Roumanians; and the Magyars, of whom they naturally knew more, kept up a lively agitation among them. Finally they themselves decided to join Czechoslovakia. They discussed their political future, albeit hypothetically, for the first time at a Congress they held at Homestead, on July 23, 1918. If complete independence should not be practicable, the idea then was that the Ruthenes of Hungary should join their brethern in Galicia and the Bukovina; should this be impossible they would demand autonomy, though under what State they did not say. But, five months later, on December 19th, they held a second Congress at Scranton, Pennsylvania, where they resolved to join the Czechoslovak Republic on a

federal basis, as a State enjoying a wide measure of self-government; and the wording of their resolution shows that it was
framed on an English model which had little in common with the
conditions prevailing in Austria and Hungary. It demanded
also that all the "originally" Ruthene or Carpatho-Russian
regions of Hungary should be included in the Ruthene State.
The various Ruthene organizations then took a referendum by
parishes, with the result that a big majority voted in favor of
joining Czechoslovakia. Dr. Žatkovič sent me memoranda on
the subject; and I, for my part, drew his attention both to
the main problems—economic, education and financial—which
the liberation of the country would raise, and to the lack of
officials, teachers and even priests able to speak its tongue.
I explained to him very thoroughly the political importance of
the Rutheneneland and the difficulties which might arise from
the vicinity of Poland, of the Galician and Roumanian Ukrainians and of the Magyars. But he and other leading Ruthenes
were convinced that, all things well considered, it would be best
for them to join our State. How the question of Carpathian
Ruthenia was dealt with in Paris, and how the Ruthenes themselves acted at home, are matters that come within the period
of the Peace Conference. I need only say that three national
Councils were set up—at Prešov, Užhorod and Hust—which
amalgamated after a time and proclaimed the final decision to
join the Czechoslovak Republic on May 8, 1919, as "Sub-Carpathian Russia."

As regards the language question, I approved of introducing
Little Russian into the schools and public offices; for even if
Little Russian be regarded merely as a Russian dialect, I think it
right, for pedagogical reasons, that it should be used. In this
I adopted the view of the Great Russians themselves, as
expressed by the Petrograd Academy of Science and by
eminent Russian authorities on education. True, I insisted
that the Little Russian language must first be developed by
popular writers on the basis of the local dialects, for I feared
the growth of a jargon, or of an artificial amalgam of words

bureaucratically put together. Nor did I see why the pro-Russian minority which professed Great Russian ideas should suffer educational disabilities. We have something similar among our own people—analogous not identical—in the use of Slovak as a written language.

MR. VOSKA

Before describing the closing stages of my work in the United States I must complete the account of our propaganda which had been organized there, from 1914 onwards, with the help of Mr. Voska. I have often mentioned it and have explained how, through him, I got into touch with the Allies at the beginning of the war. Toward the middle of September 1914 Voska went from Prague to London and thence back to New York, where he reported to my American friends, to Mr. Charles Crane particularly. He unified the action of the Czech press in America and helped to combine into one unit—the "Czech National Alliance"—the organizations which had been created in the various cities of the United States on the outbreak of war. At the same time he established relations with the American press and, soon afterwards, with the American Government itself. He built up a complete Intelligence Service. At an early stage, some of his acquainances and friends managed to ascertain that the Embassies, Consulates and agents of the Central Powers were carrying on espionage and Secret Service work in America against the Allies; and, with the aid of Allied officials, Voska took counter-measures. Mr. Steed had recommended him to the correspondent of "The Times," who, in his turn, recommended him to Captain Gaunt, the naval attaché to the British Embassy in Washington. Among the Czechs who helped him freely was Mr. Kopecký, an official of the Austro-Hungarian Consulate at New York and afterwards our first Consul in the United States.

German propaganda in America was conducted especially by Dr. Albert, the commercial attaché, who therefore came under our nouce. How his portfolio was taken from him on the New York Elevated Railway is an amusing story that was told at the time. In various factories, and in munition works particularly, the Germans were organizing strikes; and plots were being hatched against the vessels which were carrying food, arms and ammunition to the Allies. Upon these vessels outbreaks of fire were to be caused by incendiary bombs and other means. German and Austrian officers, who had been prisoners of war in Russia, were passing through the United States on their way back to Germany, furnished with passports bought from Russian officers in the prisoners' camps. There was a German-Irish plot against England and a secret understanding between Mexico and the Central Powers. All these things Voska's organization discovered, and it identified the German agent who was arranging to place orders in the United States ostensibly for Sweden and Holland but really for the Germany army. Thus the Allies were enabled to confiscate whole cargoes of contraband. Voska himself found means to secure the withdrawal of the American regulation that forbade British merchantmen, armed against German submarines, to enter New York harbor. His Intelligence Service brought about the arrest of the American journalist Archibald who was carrying papers for the Germans; unmasked the enemy plans to poison the horses that were being bought in America for the Allies; traced the organization of a German plot in India; revealed the identity of the agents in France who, in the interest of Germany, were striving to bring about a premature peace, and ascertained what sums were being paid for the purpose by the German Embassy in Washington. One of these agents was Bolo Pasha, who was arrested in France on October 1, 1917, and shot on February 5, 1918. Voska's organization also arranged for the capture of the forger Trebitsch-Lincoln, and obtained evidence that the Austro-Hungarian Ambassador, Dr. Dumba, was organizing a strike in American factories. In consequence, Dumba had to be recalled on September 29, 1915. Voska ascertained further that the German military attaché, von Papen, was intriguing not only in Canada but in the United States and in Mexico. Von Papen was therefore expelled from America. To these intrigues, particularly to those in Mexico, President Wilson referred in his Declaration of War upon Germany.

All this was done as early as 1915. How great was the political credit it gained for us in England and France as well as in America is proved by the fact that, at the end of 1915, Voska was authorized to issue Czechoslovak passports to which the Serbian, Russian and British authorities gave visas. A letter, dated September 15, 1918, which I received from the British naval attaché in America, attests the value which British official and military circles set upon his work; and it is with much gratification that I record the fact that in this Secret Service, comprising at least 80 persons, there was not a single traitor. Indeed, the same can be said of our whole work abroad.

In 1916 our Secret Service established relations with the Russian Secret Service, and thus got wind of many a German intrigue in Russia. Voska's reports repeatedly drew attention to the Germanophil proclivities of the Russian Prime Minister, Stürmer. Not only was Voska's work voluntary but he himself paid for the cost of his Secret Service. When, however, he informed me, in the autumn of 1916, that his means were exhausted, I thought it just that the expense should be borne by the Allies because the service was carried on in their interest and mainly in that of England. Accordingly, I arranged for the expenses to be paid in London and for the financing of our Secret Service to be put down officially to the account of the British Secret Service.

When the United States entered the war in 1917 the American Government perfected its own Secret Service and lightened Voska's task. In agreement with the French and British authorities he went then to Russia in order to organize a new service which was to supply information to Washington. He was recommended to all the American authorities in Russia whose help was thus secured for our propaganda there. One interesting detail was our discovery that a certain lady was in the service of Germany and was acting as intermediary for the supply of German funds to a number of Bolshevist leaders. These funds were sent through the German Embassy at Stockholm to Haparanda, where they were given to her. Kerensky, whose attention was drawn to her, had her arrested; but she was set free on the plea that she was supporting the Bolshevists from her own resources. This plea availed her only because Voska quashed official inquiries when it was found that a prominent American citizen was involved in the affair, for it was not in our interest to compromise America. This was not an isolated instance. Among American citizens and authorities in Europe there were several people of foreign origin who favored the enemy.

Voska concluded his work in Russia at the beginning of September 1917. Later on, he went to Europe and conducted a Secret Service on behalf of the Allied Countries. He was, besides, liaison officer between the American army and ours, and, in this capacity, secured for our army, especially in Italy, support from the American Red Cross and its auxiliary organizations in organizing our own Medical Corps. After the Armistice he was attached to the American Delegation in Paris which sent him, with Mr. Creel, to report upon Central Europe. By that time I was already President of the Republic and agreed that Prague should be the center of this service.

As I have said, our Secret Service in America contributed largely to win for our cause, at an early stage, effective sympathies in official and, precisely, in the most authoritative quarters. Voska was in a position to report upon our work in Europe, and upon my plans, both to Colonel House and to the leading members of the American Government, including President Wilson himself.

THE BREAKING UP OF AUSTRIA-HUNGARY

In America, as elsewhere, it was hard to convince people that it would be necessary to break up Austria-Hungary. Unlike Berlin, Vienna was not an object of immediate political enmity. As the French, the British and the Americans were fighting only against the Germans, there was not in the West the same direct hostility towards Austria as towards Germany. The Austrian front ran against Russia and Italy, yet even in those countries there were influential pro-Austrians. Austria was generally looked upon as a counterpoise to Germany, as a necessary organization of small peoples and odds and ends of peoples, and as a safeguard against "Balkanization." Palacký's original saying that if Austria had not existed she would have had to be invented, represented a view widespread among the Allies. The Allied Governments were influenced also by Austrian and Hungarian diplomatists; and in the Allied diplomatic services there were not a few pro-Austrians who had served in Vienna, some of them having family connections with the Austrian and particularly with the Magyar aristocracy.

Besides, Austria had borne herself otherwise than Germany from the first. She had only declared war directly upon Serbia, Russia and Belgium, and had let the other States declare war upon her. Not even against Italy had she declared war. In this respect Germany was more definite and downright. True, the Austrian tactics presently proved disadvantageous and caused tension with Germany, as when, in February 1917, the Emperor Charles refused to break off relations with America at the behest of the Emperor William.

Austrian and Hungarian propaganda, vigorous everywhere, could be organized without hindrance in America, since she long remained neutral. Just as the Magyars dominated the Slovaks, Ruthenes and other nationalities in Hungary, the Magyar colonies in America managed to influence, even during the war, the colonies of non-Magyar peoples in the United States. Many leaders of these non-Magyar colonies were under Magyar influence without knowing it. An effective Austrian and Magyar argument was that Austria-Hungary was a victim of Germany, by whom she had been compelled to make war against her will.

Memories of the revolution of 1848 and of the exile of Kossuth in Allied countries also stood the Magyars in good stead, while the Hapsburg Monarchy in general enjoyed the support of Roman Catholic propaganda. In America, as in France and Italy, the Catholics skilfully defended it as the greatest Catholic State. They worked behind a veil and through non-political agencies. Counter-propaganda had to be organized accordingly.

I have already referred to the policy of the Vatican at the beginning of the war; and though the Vatican cautiously modified its standpoint as the war went on, since it did not wish to be tied to the losing side, it supported Austria throughout. The relationship of the Vatican to Germany was less definite and uniform, notwithstanding the importance of the German Catholic minority and the superiority of German Catholic theology and ecclesiastical organization over those of Austria. The Catholic traditions of Austria were old, and the Austrian Catholic dynasty took precedence over the Protestant German dynasty. Gladly as the Vatican accepted the Emperor William's compliments to it and to Catholicism, most Vatican politicians were opposed to Prusso-German hegemony and hoped that, in her own interest, Austria would be a strong bulwark against Germany. In any case, the Papal Secretary of State, Cardinal Gasparri, took this view and in 1918 deprecated the setting up of new States which, he thought, would be too weak too to fend Germany off. He wished Poland alone to be liberated, albeit according to the Austrian plan. To some extent the Central Powers gained the goodwill of the Vatican by promising to support the restoration of a Papal State that should be independent of Italy; for, from the early days of the war, the Vatican had been unpleasantly conscious that its intercourse with Catholic States and organizations was not untrammened. This question was aggravated when Italy entered the war, above all by the Treaty of London which excluded Papal representatives from the Peace Conference. Thereupon, with the support of Austria and Germany, a scheme was set on foot to secure for the Roman Curia a stretch of territory along the Tiber to the sea, so that Papal diplomatists might not be obliged to pass through Italy. This scheme was zealously ventilated in the press during 1916 and 1917.

The pro-Austrian views and temper which persisted in official Allied circles up to the spring of 1918 are most clearly revealed by President Wilson's declarations. In his Message to Congress on January 8, 1918, which contained his Fourteen Points, his allusions to Austria-Hungary were still pro-Austrian. His tenth Point ran: "The peoples of Austria-Hungary, whose place among the nations we wish to see safeguarded and assured, should be accorded the freest opportunity of autonomous development"; and President Wilson invoked the British declaration of January 5, 1918, in which the Prime Minister, Mr. Lloyd George, had assured a Trade Union meeting that the destruction of Austria-Hungary was not a British war aim.

In his "Fourteen Points" President Wilson repeated more precisely what he had said on December 4, 1917, when explaining to Congress the significance of the American Declaration of War upon Austria-Hungary. Even then, in declaring war, the burden of his indictment was against Germany. Of Austria he said that her peoples, like those of the Balkans and of Turkey, must be freed from the shameless alien rule, the military and commercial autocracy of Prussia. He added: "We owe it to ourselves to declare that we do not wish to weaken or to transform the Austro-Hungarian Monarchy. How it may wish to live politically or industrially is not our concern. We neither intend nor desire to dictate to it in anything. We wish only that the affairs of its peoples, in great things and small, may remain in their own hands."

This speech expressed the view that Austria should be freed from Prussian overlordship—a view which Professor Herron, one of Wilson's confidential advisers, used to expound in Switzerland. As late as the autumn of 1918, Herron told an Austrian emissary, Dr. Lammasch, that America opposed Austria solely because Austria stood by Germany, but felt no hostility whatever against Austria herself. President Wilson's view of the Austrian relationship to Germany is the only explanation of the significant fact that the United States did not declare war upon Austria-Hungary until December 4, 1917—seven months after the declaration of war upon Germany. But the statement in the book of Prince Sixtus of Parma, that it was my continual pressure which induced President Wilson to declare war on Austria-Hungary, requires correction. It is true that, through mutual acquaintances, I recommended President Wilson to take this step as the logical consequence of the war with Germany, but I doubt whether, at that moment, my recommendation can have sufficed. As far as my own information goes, Italy urged the United States to declare war on Austria after the Caporetto disaster, in order to strengthen the position of the Italian Government at home. The request was forwarded to President Wilson by Mr. Sharp, the American Ambassador in Paris.

In England, too, there was much friendliness towards Austria. Though Lord Palmerston had uttered his famous and very trenchant opinion of the Austrians in 1849 when he called them "brutes"; though Gladstone had declared in 1880 that nowhere in the world had Austria ever done good, while Lloyd George had called her a "ramshackle Empire" in the autumn of 1914, many influential Englishmen felt sympathy with Austria, or with Vienna and Budapest, or were of opinion that, good-for-nothing as she might be, Austria was still better than a lot of small peoples, since she prevented both the expansion of Germany and the "Balkanization" of Europe. How deeply rooted was this pro-Austrianism can best be seen from the fact that though the Italian Foreign Minister, Sonnino, demanded portions of Austria for Italy, he worked for the preservation of Austria-Hungary itself. This was at once an effect of the political Conservatism that feared the "Balkanization" of Central Europe, and, in Sonnino's special case, the consequence of a policy antagonistic to the unification of the Southern Slavs.

Finally, Austria found defenders in the Socialists, the Marxists particularly. They, too, deprecated "Balkanization" and therefore thought Austria worth preserving, despite her backwardness. Besides, the German Marxists agreed with German policy in regard to Austria, although the founders of German Socialism, Lassalle and Marx, had roundly condemned her. Lassalle looked upon Austria as an embodiment of the principle of reaction, and as a consistent enemy of aspirations to freedom. In the interests of democracy, he said, Austria "must be torn to pieces, broken up, destroyed, pulverized, and her dust be scattered to the four winds." And though Marx looked upon Russia as the home of reaction, he too denounced Austria.

It was this pro-Austrian atmosphere that the Emperor Charles—with the help of his brother-in-law, Prince Sixtus of Parma who, like his brother, was serving in the Belgian army—opened the peace negotiations with the Allies to which I have already referred. Overtures were begun at the end of January 1917—though initial steps had been taken a month earlier—by the mother of Prince Sixtus, whom the Emperor Charles had sent to Switzerland, and they were afterwards continued by other persons in the Emperor's confidence. Prince Sixtus himself went to see the Emperor at Vienna; and, in a letter dated March 24, 1917, which was intended for President Poincaré, the Emperor Charles promised to do all in his power to persuade Germany to give up Alsace-Lorraine. For himself he demanded that the Hapsburg Monarchy should be preserved within its existing frontiers. After the negotiations, Prince Sixtus saw President Poincaré five times in the course of 1917. M. Briand approved of the scheme, as did Mr. Lloyd George whom Prince Sixtus saw more than once. The Prince was received also by the King of England.

I need hardly go into details. Disputes and differences arose between the Emperor Charles and the Austro-Hungarian Foreign Minister, Count Czernin, whose references to France at the

Vienna Town Hall were anything but straightforward. He alleged that, before the new German offensive began, Clemenceau had sent a negotiator to him; whereupon Clemenceau answered "Count Czernin has lied." The Austro-Hungarian Government went on lying and, finally, the Emperor Charles sought to defend himself by lying repeatedly to the German Emperor and by attacking Clemenceau—until the publication of a photographic facsimile of the Austrian Emperor's letter put an end to the lying. Clemenceau drastically disposed of him and of Czernin in an exclamation which pertinently described the Austria of the Hapsburgs—"putrid consciences!" Mainly through the writings of M. Ribot and of a person in the confidence of Prince Sixtus these things are now sufficiently cleared up, and the mendacity and infinite clumsiness of the Hapsburgs adequately exposed. The significance of Prince Sixtus's negotiations lay in the circumstance that the most influential persons on both sides were directly concerned in them. The Emperor of Austria himself wrote to the President of the French Republic; and Briand, Lloyd George and the King of England took part in them, as well as the French General Staff. Had the Revolution not broken out in Russia, Prince Sixtus would have negotiated also with the Tsar at the wish of the Emperor Charles.

The Viennese overtures began, so to speak, concentrically from several points. At first Count Czernin approached the Entente, ostensibly on his own initiative, through his friend Count Revertera, a former Austro-Hungarian Counsellor of Embassy, and other acquaintances. Revertera met Count Armand, the Chief of the French Intelligence Service, at Freiburg in Switzerland, the negotiations lasting from July 1917 until February 1918. Mr. Lloyd George was informed and approved of the suggested policy. In the spring of 1918 Dr. Beneš was in touch with Count Armand who, at that time, hoped for a revolution in Austria-Hungary and perhaps worked for it in the expectation that it would increase Austrian readiness for peace. The French General Staff, and even Marshal

Foch, knew and approved of Count Armand's negotiations. On the French side they had been authorized by Painlevé and Clemenceau. Meanwhile, conversations between Austria and the Allies were also carried on by the former Austro-Hungarian Ambassador in London, Count Mensdorff, and General Smuts, who discussed peace in September and December 1918 and, according to some accounts, as late as January 1918. Dr. Seton-Watson suspects that Mensdorff's proposals were communicated to the Allied Governments, and that Lloyd George's pro-Austrian declaration, which President Wilson cited in January 1918 was prompted by them.

Before I left London for Russia in May 1917 I had heard of the negotiations begun by Prince Sixtus. They had been talked about in Berlin, whence some account of them had reached England. I did not hear nor did I need to hear the full story; it was enough for me to know that Austria was already in direct touch with the Allies. I could guess what Vienna wanted and was probably proposing. The details I learned later.

My own view of the overtures was that, from the outset, the Allies had thought it feasible to detach Austria from Germany. They would have been prepared to make peace with Austria but would have gone on fighting Germany until she was completely beaten. To this conclusion I was led in the winter of 1914 by reports from London, and it was confirmed everywhere by Allied official views about Austria. Austrian propaganda worked in the same sense, letting it be understood that Austria was acting under German compulsion and was at heart opposed to Germany. The Emperor Charles himself said this in so many words; and, after Francis Joseph's death, the circumstance that Charles had not been responsible for the war strengthened his position in France and England. His continual protestations of readiness to make peace gained him Allied sympathies.

German military successes, Russian defeats and, subsequently, the Russian Revolution accentuated the idea of dividing Austria-Hungary from Germany. In 1916 we noticed suddenly that our Russian friend and fellow-worker, Svatkovsky, was harboring conciliatory views about Austria to a disquieting degree; and, under the influence of the Stürmer régime, he advocated outspokenly an agreement with Austria and, if necessary, even with Germany. Not a few influential French journalists who had previously supported us against Austria thought likewise. Hence I concluded that his view was shared in official circles and I kept my eyes open. The fact that the French Ambassador in Petrograd, M. Paléologue, submitted to Sazonof on January 1, 1915, a detailed scheme (to which I have already referred) shows that the idea of turning Germany against Austria had been fairly widespread in France from the first. In fairness to Paléologue it must be added that he described the scheme as personal, not official. Therefore I treat it only as a symptom. In addition to the old French liking for Austria, and particularly for Vienna, the military tendency came into play—to weaken and vanquish the Germans militarily by means of a separate peace with Austria. The unfavorable military situation of the Allies also played a part. It explains why Briand, who, in February 1916, had accepted our program which culminated in the destruction of Austria-Hungary, gave ear a year later to the proposals of Prince Sixtus. Nor was Briand alone. A number of important men, such as MM. de Freycinet, Jules and Paul Cambon and William Martin, Chief of the Ceremonial Department of the French Presidency, were of the same mind as Briand and Prince Sixtus, that is to say, the Emperor Charles. The standpoint of the French General Staff and of Foch seems to confirm my view; for, after the failure of General Nivelle's offensive in the spring of 1917, the General Staff took up the idea seriously. What Clemenceau thought I do not know. When I first came into touch with official Paris, I heard he was unfavorable to us. In America I was told that he had wished to negotiate with Austria in the spring of 1918 and had opened communications with her, apparently through a well-known journalist, but that he had been frightened by Viennese clumsiness. However this may have been, it was precisely from Clemenceau that we received notable help.

Our people were often put out by these pro-Austrian tendencies. But is it not true that we ourselves had long given countenance to the very policy which the French and the other pro-Austrians now recommended? Who was it, beginning with Palacký's original view that if Austria did not exist she would have to be invented, who proclaimed pro-Austrianism among us and the doctrine that Austria was a bulwark against Germany? And, up to the year 1917, what was the bearing of official Prague? Like us, the French had to unlearn and to change their outlook; and some of them changed it thoroughly—Chéradame, for instance, with whom we were in touch. Before the war he had urged the preservation of Austria against Germany. During the war, he recognized that Austria could no longer withstand the German Empire. The negotiations opened by the Emperor Charles were foredoomed to failure, and the fact that they took place as they did is merely an instructive sign of the extent to which official quarters on both sides were groping in the dark. After all, the Allies had bound themselves by the Treaty of London to get for Italy considerable territorial concessions at the cost of Austria. They had done the same with Roumania in regard to Transylvania; and they had promised Serbia, as a minimum, Bosnia-Herzegovina and free access to the sea. How much of Austria-Hungary would then have been left? True, Austria—the Emperor Charles in particular—was prepared to make over the whole of Galicia to the projected Polish Kingdom under German control; and it is a further sign of official bewilderment that the French General Staff should have supported a scheme to give Prussian Silesia or Bavaria to Austria by way of compensation.

To the concrete difficulties arising out of the earlier engagements I attributed the caution with which the French Prime Minister, M. Ribot, approached the Austrian proposals. He declined to negotiate without Italy. Though the Emperor Charles and his representatives affirmed that the Italian Commander-in-Chief, General Cadorna, and the King of Italy had offered Austria peace about the time when Prince Sixtus became active, I doubt the truth of these statements in this form. Some Austrian negotiators sought to add weight to their offers by asserting that, on behalf of post-Tsarist Russia, Prince Lvoff had approached Austria, but their statements no longer impressed France and England. In Paris it was reported, on the other hand, that Count Czernin had offered peace to Russia; and while I was in Russia I learned, in August 1917, that a Dutch correspondent had brought the Russian Foreign Minister, Tereshtchenko, a confidential message to the effect that Austria was prepared to make a separate paece. As far as my information goes, Tereshtchenko did not reject this overture. At that time, however, the Russian Government had neither the strength nor the courage to follow it up.

How chaotic were the Allies negotiations with the Emperor Charles may be judged by the following facts. In mid-December 1917, when Austria was negotiating with the Allies through Count Revertera, Count Mensdorff and Prince Sixtus, the French Government recognized our National Council as the Head of the Czechoslovak army established in France; and the decree authorizing the establishment of our army was promulgated on January 7, 1918, a day before the announcement of President Wilson's "Fourteen Points" and two days after Lloyd George's pro-Austrian speech. Nor should it be forgotten that, twelve months earlier, the Allies had, at the instance of the French Prime Minister, M. Briand, demanded our liberation in their reply to President Wilson.

On the other hand it was no surprise to me that Austria and the Emperor Charles should have behaved as they did. By 1917 Austria was already aware of her own weakness. Therefore she put forward her hollow anti-German proposals. As early as April 1917 Count Czernin drew up—at the command of the Emperor Charles after his meeting with the Emperor William at Homburg—the famous report for the Emperor William and the German High Command on the position of Austria.

Of this report the Allies soon got wind and it naturally diminished the effect of the Austrian peace overtures. But after Clemenceau had dealt so vigorously with Czernin, Germany and the Emperor William let it be known that the Emperor Charles had gone to Canossa. Ludendorff—a somewhat untrustworthy authority as regards facts and their critical interpretation— asserts that the Austrian Emperor acted with the knowledge of Germany. Certainly, at the time when Prince Sixtus was negotiating, Bethmann-Hollweg, the German Chancellor, was not unwilling to cede at least a part of Alsace-Lorraine to France.

For us it was, indeed, important that Clemenceau should have dealt so sharply with Vienna at the beginning of 1918. By revealing what the Emperor Charles and Czernin had done and by convicting the Austrians of double-dealing, he furthered our cause and facilitated the anti-Austrian work which I took in hand as soon as I reached America. There, despite Clemenceau's disclosures, strong pro-Austrian tendencies still prevailed in the official world and among the general public, and they gave us not a little to do. Nevertheless our propaganda went well throughout the United States. The argument that our State had never lost its historical rights and had as good a claim as Hungary to existence was politically effective. On this point we could invoke President Wilson's book, "The State," in our support. Further demonstrations of the electoral privileges of the nobility, of the anti-democratic institutions of Austria-Hungary, and of the fact that the Germans and the Magyars, a minority, oppressed the majority of the Hapsburg peoples, never failed to make a deep impression. Not less telling were the reports of Austrian and Magyar cruelties against our own and other peoples. We took full advantage, too, of the openings given by German and Magyar falsehoods. For instance, a Magyar propagandist declared in a pacifist meeting that the Hungarian Parliament had protested in 1870 against the annexation of Alsace-Lorraine. I caught him out by proving that it was the Bohemian Diet which had protested, while the Hungarian Parliament, under the leadership of Andrássy, had kept Austria-Hungary neutral and had helped Prussia. I showed, too, that the same Andrássy had then gone hand in hand with Bismarck and that the Magyars had, in reality, laid the foundations of the Triple Alliance and of its policy. I was often obliged to use this argument against Magyar propaganda which, like the Austrian, cast all the blame for the war upon Germany. Our demonstrations that Austria-Hungary was very largely responsible for the war were very effective, and our hands were strengthened by the participation of all the other Austro-Hungarian peoples—except the Magyars and the Germans—in our work. We stood up for them, and they for us.

We sought, above all, to impart to the Americans some knowledge of our political history and of our civilizations. They had heard of the Czechs, and of the former Kingdom of Bohemia, but found it hard to understand that the Slovaks were comprised in our race. We had also to convince the Americans that we meant to be free and were fighting for freedom. Again and again we were told that the Czech leaders at home were not in opposition to Austria, and the disavowal which we had received in January 1917 was constantly thrown in our teeth, since it seemed to confirm President Wilson's view. We replied that the disavowal had obviously been extorted by pressure, and pointed to the subsequent declarations at home. Weight was added to this argument in December 1917 when the Germans raised the question of Czech loyalty in the Austrian Parliament. Their action served to prove that our people were really in revolt. Similarly, we were able to utilize on behalf of the Slovaks the manifesto at Liptovsky St. Nicholas on May 1, 1918, although the text which reached us in America was obviously incomplete or had been falsified by the Magyar censorship. To the objection that the Emperor Charles and his Government had made promises to the Austrian peoples, and to us Czechs in particular, our answer was that they were insincere and inspired by weakness. We showed that the Austrian Minister, Seidler, and the Austro-Hungarian Foreign Minister, Count Czernin (the latter at Brest-Litovsk), had stood out against President Wilson's demand for the self-determination of peoples. In the autumn of 1917 the Emperor Charles had thought of being crowned King of Bohemia. The Lord-Lieutenant of Bohemia, Count Coudenhove, had supported the project but the Vienna Government had rejected it. Moreover, Czernin had sent a brusque reply to Wilson's peace terms—a reply with which we dealt very sharply. But all our arguments would have served us little had not our political position been changed for the better by the recognition of our National Council in Allied countries, thanks to the formation of our Legions in three of them. And, in America, we were helped most of all by the way in which the march of our men through Siberia echoed round the world.

THE "ANABASIS"

Of that march, the famous "Anabasis," I need only to say enough to make it comprehensible and to complete my account of our work abroad.

I was in Japan at the time of the fateful incident at Tchelyabinsk. According to the report which reached me, a German prisoner wounded one of our men at Tchelyabinsk on April 14, 1918, and was killed on the spot. The local Bolshevists sided with the German and Magyar prisoners, and in the end our troops took possession of the town. The affair was a consequence of earlier differences that had arisen between the local Soviets, Moscow and our army, which was on its way to Vladivostok by rail. On April 21, Maxa and Čermák, the representatives of the Branch of our National Council in Russia, were arrested at Moscow.

Of these events and their sequel I learned only in America. Towards the end of May our detachments agreed at Tchelyabinsk to march through to Vladivostok as a military force; and on May 25th the fight, the armed warlike "Anabasis," began. The first vague reports of successes against the Bolshevists came at the end of May, particularly the news of the capture of Penza on May 29. Then followed the tidings that other towns on the Volga, like Samara and Kazan, and places in Siberia and on the Trans-Siberian railway had been captured.

The effect in America was astonishing and almost incredible —all at once the Czechs and Czechoslovaks were known to everybody. Interest in our army in Russia and Siberia became general and its advance aroused enthusiasm. As often happens in such cases, the less the knowledge the greater the enthusiasm; but the enthusiasm of the American public was real. Political circles, too, were affected by it. Our control of the railway and our occupation of Vladivostok had the glamour of a fairy-tale, which stood out the more brightly against the dark background of German successes in France. Even sober-minded political and military men ascribed great military importance to our command of the railway. Ludendorff induced the German Government to protest to the Bolshevists, alleging that the march of our men had prevented the German prisoners from returning home to strengthen the German army. And in America the political effect was all the greater because the "Anabasis" was making a similar impression in Europe. Certainly it influenced the political decisions of the American Government. Thanks to the direct cable, news from Siberia reached the United States sooner than Europe, and the echoes in America were louder. By the beginning of August 1918 our Legions were popular in America as they were, somewhat later, in Europe, though the attention of European political and military circles was more closely concentrated on the main theater of war.[1]

---

[1] To show the American view of our Siberian "Anabasis" I may quote a passage from a letter written by the late Mr. F. K. Lane, who was then Home Secretary in President Wilson's Administration: ". . . Isn't this a great world? And its biggest romance is not even the fact that Woodrow Wilson rules it, but the march of the Czechoslovaks across 5,000 miles of Russian Asia —an army on foreign soil, without a Government, without a span of territory, that is recognized as a nation. This, I think, appeals to my imagination as nothing else in the war has done since the days when King Albert of Belgium held out at Liége." ("The Letters of F. K. Lane," 1922, page 293.)

In the name of England Mr. Lloyd George wrote on September 11, 1918:—

To the President of the Czechoslovak National Council, Paris.

On behalf of the British War Cabinet I send you our heartiest congratulations on the striking successes won by the Czechoslovak forces against armies of German and Austrian troops in Siberia. The story of the adventures and

As must happen in any war, it was not long before tidings less favorable came to hand—at first in the form of reports that all was not quite in order among our men. From August onward the towns taken on the Volga had to be evacuated. To have taken them at all was, doubtless, a strategic mistake, for it was hard to hold a front so extended. Then the propaganda of the Bolshevists and of our other political enemies began to make itself felt, and hostile accounts of the moral condition of the army were spread. These impressed me less than the way in which Allied officers, returning from Russia and Siberia, spoke of the decline of our military discipline. Little publicity was given to these stories but, of course, they did us harm, though by far the greater part of public opinion and official circles continued to support us.

After I had sought the help of the American Government for our lads, President Wilson and the American Red Cross took action and a military relief expedition was sent to Siberia. On August 3, 1918, America and Japan agreed that each should send a few thousand men to Vladivostok "to render the Czechoslovaks such assistance and help as might be possible against the armed Austrian and German prisoners of war who are attacking them." From the funds at his personal disposal, President Wilson granted a credit of $7,000,000. The money was entrusted to a special committee—one of its members being a Czechoslovak—which was formed *ad hoc*. Moreover, a number of eminent men, whose names I gratefully record, lent us a hand. Mr. V. C. McCormick spent not a little time in working for our Legions and urged the President to grant the credit. Mr. Vauclain likewise espoused our cause; and, as regards the army in Siberia, both of Mr. Lansing's Under-Secretaries of State,

triumphs of this small army is, indeed, one of the greatest epics of history. It has filled us all with admiration for the courage, persistence and self-control of your countrymen and shows what can be done to triumph over time, distance and lack of material sources by those holding the spirit of freedom in their hearts. Your nation has rendered inestimable service to Russia and to the Allies in their struggle to free the world from despotism; we shall never forget it.

LLOYD GEORGE.

Messrs. Polk and Long, gave us assistance, while Mr. Landfield, a special assistant in the State Department, who was deeply interested in all Russian matters, was devoted to us. General Goethals, the builder of the Panama Canal, who was Chairman of the Buying Department of the American army, and General March, the Chief of General Staff, also lent their aid, as did Colonel Sheldon, whom the General Staff appointed to be liaison officer with our military attaché, Colonel Hurban. Nor should Captain Blankenhorn, one of the first officers with whom I came into touch, be forgotten. This bare list of names suffices to show how the Siberian "Anabasis" had carried our cause into the highest and most authoritative official circles. The American Red Cross intended, indeed, to let us have material and supplies to the value of $12,000,000; but its help, and the relief work as a whole, turned out to be less effective than we expected because the difficulty of communications with Siberia and of shipping supplies from America was so great as to make practical assistance almost impossible. Besides, the American military expedition to Siberia changed its plans and took no part in the fighting against the Bolshevists—out of regard for Japanese susceptibilities and in consequence of other complications. Nor were my efforts to adapt myself to the views of the Allied and Associated Governments and of their military authorities attended by much success; the Governments were not agreed among themselves, and their narrow and inadequate political and military plans were too different from my own view of what the Russian situation demanded.

This situation obliged us to keep up a service of information upon events in Siberia. Thanks to my knowledge of Russia and of our people, and to the reports brought to me by messengers, we were able to inform the Governments, the press and a number of public men. For instance, when false accounts were given of the adventurer Semyenoff and of his relationship to our army, I submitted to the Government and to the President a memorandum (written by Colonel Hurban) that showed him in his true light. Though some of our own people had taken a quite unnecessary interest in him, the course of events proved the accuracy of our memorandum, which the American General Churchill presently confirmed entirely. Thus our authority was again strengthened.

This is not the place fully to examine the question whether we or the Bolshevists were to blame for the fighting in Russia and Siberia. The opinion of the French officer, Captain Sadoul, who afterwards joined the Bolshevists, seems to me to cover the whole matter. As early as February and March 1918 and, later on, when the fighting began, Sadoul saw quite clearly that the Bolshevist Government in Moscow misjudged the position and unjustly attributed reactionary tendencies to our army— an accusation that was neither true nor sincerely made, particularly on the part of Trotsky who, in March 1918, was still looking for Allied help against Germany. Sundry local Soviets, and individuals lacking in political judgment, stupidly made matters worse. To our agreement with the Soviets on March 26, 1918, I have referred. In accordance with it Stalin then ordered the local commissary at Penza—in the name of the Moscow Soviet—to grant our men free passage to Vladivostok; but, two days later, on March 28, our men intercepted telegrams from the Omsk Soviet demanding that our troops be disarmed and transported to Archangel. Ultimately Moscow gave way. Our men had loyally assented to the partial disarmament which Moscow had demanded on the plea that their weapons were Russian property. They understood the difficult position of the Moscow authorities after the peace of Brest-Litovsk which bound Russia not to tolerate the existence of armed anti-German forces on Russian soil. But, at the same time, they felt keenly that Moscow was not keeping faith. It was perfidious on the part of the Bolshevists to propose to the Germans, as they did in June 1918, that the German prisoners should be armed against our troops in Siberia; and it must be said that the Germans were more honorable, for they declined the suggestion. On the other hand, it is true that Moscow was influenced by the treacherous conduct of some Czechs who had joined the Bolshevists. In order to counteract biased reports, I sent Tchitcherin towards the end of June an explanatory telegram in this sense which was published in the American and European press. Our campaign in Siberia was not an anti-Bolshevist undertaking nor was it inspired by any interventionist policy. It was forced upon us by the obligation of self-defense. Equally false is it to ascribe to us any, no matter how unintentional, responsibility for the murder of the Tsar and of his family by the Bolshevists at Ekaterinburg on July 16, 1918. The first official report of the murder issued at Moscow stated, for instance, that the local Soviet had ordered the Tsar to be shot lest he escape or be carried off by the Czechoslovaks. The truth is that our troops entered Ekaterinburg only on July 25 and, what is more to the point, they never had the slightest intention of liberating the Tsar. The unfortunate man had been abandoned by his own reactionaries, who had even thought of having him "removed," by murder if necessary. The Bolshevists did what the Monarchists had thought of doing. History is full of such ironies.

On leaving Russia I had given strict orders that there should be no departure from the principle of non-intervention, but I had expressly dwelt upon the duty of self-defense in case of attack from any quarter, Russian or other. The passage in my proclamation of March 7, 1918, ran: "As long as you are in Russia maintain, as hitherto, strict neutrality in regard to Russian party dissensions. Only those Slavs and those parties who openly side with the enemy are our enemies." In speaking of "Slavs" I had in mind the possibility of complications not only with the Russians but with the Ukrainians and Poles. To this effect I left written instructions with Secretary Klecanda. But from Washington it was impossible to give the army political, let alone military orders. The Branch of our National Council in Russia and the various military units had to decide things for themselves according to circumstances, and I could only trust their judgment and goodwill—a trust not misplaced. Our men themselves felt that they lacked political leadership, as was shown by a telegram—signed by Gaida and Pateidl—asking for a trustworthy political leader. It reached me in Washington towards the middle of June. There was no such leader on the spot, and leadership from Washington was impossible.

I cannot and do not wish to defend all that was done, politically and strategically, in our army after my departure. I perceived that there was some lack of cohesion, political wavering, outbreaks of an adventurous spirit and, often, fits of bewilderment in various units; and I deplored that our command in Siberia should not have recognized forthwith the incapacity of Koltchak and of his pro-German surroundings. But, on the other hand, I must say that the Bolshevists were not straightforward. Our men believed them to be under German and particularly under Austrian and Magyar control, and thought that to fight them was really to fight against Germany and Austria. All reports spoke of the part which German and Magyar prisoners took in the Bolshevist attacks upon us. Moreover, the policy of the Allies in Siberia was anything but clear. For example, the French Commander, Guinet, sought to hold a front on the Volga in the expectation that a mythical Allied army would turn up at Vologda; and our own fellows imagined that the formation of a Czech-Russian front on the Volga would mean a renewal of the war against Germany and Austria.

Yet, on the whole, things turned out well, better than our enemies, better even than our fairer critics pretend. As regards discipline, the prolonged inactivity of our army, its dispersal through Siberia from the Urals to Vladivostok and the general nervousness in Russia must be taken into account; while the military shortcomings of an improvised army are self-evident. Nor should the lack of unity and the indecision of the Allies and afterwards of America in regard to Russia be forgotten. It was, for example, the French Military Mission which recommended our Branch National Council to send our troops to France not only by way of Vladivostok but also from Murmansk and Archangel—a course that would seriously have weakened its cohesion and its strength. Among men who had long borne material privations with good humor, and had suffered morally by separation from their homes and families, some relaxation of discipline was only to be expected. Yet, despite all this and notwithstanding many disappointments, the army was not demoralized. Some of its units passed through severe crises, as is proved by the suicide of Colonel Švec—a tragedy that had a wholesome effect. Nor must the spirit of our army in Siberia be judged solely by its military activity. Alongside of their military duties our men did industrial and economic work. In August 1918 they organized Working Associations and, somewhat later, a Chamber of Commerce, a Savings Bank, a regular bank and a well-developed military postal service. These things—not only the glamour of an heroic "Anabasis"—must be borne in mind when we speak of our army in Russia and Siberia. It was no mere nine days' wonder. And it ought not to be forgotten that in Siberia even the Germans of Bohemia began to join our army. They were formed into labor contingents.

Finally we must remember the remarkably good order in which our men returned home from their journey round the world and, above all, the fact that by their discipline and their behavior at the various stopping-places they made known the name of Czechoslovakia to peoples who had never heard it before. In this regard delightful reports reached me from the American and other Captains of their transports. Without discipline, this could not have been. Then, organizing skill and ability were shown in the whole technique of the transport question. Few people can imagine how fine a technical achievement was this return from the Far East round the greater part of the world. For its triumphant accomplishment in so short a time— the first transport sailed from Vladivostok on December 9, 1919, the General Staff reached Prague on June 17, 1920, and the evacuation was completed on November 30, 1920—we have to thank the friendliness of the Allies who lent us ships, and Dr. Beneš to whom belongs the credit for the successful conduct of the negotiations.

My plan had been to get the army to France in 1918 and to bring it into action there in 1919. It never reached France, but we had an army and it made itself felt. That was the main thing. The "Anabasis" proves that I was right to insist upon having a large army. Small non-military or political units, such as our people in Russia and the Russian Government itself desired, would have been swamped in Russia and would have been dissolved in Bolshevist acid. Historians and politicians may be left to speculate upon what would have happened had we succeeded in getting the army to France on the eve of peace. Much virtue in "if." In any case I should have managed to turn it politically to good account.

A Summary

What I have said hitherto of the formation of our army abroad, and of its political and international significance, may be condensed as follows:—

When the war began, a spontaneous anti-Austrian movement to join the Allied armies arose in all the Czech colonies abroad. Czechs who had been naturalized in belligerent countries were naturally liable to military service; the others joined as volunteers.

At first, France accepted our men only as recruits for the Foreign Legion. This they disliked. They wished either to gain admission to the regular army or to form an independent unit. But the number of Czechs in France was small and, at the outset, negligible. Not until volunteers reached France from Russia and America could a separate Czech division be created. Yet France was the first country to see what our Legions meant and to foster their formation both on her own soil and in Russia. As the French had to deal with a large number of volunteers from Alsace and Lorraine, they showed more enterprise in our case as well.

In Russia conditions were different. Our colonies there were larger and a separate unit was therefore conceivable. Thus arose the "Družina," albeit as part of the Russian army. The idea of forming an independent Czech force only took shape when a considerable proportion of our prisoners of war expressed a wish to join the "Družina."

In Italy there were no Czech colonies, merely a few individuals or groups in some cities. Nothing could be done to form a Czech Legion until the numbers of our prisoners grew. Successful efforts were then made, though somewhat later than elsewhere.

In London our colony was small, but at a very early stage it began to work efficiently for the admission of its members into the British army. With the help of Mr. Steed it was not long before Kopecký got permission for Czechs to enlist.

In America, where our people were most numerous, it was impossible to form a military contingent as long as the United States remained neutral. Therefore many of our people joined the Canadian army and organized themselves as Czech volunteer companies—a difficult matter because the American Government enjoined strict neutrality upon its citizens. After the American declaration of war in April 1917, Štefánik recruited men for our Legion in France, with the assent of the Government, though I hardly expected much from its efforts because thousands of our young fellows went direct into the American army.

Even in December 1914 before leaving Prague I had sought to create the nucleus of an army abroad. Through Mr. Voska, who delivered the message in London, I asked Russia to welcome our prisoners and deserters from the Austrian army. Most of our prisoners were in Russia; and there, with infinite difficulty, we ended by creating a real army; and from Russia we sent a small contingent to France.

The growth of our Legions raised not only the question of the relationship of the Czechoslovak force to the army of the country on whose territory the Legions were formed but the further question of the relation of our troops, and of the troops of other States, to our National Council as the leading political organ of our struggle for freedom. These questions arose in Russia, France, Italy, America and England, since the British and American forces might, at any moment, find themselves alongside of our men on the field of battle in France—as actually happened. In the case of America, the problem was complicated by the circumstance that the Czechoslovak recruits from America, some of them naturalized American citizens, were serving in our ranks. Hence it had to be dealt with internationally in all Allied countries, and even in Japan and China, as early as the winter of 1917. It was only in Soviet Russia that the position became uncertain, since Russia was neutral after the peace of Brest-Litovsk and all international arrangements with her were of doubtful value.

Everywhere the same solution was adopted—Allied Governments assented to the formation of our units on Allied soil, and to the recruiting of volunteers among prisoners of war and non-prisoners alike; and, at the same time, they recognized our National Council as the political organ of our movement and consequently as the Supreme Command of our army. In other words, while forming a part of the Allied forces, our army was autonomous and subject to the authority of the National Council. I was Commander-in-Chief, or "Dictator," as our men in Russia proclaimed me. But I was not the military leader. My relationship to the Legion was like that of a sovereign to his army which is led by its commanders and officers. These commanders were, in point of fact, French, Italian and Russian generals.

This recognition of the National Council as the Supreme Authority entailed recognition of the unity of our army as a whole, that is to say, of all the Legions in the various Allied countries; and, since our army in Russia became part of the French army when the Russians withdrew from the struggle, the French Commander-in-Chief held the High Command, and he appointed General Janin to command all our Legions. As I have said, General Janin had belonged to the French Military Mission in Russia. He had learned Russian, knew Russian military conditions and had seen our men. On behalf of the National Council, he directed, at the beginning of 1918, the recruiting of our men in the French camps to which our prisoners of war had found their way from Serbia through Italy; and, on his way to Siberia to take over his command, he stayed with me in Washington where we agreed upon what our army should do in given circumstances. He discharged his hard task with uprightness and prudence. In practice, it was not possible for him to act fully as the effective commander-in-chief of the whole army, since our Russian Legions were in Siberia, and the contingent which had been sent from Russia to France had been united with the original volunteers from France and America. Moreover, the Legion in Italy, which was much larger than the Legion in France, remained separate except in the case of a small detachment, a battalion, I believe, which was sent to France in order to demonstrate the unity of the army.

Since our army was created somewhat late in the war, the first thing had been to secure recognition for our political program as represented by the National Council. At the beginning the Allied Governments would recognize only the principle of legitimacy—and our movement was revolutionary. Thus, recognition came gradually and by no means easily. It began informally by the personal recognition of me, Dr. Beneš and Štefánik through intercourse or negotiation with us, or by events like the consent of the British Prime Minister, Mr. Asquith, to take the chair at my lecture in London. Things took much the same course in the military sphere. In the early stages of the war difficulties arose from the international legal position. In the eyes of the Allies our prisoners were, internationally speaking, Austrians; and it was long before people in Allied countries could understand the difference between Czechs and Slovaks, on the one hand, and Austrians on the other. Even in Russia— and there most rigidly—this constitutional and international technicality was observed. It led to disagreeable incidents in many countries, for our own people could not understand it; and we felt we had made some headway when the several Allied States began to treat more leniently our prisoners and those of the other non-German and non-Magyar races of Austria-Hungary.

The French Prime Minister, M. Briand, was the first to recognize our national program, expressly and officially, on February 3, 1916. His decision was made known in an official *communiqué*. In pursuance of this recognition the Allies included in their reply to President Wilson's request for a statement of their war aims a demand for the liberation of the Czechs and Slovaks from alien rule. This was in January 1917; and, once again, it was due to M. Briand's good offices. But the year 1917 was rendered dangerous to us by the efforts of the Emperor Charles to save his Empire by means of a separate peace. With them I have already dealt. They failed, and were more than outweighed by the creation of our Legions in Russia, France and Italy and by our military agreements with France from December 1917 onwards. The summer of 1918 brought us final recognition by all the Allied and Associated Powers. The chronological table given in an appendix can, however, convey no idea of the amount of work, thought, anxiety and emotion which the process of recognition caused us, what wanderings through the whole world, what petitions and interviews in the various Ministries of Paris, London, Rome, Petrograd, Washington and Tokio, how many visits to leading personages, how many memoranda, telegrams, letters, lectures and articles, how much help from Allied Ambassadors and from our political friends! But without our propaganda abroad, without our diplomatic work and the blood of our Legions we should not have achieved our independence. How our Legions and the part they took in the common struggle were appreciated may be seen from the official declaration made by Mr. Balfour, the British Foreign Secretary, on August 9, 1918:—

DECLARATION

Since the beginning of the war the Czechoslovak nation has resisted the common enemy by every means in its power. The Czechoslovaks have constituted a considerable army, fighting on three different battlefields and attempting, in Russia and Siberia, to arrest the Germanic invasion.

In consideration of its efforts to achieve independence, Great Britain regards the Czechoslovaks as an Allied nation and recognizes the unity of the three Czechoslovak armies as an Allied and belligerent army waging regular warfare against Austria-Hungary and Germany.

Great Britain also recognizes the right of the Czechoslovak National Council, as the supreme organ of the Czechoslovak national interests, and as the present trustee of the future Czechoslovak Government, to exercise supreme authority over this Allied and belligerent army.

On the basis of this declaration Dr. Beneš negotiated and signed, in the name of the National Council, our first Treaty with Great Britain on September 3, 1918; and, after the end of the war, the President of the French Republic tersely defined the political significance of our Legions in his opening speech to the Paris Peace Conference by saying: "In Siberia, France and Italy, the Czechoslovaks have conquered their right to independence." The fighting strength of our forces in those three countries was approximately——

In Russia	..	..	..	92,000 men
In France	..	..	..	12,000 "
In Italy	..	..	..	24,000 "
	Total	..	..	128,000

If to this number of combatants be added the 54,000 reserves who were organized in Italy after the Armistice, the grand total is 182,000. These figures correspond to the data collected up to February 1923. As far as I can estimate, we actually lost 4,500 men in Russia and Siberia, France and Italy —the price in human life which we paid for the recognition of our independence. These rough figures give, I think, an idea of our military work and its political importance. The size and the quality of the Legions explain why the Allied Governments and armies recognized them and us, and why they looked upon our movement with respect and goodwill. Moreover, the Legions retained and will retain their value at home; for if we reckon the families, relations and friends of the individual legionaries, we find that there are at least a million people directly interested in them. Thus they remain a considerable and significant source of political strength in our State.

THE DECISIVE HOUR

How crucial for us were the end of 1917 and the events of 1918 appears from the foregoing summary. The year 1918 was, indeed, decisive for all the belligerents and for the war itself which, economically and strategically, was won in the course of that summer; the expectation that it would last into 1919 was not fulfilled.

After the Treaty of Brest-Litovsk with Russia and the peace with Roumania in 1918 it was clear that Germany would attempt to use the forces thus released for a decisive blow in the West before America could increase the number of her troops in France. At first, it appears, the Germans assumed that America would be unable to send any troops at all, "verifying" their assumption by experiments in their own waters. When they found out their mistake they tried all the harder to bring about a decision in the spring of 1918. Doubtless they perceived that many prominent generals in France were anxiously awaiting the arrival of American reenforcements; and from England reports reached them of a growing pacifist movement and of the readiness of leading public men to bring the war to an end. In numbers, the German army was quite equal to the Allied forces. Thus the offensive began; and, in order to enhance its effect, Paris was bombarded with long-range guns from March 23 onwards. Though they gained ground and made large numbers of prisoners—reaching a point only 85 kilometers from Paris and making some people (not M. Poincaré) wonder whether the seat of the French Government ought not to be moved—the Germans failed to force a decision.

The Allies, for their part, managed at last to unify their supreme command under Foch, who began a counter-offensive in July. On August 8 the Germans were heavily defeated near Amiens and their final overthrow was assured. Their armies withdrew steadily before the victors. They had opened hostilities on August 4, 1914, in Belgium and France. Four years and four days later, on August 8, 1918, they began to retreat, a beaten host. Despite some talk of treason, the more critical Germans now began to doubt the military capacity of Ludendorff, and to admit that the offensive of 1918 was foredoomed to failure.

From June onwards the successes of the Italian army and the overthrow of the Bulgarians helped to weaken the offensive spirit of the Germans; while, by the autumn (October 24–November 3) Austria was thoroughly worsted and her army demoralized. The Bulgarian disaster had an especially demoralizing effect upon Austria since she had begun the war in the Balkans for the Balkans, and defeat in the Balkans hastened the Allied triumph. Both in Austria and Germany disintegration was apparent in the field and on the "home front"; and both Powers were compelled to sue for an armistice and peace. Yet, untrustworthy as ever, Austria-Hungary made peace proposals to the Allied belligerents on September 14, without the consent of Germany, and asked that Allied delegates, empowered to discuss all questions might be sent to a neutral country. Clemenceau answered the Austro-Hungarian offer in the French Senate on September 19 by saying that no negotiations were possible between right and wrong, while the Foreign Minister, M. Pichon, transmitted Clemenceau's speech to Vienna through the Swiss Minister. President Wilson likewise rejected the offer, declaring that, inasmuch as the United States had frequently expressed its views on peace in the clearest terms, it could accept no proposal for a Conference. Even more negative than the substance of this reply was its form—sixty-six words in all—a cutting and by no means unintentional terseness. Indeed, the German and Austrian press thought the American answer contemptuous.

Bulgaria capitulated finally on September 21 and concluded an armistice with the Allies on September 29, the very day on which the German military command requested the Government to sue for an armistice and peace. The Allied Governments, too, were weary, especially the French; and in England the pacifist movement was growing. Readiness for peace was general. We, for our part, were prepared for peace negotiations and our people at home had realized the situation. The gathering of all the oppressed Austrian peoples at Prague in mid-May 1918, on the occasion of the jubilee festival of our National Theater, had been very effective. Even the Austrian-Italians were present. There was an evident analogy between this gathering, the Rome Congress in April, and the work of the Mid-European Union in America; nor were the Austrian reprisals which followed it a sign of strength. On July 13 our people at Prague set up a new Czechoslovak National Committee, a significant act which was in itself equivalent to a national manifestation, inasmuch as there had been violent opposition to the former National Committee. Though its program was, juridically, somewhat vague it was satisfactory on the whole. The new Committee read aright the signs of the times and took its stand firmly on our claim to independence. Noteworthy, too, was the meeting at Lubljana, the Slovene capital, in August, and its resolution that all Slavs should work together for freedom.

Though I could not quite understand why a Socialist Council should have been set up at the beginning of September alongside of the new National Committee, the declarations of our members of Parliament on September 29, the speech of the Chairman of the Czech Association in Parliament on October 2, and the manifesto of the National Committee on October 19—in which our work abroad was, for the first time, expressly and publicly recognized at home—strengthened my conviction that the days of public pro-Austrianism among our people were past and gone. The question was rather how Austria-Hungary would be liquidated than whether she would be liquidated, for the Austrian-Germans as well as the Magyars had turned against the dynasty. True, it was to be expected that at the last moment Vienna would make—promises. Indeed, I knew that the expediency of granting us national autonomy, in one form or another, was being canvassed there. For this reason we forestalled Vienna by proclaiming our own National Council abroad as a Provisional Government. Beneš and I had often thought of this so as not to be caught napping when the time came. Now the time had come. On September 13 Beneš let me know what the position was in Paris, and proposed that the National Council should be transformed into a Provisional Government; and on September 26 he received my full assent. After negotiations to make sure of recognition by the Allied Governments, Beneš informed them on October 14 that the Provisional Government had been set up with its seat in Paris. I became President, Prime Minister and Finance Minister, Beneš was Secretary for Home and for Foreign Affairs, and Štefánik Secretary for War. Simultaneously, Dr. Osuský was appointed Minister in London, Dr. Sychrava in Paris, Dr. Borský in Rome, Pergler in Washington and Pavlu in Russia. The French Foreign Minister, M. Pichon, recognized the Provisional Government next day and the other Allied Governments soon afterwards. Thus we were independent and free *de facto* and *de jure*. The Emperor Charles's manifesto came too late.

It came too late also in another respect. Though Vienna had continually sought to influence pro-Austrian circles in Allied countries and in Switzerland, Holland and Sweden, and though some French politicians would have been disposed to recompense Austria had she, even at the twelfth hour, turned her back upon Germany decisively, Austria feared Germany and the Austrian Germans. Therefore she hesitated. Consequently the Emperor's manifesto, the Cabinet of Dr. Lammasch, and Count

Andrássy's acceptance of President Wilson's new Austrian program were all belated. "Toujours en retard."

THE LAST HOURS OF AUSTRIA

German and Austrian writers, military as well as political, agree that President Wilson's answer on October 18 to Austria's offer of peace, sealed her fate and settled likewise the question of our freedom. Both personally and as the representative of the United States, Wilson had become a great moral and political figure in Europe. His words carried the greater weight because America had entered the war without territorial ambitions; and the American army was a decisive factor in the Allied forces. As I have said, the German military command requested the German Government on September 29 to offer the Allies an armistice and peace. The German generals had grasped the position and acted promptly in order to forestall a capitulation of their troops. On October 5 the German Government asked President Wilson for an armistice; and following suit, Austria and Turkey sent a similar request on the same day. On October 8 Germany received a preliminary answer in the form of a question as to the real meaning of her proposal which was finally declined on October 14. But it was not until October 18 that President Wilson answered Austria-Hungary who, in her offer, had expressly accepted Wilson's Fourteen Points and his other declarations, particularly his speeches of February 12 and September 27. In the former of these speeches President Wilson had reported to Congress upon the exceptions taken to his Fourteen Points, and to the War Aims Speech of Lloyd George, by the German Chancellor (Count Hertling) and the Austro-Hungarian Foreign Minister (Count Czernin); and had boiled down his program to four principles. On September 27 he had enunciated five principles for the conclusion of peace and as many in regard to the organization of the League of Nations.

People in Vienna believed that Austria-Hungary could gain President Wilson's goodwill by appearing submissive. They had failed to understand his curt rejection of their peace offer in September; and since America left the offer of October 5 so long unanswered, the greatest excitement prevailed in Vienna and in pro-Austrian circles generally. Inquiries into the reason for the delay were even made in Washington through indirect channels. When the answer came at last it was a surprise.

Simultaneously I heard that the Emperor Charles was preparing a manifesto in which he would promise to transform Austria—not Hungary—into a federal State. He was a drowning man clutching at a straw. Nevertheless his idea was dangerous, and it was necessary to forestall the effect which the manifesto might have in quarters that still retained considerable sympathy with Austria. Therefore I issued at that moment the Declaration of Independence which I had long had in mind. Logically, the Declaration was a consequence of the establishment of our Provisional Government which had been notified to the Allies on October 14; and it was cast in a form calculated to remind the Americans of their own Declaration of Independence. It had also a tactical value; for by the time the Emperor Charles's manifesto was published, the colors of the free Czechoslovak State were already flying from the house where I lived as President of our Provisional Government.

In the Declaration of Independence I rejected the Emperor Charles's belated effort to transform Austria into a sham Federation, and outlined the fundamental principles on which the Provisional Government would build our new State. I submitted the first draft of it to a number of friends, among them Judge Brandeis and Mr. Ira Bennett, the Editor of the "Washington Post," whose criticisms of substance and form were reviewed by a small committee which put the finishing legal and formal touches to it. Of this committee Mr. Calffee, the well-known legal authority, was a member. It was a good instance of harmonious cooperation and, at the same time, the first act of State on a grand scale to be accomplished under my leadership.

I handed an advance copy of the Declaration to the Secretary of State, Mr. Lansing, so as to secure the approval of the

American Government and also in order to remind President Wilson of our standpoint on the eve of his reply to Austria-Hungary. This had the desired effect. The Declaration was a great success not only in the press and with public opinion but in Government circles and especially at the White House. President Wilson wrote me that the Declaration had moved him deeply, as we should see from his reply to Austria-Hungary. Indeed, his reply was in harmony with our Declaration of the same date. In it President Wilson stated emphatically that the United States had changed its view of Austria-Hungary and of the relationship between Austria-Hungary and America, a change indicated by the recognition of the Czechoslovak National Council as the *de facto* Government of the Czechoslovak nation. Likewise the United States recognized the national aims of the Yugoslavs. Hence the President could not accept any mere autonomy of these peoples as a basis of peace, as he had thought feasible when formulating his Fourteen Points in January. Not he but these peoples themselves must be judges of the means by which the Austro-Hungarian Government should fulfil their wishes and satisfy their conceptions of their own rights and destinies.

There can be few examples in diplomatic literature of so manly and honorable a retractation of an earlier view; and for this very reason its effect was so great. President Wilson never concealed the fact that his opinions had changed during the war. For example, Colonel House informed the German Ambassador, Count Bernstorff, in January 1917, that the President not only did not agree with the war aims set forth by the Allies but thought them impossible. Yet, four months later, on April 6, he resolved to declare war upon Germany and was led to revise his European policy.

This revision was gradual. Mr. Lansing's declaration on May 29, 1918, merely accepted the resolutions of the Rome Congress of the Oppressed Austro-Hungarian peoples, and assured us and the Southern Slavs of the sympathies of the United States. The declaration had been preceded by a speech of the American Ambassador in Rome, Mr. Page, who referred warmly to us when presenting colors to our Italian Legion in Rome. The late American Ambassador in Paris, Mr. Sharp, also worked in our favor. I had some discussion with Mr. Lansing about his declaration; and my criticism of it, and interviews with other members of the Government, led to the statement (explanatory of his May declaration) which Lansing issued on June 28. The Serbian Minister, I ought to add, also presented a memorandum to Lansing upon the May declaration. In his explanatory statement Lansing insisted that the previous expression of sympathy with us and with the Southern Slavs signified the desire of the United States for complete liberation of all Slavs from Austrian and German rule. This was a great step forward, really our first big success in America, where official circles, notwithstanding their goodwill towards us, were not a little embarrassed by our problem since there was no international precedent to serve as a guide in solving it.

After our recognition as an Allied and belligerent nation by the British Foreign Secretary, Mr. Balfour, on August 9, we had been granted clearer and more definite recognition in America on September 3. Lansing and I agreed upon it; and, in pursuance of our agreement, I handed him on August 31 a lengthy memorandum setting forth the necessity of our being recognized by the Allies. At that time the negotiations for the relief of our army in Siberia were going on, and Lansing drew up his declaration in this sense, taking Mr. Balfour's declaration as a model. The American document recognized that a state of war existed between us and the German and Austrian Empires; it acknowledged our National Council as the *de facto* Czechoslovak Government which was waging regular warfare and had full power to direct the political and military affairs of the Czechoslovak nation. Mr. Lansing kindly showed me the document before it was published. I expressed my gratitude to him and thanked President Wilson in writing for his political high-mindedness, justice and wisdom. Wilson's answer convinced me of the great change and of the improvement in the views of the White House upon Austria-Hungary.

The fourth and decisive act of recognition came on October 18 in the acceptance of our Declaration of Independence. The subsequent course of events in Austria and in Hungary proved to President Wilson and to other American statesmen that my view of Austrian conditions, and my judgment both of the internal collapse of Austria and Hungary and of the whole course of the war, had been accurate; and this proof impressed them. I myself was more than satisfied that events showed me to have been right. Thus the confidence of American statesmen was strengthened not only in me but in our cause, and valuable foundations were laid for the impending peace negotiations.

My Relations with President Wilson

In public discussion of President Wilson's reply to Austria-Hungary the question has often been raised why it was that Wilson departed so quickly from his pro-Austrian standpoint; and all sorts of legends were spread in America about my relations to him. I will therefore state briefly the principal facts.

My personal relations with President Wilson began somewhat late. Though I reached Washington on May 9, 1918, I saw him for the first time on June 19, Mr. Charles Crane having brought me an invitation to meet him. In all my propaganda work abroad, I sought to influence statesmen in the first instance by public declarations, articles and interviews; and before I met the President I saw a number of people whom he was wont to meet and who had a certain influence with him. Discussion with men whose minds have thus been prepared is, naturally, more fruitful and takes less time.

At the beginning of the war President Wilson was made aware of our movement abroad by his Ministers, whom Mr. Voska informed. Unless I am mistaken, Voska also saw the President in person. In 1915 Wilson received a copy of the memorandum—containing a full account of our aims—which I had drawn up for Sir Edward Grey; and when General Štefánik went to America in 1917, he supplied the President and American official quarters with information. Moreover, Wilson heard of our efforts and of our work from me and through Mr. Charles Crane; and I telegraphed to him from Kieff, at the end of January, an exhaustive analysis of his Fourteen Points. It was substantially identical with what I wrote in "The New Europe." In addition, President Wilson received from Tokio in April 1918 the memorandum in which I expressed my views on Russia and on relations with the Bolshevists. Finally it must be said that the Siberia "Anabasis" of our troops had attracted his attention and had awakened his goodwill.

After reaching Washington in May, I was soon in regular touch with those members of the President's Cabinet (and with their secretaries) who had to deal directly or indirectly with matters concerning us. The principal of these were—besides Mr. Lansing—Messrs. Baker, Philips, Polk, Long, Lane and Houston. Mr. Richard Crane was secretary to Mr. Lansing and with him, as with his father, my relations were constant. Nor must I forget either the French Ambassador, M. Jusserand, who helped us everywhere and in every way, even with the President; or Colonel House, the influential adviser and confidential friend of the President, with whom I discussed very thoroughly the problems of war and peace. And over and above this personal intercourse, I supplied Mr. Lansing and other Ministers, as occasion arose, with memoranda or notes upon the weightiest questions at issue and expressed my views upon them.

My own relations to the President were purely matter-of-fact. Throughout our movement, I relied upon the justice of our cause and the force of my arguments. I believed and believe that upright, educated people can be taught and convinced by argument. Therefore, in oral discussion with the President and in my memoranda and notes, I trusted solely to argument and to the weight of carefully verified facts, linking them with the President's own declarations and writings. What he had written upon "The State" and the development of the American Congress, I had known before the war; and as I read his speeches carefully, I was able to cite passages from them in support of my contentions. Thus I was able, step by step, to persuade the President and Mr. Lansing to accept our program. But this was by no means the result of my personal influence alone. The work and propaganda of our people won us public goodwill—and Austria-Hungary lost it. The change in the situation could be seen from the fact that the head of the Near Eastern section in the State Department, Mr. Putney, a well-known writer on legal questions, had upheld our view of the Austrian problem in the memoranda which he wrote for Mr. Lansing about the time I reached America. Mr. Putney was acquainted with our anti-Austrian literature and was in touch with my secretary, Mr. Pergler. The subsequent drift away from pro-Austrianism was revealed in the degree of recognition which the United States gradually accorded us.

It was upon Austria and the Hapsburgs that my conversations with President Wilson presently turned, Clemenceau's revelations of the Austrian peace maneuvers supplying a welcome opportunity. I pointed out the sorry behavior of the Emperor Charles toward his Germany Ally, saying that, soon after the war began, Germany had saved Austria from the Russians, for a time at least; and, later on, had driven the Russians eastward and had cleared the whole border from Finland to the Ukraine. Willy-nilly, Germany had also been obliged to help Austria against Italy. The Hapsburgs had nevertheless stabbed Germany in the back. President Wilson admitted that the Hapsburgs had behaved dishonorably, though he disliked the subjection of Austria to the over-lordship of Prussia-Germany. In our view of Prussian Tsarism, as I called it, we agreed fully; and, in his answer of October 23 to the German Note of October 20, the President dwelt very effectively upon this view. While we were discussing it, we touched upon the old idea of the European Allies that Austria might be detached from Germany, a plan really based upon the assumption that Austria would betray her ally. This aspect of the Hapsburg character had marked influence upon Wilson and other statesmen. In addition, I drew the President's attention to the responsibility of Austria in provoking the war, and he recognized that Austria had not been driven into war by Germany.

When the peace offers began and the question of arranging an armistice arose, I expressed to the President my conviction that the war ought to be continued until the Allies had compelled the German army to lay down its arms and that, if necessary, they should enter Berlin. I argued that this course would not cost more lives than would be lost by an indecisive peace. I admitted that the decision of the German command to ask for peace showed that the war had already been won strategically; but, as I knew how strongly the masses of the German people believed in the invincibility of the Prussian-German army and its commanders, I feared that German public opinion in general would not be convinced that Germany and Austria had been strategically defeated. I reminded the President that he had sent his friend Colonel House to Europe in order to discuss with the Allied leaders how a lasting, not a fleeting, peace could be secured, as the President himself had rightly said a year before in a speech to workmen at Buffalo; and I recalled to his mind the way in which he had justified to Congress the American declaration of war on Austria-Hungary, though he did not at that moment think of destroying her. He had demanded the destruction of Prussian militarism which, in my opinion, could best be achieved if Marshal Foch were to lead the Allied armies across the Rhine.

President Wilson was perhaps a stronger pacifist than I, and he certainly knew the mood of the American people and had to take it into account. When I saw the spontaneous celebration of the Armistice in New York—started by a premature report— I understood the President's views, which Colonel House represented in Paris before the President arrived there. But, even now, especially after the peace and its sequel, I think my view was right.

On points of detail I may say that President Wilson wished the Danzig question to be settled more or less in the way in which it was settled, and that he was not in favor of giving Danzig to Poland. To this I objected that any kind of condominium would create more friction between the Germans and the Poles than the definite attribution of Danzig to Poland, and would keep alive German discontent with the corridor between Germany and the enclave of East Prussia. The President was well-disposed both towards the Poles and the Yugoslavs; and, from several things he said, I got the impression that he did not agree with the Treaty of London on the basis of which Italy had entered the war. I heard afterwards from Paris, when the Italo-Yugoslav conflict became acute, that he knew nothing of this Treaty; but, on the other hand, it was stated on American authority that he had known of it and had forgotten it. I well remember having discussed the Treaty of London with Mr. Lansing, who certainly knew of it. It would assuredly be an interesting and instructive proof of the lack of American interest in European affairs if this Secret Treaty, which the Bolshevists had trumpeted throughout the world and American newspapers had published, really attracted so little attention in the most official American quarter. I know, however, that the Italo-Yugoslav controversy—which turned on the Treaty of London—was brought before the President and the State department by Yugoslav protests while I was in Washington.

When the question was raised in official circles and in the press whether President Wilson in person should take part in the peace negotiations in Europe, I advised him not to do so or, at least, not to remain in Europe after the opening of the Peace Conference. Knowing Wilson's character and his enthusiasm for the League of Nations as the chief point in a peace settlement, knowing also the personal qualities of the European peace negotiators, I feared that each side would be disappointed with the other. The war had lasted so long and had put so severe a strain upon the minds and nerves of all the men who would meet at the Peace Conference, that disillusionment might easily be aggravated by personal weaknesses. Thus, I thought, the high authority which President Wilson had gradually won in Europe might be lessened or entirely lost. But he, who was conscious of the great importance of the Peace Conference, wished personally to uphold his own and American ideals during its work. He believed that the mission of America was to lead mankind toward unity and that he could do it.

In our talk we touched upon the question why he had not formed a Coalition Cabinet when war was declared, as the Governments of the Western Allies had done in Europe, but had chosen his Ministry solely from the Democratic Party. I asked him in particular whether it would not be well to take representatives of the Republican Party with him to the peace negotiations in Paris. He thought that, in Paris, differences would arise between the members of the two parties, and confessed that he had no talent for coalition or compromise. "I tell you frankly"—this was how he put it—"I am descended from Scottish Presbyterians and am therefore somewhat stubborn." My own explanation was different. In America, as elsewhere, the war had set up a sort of dictatorship and had given decisive power to individual statesmen, even though, under Wilson, the contact between the President and Congress had become closer than it was before. I had watched this development the more keenly because I knew Wilson's views about the centralization of Congress—the growth of which, in my view, greatly strengthened the constitutional position of the President, whereas the American Constitution gives the President a position corresponding too closely to the English monarchical model. And, while I agree that President Wilson was, to some extent, oversensitive and intolerant of criticism, it did not seem to me that he had been partial in his choice of military and naval commanders. On the contrary, he gave a number of appointments to Republicans, and showed in this respect a notable sense of realities.

Our people at home recognized spontaneously and well the significance of Wilson's stand against Austria. The buildings, streets, squares and institutions which have been named after him throughout Czechoslovakia are a visible proof of our gratitude. To portray his character as man and statesman would be for me an easy task. I heard much of him from people who stood close to him; I read his speeches with great care and let his ideas and the style of his mind sink into me. I observed the warmth with which he was at first received in Allied countries and the way it afterwards cooled off. The Germans, too, took him up and then turned against him. From the outset I saw in him a conscious, straightforward exponent of Lincoln's conception of democracy and of American spiritual and political ideals in general. How he looked upon the fateful part which America was called upon to play, I have already indicated; and, if he had known more of Europe and European difficulties, he would have given more practical expression to those ideals. Between the "Allies" and America—whom he termed only an "Associated" Power—he distinguished consistently; but the continental character of the United States misled him into dealing too abstractly with the politics of Europe. Even his great watchword of the "self-determination of peoples" was far too general to serve as a guiding principle in Europe; and he was to some extent to blame if his idea of the League of Nations was not fully understood. It was a magnificent and a just conception, above all in its postulate that the League should form an essential part of the Peace Settlement. On the whole, my impression is that, for an American, Wilson was theoretical rather than practical, and that his thought was more deductive than inductive. If, as rumor had it, he preferred to correspond with his Ministers instead of conferring with them, typing his decisions and suggestions with his own hands—he was evidently of a somewhat retiring disposition—I cannot blame him for it, since it indicated a calm and matter-of-fact judgment of political affairs. This, I think, he showed in his treatment of Germany and in his decision to declare war upon her. Though he did not overlook details he would not allow them to excite him; and when enough of them had accumulated, he declared war very firmly. The American people followed him. Quite as firmly did he conduct the war; and it was for this reason that the Germans turned so sharply against him. Ludendorff was under no illusion about the gravity of Wilson's replies to the German proposals for an armistice and peace; and, in my view, it is unjust to contend, as Roosevelt and others did, that he ought to have declared war earlier.

Wilson was and remains one of the greatest pioneers of modern democracy. In his very first political campaign for the governorship of New Jersey he proclaimed his faith and belief in the people as the basis of democracy, in opposition to aristocracy and monarchism. Nations are regenerated from below, not from above; and monarchism and aristocracy lead always and everywhere to decline. This the world war proved on the grandest scale; for, in it, three great monarchies with their aristocracies went down in the conflict with democratic nations.

PRESIDENT WILSON AND PROFESSOR HERRON

My account of President Wilson's change of mind in regard to Austria-Hungary would be incomplete without some reference to another quarter from which he received information—Professor Herron, to whom I have already alluded. Herron's ideas may be gleaned from his writings. He is one of those American idealists for whom democracy is not merely a political but a living and moral program. Unless I err, Professor Herron had not known President Wilson personally in America or, at least, had seen little of him. The two men were brought together by Herron's writings, which Wilson recognized as accurate and to the point. Herron had been living in Europe before the war. When it broke out he settled in Switzerland where, from the autumn of 1917 to the end of 1918, he carried on negotiations with a number of Austrian and German politicians as Wilson's unofficial representative.

While I was in Switzerland I read the writings of Professor Herron—of whom I had known something before the war—and watched his literary and journalistic work; and then, through Dr. Osuský, a curious chance brought me into direct touch with him. As I have said, Osuský was a young Slovak who had come to Europe from America in 1916. He had wished to do something as soon as the war began, and felt he must come to Europe since America was then neutral. As submarines prevented ordinary vessels from sailing, he managed, in July 1916, to sail on a cargo-boat laden with munitions. When he came to me in London I thought he could help in our propaganda, and agreed that he should join Dr. Beneš and learn French. The Slovak League in America had given him certain instructions; but, as they had been drawn up at a distance and in ignorance of actual conditions, they could scarcely be binding upon him. In 1917 he thought of joining the army. In July of that year he went, however, for a while to Switzerland where, he believed, anti-Austrian propaganda could be carried on more effectively than in Paris, inasmuch as letters from Austria and Hungary reached Switzerland more regularly than France. When, in October 1917, the news reached Paris that the Hungarians, Count Károlyi and Dr. Jászi, would attend a Peace Conference which was being arranged at Berne in November, Osuský went definitely to Switzerland. As an American citizen, he came into touch with the American Legation at Berne; and, on hearing that a number of intermediaries were in the habit of visiting Professor Herron, he presented himself to him, and their common interests soon led them to work together. Osuský knew Magyar as well as German, and thus became indispensable to Herron and to the American Legation. He rendered a service to the Legation and to several newspapers by convicting a Hungarian interpreter and correspondent of falsifying news from Hungary, just as he had already helped Seton-Watson to expose the Hungarian correspondent of the "Morning Post." He was soon in a position to furnish the American Legation and Herron with reports that were sent to the State Department in Washington, and some of them to President Wilson direct. Thanks to his knowledge of the affairs and public men of Hungary, he was able to correct inaccuracies into which Károlyi and Jászi fell at that time— for, in the excitement of the war, and trusting, perhaps, to French and English ignorance, even the best Hungarians were guilty of erroneous statements—with the result that pro-Magyar newspapers which the Magyars wished to influence recognized and condemned Magyar insincerity. Dr. Osuský will, I hope, publish a full account of what he did and of his personal relationships. Naturally he kept me informed, and I can therefore say something of the matter. From other quarters, too, I heard the names of the people with whom Professor Herron was in touch, and he himself made no secret of the matter. His Austrian, Magyar and German visitors interested me principally. Among them were Professor Lammasch (both he and Herron have published accounts of their negotiations); the Viennese industrialist, Julius Meinl; Professor Singer of the Viennese "Zeit," and Dr. Hertz; Professor Jaffe and Dr. De Fiori, both of whom came from Munich (De Fiori's negotiations, which were ostensibly carried on in the interest of the Bavarian Court, have recently been mentioned in the German press); Herr Haussman, a German member of Parliament who was connected with Prince Max of Baden; Professor Quidde, Herr Scheidemann, Count Károlyi, Dr. Jászi and others. A former Dutch official, Baron de Jong van Beck en Donc, of whose propagandist work and relations with Austria I heard repeatedly, served on occasion as intermediary; and Profesor Herron was visited also by Southern Slavs like Dr. Trumbitch.

In Washington I heard something of Professor Herron's reports. For me the important thing was that President Wilson sent on parts of them to Mr. Balfour; and that, later, with the assent of the President, Herron sent most of his documents direct to Mr. Balfour who communicated them to a small official circle. Not only did Professor Herron understand and appreciate the significance of our Legions, not only did he observe how, on this account, the Allied Governments recognized our National Council and gradually adopted our anti-Austrian program, but he became convinced that our movement for freedom was genuine, and estimated accordingly the importance of our people's task in the reconstruction of Europe and of Eastern Europe in particular. He saw how artificial and, indeed, impossible Austria-Hungary was, and he rightly discerned a specifically Hapsburg insincerity in what Dr. Lammasch, Dr. Hertz and others told him for the benefit of President Wilson. He understood that the Emperor Charles and his agents wished to use the President and America for their own ends.

For instance, Lammasch described the Emperor Charles to Herron, at the beginning of February 1918, as an opponent of Prussian and Magyar domination, and wished President Wilson to express satisfaction that Count Czernin's speech of January 24 should have revealed Austrian readiness for a policy of reconciliation with the Hapsburg peoples. When this had been done, Lammasch suggested, the Emperor Charles would write to the Pope a letter, which would be published, promising to grant autonomy, in principle, to the Austrian races. These roundabout suggestions displeased Herron, who demanded that the Emperor himself should come forward honestly and take in hand the transformation of his Empire. Only on this condition could the President and America accept and support the plan.

The trick was transparent. The Emperor was to promise to the Pope, not to his own peoples, a system of autonomy, and was to do even that only "in principle." His chief care was for his own prestige. President Wilson was to welcome Czernin's speech in which, according to Lammasch, the Emperor himself felt his ideas had been inadequately expressed, though it was alleged to have been made at the Emperor's direct wish. The same care for prestige came out again in the Emperor's letter of February 17 to President Wilson, in which he asked the President to send a special personal envoy to him. As may be seen from the President's negative answer of March 5, this request made a bad impression on him; and when, on October 14, Lammasch promised the transformation of Austria into a federal State, neither Herron nor Wilson would listen. A few weeks earlier, in September 1918, Dr. Hertz gave Herron a more detailed program. He promised that Austria would detach herself from Germany and become democratic, and that Austria-Hungary would be changed into a federation of self-governing

States. He did not say clearly how the Czechs, Poles and Southern Slavs were to be organized as States alongside of the Germans and the Magyars. The Slovaks were to be kept apart from the Czechs, the argument being that Slovakia would presently join the Czechs "by herself." Poland was to be linked with Austria in a dynastic union, that is to say, Russian Poland and Polish Galicia. Posen, or Prussian Poland, was to remain German. Transylvania would get autonomy. The Southern Tyrol would go to Italy—after a plébiscite; and Trieste would form a Free State in economic alliance with Austria-Hungary. The Ruthene, or Little Russian, part of Galicia would be given to the Ukraine. Finally, Serbia would be allowed "on certain conditions" voluntarily to join the Austro-Hungarian Southern Slav State.

In this fashion Vienna still dreamt of expansion even at the end of September 1918; and Dr. Hertz ingenuously said that an Austria thus aggrandized would be democratic and anti-German! It sounds like a farce when, in speaking of the voluntary adhesion of Serbia to the new Southern Slav State, Dr. Hertz added: "In no circumstances must pressure be applied." I am ready to admit that Dr. Hertz said on behalf of Austria everything that it was possible for an Austrian to say. In words, Vienna and Budapest paid homage to Wilson's ideas, but in reality they wished to continue and even to strengthen their rule over us and over other peoples. Herron saw through the sort of autonomy that was promised, and let President Wilson know what he thought at every important stage, never hiding his conviction that America could not make terms with Austria. He reiterated this view emphatically when Mr. Lansing informed us officially, in the name of the President, that the United States had recognized our National Council and its policy; and, after the Austrian peace manifesto of September 14, which Clemenceau answered so drastically, Herron sent a note to Washington no whit less vigorous than Clemenceau's own opinion. On the same day Washington sent the laconic reply to which I have referred; and President Wilson's final answer to Austria-Hungary was written in the same spirit.

Yet it was not I or Professor Herron who prejudiced the President against Austria. American democratic ideas turned his mind not only against Prussian Germanism but also against German Hapsburgism. The war was a moral question as well as a question of power, strategy and politics. True, Vienna was incapable of comprehending a moral issue and took no account of it. Thus it came to pass that American democracy, and democracy in general, buried the Hapsburg Monarchy and the Hapsburgs with it.

INCIPIT VITA NOVA

After President Wilson's answer to Austria-Hungary and our Declaration of Independence on October 18, a new situation had to be faced. It gave us no little work. Austria, false to the last, left Germany in the lurch and begged Wilson for a separate peace on October 27; she accepted the humiliating condition he made in regard to us, but sought to interpret it to her own advantage. On this point I sent Secretary Lansing a Note—the last—to expose the cunning of Austrian policy; and Professor Herron advised the President direct to have nothing more to do with Austria since she was already a political corpse. For all eventualities I sought recognition from Belgium and Greece, after having received that of the other Allies, and took the necessary steps at their Legations in Washington on November 13. The recognition came from Athens on November 22 and from Brussels on November 28.

During the last fortnight of October and the first fortnight of November 1918, public attention was absorbed, in America as in Europe, by the rapid sequence of the scenes in the world-historic drama of which the last act had begun with the Russian revolution. Austria-Hungary collapsed and Prussian Germany was overthrown. On October 21 a revolution broke out in Vienna and also in Hungary. Count Tisza was murdered on

October 31. Independent Austrian, Czechoslovak, Yugoslav and Magyar States arose out of the Austria-Hungarian ruin. In Germany the revolution began on October 28 with a mutiny in the fleet; at the beginning of November, Hamburg, Lübeck, Bremen, Munich and Berlin revolted. The Reichstag changed the Constitution and Parliamentarized the country, Ludendorff resigned, the Emperor William and the Crown Prince abdicated —the Kaiser fleeing to Holland—and all German dynasties were swallowed up. At last, even the Emperor Charles abandoned his throne. On the same day, November 11, Herr Erzberger, Marshal Foch and Admiral Wemyss signed the Armistice which saved Germany from the capture of her army and capitulation. The Austrian army was totally demoralized, especially on the Italian front, whereas the troops of Germany went home in fairly good order. Nor were these great events without their symbolical and ironical side. On October 20 Berlin University came out in favor of the new régime and went almost Social Democratic. The "Frankfurter Žeitung" was the first to demand the abdication of the Kaiser on October 24, the Social Demcrats following suit four days later. The Chairman of the Social Democratic Party, Herr Ebert, became Chancellor, Herr Scheidemann proclaimed the Republic from the steps of the Reichstag, and the Social Democrats took over the Government.

Through all these events my interest lay mainly in the developments at home, and particularly in our revolution of October 28. The first accounts of it were confused and incomplete, and not entirely satisfactory reports reached me of the meeting between the delegation of our new National Committee and Dr. Beneš at Geneva. Our pro-Austrians comforted themselves with the hope that the Hapsburgs might still remain. But Dr. Beneš's initial report on November 5 cleared up the position to some extent; and, at last, the abdication of the Emperor Charles justified, even in the eyes of our pro-Austrians, the policy we had followed abroad. The reports from Dr. Beneš urged me, however, to return home with all speed. Therefore

I made ready to go. The news of the Slovak declaration at Turčansky St. Martin on October 30 was very welcome, though, on the other hand, the story that the Germans of Bohemia had begun a separatist movement and were trying to organize a German Bohemia made me uneasy. But when I heard that regions calling themselves a "Sudetenland" and afterwards a "German South Moravia" and even a "Bohemian Forest District" were being set up, my fears vanished. The very idea of such sub-division was a strong argument against German separatism. Nevertheless the question of the German Bohemians was always serious, and the Americans and the British insisted upon abstract definition of the "right to self-determination." To the resolution of the Provisional Austrian-German Parliament on November 12, that "German Austria is a part of the German Republic" I paid special heed as, indeed, to the strange rumors from Switzerland in regard to our Prague delegation. I heard that Vienna was negotiating with its members and wished to negotiate with me. Therefore I sent from London a special envoy to Switzerland to get trustworthy information of Austrian intentions.

In Washington I had heard that the Emperor Charles had made his last offer to President Wilson in agreement with the Vatican. True, the general situation made it seem improbable that the Vatican would run risks for the sake of Austria; and though the Emperor Charles and those about him sought solace during dark hours in their relations with the Pope, Vatican policy had in reality already become circumspect. According to later reports, the Emperor Charles sent Andrássy's Note to the Pope at the same time as he sent it to Wilson, expecting doubtless that His Holiness would do something for him; but whether there were any preliminary negotiations I have been unable to ascertain.

As soon as the Republic had been proclaimed at Prague and I had been elected President on November 14, I sent an Army Order to our troops in France, Italy, Russia and Serbia, informing them of the establishment of our State and defining the task of the army. It announced that the Legions in France and Italy would shortly return home, and commanded those in Russia and Siberia to stand by the Allies. Our Branch National Council in Russia was dissolved on November 14, since the National Council itself had become the Provisional Government which the Allies had recognized. General Štefánik as Minister for War, became the chief administrative military authority for our forces in Siberia.

On November 15 I paid my last visit to President Wilson in order to thank him heartily and to assure him of the gratitude of our whole nation. Of all our political friends and well-wishers I took a warm farewell, especially of M. Jusserand and his wife and of his colleagues; and I naturally said good-by to Secretary Lansing, to the other principal members of the Government and to the chief officials. The preparations for the Peace Conference were practically complete, and Mr. Lansing informed me that he had drafted, for his own use, a peace program which, in general character, resembled our own.

The newspapers, a long list of them, sought interviews with the new President. Obviously, propaganda was not yet at an end! The American Government granted me a credit after my election to the Presidency. Alongside of ideal motives and feelings, a State debt is sometimes an effective background for political relations; and I negotiated with American financiers on the subject of eventual loans, signing an agreement for a first loan of $10,000,000 before I sailed.

At noon on November 20 our boat, the "Carmania," steamed out of New York harbor. On leaving the Vanderbilt Hotel I was surprised to find a detachment of American sailors awaiting me. They had been sent to render me my first military honors as President—those military honors that were henceforth to be paid as I came and went, everywhere and always, compelling me again and again to realize that I had ceased to be a private individual.

CHAPTER VIII

GERMANY AND THE WORLD REVOLUTION

(FROM WASHINGTON TO PRAGUE. NOV. 20–DEC 20, 1918)

The Slavs themselves will not seek this fight. Should it come, the fortune of war may waver for a while; but I am sure that, at last, the Germans will be crushed by preponderant foes in East and West. And the hour will be at hand for them to curse even the memory of the five-milliard genius[1] whom they extol—when those five milliards have to be paid back with usury.—FRANCIS PALACKÝ, "Memoranda." Epilogue to the year 1874.

AT sea again, and no German submarines to fear! At last chance to rest and reflect—if I were not President! Not only on land but at sea I felt at every turn that my personal freedom and private life were gone. Now I was a public, official personage, always and everywhere official. Thus it had to be, since my fellow-citizens, and foreigners too, demanded it; and even on board ship the secret police of Governments kept watch over the new-born Head of a State.

By a happy chance I sailed on my wife's birthday. My daughter Olga and I kept it quietly amid roses as ever, and memories—no, not memories, for the thoughts and feelings of two souls which, despite distance, cleave to each other, are something more than a memory.

The sea, the sea! Rest for nerves and brain. Naught but sea and sky by day and night. The throb of the engines and propellers goes unheeded. In my exile I had lost the habit of regular sleep. I doubt, indeed, whether I slept well for five consecutive nights during the whole four years. My brain was

---

[1] Bismarck, who compelled France to pay an indemnity of 5,000,000,000 francs after the war of 1870-71.

ever working, like a watch, considering, comparing, reckoning, estimating, judging what the next day would bring forth on the battlefields or among Governments, a constant measuring of distances and of deviations from the goal. The sea lulls. Even the life on board is soothing. I went over the "Carmania" and the officers explained to me the progress in the art of navigation. I thought of my first voyage from France to America forty years before and of the old fashioned steamers of the time. Then I had traveled as an unknown man with no position, yet full of hope and enterprise. Now I was returning from the same New York, perhaps on the self-same course, as President of a State, and equally full of hope that my work would prosper. In America, and afterwards in England and everywhere, numbers of people asked me what it felt like to be President since I had secured independence for our people. They took it for granted that I was the happiest man on earth. In Prague a well-known German writer visited me so that, as he said, he might see with his own eyes a really happy man. Happy?

As President I thought only of going on with the task in hand, and of the responsibility which all of us who were capable of thinking politically would have to bear. I felt neither happy nor happier than before, though knowledge of the inner consistency, of the internal logic of my long life's work gladdened me. From a review of my own life and of what I had done abroad, I went on to review the world war, the political evolution of Europe since 1848, that is to say during my lifetime, and sought to trace amid a multitude of details the scarlet thread of cause and effect.

"So we are free, shall be free. We have an independent Republic! A fairy-tale," I said to myself, again and again, now unconsciously, now consciously and aloud, "that we are really f-r-e-e and have our own Re-pub-lic!"

Yet, in my mind, stillness reigned. Day after day I paced the deck, gazing across the waves; though the sense of new duties, new tasks, knocked ceaselessly at the door of my brain; anxieties about the peace negotiations and their outcome, care upon care. One thing was clear—despite science and philosophy, reason and wisdom, prudence and foresight, the lives of men and of peoples run, in large measure, otherwise than they will and wish. Still there is in them a logic which they perceive retrospectively. The efforts and plans of the most gifted political leaders, of the men who make history, reveal themselves as *vaticinatio ex eventu.*

The whole war through I had compared the plans and efforts of each belligerent party with those of the other. On the German side there had plainly been preparedness, a thoroughly thought-out undertaking on a large scale, with bold intent to fashion the future development of Germany, of Europe and of the world; but the outcome had shown the fatal mistakes of a people undeniably great, a people of thinkers qualified in many ways to teach all nations. On the other side, the Allies had lacked unity, both singly and as a whole. They had no positive plan—both sides wished to win, but that is no plan—they made big political and strategical blunders, and were nevertheless victorious not only by reason of their own superiority but thanks also to the errors of the foe. To me, the battle of the Marne seems an example of this human blindness on a large scale. If we assume that the French themselves did not expect to win it, as several French strategists have admitted, and that the Germans lost it only through the mistake of a subordinate officer, Colonel Hentsch, whom the literature of the Marne Battle has made notorious, does not the question "Why?" seem the more insistent? Or, to take another example: In 1917 and at the beginning of 1918 the Austrians and, perhaps, the Germans as well, could have got from the Allies peace terms under which we and the other nations, now liberated, would have won far less. The Allies were disposed to make peace; some of them too much so; a clear, honest word from Vienna about Belgium, and an open breach with Germany would have softened the hearts of England and France towards Austria-Hungary. But the insincerity of the official policy pursued in Vienna and Berlin, and their incorrigible arrogance and blindness, helped

the Allies to hold out and to conquer. Who, at the beginning of
the war, expected the overthrow of Russia and the establishment of a Communist Republic? Who foresaw the Revolution
that came forth from the war and altered the political face of
Europe and of the whole world? Shakespeare has put it very
wisely:—

> Our indiscretion sometimes serves us well,
> When our deep plots do pall; and that should teach us
> There's a divinity that shapes our ends,
> Rough-hew them how we will.

Yet a belief that Providence watches over us and the world
is no reason for fatalistic inactivity but rather for optimistic
cencentration of effort, for a strict injunction to work deter-
minedly, to work for an idea. Only thus are we entitled to
expect the so-called "lucky accident" that springs from the inner
logic of life and history, and to trust in God's help.

In my work abroad and throughout my life I remember
case after case in which my plans failed, and the result was
nevertheless better than my original design. How impatient
I was, for example, whenever the Allied armies made slow
progress; yet the very protraction of the war enabled us to make
ourselves known by propaganda and to enter the field with our
own forces! Had the Allies triumphed speedily we should not
have won our independence. Austria would have survived in
one form or another. In my messages to Prague I urged that
members of Parliament and journalists should be sent abroad
to help me. They were not sent, the work was done without
them and, as I saw on reflection, it was better that we should
have been alone and obliged to strain every nerve in systematic
and united work. The Siberian "Anabasis," and many another incident, helped us unexpectedly in much the same way. Going
back still further, I often think how unwillingly I left Vienna
in 1882 to settle in Prague, what epoch-making plans I then
had and how, instead of pursuing them, I was compelled in
Prague to study our people thoroughly and to enter political

life at an early stage.   The whole of life is shot through with
paradox.   Many a "lucky accident" befell me at home and
abroad.   It was by accident that, after the outbreak of war,
I was able to justify my journey to Holland in the eyes of the
police and that I had a passport, good for three years, which
had been issued just before the war.   (It seems that the police
superintendent in Prague, Křikava, fell into disgrace because
he allowed me to travel abroad.)   Only by a lucky chance did
I get over the frontier to Italy; the frontier official was very
doubtful whether he should let me pass, and before his tele-
graphic request for instructions could be answered I had got
away.   From Switzerland I wanted to go home once more and
had asked for a visa, but friends in Prague heard, in the nick
of time, that I should have been arrested and condemned immediately.   Again, in 1916, when I was in London, I was to
have crossed the English Channel on the "Sussex"; but the date
did not suit Dr. Beneš who telegraphed me to postpone my visit
to Paris.   The "Sussex" was sunk by the Germans—the incident
evoking an emphatic American protest.   When I was going to
Russia in the spring of 1917 the ship was only saved from a
German mine during the crossing from Scotland to Norway by
the Captain's presence of mind at the very last moment.   And
by how many lucky accidents did I not profit during the Russian Revolution and the fighting in St. Petersburg, Moscow and
Kieff!   Were I more superstitious than I am, I might fall into
the Emperor William's error and think myself a special instrument of God.   But theological belief, I repeat, ought not to
seduce us either into fatalism or into pride, and we should never
forget that Providence has to care for others as well.   Dr. Beneš
is also entitled to claim good fortune.   He succeeded in carrying
on the work in Prague under the eyes of the police, in organizing the "Maffia" and in crossing the frontier—with such a passport that I was horror-stricken when I saw it.   It had been
"arranged" so amateurishly that it would have aroused my
suspicions at the first glance—but the German frontier official
never noticed it.   Nor was Huza touched when he often passed

with me unscathed through the street fighting in Russia. Once we were going with Klecanda to the Kieff railway station to see Muravieff, when a shot was fired, the bullet striking a telegraph post in front of us. So close to us did it fly that we felt the air it displaced. The same Providence watched over us both.

People often made merry over the idea that Professors like Wilson, Masaryk and Beneš, and men of science like Štefánik, should decide questions of international policy. Our professorships mattered little; and there are professors and professors. What mattered was that we, at least we three Czechoslovaks, had won our positions by work and diligence, and that I was born poor and never grew rich. Thus I gained knowledge of men and of life and, with all my theorizing, remained practical. The same is true of Beneš and Štefánik. I never wanted to be a professor; I wanted to be a diplomatist and a politician. In Vienna, when I was unable to enter the Oriental Academy and to take up a diplomatic career, I was very unhappy; yet I ended by becoming a politician and a diplomatist! Though I wished not to be a professor, fate soon made a teacher of me. After a short apprenticeship as an artisan, I had to give lessons in order to earn my living as a high school and university student. Nor, later, was I to be spared a professorship; yet it did me no harm and even helped me politically.

In philosophy I strove to attain scientific precision, concreteness and realism. The philosophy of the schools estranged me, for it was a survival and continuation of medieval Scholasticism. Metaphysics I did not like, for I found no satisfaction therein. In my eyes philosophy was, above all, ethics, sociology and politics. I might be styled, in the jargon of the learned, an "activist" or, perhaps, a "voluntarist," for I have always been active: a worker. I have never recognized an antagonism between theory and practice, that is to say, between correct theory and right practice; and just as I opposed one-sided intellectualism I stood out against practice divorced from thought. Plato was my first and chief political teacher; then Vico, Rousseau, Comte, Marx and others. My first considerable work "On Suicide" gives in a nutshell a philosophy of history and an analysis of our modern era; and in it I first laid stress upon the importance and the necessity of religious feelings in modern men and in society. Metaphysical experience I found in art and particularly in poetry; and poetry, albeit realistic poetry, helped me in political life. I have always been a reader of philosophic and scientific works, without neglecting pure literature and literary criticism. My imagination I exercised deliberately and, thanks to scientific precision, I escaped becoming fantastic. In science, it is a question of acquiring an accurate method. I sought to develop a critical faculty as a preservative against shallowness, and insisted on strict and pitiless analysis, even in history and sociology; but the analytical method was for me a means, not an end. The end was synthesis and organization, as all my writings show. Nor do I regret my critical work or my exposure of the Königinhofer and Grünberger manuscripts, though they had long been regarded as one of our national treasures. I regret only the mistakes which I made. My opponents deplored my rationalism, claiming that the Fatherland and the national consciousness of our people were being endangered, although I was on principle hostile to the one-sided rationalism that takes no account of the feelings and of the will, or of their psychological and ethical significance. True, I did not recognize the rightness of all feelings; and the lengths to which parochialism could go was shown when I was obliged to demonstrate in a court of law that my work "On Suicide" did not advocate suicide.

In political life I studied and observed men in the same way as I study characters in novels or in modern poetry. One must know men, select them and assign to them suitable tasks if one is to organize them politically. At an early stage I acquired the habit of observing the people with whom I had to deal, or who were prominent in public life, as though I intended to write a book about them. I collected all possible data upon friend and foe, and gathered biographical material upon those who played an active political part. Before meeting statesmen and public men, I read their writings or speeches and got as much information as I could about them. This habit really began in childhood. At the age of fourteen, when I was about to become a teacher, Lavater's "Physiognomy" fell into my hands. I read it eagerly and grasped its importance for teachers. Hence, possibly, my continual study of men—and of myself.

Soon after settling in Prague I was drawn into politics and came into touch with all our leaders. My first experience as a member of the Austrian Reichsrat and of the Bohemian Diet (1891-93) gave me pleasure but did not satisfy me. I was oppressed by the partisanship, the narrowness, the sectarian spirit of the small parties and groups; and, above all, I felt the need of a better political education and of getting others to work with me. I was still immature. In Parliament I was concerned not only with party politics but with culture, that is to say, politics in a broader sense, unpolitical politics, and with journalistic work. After my first brief experience of Parliament I gave myself up therefore to the study of our national rebirth, of Dobrovský,[1] Kollár, Palacký, Havlíček and their contemporaries. From them I learned how our people could evolve, and what our aim and our essential task in future would be.

The Czech question I always conceived as a world-problem. Therefore I constantly compared our history with that of Austria as a whole and of Europe. The object of all my journalistic writing and of·my books was, so to speak, to fit our people into the structure of world-history and world-politics. Since we lived under the sign of Austria, Europe knew little of us. Hence my journeys throughout Europe and America and my eagerness to study the chief civilized countries and their history, philosophy and literature. I traveled in Austria, Germany, America, England, Russia, the Balkans and Italy. To France I did not go because I had learned her language and followed

---

[1] Joseph Dobrovsky (1753-1829), a Liberal Czech priest, ex-Jesuit and Freemason who was among the "awakeners" of the Czech national spirit at the end of the eighteenth and the beginning of the nineteenth centuries. In fearlessness and love of truth he resembled Hus.

the course of her culture since my schooldays. The value of this experience of the world proved itself during the war, as did my knowledge of languages.

In the second period of my membership of Parliament, from 1907 onwards, I made Austria and the whole Austrian structure the subject of careful investigation. In Vienna and elsewhere I collected information upon the Emperor, the Court and the Hapsburg family, observing very keenly the principal Archdukes, like Francis Ferdinand and Frederick. During the sittings of the Reichsrat, which I did not fail to attend, I often read political works and memoirs; and, as a member, I made myself familiar with the mechanism of the State and of public administration. Nor did I forget the army. When people began to talk of General Conrad von Hötzendorf, I gathered facts about him, and had more than one dispute with Machar, whose opinion of Conrad was more favorable than mine. In the army I had a number of acquaintances and friends who had passed through the Vienna military academy and were thus able to explain to me the whole composition of the Austro-Hungarian forces and of the higher command. And I was well-informed of Austrian military designs.

Why did I do all this? Thoughtful people might have gleaned the reason from the constant interest I took in the problem of revolution, and from my views on historical and natural rights in conjunction with the problem of what constitutes real democracy. On this account I came into conflict with the Government party, and also with our Radicals in regard to tactics. I could not tell them why the question of revolution interested me so deeply and, indeed, disquieted me; for I expected circumstances to arise in which I should have to settle the question practically; and I confess that I hoped the cup would pass from me. I may have been unjust to our Radicals in connection with the "Youth" movement, for it was a beginning, a first essay which exerted a certain educational influence. In principle, I still disagree with Radicalism; for an experienced man, who is capable of historical and political thought, draws his program from the observation and study of contemporary history and carries it out consistently. A political man, a statesman, goes his own way and puts his ideas into practice, whereas Radicals are often as blind as Reactionaries. Both do the opposite of what their opponents do, and live by contrariness. Neither did nor do I believe in the so-called "golden mean," the unthinking policy and tactics of living from hand to mouth.

It was because I knew the Slav world, and the Southern Slavs and Russia in particular, that I came into collision with Aehrenthal [1] over the Balkan policy of Austria-Hungary. For our current Slavism I had little liking. The pro-Slav "twaddle" —as Neruda once called it—was repugnant to me; and I could not stand the "patriots" and "Slavophils" who had not even learned the Russian alphabet and were obliged to speak German with Russians and with foreigners generally. I remember vividly how angry my nearest colleagues were when I began a discussion on the Slovak question and gave much space to it in the "Naše Doba" and in the "Čas." To me, an abstract and narrow political allegiance and patriotism, coupled with ignorance of our real people in Bohemia, Moravia and Slovakia, seemed totally inadequate. From childhood I thought it my duty towards the Czechs to acquire concrete understanding of the character, views and life of our people in Slovakia as well as in Moravia and in Bohemia. The rights of Prague are assuredly as good as those of any Slovak village—though too many people in Prague do not live the life Neruda lived, but content themselves with coffee-house theories and pothouse imaginings. As a Czechoslovak and a Slav I feel at home with the country-folk and with their dialects; and, philosophically, I stand with Hus, Chelčický [2] and Žižka, down to Havlíček and his successors. At home and in Vienna parochialism oppressed me, the parochialism of Prague and the characteristic parochialism of Austria.

---

[1] Count Aehrenthal, Austro-Hungarian Foreign Minister, 1906-1912.

[2] Peter Chelčický, a disciple of John Hus and founder of the Bohemian Brotherhood Church in the fifteenth century. He was opposed to war on moral grounds and preached the doctrine of conquest by meekness and humility.

Pettiness does not proceed from geography but from men, characters, manners. One does not become a citizen of the world merely by travel of the ordinary sort, or by official international intercourse, but by penetrating spiritually into the life of individuals, of nations and of mankind. It was my own great good fortune and happiness that, in my journey through life, I met Charlotte Garrigue, in whom French blood and American vigor were united. Without her I should never have seen clearly either the sense of life or my own political task. Thus France and America helped me and, through me, helped our nation to win beneficent freedom.

I can only indicate, not describe, how life prepared me for the work that fell to my lot during the world war, how I conceive purposefulness in individuals, in nations and in humanity, and how single lives are organically combined with the life of whole communities. Despite my political vigor I can say, with a clear conscience, that I never came forward unbidden, that I never sought prominence. I was begged and driven to take up the matter of the Königinhofer manuscripts; I was challenged to make a stand in the Hilsner affair; into the conflict over the Agram High Treason and Friedjung trials and with Aehrenthal, my Croat university students literally dragged me. Even my literary work consists largely of answers to questions that were forced upon me. There is deep truth in the words "He lives well who is well hidden," and they apply not only to monks but to politicians. And, if it be permissible to compare small things with great, God guides the Universe and none sees Him. He never shows Himself, and takes, assuredly, no delight in the praise of countless priests.

A second wholesome rule, which many ignore, is not to want always to be first. It is enough to be second or third. I am a very strong individualist, yet I know that others exist besides me, that I do not live by myself alone but by the life and work of my fellow-men and of those who have gone before. An observant public man and practical politician soon sees that few things are new in the world and that he brings little that is new into it. Moreover, in political life we must think not only of organizing, leading and doing but of coordinating, working together and disciplining ourselves. Perhaps everybody would like to be a small Napoleon, but normal men like equally to obey, and obey gladly. Above all, patience is necessary, everywhere, in everything and especially in politics. Without patience there is no true democracy. A democrat may be dissatisfied, uneasy, but he must not be impatient. Patience is a pledge of humaneness.

THE ERRORS OF GERMANY

The wireless news from Europe which reached us on board ship necessarily turned my thoughts once again to the war. Among the items were the documents published by the Bavarian Government on the war-guilt question and the statement they evoked from the German ex-Chancellor, Bethmann-Hollweg; the entry of Marshal Foch into Strasburg on November 25, and, finally, the solemn abdication of the Emperor William in Holland. The Kaiser's manifesto was more than an abdication: it was a recognition of the Revolution.

The theory that Germany was "stabbed in the back" and that the Allied victory was solely due to the demoralization of the army, to Socialist agitation and to internal revolution is untenable. Even were it sound, it would furnish new proof of the Germans' shortsightedness and ignorance of their own domestic conditions. If the influence of the German Social Democrats is to be taken into account, the influence of Socialists and pacifists in Allied countries cannot be ignored; and the French have likewise a theory of a "stab in the back" which, according to some of them, prevented Foch from crossing the Rhine into Germany. The truth is that war-weariness grew simultaneously in all belligerent countries, and grew for the same reasons.

Attentive observation of the development of the belligerent armies, and of the strategy and tactics on both sides, led me to the conclusion that the strategy and tactics of the French were superior to those of the Germans. At first, I had feared that the Germans would be superior; but the course of the war convinced me that their very Prussianism, that is to say, their outward orderliness and their mechanical precision, rendered them militarily weaker than the French. Prussian absolutism and, towards the end, the Kaiser's influence, did harm even to the army, which grew stiff and relied bureaucratically upon its organization, upon numerical preponderance and upon sundry technical advantages such as the rapid movement of troops on well-built strategic railways. The French army, on the other hand, had benefited by being republicanized, by being permeated with a greater spirit of freedom and by being criticized in the same spirit. German tactics, based upon phalanxes in close formation and on the idea of turning the enemy flank, proved less effective than the French system of advancing in shorter columns marching in echelon. Even militarily, the Germans were centralist and absolutist, while the French were individualist and republican. During the war the French called their field tactics "le système D.," that is, "se débrouiller" or "Use your wits." And French soldiers, both individually and as leaders, knew how to use their wits.

English and French military experts often told me that General von Schlieffen's strategical plan was good in itself but unsuited to the world war, perhaps because it was inaptly amended by General von Moltke, the German Chief of General Staff, who extended the Western army as far as Switzerland, whereas, according to Schlieffen, it should have reached only as far as Strasburg; or, as I am inclined to think, because the plan had been bureaucratized. My interest in it, as providing for a war on two fronts, and my inquiries about it among military experts, were prompted in part by the similarity between the geographical position of Germany and that of our future State. I had long noted the differences of opinion and the waverings in the German Supreme Command. The question was whether the main effort ought to be made on the West or on the East, against France or against Russia. In answering it the

Germans were influenced by their leading military authority, Clausewitz, who taught them that the enemy's strongest point must always be their objective. But who were the stronger, the Russians or the French? The elder Moltke wished, in his later years, to stand on the defensive in the West and to take the offensive against Russia with the whole strength of the German army. His plan, which was worked out in detail in the eighties of last century, was in accordance with the political situation, for England was then hostile to Russia. Bismarck and General Count Waldersee, who succeeded the elder Moltke as Chief of General Staff, agreed with it. Schlieffen, who succeeded Waldersee in 1891, found it no easy task to withstand Moltke's authority, though he was disposed to think that the main attack should be directed against France and that Austria should deal with Russia. Under him, the General Staff and the Kaiser decided in this sense; and, according to some accounts, the Emperor William was really the author of Schlieffen's plan.

But in 1914 the political situation was essentially different. England stood with France and Russia, and Italy and America presently joined the Allies. The balance of forces and their disposition were other than they had been in the time of the elder Moltke. The occupation of Belgium led, moreover, to tactical changes that were not in harmony with Schlieffen's main postulates. Moltke the younger took over Schlieffen's plan for the war of 1914 but gave it up after the battle of the Marne and returned to that of his uncle, Moltke the elder. It was then too late, and the change merely shows the perplexity of the German Supreme Command. To some extent the Germans were carrying out the concept of the elder Moltke when they beat the Russians in the East and waged a war of movement, while they fought a war of position in France and were really on the defensive. The French adapted their tactics to their own numerical inferiority, whereas Germany trusted too much to her traditional numerical preponderance; and she failed to change strategy and tactics when the other Allies came into the field alongside of the French. At the moment of the final German offensive in 1918, the Germans possessed numerical superiority or, at least, equality of numbers. Yet they lacked mobility and the gift of improvisation. True, they sprang some surprises in detail upon their enemies, as, for instance, with their long-range guns; and though they had conscientious Generals, they lacked real military leaders. Hence their incapacity for unitary action on a grand scale and their addiction to small sporadic enterprises and partial successes which served only to mislead them. It was always a puzzle to me why they besieged Verdun so violently and obstinately. What might they not have done had they thrown the greater part of their army into Russia when Stürmer was in power in 1916!

It may be that, in this war, the military leaders, not on the German side alone, were not masters of the situation. For the first time the war was literally a war of masses, of whole peoples, a democratic war if the term is not inappropriate. It would almost seem that, in democratic war, the leader of an immense host cannot take decisions by himself but has to consult other leaders, since battles and the war as a whole can only be won by the coordination of separate armies. Voltaire wrote long ago that the biggest armies can do nothing big, that they neutralize each other, and that such war brings naught save woe to peoples. In high degree this is true of the world war.

But the defeat of Germany was not due to military deficiencies alone. As Clausewitz rightly said, war is the pursuit of political ends by other means; and the whole German estimate of the situation in Europe and in the world, and even of the situation in Germany, was wrong. The pan-German scheme —the German army and its corps of officers were pan-German in tendency—was erudite, but of dubious quality. The Germans miscalculated the balance of forces, political, military and economic; they over-estimated themselves and their allies and under-estimated their foes. At the outset they under-estimated England, and until the last moment, they disbelieved obstinately in the military mobilization of America. By experiments they proved to their own satisfaction that the Americans could not cross the Atlantic; and in their own imagination they exaggerated the power of submarines, of which, in any case, they had too few. The way they deceived themselves about Austria is almost incomprehensible, for they must have seen, at a very early stage in Galicia and Serbia, how incapable the Austrian commanders were. To my mind, the campaign against Italy likewise reveals the incapacity of Austria, and of Germany too; for a better and more vigorous leader of the Austro-Hungarian and German troops would have utilized Northern Italy more effectively against France. On the Allied side only the French and, to some extent, the Italians were in a position to take the field with armies already organized on the basis of compulsory military service and animated by military traditions, whereas the British and American armies were largely improvised—conclusive proof of the inefficiency of Prussian militarism. Even in a military sense, absolutist monarchism was defeated by democracy.

Nor did the Germans take the industrial supremacy of the Allies sufficiently into account. The British were soon able to cope with the German submarines. The Americans invented deadlier gases than the Germans but refrained from using them for reasons of humanity. Edison helped the army by a number of successful inventions which accomplished more than the miracles people expected him to perform, for they increased the fighting efficiency of his fellow-countrymen. And just as the Germans relied too much on material forces and on the mechanism of organization, so they failed to comprehend moral forces and to understand the ethical strength of England and America, Italy and Serbia. They believed France degenerate and were blind to the degeneracy of Austria-Hungary. In fact they were beaten in the field by their own science, their history, their philosophy, their policy, and by Prussian militarism.

In saying this I do not belittle the military achievements of the Allied armies, all of which helped the French to gain the final victory. The British navy kept the seas open for the Allies and made it possible for food-stuffs, munitions and raw materials to reach them. As soldiers, the British distinguished themselves by their power of resistance and exemplary tenacity; and when Field-Marshal Haig attributes the Allied victory to a miracle, he recognizes the severity of German pressure but criticizes at the same time the lack of unitary leadership among the Allies. True, enemy leadership was not unitary, but the Germans managed at least to keep the politicians and strategists of Vienna within bounds. And during the whole war the Germans certainly showed admirable endurance, efficiency and skill in details. They stood out stubbornly against the greater part of the world. All respect to them!

The American share in the victory is generally recognized. It consists not only in the contribution of fresh and valiant troops at a critical moment but in the circumstance that the United States joined the Allies at all. Before coming into the war America had helped them by supplying food-stuffs and war material; afterwards she helped them by the great authority which President Wilson acquired throughout the world. In no respect was the shortsightedness of the Germans so obvious as in their treatment of America in America, and in their failure to understand the situation after the American Declaration of War.

Neither ought we to forget the other Allies, above all unhappy Russia. Her share in the successful defensive operations at the beginning of the war deserves to be dwelt upon, for Russia, with France, bore the brunt of the fighting before England had created big armies, Italy had joined the Allies and America had decided upon active intervention. Though outward and quantitative, not inward and qualitative, the power of Russia inspired the West with hope in dark hours, as it inspired likewise the Austrian Slavs, Serbia and Roumania. It formed a moral armament and enhanced endurance and pertinacity. The initial Russian successes against Austria had at once a military and a politico-psychological importance which found expression in the first phases of our revolution. Our joy in Russia's share in the victory and in the services she rendered is clouded to-day not only by the thought of the defeat and catastrophe that befell her afterwards—mainly in consequence of her internal rottenness—but also by critical knowledge of the moral quality of her merits and sacrifices. Her sacrifices were not made consciously for ideal aims in the same degree as those of the other Allies. Most of the Russian dead fell less in the service of an ideal, of a nation, of a State, than as the passive victims of ambitions which they neither knew nor understood. The greatest of Russian wars was fought by the old Tsardom, for whose sins and crimes hecatombs of human sacrifices had to pay; and the origins and aims of this Russian war are to be sought in the unhappy un-Russian policy of old Russia. Thus, despite the sad tragedy of them, the remarkable efforts and sufferings of Russia are depreciated in our eyes, and the only compensation is that, without them, Russia might not have been freed so soon and so completely from the bad old system. But at what a price had this freedom to be bought!

Italy, too, played her part in the victory early and late in the war, and Roumania and Greece brought welcome help to the greater Powers. And what shall we say of Serbia who, despite disaster, held out to the end against enemy superiority, suffered all the horrors of which the Austro-Magyar soldiery were capable, retreated valiantly through the Albanian mountains and stood loyally side by side with the Allies on the Salonika front till she finally reaped the fruit of her heroism?

Why the War Came

What is the meaning of the world war, of so immense a mass phenomenon in the history of Europe and of mankind? · The Marxist explanation is inadequate. Materialism is scientifically impossible, and the economic doctrine of historical materialism is one-sided. The way it is expounded in relation to capitalism is not wholly wrong, but it is partial, incomplete and vague. The conception of capitalism itself is indefinite. Assuredly, there were wars long before the capitalist system, and nobody has shown in what measure this system engenders or develops war.

Are we to understand by "capitalism" the economic system as a whole? Or finance, financiers and banks in particular? Or heavy industry? If so, in what countries? Capitalism exists in all countries, and thus capitalism would be fighting capitalism. Then which capitalism is the decisive factor? We are brought back to the main question—which of the belligerent parties took the offensive and which were on the defensive?—a point of great weight in determining the character of the war.

Nobody doubts that economic interests or, more precisely, *auri sacra fames,* has always been an incentive to war; but other motives also play their part. Do not historians, including Marxist historians, constantly maintain that, in modern times, States and their rulers and leading statesmen have waged war to increase their power, authority and prestige, to extend their territories at the expense of neighbors, to subjugate peoples and to acquire colonies? Large States are taxed with "Imperialism"; and, as aims of offensive war, love of power, ambition, greed, racial and national hatreds are alleged.

Nor is it enough to explain the world war as a result of nationalism. Otherwise we should have again to ask—what nationalism? There is nationalism in all countries. What is the substance of the nationalism that is supposed to have caused the war? Who attacked and who merely resisted attack? Certainly national antagonisms were among the causes of the war, but one cannot regard them as its sole cause. Economic and other motives entered into it. The peoples themselves were not legal parties to it but were involved in it indirectly in so far as they were organized into and represented by States. The States themselves did not appear to pursue a solely national policy; they were influenced by all kinds of complicated factors—dynastic aims, the interest of Governments, the influence of statesmen and politicians, of journalists, of Parliaments, of parties and of various intellectual tendencies. It is precisely the task of history and of the philosophy of history—which will have to be sounder than the pan-German and nationalist philosophy—to establish with scientific precision who directed and determined the policy of a State, who took the decision at a given moment and for what reasons. England and America certainly did not join in the war from motives of nationalism, though they recognized the principle of nationality and above all the right of the small European peoples to independence and freedom. For this reason the war cannot be described as a struggle between Germans and Slavs or Germans and Latins. It was a world war. Its origin and development show plainly that nationality or even national chauvinism was but one of several factors, another of which was religious. Yet the war is rarely interpreted as a fight between Churches and creeds, although the Orthodoxy of the Russians and the Serbians, the Catholicism of Austria, the Protestantism of the Germans and the Catholicism of the French, played a part in it. Indeed, none of the usual stereotyped definitions are applicable to it. It cannot be called a war of dynasties, of prestige, of religion, of liberation, of races, of expansion or predatory or colonial. Therefore the quantitative description a "world war," indicates its special character and meaning.

THE RIVAL WAR AIMS

The character of the world war is, to a great extent, discernible in a comparison of the respective war aims of the two belligerent parties and of their programs—the program of the West, which was that of the immense majority of mankind, and the program of Germany, which was supported by a minority grouped round the Central Powers. This division of nations into two camps had not merely a temporary military significance but corresponded to different conceptions of civilization, to divergent ideas and views of life and conduct.

I am well aware that an attempt tersely to define racial and national aims, or conceptions of civilization, is bold even to rashness. Yet an analysis of the war in the light of history seems to warrant it. The universal Theocracy of the Middle Ages, centralized under the leadership of the Papacy, gave place, during the modern era, to the growing independence of individual States and Nations. The Reformation, classical Humanism, Science, Art and Philosophy, striving toward a fresh comprehension and knowledge of Nature, of men and of social relationships, established new spiritual and ethical ideals and foundations for the organization of society. By the Reformation, by Humanism, Science, Art and Philosophy, the Great Revolution in England, France and America was prepared, and its main result was that the Church, or, rather the Churches, were separated from the State. In the West, in Europe as well as in America, the tendency toward the separation of the Churches from the State gradually became general. Religion lost nothing by it; on the contrary, it gained, as politics gained; and, like the State, public institutions and social arrangements shed, little by little, their ecclesiastical character. Science and Philosophy, Education, Ethics and, largely, even Religion were divorced from the Church. In regard to the State which, after the Reformation, had assumed the leadership of the community and, like the Church before it, had become absolutist, the French Revolution proclaimed the principles of "Freedom, Equality, Fraternity." The rights of men and of citizens were enunciated and codified, France and America became Republics, England—and, presently, for a time —France also, became a constitutional monarchy. Against the old aristocratic system—monarchism is but a form of that system —Democracy developed in various shapes, degrees and qualities.

The revolutionary process was not exhausted in the French Revolution. A series of revolutions followed; and we are still in the midst of this phase of development, for other revolutions arose in and through the world war. Not in the political sphere alone but in all domains the revolutionary tendency showed itself as a perennial phenomenon. Yet it is possible that, in the world war, the transitional period of revolution came to an end, not the old régime alone.

The ideal of the French Revolution was humanity, that is to say, ethical sympathy, respect of men for their fellow-men, a recognition of human personality, the principle that human beings must not be used merely as tools or chattels by other human beings. Politically and socially, these principles imply equality between all citizens of a State, and the bringing of nations and State nearer to each other on the basis of a common humanity. Juridically, the existence of an equal natural right to freedom and equality was believed in; and individuals, as well as communities and nations, were recognized as possessing this right. The idea of natural right is ancient. We inherit it from the Greeks and the Romans, and it was sanctified by the Church and the Churches. Gradually its essence was defined, politically and socially. And closely bound up with the humanitarian ideal was the yearning for enlightenment, knowledge and culture. Hence the general recognition of Science during the past century and the efforts to found a new scientific philosophy; hence the constant attempts to organize education, to make schooling compulsory, to popularize scientific knowledge; hence also the growth of journalism and the diffusion of the press.

The Great Revolution, and the mighty changes in life and thought which it entailed, allowed the idea and the ideal of progress in all departments of human effort to take root—the belief that individual peoples and the whole of mankind have the power gradually to attain a higher, nay, the highest plane of perfection and contentment.

These, it seems to me, are the leading ideas of the European West. (I say "the West," though I may be thinking in the first place of France; for the West—France, England, America, Italy and the other Romance nations—form a civilized whole, as is clearly shown by the reciprocal influence of the Western peoples upon each other and by their political evolution.) To put it briefly: During the Middle Ages, mankind—mankind being then the Europe of the Holy Roman Empire—was organized extensively by the Roman Catholic Theocracy. Democracy arose through the Reformation and the French Revolution, Democracy being an attempt to organize mankind intensively. Democracy is, in my eyes, the antagonist of Theocracy. We are now in a period of transition from Theocracy to Democracy on a humanitarian basis.

In the Middle Ages, German thought and culture formed part of those of Europe; but in more modern times they were increasingly differentiated and isolated. The Prussian State, which the Reformation strengthened, was aggressive from the outset and dominated Germany. The idea of the State, the so-called "Statism," prevailed also in Western Europe, though there the State became an organ of Parliament and of public opinion. In Germany, on the contrary, the monarchical State was literally deified, and its absolute power generally recognized. Indeed, it was not until the end of the world war that the King of Prussia, in his capacity of German Emperor, decided in favor of the parliamentarization of Germany. Prussia and Germany were really an organized Caesarism; and Frederick the Great, Bismarck, William I and William II, were, unlike Napoleon, strange Tsarist Caesars. The word "Tsar" is of course derived from "Caesar," but how widely the word differs from the idea it ostensibly expresses! The Prussian officer, the soldier, became the German criterion for the organization of society and, indeed, of the world. The soldier and war were regular institutions. Nor did the Reformation, classical Humanism, Science, Art and Philosophy prevail over Theocracy in Germany so thoroughly as they prevailed in the West; for the German people accepted the Reformation only in part, and the German Lutheran Reformation adapted itself to Catholicism. Thus there arose a sort of Caesaro-Papism, albeit distinct from the Russian Caesaro-Papism. In course of time pan-German Imperialism took the place of Lessing's, Herder's, Goethe's, Kant's, and Schiller's humanitarian ideals, which were derived from secular and Western evolution and from participation in it. The catchword "Berlin-Baghdad" represented an endeavor to secure mastery over Europe, and thus, eventually, over Asia and Africa also—an endeavor which, in itself, expresses an ideal of the ancient world. Germany cherished and sought to realize, even geographically, the ideal of the Roman Empire. The Western ideal tends, on the contrary, to organize the whole of mankind and, above all, to link Europe with America and with other continents. In the world war they were thus linked.

In doctrine and policy pan-Germanism declined to recognize the right of peoples to independence; Germany was to be lord and master over all. In its expansiveness, pan-Germanism proclaimed the multi-racial State as ideal, an ideal of which Austria-Hungary, alongside of Germany, was to be a living exemplification—without forgetting the Russian State which had been fashioned, in so remarkable a degree, after the Prussian model. The Allies, on the other hand, proclaimed the right of all States, small as well as big, to independence; and the outcome of their program is the League of Nations, which is the culmination of the democratic ideals formulated and, to some extent, realized in America.

Philosophically, the Germans rejected the idea of natural rights and substituted for it that of historical rights. Though Kant was recognized as the leading philosopher, his inclination towards natural right and towards the standards of Rousseau was spurned as humanitarian; and Darwin's doctrine was invoked in support of historical right and of the theory of mechanical evolution founded on the "survival of the fittest," or strongest. Thus war and the waging of war came to be looked upon as divine ordinances. The English naturalist's theory was invoked by Prussian militarism in support of its aristocratic military postulates, of which the main outcome was the so-called "Realpolitik," the claim that all right is born of might—might, in its turn, being identified with violence. In the name of this doctrine, the German people were declared to be the ruling race. Even since the war, the pan-German identification of might, or power, with violence has been upheld by Professor Schäfer in his "State and Society," published in 1922. He maintains that right, or law, is solely the expression of might (page 264) and he subtly treats might as equivalent to force. He writes: "The thing cannot be otherwise; force and might can create right."

GOETHE OR BISMARCK?

The Germans themselves have sometimes expressed the difference between the new Germany and the old in the catchwords "Weimar or Potsdam? Goethe or Bismarck? Kant or Krupp?"

The Prussianization of Germany was political in the first instance. Taking advantage of the decay of the "Holy Roman Empire of German Allegiance," that remnant of Roman Catholic theocracy, the Prussian theocracy dominated Germany and Austria by its strong, unitary, military and administrative organization. Little by little Prussianism secured control of all efforts to advance education and culture, and made of Germany outwardly a well-ordered Empire. Not only in politics, philosophy, science and art, but even in theology this Prussianism expressed itself. As soon as the leading men and classes in a nation begin to rely on might and violence, the wells of sympathy dry up. People lose interest in knowing the feelings and thoughts of their neighbors, since the mechanism of the State, the word of command, the fist, suffice for all purposes of intercourse. They cease to think freely and their learning becomes barren of living ideas.

This is the explanation of the great errors and faults of German history and in German thought before and during the war. Bismarck, with his overbearing treatment of those about him, is the type of the domineering Prussian. Were I to make a diagram of the development of German ideas it would be:—

Goethe—Kant—Frederick the Great

Hegel

Moltke—Bismarck—William II—Lagarde—Marx—Nietzsche

I look upon Hegel as a synthesis of Goethe and Kant and an anticipation of Bismarck. He accepted the Prussian idea of the State as the highest expression of nationality and a guide for the whole community. His pantheism and fantastic philosophy are a transition from the idea of the Universe held by Goethe and Kant to the mechanical materialism and violence of Prussianism. By his doctrine of "Absolute Idealism" Hegel supported the claim of the Prussian State to absolute authority, forsook the universal outlook and humaneness of Goethe and Kant, and created the basis for a policy of force in theory and practice. It was not for nothing that Hegel was originally a theologian; and even in theology he propounded the principles of the Prussian theocracy. Bismarck and the Emperor William were always calling on God, the Prussian God; and Bismarck and Bismarckianism swallowed up Goethe. The Prussian State became the infallible director of the nation and of its spiritual life and culture.

Marx, for his part, after running through Feuerbach's philosophy that "a man is what he eats," turned Hegel's pantheism and Absolute Idealism into materialism. He took over the mechanism of the Prussian organization, with its State authority and almighty centralization, even though he conceived the State itself as subject to economic conditions. His relationship to the method and the tactics of Prussianism explains the circumstance that, in the world war, the German Marxists associated themselves for so long with the pan-Germans and gave uncritical support to Prussian policy despite their Socialism and their revolutionary tenets. Indeed, the undemocratic notion that large economic units are indispensable corresponds to Prussian "supermanishness"; and Marx's own view of the Slav peoples was not different from that of Treitschke or Lagarde. And Nietzsche sought refuge from egomaniac isolation—from "solipsism"—in the Darwinian right of the stronger. The sway (and the Church) of a new aristocracy were to be founded upon the "blonde beast," Christian theocracy being replaced by a theocracy of the superman.

Yet I do not conceive the antithesis between Goethe and Bismarck, Kant and Krupp in the sense of a Parsee dualism, for a psychologist might find elements of Prussian "Realpolitik" even in Kant and Goethe.   The real antithesis would be between Beethoven and Bismarck.   In Beethoven I see a German genius unspoiled by Prussia.   His art springs from pure, true inspiration.   It speaks from heart to heart, as Beethoven sometimes thought it did.   The Ninth Symphony is a hymn of humanity and democracy.   Let us not forget how Beethoven upbraided Goethe, the Olympian of Weimar, for bowing low before the seats of the mighty.   And "Fidelio" is unique.   Shakespeare alone has expressed the love of man and wife with equal strength; nor in the whole literature of the world is there another instance of conjugal love, so pure and strong, for even the greatest poets have taken as their theme the romantic state of pre-nuptial love.   In the "Missa Solemnis," too, Beethoven pours out his passionate religious faith, the faith of the modern man rising above traditional ecclesiastical forms to heights undreamed of save by the maturest spirits of our time!   Yet Haydn taxed Beethoven, albeit in friendly fashion, with disbelief in God!

And with Beethoven I couple his great teacher, Bach, and Bach's religious music; and, in philosophy, Leibnitz, whose yearning to melt the Churches into one is the natural outcome of his doctrine of the Monads and of his fundamental conception of universal harmony.   Pan-German chauvinists see in Leibnitz's humanitarian aspirations an effect of his Slavonic blood.   I, however, look upon his philosophy as a continuation of Platonism, albeit with strong traces of the subjectivism which Kant and his followers were presently to overdo.

I regret that my musical education is not sufficient to permit me to detect the workings of the German spirit in the brilliant line of great musicians—Bach, Handel, Gluck, Haydn, Mozart, Beethoven, Schubert and Schumann; but the Prussian spirit certainly found a musical exponent in Richard Wagner, a genius whose work is a synthesis of decadence and Prussianism.   Alas! the splendid, noble and beauteous music of Germany took too light a hold on the hearts of peoples; the effects of Prussification were stronger.

THE DECLINE OF GERMAN THOUGHT

After Kant, and in large measure through his influence, German thought took the wrong road. He strove against the one-sidedness of English empiricism, and particularly the skepticism of Hume, by means of the equally one-sided intellectualism of an ostensibly pure creative reason. He built up a whole system of *a priori* eternal truths, and thus opened the door to all the fantastications of German subjectivism, or "Idealism," which necessarily led to egomaniac isolation, or "solipsism," to aristocratic individualism and to supermanishness based on force. From a skepticism born of his dislike of theology and metaphysics, Kant—like Hume before him—returned at last to ethics and worked out an essentially moral view of the Universe. But his followers held fast to his earlier subjectivism and, in the name of "Idealism," gave themselves up to arbitrary constructions of the Universe, to a metaphysical Titanism, or cult of the gigantic, which necessarily led the German subjectivists into moral isolation. The fanciful imaginings of Fichte and Schelling brought forth the nihilism and pessimism of Schopenhauer. The Titans grew angry and ironical—though anger and irony in a Titan are a contradiction in terms—and finally fell into despair. Hegel and Feuerbach sought refuge in a sort of State police and in a materialism which helped them to escape from metaphysical cobweb-spinning. They subordinated themselves to the Prussian corporalism which had already found strong expression in Kant's "categorical imperative"; and the German universities became the spiritual barracks of a philosophical absolutism that culminated in Hegel's deification of the Prussian State and Monarchy.

For his State absolutism Hegel provided—under the title of dialectics and evolution—a Machiavellian doctrine based on denial of the incompatibility of violence and right; for he deduced his right from might and force. Both Nietzsche and Schopenhauer rejected this doctrine verbally. In reality, it was Nietzsche who became the philosophical product of the Hohenzollern parvenus and of pan-German absolutism. Nor did Hegel proclaim only the infallibility of the State. He preached the saving virtue of war and militarism as well. Then Lagarde and his disciples conceived the philosophy and policy of pan-Germanism—the policy which the war overthrew on the battlefields of France.

With the fall of the Prussian regiments fell also the philosophy which (in von Hartmann's words) had preached the extermination of the Poles or (in those of Mommsen) the smashing of the hard Czech skulls, the suppression of the decadent French and of the haughty English. The war, which answered the question "Goethe or Bismarck?" "Weimar or Potsdam?" weighed Prussian pan-Germanism in the balance and found it wanting.

In repudiating the one-sidedness of German thought, from Kant onwards, I do not say that German philosophy or all German thought is dubious, nor do I say that it is feeble, superficial or uninteresting. On the contrary, it is interesting and deep, though deep because it was not and could not be free. It is a scholasticism like that of the Middle Ages, conditioned and limited by a ready-made creed laid down in advance. Just as the Prussian State and Prussianism are absolute, so German philosophy and German idealism are absolute, violent and untrue. They mistake the hugeness of a colossal Tower of Babel for the grandeur of a humanity united in Freedom.

German Decadence

The dilemma "Goethe or Bismarck?" had a strong influence upon my personal development. I received my secondary education in German schools, I wrote and published a number of my works in the German language, and I knew German literature well. It was more accessible to me than other literatures, and Goethe was my first and principal literary teacher. Alongside of Goethe I studied Lessing, Herder, and something of Immermann. As a man and as a character Schiller appealed to me more than Goethe, but I preferred Goethe as poet, artist and thinker, though his boundless egoism is a golden bridge to Prussian pan-

Germanism. From these names it may be seen that, while I could not altogether escape German Romanticism, it attracted me far less than French Romanticism, and that its influence upon my culture was transient, not fundamental. Its reactionary quality repelled me. And though I read modern German literature and studied the development of the drama, I found English and French literature of the same period more nourishing. There is more in them for the modern man.

But it was Goethe who gave me a standard by which to measure all literatures—including our own. His searching analysis of the modern man, especially the modern German man, set his successors, in Germany and elsewhere, a principal and weighty task—that of overcoming Faustism, of doing in literary art what Kant would fain have done in philosophy, of vanquishing skepticism, subjectivism, pessimism, irony and their corollary—violent supermanishness. Indeed, the word "superman" was coined or given currency by Goethe.

German literary critics rightly date modern literature from Hebbel, who analyzed the conditions of the period following the French Revolution, grew up in the era of Reaction and saw through it. Yet he bowed to it in so far as he overvalued the State in too Hegelian a fashion, and sacrificed—unnecessarily—the individual to it. His conception of the State is, in fact, Hegelian. Hence his lack of sympathy with the Revolution of 1848, though he himself was in revolt against society as then constituted, a revolt in which one feels nevertheless some indecision. His observation of contemporary social problems and of the moral fissures in aristocratic and middle-class society was keen. Problems like those of suicide, of the relationship beween women and men, of love, he pondered much and presented in many forms. Here, again, his peculiar waverings revealed themselves. He rejected the antiquated view of women but feared to fall into the extreme of advocating their emancipation.

True, such indecision is characteristic of transitional periods. It affected Hebbel's art as well as his views. As a dramatist he is downright and realistic while bearing in himself the elements of Romanticism and delighting in the unusual. To historical figures, such as his "Judith," he lends new significance by fresh interpretation; but in his lyrics his artistic indecision crops up again. There is too much reflection in them, too little lyrical poetry. Therefore he cannot, in this respect, be compared with Goethe. None the less his relationship to Goethe interested me, particularly the way in which he lends to the Titanism of Holofernes and Herod certain of the attributes of a State. He took a narrow, a gross, one may almost say a Prussian view of them. As regards form he seems to have imitated Goethe; for, in his later dramas at least, his art approaches the classical form of "Iphigenie."

One reason why I read so much of Hebbel was that he had lived in Vienna, where I still found living memories of him. To me it seemed that the unhappy influence of Austria and Vienna could be most clearly traced in the work of this North German. In Vienna, too, the theater led me to pay heed to the Austrian poets, particularly Grillparzer, in whom the Austria of Metternich and her fatal influence on great men can be best studied, as Grillparzer's autobiography proves. A similar case is that of our Bohemian-German writer, Stifter. The same fatal influence I detected also in Raimund, Bauerfeld, and Anzengruber; while Nestroy expressed the spirit of Vienna. All of them wrote in Austrian handcuffs. To Grillparzer, Vienna was a "Capua"; and, to Anzengruber, Austria was a "murderess" of the mind.

Under the absolutism of Prussia and the Hapsburgs, and especially under the Metternich system after the Revolution, no free, liberating literature could blossom. The most gifted men were either vanquished by Reaction, as in the case of Hebbel, or broken, as Grillparzer was broken. The discontent of smaller men found utterance in mere protests, after the fashion of Stirner and Nietzsche. Heine fled to France, while Richard Wagner made his peace with Imperialism and its outward brillance. Finally, the younger writers adapted themselves too lightly to the successive phases of Prussian policy, or bowed their heads in non-political retirement. All eyes were dazzled by the triumph of Prussia. Indeed, the exaggerations and vulgarities of German "Naturalism," "Modernism," Decadence and Symbolism—as the various literary fashions were named—the incoherence of Impressionism and the feeble megalomania of the so-called "Expressionism" reflect the moral crisis and the decay of the new German society after 1870.

In Prague I had followed the course of German literature, and, by comparing it constantly with Czech, French, British, American, Scandinavian and Russian literature, I became convinced that German civilization and culture were passing through a real crisis in which their weakness, their inadequacy, not to say their breakdown, were revealed. To this weakness may be attributed both the striking influence of Scandinavian, Russian and French writers upon them and the perpetual German attempts to return to the past and, above all, to Goethe. From such an attempt, in which weakness and strength were strangely mingled, the writings of Gerhart Hauptmann seem to have sprung.

"Expressionism" is preeminently German, an aspect of German subjectivism, and therefore damned from birth. The Expressionists are nothing but interpreters of Kantian or neo-Kantian doctrine and of subjectivism after the manner of Nietzsche. Expressionism, as Herman Bahr describes it, creates a universe of its own. The expressionist poet and critic Paulsen—it is something more than an accident that he should be the son of the philosopher Paulsen who was a follower of Kant—explains that the poet bears in himself the "finished forms" (a Kantian term) out of which the whole world grows. This is subjectivism in all its violent absurdity. Paulsen says rightly that expressionism is essentially German. And I do the Germans no wrong if I say that, during the war, their literature was more chauvinistic than any, in quantity and quality, or that German writers and journalists drove their people towards war in Berlin, Vienna and Budapest. There were exceptions, like Stilgebauer, Unruh, Förster, Schücking, Nippold and Grelling, but they were exceptions.

MILITARISM AND SUICIDE

There is an essential connection between "supermanishness," "militarism," war and suicide. In my first work on "Suicide as a Social Mass-Phenomenon of Modern Civilization," which appeared in 1881, I essayed an explanation of the surprising and terrible fact that, in modern times, from the end of the eighteenth century onwards, the number of suicides has increased everywhere in Europe and America, particularly among the most enlightened peoples. This increase has been so marked that suicide must be regarded as a pathological condition of modern society; and the disposition of modern human beings to commit suicide is linked with their growing psychosis, or mental morbidity.

Careful analysis of motive in individual cases of suicide led me to the conclusion that its chief cause is a weakening of character consequent upon loss of religious feeling. Viewed in historical perspective, modern suicide and modern mental ailments appear as effects of a period of transition, of immaturity in the modern outlook on life and of a resulting inadequacy in the organization of society.

Throughout Christendom, the Catholic theocracy of the Middle Ages established a unitary view of life and a political system in harmony with it. But in the modern era—which is modern for that very reason—Catholic theocracy fell into decay and is still decaying, the transition from the Middle Ages to modernity being marked by a revolution in religion, science, philosophy and art. The new era was, and is, clearly one of transition, a phase of spiritual and moral anarchy; and alike in their philosophical skepticism and in their efforts to overcome skepticism, Hume and Kant were both interpreters of this modern phase. The permanent ecclesiastical authority, once so generally recognized, lost its power—was, indeed, bound to lose it—by reason of its absolutism, of its premature, artificial and forcible establishment of a universal outlook and political system. Against this spiritual absolutism, revolution broke out along the whole line, within the Church and outside it. A real consensus of view, that is to say, catholicity, lasting catholicity of outlook, could not be dictated from above or imposed by force; it could have been attained only by free agreement in the light of experience and reason.   Men withstood infallibility, absolutism and the inquisitorial spirit, and rebelled against them.   Exaggerated, revolutionary individualism and subjectivism sprang up; and they, in their turn, led to egomania and "solipsism," to spiritual and moral isolation, to general anarchy in place of the earlier systematic Catholicism.   Belief and the disposition to believe were vanquished by skepticism, criticism, irony, negation and disbelief.   Men lost their peace of mind, grew restless, inconstant, nervous.   Some sought in Utopian dreams outlets for their artificially stimulated energies—and in their seeking and doing suffered disillusionment after disillusionment.   Idealists gave themselves up to the pursuit of pleasure, yet found in it no contentment.   Pessimism spread, theoretically and practically, joylessness and discontent, vexation and despair —the parents of weariness, nervousness, morbid introspection and suicidal mania.

From a psychological standpoint, modern society is pathologically irritated, torn asunder and divided.   It is in process of transformation.   The statistics of suicide form, as it were, an arithmetical table of this mental and, at the same time, moral and physiological sickness.   In Europe and America the average number of suicides is about one hundred thousand a year, the increasing proportion of child suicides being especially characteristic.   For the benefit of those who are impressed only by big figures, we may say that, in ten years, one million, and in fifty years, five million people do away with themselves.   Yet the total of war losses horrifies us—as though the suicide of one child despairing of life and of itself, were less tragic and less significant of the modern life of civilized peoples than the death of men in war!   What are we to think of a society, of its organization, of its humanity, if it can look upon this state of things with calm indifference?

Murder and blood-lust are, psychologically, the opposites of suicide and suicidal mania; for suicide is violence done to itself by an introspective, self-centered soul, whereas murder is violence done by the soul to others; it is an abnormal "objectivization." Subjective individualism, which becomes intensified into superior self-sufficiency and Titanic pseudo-godlikeness, ends by being unbearable. In the last resort, men of this temper do violence either to themselves or to their neighbors, and commit suicide or murder.

THE PSYCHOLOGY OF SUICIDE

It was the study of modern revolutionary tendencies and of the specifically Russian terrorist anarchism that forced me to reflect on the psychology of suicide and murder. True, poets and thinkers, from Rousseau and Goethe onwards, have long dwelt upon it, and modern statisticians, sociologists and psychiatrists have zealously analyzed what are called "moral statistics." Yet European society still fails to realize the gravity of the problem, and literary critics have been unable to grasp the main ideas of great thinkers. Rousseau's Saint-Preux is the first well-defined type of the superman; and though Rousseau merely toys with the subject, he reveals the moral sickness that drives his superman to suicide. Faust, Goethe's full-blooded superman, is actually holding the phial of poison to his lips when his omniscient discontent is checked and he is saved by the happy accident of the sound of Easter bells falling on his ear. Goethe himself confesses that he once fell into this mood. But another of his heroes, Werther, could not be saved and ended his romantic sickliness in death. For post-revolutionary France, de Musset analyzes the *mal du siècle;* and his hero, Rolla, the god-slayer, is likewise driven to suicide. In Manfred, Byron lays bare this modern malady for English readers; while, among the Russians, we have an almost cruel analysis of intellectual distraction, from Pushkin's Onegin to Tolstoy's Levin, an analysis which Dostoyevsky enhances by implacable realism and illustrates in characters of drastic brutality. Dostoyevsky's short sketch "The Condemned" is an attempt to turn the modern logic of suicide into a syllogism. The Scandinavians—Jacobsen, Garborg and practically all writers since Strindberg—take these weary modern souls to pieces, performing, indeed, the operation on their own souls. And, among the most modern German writers, Wasserman shows how devoid of piety the younger generation are, how they identify freedom with insolence, godliness with courage, and pleasure-seeking with strength; how they denounce "bourgeois narrow-mindedness" yet are fearful of microbes; how loveless, neutral and heartless they are. Naturally, Wasserman's hero commits suicide. Wasserman knows his Dostoyevsky, as Kasimir Edschmid, a leader of the "Expressionists," knows him, although the latter defines "Expressionism" as a struggle of dwarfs against God, a struggle that necessarily ends in their conversion and regeneration under the influence of the watchwords "Love, God and Righteousness."

Modern militarism, especially Prussian militarism, is a scientific and philosophic system of objectivization, of compulsory escape from morbid subjectivity and suicidal mania. I repeat "modern militarism"; for the fighting spirit of savage and barbarians, or even the fighting spirit of medieval knights and mercenaries is, psychologically and morally, very different from the scientifically coordinated military system of the modern absolutist State. Savages and barbarians fight from aboriginal savagery, or driven by want or hunger; but, in the world war, disciples of Rousseau and Kant, Goethe and Herder, of Byron and de Musset stood in the trenches. And when, in the spirit of Hegel, Werner Sombart praises German militarism and boasts of the Fausts and Zarathustras in the trenches, he fails to understand how severely he is, in reality, condemning German and European civilization. The fighting of these modern, civilized men is a violent effort to get away from the perplexities that arise in the ego of the superman; and, for this reason, the *intelligentsia* were no whit behind the peasants and workmen in fighting spirit, but rather outdid them. This phenomenon struck me first when I saw the Serbian *intelligentsia* in the Balkan wars.

In modern war, adversaries do not face each other eye to eye, hand to hand. They destroy each other from a distance, abstractly, invisibly, killing through and by ideas—German idealism translated into the tongue of Krupp. Even defensive war, which alone is morally admissible, thus becomes repugnant; and this is why Democracy has so hard a task in training democratic soldiers, in building up a democratic army composed of soldiers consciously on the defensive, not seeking to conquer and to subjugate by main force, yet brave and ready to sacrifice their own lives. Militarism and modern war are of a piece with Rousseau's "State of Nature," with Comte's lapse from Positivism into Fetishism, and with the Romanticist yearning for an unreasoning, animal, vegetative life. Neither the great theorist of modern Democracy nor the founder of Positivism nor the Romanticists saw that the "State of Nature," Fetishism and animality signify barbaric blood-lust and a war of all against all. The natural man knows naught of suicide from modern weariness of life, exhaustion and neurasthenia. If he ever kills himself it is in rage at some affront or at the failure of some vigorous effort, whereas the modern man suffers from morbid suicidal mania, from lack of energy, fatigue or dread born of mental and moral isolation, of barren megalomania, and supermanishness. Militarism is an attempt of the superman to escape from diseases which nevertheless it aggravates. The German "Nation of Thinkers and Philosophers" had the greatest number of suicides, developed the completest militarism and caused the world war.

At the same time the psychological contrast between suicide and slaying, between the killing of self and the killing of others, explains why the number of suicides decreased everywhere during the war, especially in the victorious countries. Attention was riveted upon the actual fighting. Men became more objective, less subjective. Indeed, I believe that the moral significance of the world war stands out clearly as an effort to find, in objectivism, freedom from exaggerated subjectivism. The war and the way it was waged grew out of the ethical and mental condition of the modern man and of his whole culture, as I have briefly described it; and the modern antagonism between objectivity and subjectivity is a protracted historical process which was revealed in the war and in its long duration. The universality and the length of the war gave it its peculiar character.

It was, as I have said, a war of peoples, not between the standing armies of former days but between new armies formed on the basis of compulsory military service, armies of reservists. Professional soldiers were comparatively few, though the Kaiser and his Generals and a proportion of their men were soldiers of the old type. The war took on a visage of its own, and the characteristics of the belligerent nations came into play because it was a war of masses. The character of war depends upon the character of the soldiers. If, as pacifists tell us, war lets loose all evil impulses—rage, hatred, and blood-lust—it was not the war itself that engendered them; they were present in the belligerent nations before the war. The devils of 1914 were not angels in 1913. Besides, as I have said, the world war bore an abstract scientific impress. It was a war of position, not a war of movement; it was marked by anonymous and invisible killing until ultimately victory was won in great part by superiority in scientific war-industry and by the mathematical utilization of great masses. But post-war military literature upon the philosophical significance of the war proves conclusively that, on account of its long duration, the decisive factor in it was the general moral condition of the belligerent peoples and armies, not the military training and skill of their leaders. Modern men waged it. And it behoves us to recognize the good qualities of the fighters on both sides, for the very length of the war brought out their great moral strength, their heroism, tenacity and devotion. It showed what modern men are capable of and what they could do were they to rid themselves of the desire to rule over others, and were they not to suppress in themselves the fellow-feeling that is born in every man. True, they would need also to overcome the whole modern hankering after Titanism, and the selfishness of morbid subjectivism and individualism; for supermanishness necessarily ends in suicide and war.

Inadvertently, my analysis is confirmed by the German historian, Lamprecht, who sought, with so much vigor and enthusiasm, to vindicate the Germans in the war. In his history of Modern Germany, written before the war ("Zur jüngsten deutschen Vergangenheit," published in 1904), he rightly describes the epoch as one of "irritability," and adduces both the Emperor William and Bismarck as its characteristic types. In truth, the German superman, the Titan, is a nervous creature who seeks relief from chronic excitement in death or in war, that is to say, in an excitement still more acute.

However true this may be of all nations, it is especially true of the Germans. Their philosophers, artists and other active minds pushed subjectivism and individualism to the point of absurd egomania, with all its moral consequences. Nietzsche's superman, the Darwinian "beast," was to prove a remedy for the inhuman folly of "solipsism." In their spiritual isolation, the German philosophers and men of learning, historians and politicians, proclaimed German civilization and culture as the zenith of human development; and, in the name of this arrogant claim to superiority, Prussian pan-Germanism asserted its right to expansion and to the subjugation of others by sheer force. The Prussian State, its army and its fighting spirit became antidotes to morbid subjectivism. Prussian pan-Germanism is answerable for the world war, morally responsible for it, even if the Austro-Hungarian system shared its guilt and was, in a sense, still guiltier. The people of philosophers and thinkers, the people of Kant and Goethe, which claimed for itself the proud task of enlightening the world, was not entitled to seek in war a way out of the blind alley into which its one-sided, albeit highly refined, culture had led it. Nor could it honestly adopt and support the deceitful and short-sighted policy of the degenerate Hapsburgs. *Corruptio optimi pessima.*

WAR AND RELIGION

The awakening of a religious spirit during and after the war bore out my reading of the war itself. The modern tendency towards suicide is, in the last resort, attributable to the decline of religion and of spiritual and moral authority. When, in so many quarters, men call so earnestly for a religious revival, is it not a sign that they are becoming aware of the singular moral condition of European society out of which the war arose? What a fiasco, what a relapse into Rousseau's "State of Nature" after all our boasting of progress, of our having escaped from the Middle Ages! But when we speak of religion we need to say exactly whether we mean positive, official, ecclesiastical, or non-ecclesiastical faith. No catchword can suffice to define so intricate a matter. In all the countries where I happened to be during and after the war I observed the religious phenomena to which it had given rise and noted the positive and literary forms in which they found expression. I watched the soldiers, comparing the influence of army chaplains upon them, and upon the wounded and the dying, with that of doctors, nurses and laymen. I felt that there was a yearning for religion but that the creeds of the Churches had, and have, far less influence than was supposed. Among our Legionaries in Russia there was a temporary disposition, political rather than religious, to embrace Orthodoxy; but I met not a few soldiers in whom experience of the war had stimulated religious feelings and reflections. Only a small minority of them were satisfied with ecclesiastical dogma.

And the question remains whether and in what degree the religion of the Churches can suffice. Why have the Churches and their creeds lost ground? Why do men—the *intelligentsia* in the first place but also the masses—turn away from them? Why are medieval theocratism and its organization of society declining? In the world war three of the oldest theocracies—Austria, Russia and Prussia—fell. Catholicism failed to save Austria-Hungary, Orthodoxy did not save Russia, nor did Lutheranism avail Prussia. Catholicism, Orthodoxy and Lutheranism failed to prevent the war, just as they had failed to impede the genesis and the development of the general moral condition out of which the war arose—though, like the medieval Church itself, these Churches wielded spiritual authority over society and, in conjunction with the State, temporal authority as well. Why did they lose their influence?

We are, in truth, faced by the great antagonism between the Churches and modern thought, modern feeling and aspiration, in philosophy, art, science, ethical and political ideals and, in a word, modern culture as a whole; and also by the question how this antagonism can be got rid of. To say that the modern man has been led astray by pride and that he must repent in sackcloth and ashes is no solution, for it has been recommended fruitlessly for centuries by orthodox theologians. After the French Revolution and the Napoleonic wars, the old régime and ecclesiastical religion were alike restored without effecting any real improvement. New revolutions supervened in ideas and in politics until finally another revolution was wrought by the world war. And, whatever might be the result of attempts at restoration now, they would assuredly not mend matters.

Let us examine the various elements and factors in religion. Among them are views upon the transcendental, views upon God and immortality, the teachings of theology and of metaphysics, worship, the sense of the relationship of man to God and the Universe, ecclesiastical organization and authority— the priesthood and its hierarchy or theocracy—and morality or the relationship of man to man alongside of his relationship to God and the Universe. The concept of religion is identified with the concept of faith, of childlike faith, and this faith is placed in opposition to reasoned critical scientific knowledge, theology *versus* metaphysical philosophy. As against determinist science and scientific philosophy, religion offers the believer a non-determinist faith in the miraculous. Religion identifies itself with mysticism, with belief in the possibility of direct communication of human souls with God and with the transcendental world; and this mystic communion is set above mundane morality. What do we mean when we say that we need religion and build our hopes upon it? Do we wish to return to the creeds and the doctrines of the Church? If so, of which Church? Is there to be a complete return, a philosophical Canossa? Even though war and revolution have strengthened the religious spirit, has morality, personal and social morality, also been strengthened? In most countries, complaints may be heard of the demoralization caused by the war, not merely among people whom the war made rich but of widespread laxity, slothfulness and dishonesty, and of the decline of morals in the young. If morals are a weighty element in religion—as they certainly are—it is not so easy to assert that religion has been fostered by the war. I have noticed and notice that many people, even those scientifically educated, have fallen into divers forms of mysticism, spiritualism and occultism. But is this type of religious re-awakening really desirable? It seems to me that, religiously, we are in much the same position after the war as we were before it.

The crisis of the modern man is general. It is a crisis involving the whole man, and the whole of spiritual life. Modern life in its entirety, all its institutions, its whole outlook on the world and on the problem of existence need to be revised. An inner lack of unity, an atomization in individuals and in society, a general mental anarchy, a struggle between past and present, fathers and children, the antagonism of the Churches toward science, philosophy, art and the State, permeate the whole range of modern civilization. If we seek peace of mind for ourselves, where and how are we to find it? In the effort to attain spiritual freedom, many fall into excessive individualism and introspection. Hence their spiritual and moral isolation. Many give themselves up to materialism and to a mechanical conception of the Universe. Maybe, we have all cultivated the intellect too one-sidedly and have forgotten the harmonious cultivation of all our spiritual and physical powers and faculties. In their opposition to the Churches and religion, not a few were satisfied with mere skepticism and negation, and thought it enough to be political revolutionaries. Though they were convinced that no lasting organization of society is feasible without agreement on the primary conceptions of life and of the world, they revolted against ecclesiastical discipline, only to become the slaves of parties, groups and factions. Any talk of or call for morality and moral restraint they denounced as antiquated moralizing, and piety and a religious life as superstition. Restlessness, discontent and skepticism; weariness born of disjointedness; pessimism, irascibility and despair ending in suicidal mania, militarism and war—these are the dark sides of modern life, of modern man, of the superman.

After the war a conviction spread that Europe and civilized peoples were in process of final decline. While the pan-Germans often proclaimed, before the war, the decline of the Latin races and of the French in particular, German philosophers of history, like Spengler, now announce the decline of the Germans likewise and of the whole of the West. Some look for salvation to Russia or to the Far East, though Russia suffered overthrow in the war as well as Germany and Austria; and it is certainly characteristic of German literature that Russian influence upon it has grown, an influence noticeable also in France, England and America.

I do not believe in a general and final degeneration and decadence of our civilization. The war was an acute crisis within a chronic crisis for which not we alone but our forefathers are to blame. We were bound to change what they bequeathed to us; but in changing it we erred again and again. Yet honest confession of error is the beginning of improvement. The war and its horrors excited us all, and we stand helpless before the mighty historical riddle of an event unprecedented in human history. But excitement is not a program. We need calm and frank analysis and criticism of our civilization and its elements, and must make up our minds to reform concentrically every sphere of thought and action. There are enough thinking people in all enlightened countries to set about these reforms, hand in hand.

A PHILOSOPHY OF THE WAR

Thus far I have tried to grasp and to explain, psychologically and sociologically, the crisis through which modern men and European civilization and culture are passing. Now I wish briefly to review it in the setting of its historical development. The philosophy of the war which I am propounding was conceived as soon as the war began. It forms a synthesis of my pre-war contributions to the philosophy of history, and I am now expressing it tersely in the shape in which I finally sketched it out during the voyage across the Atlantic on my way home. Afterwards I developed it, particularly by means of a thorough analysis of representative personalities of the modern era, like Rousseau and Goethe, and by a more precise definition of various mental and spiritual tendencies. I may perhaps publish this work separately. For the moment, this summary of it must suffice, so as not to distort the proportions of the present volume.

The fight between the Central Powers and the Allies was a fight of Theocracy—albeit an enfeebled and expiring Theocracy —against Democracy. The Central Powers were led by Prussia which, in recent decades, had adopted the program of Bismarck, the most skilful and consistent warden of the old medieval political and ecclesiastical régime. The political idea of Germany, a Germany Prussianized and led by Prussia, culminated in the principle of a Prussian Monarchy independent of the people, and forming, in Bismarck's eyes, the antithesis to modern Parliamentarism and Democracy. The Emperor William went so far as to declare himself expressly an instrument of God, and his official style "By the Grace of God" took on an anti-democratic sense and meaning. The Monarchy by Divine Right and Divine Grace stood over against the democratic principle "of the people, by the people, for the people."

This absolutism was a continuation of the medieval conception of Empire. The *Imperium* bequeathed by Rome to the Germans was administered by the bigoted Hapsburgs who, amid the religious and political excitement of the Reformation, carried through a violent Counter-Reformation. Prussia became Protestant and strove with Austria for overlordship in Germany until Austria was finally expelled. Then Germany took over the Roman *Imperium*, the Imperial dignity, on her own account. It is one of the many perversities of history—though when we talk of "history" we really say "human beings"—that the Roman Catholic supra-national—and therefore really "Catholic"—Imperialism of the Holy Roman Empire was carried forward by a Protestant and national German State, and that the Roman Catholic State which had stood at the head of the Catholic *Imperium* renounced its Holy Roman Imperial dignity, proclaimed itself a secularized Austrian Empire and ended by accepting a subordinate position as the advance-guard of Germany in the East. Hence the senselessness of Austrian and Prussian policy in the modern era.

Under Prussia, Germany turned the Catholic idea of the Holy Roman *Imperium* into a pagan Roman and German national ideal. By means of pan-German philosophy it developed its forcible "Urge Toward the East" into a general program, that is to say, into an aspiration to rule over the Old World of Europe, Asia and Africa. To this end its colonial policy and its alliance with the declining Ottoman Empire were alike directed.

After a first attempt to form a "League of the Three Emperors" the Triple Alliance was founded under the economic and political pressure of Prussia. In it, Italy had no organic position, for the Triple Alliance really signified German domination over Austria-Hungary. It is characteristic that the beginnings of the Triple Alliance are to be found in Bismarck's negotiations with the Magyars or, rather, with Andrássy, as I have pointed out in speaking of Magyar propaganda in America; and, as Austrian Catholic politicians have insisted, the Magyar State was in the hands of Calvinists—of whom Tisza was an outstanding example—and of Freemasons For this reason the alliance of Hungary with Prussia was by no means incompatible with the postulates of pan-Germanism, false though they were. Nor is it of little moment that, from 1849 onwards, the Magyars were antagonistic to Russia and that, as an Asiatic people, they were doubtless prepared to fall in with German ideas of expansion eastwards. For the same reason it was easy for Germany to secure Turkish acquiescence. I cannot say whether the non-Slav element in the mixed blood of the Bulgars predisposed them also to join the Turks and the Germans in the war. By religion, the Bulgarian dynasty was Catholic; politically, it was Austrian and therefore also German; and, like the other Allies and friends of Prussia, the Bulgars were subject to German educational influences.

Similarly, the initial uncertainty and wavering in the attitude of the Vatican towards the struggle between Germany and the Allies was determined by the old relationship between Austria and Papal Rome, and by consideration for the large Catholic minority in Germany. Practically and historically, the Triple Alliance represented the Middle Ages and the absolutist monarchical régime as it evolved after the weakening of ecclesiastical absolutism during the modern era; and, politically, pan-Germanism became the chauvinistic program of Prussian militarism. Against it France, Russia, the British Empire, Italy, the United States and the other Allies took their stand, all of them, with the exception of Russia, being democratic, constitutional or republican States. Modern Democracy ranged itself against Theocracy.

In contra-distinction to Germany and Austria, the Allies accepted the modern principle of nationality for all peoples and supported the cause of small States and nations, a cause of far-reaching importance, as I have shown when referring to the zone of little peoples who lie between the Germans and the Russians. The democratic principle implies that small States and nations stand on a footing of equality with the big, just as the rights of the so-called "small man" within his own community are, in theory, equal to those of the wealthy and powerful. In foreign affairs the consistent application of the democratic principle is, however, only beginning; and even in the domestic affairs of individual States it has hardly gone beyond the initial stages. But, by accepting the principle of nationality, the Allies guarded themselves against Chauvinism. True, Germany too was "national," though she conceived her "nationality" as something superior to the "nationality" of others. The Allies, on the other hand, recognized both the principle of nationality and also the "catholic"—in the sense of "universal"—principle of humanity, and were bound to recognize it if only by reason of the support given to their cause by the great majority of the national States throughout the world. Thus five continents, and the nations inhabiting them, were *ipso facto* united by the "catholic" humanitarian ideal—which postulated the organization of mankind into a friendly whole—against national-chauvinist pan-Germanism with its spiritual, ethnographical and geographical limitations. President Wilson's League of Nations, organically interwoven with the Peace Treaties, is the first great practical attempt to set up a world-organization which, in virtue of its very dimensions and of the idea it represents, excels and refutes the pan-German program of subjugating the Old World. In the war, the New World and, indeed, the whole world, resisted the pan-German conception of the future of the Old World. As a result, the democratic principle spread from the field of domestic politics into that of international relations. The war overthrew the three centers of theocratic absolutism (the Russian, the Prussian and the Austrian); new Republics and new democracies arose and, with them, the fundamental principles of a new international policy. The League of Nations grew politically stronger and was adopted as a program by all modern and truly democratic politicians and statesmen. The "United States of Europe" ceased to be a Utopia. The dream that one great Power should rule the continent of Europe, and that a number of States and nations should ally themselves against other States and Nations, paled before the establishment of a pacific society of all States and Nations.

In this way the war and the Allied victory altered the face of Europe and of the world. The Caesarism of the three greatest States and of two of the greatest nations in Europe is gone. Numerous smaller peoples—the Czechoslovaks, the Poles, the Yugoslavs, the Roumanians, the Finns, the Letts, the Lithuanians and others—have been liberated and, through the League of Nations, provision has been made to assure the future of racial minorities. May we not hope that these political changes will stimulate endeavors to bring about a renascence and regeneration in ethics and culture? Is there no warrant for this hope in the changes that took place, during the war and the revolution it entailed, within the belligerent countries themselves and among other peoples? The flower of those peoples were in the field, lay in the trenches and were forced to reflect upon the war and its meaning; nor did they alone experience the horrors of war. Their wives and children, mothers and fathers, felt them too. Is it conceivable that, after such experience, a considerable majority, at least, of honest minds should not espouse the new ideal, the ideal of democracy and humanity, and should not strive for regeneration? Along the whole line the trend of events is against the old régime. This is the true meaning of the war and of the post-war era; for the war has freed even Germany from the old régime and, in her freedom, Germany will escape from her spiritual isolation, will win a moral victory over Bismarckianism and will return to the ideals of her Goethe, her Kant and, above all, to those of her Herder and Beethoven.

IN LONDON AGAIN

These and like thoughts were in my mind as we drew near the English coast on November 29, 1918. On reaching harbor, and at the railway terminus in London, military and diplomatic honors reminded me once more that I was the Head of a State. That evening I spent with my dear friends and fellow-workers, Steed and Seton-Watson. But what a difference between the position then and the position in May 1917 when I started from London on my—unforeseen—journey around the world! Yet my cares had not grown fewer; for, if old cares had lifted, new cares had filled their places.

In London I stayed till December 6 and saw many friends, Dr. Burrows, Lord Bryce, Mr. R. F. Young, Lady Paget and others; and, at a lunch to which Mr. Balfour, the Foreign Secretary, invited me, I met a number of political personages, among them Lord Milner, Mr. Churchill and the Secretary of the King, for the King himself was not then in London. The Germans had just proposed to the Allies that a commission should be set up to investigate the question of war guilt. Naturally we talked of the whole political outlook, the end of the war and the task of the impending Peace Conference, though my conversation with Mr. Balfour turned chiefly on the philosophy of religion. Mr. Churchill showed great interest in Russia and in our Legions there, and he was especially pleased that I had stopped Bolshevist agitation among our men without using force. I could not help comparing the standpoint of British with that of German statesmen. What a difference between a really constitutional and Parliamentary spirit and the declining Caesarism of Russia, Prussia, and Austria!

While I was in London, conferring with Foreign Office officials who were likely to take part in the Peace Conference— Sir William Tyrell, Sir Eyre Crowe, Lord Hardinge of Penshurst and my old acquaintance, Sir George Clerk, and was visiting the chief members of the diplomatic corps—I had my first experience of a characteristic diplomatic incident. The column erected at Prague in honor of the Virgin Mary (as a monument of the Hapsburg victory over our people in the Battle of the White Mountain during the Counter-Reformation) had been thrown down, and the Vatican took occasion to draw attention to the matter in London. I do not know in what form the Vatican communication was made, as I was not officially notified; and, though I was unaware of the details of the incident at Prague, I knew that the removal of the column had often been demanded by our people who had doubtless thrown it down in a moment of political excitement, not in a spirit of religious intolerance. In this sense I was able to explain it.

Meanwhile, events on the continent were proceeding apace after the defeat of the Central Powers. On December 1 the British troops crossed the German frontier, and I well remember what an impression the news made in London. On the same day the German Crown Prince renounced all his rights to the Prussian Crown and to the German Imperial dignity; while, in Serbia, Prince Alexander took over the Regency and the Serbo-Croat-Slovene State became a reality. Tidings of the last days of the Austrian Empire reached me also in London— particularly, by special messenger, an account of the way the Austrians had sought to turn to account the meeting of our delegates at Geneva. Some Austrian agents had tried to pry into our delegates' political disposition, and more than one member of our delegation seemed to have fallen into the trap and to have dilated upon the difference between my views and those of Dr. Kramář and his followers. Reports that these delegates were wavering in their opposition to Austria were then sent by the Austrian agents to Vienna; but Dr. Beneš soon came from Paris and cleared up the position in unmistakable fashion. Yet the episode served to remind me of the position I had held in our political world at home before the war, and to make me feel that men rarely undergo a thorough change of heart. They would doubtless say: "Masaryk as President! Good; but he has no Party behind him. He is an idealist, more of a philosopher than a politician." Would not the old antagonisms be revived? Would all political men and parties be able to forget past conflicts and controversies? Very soberly I weighed the pros and cons, and examined the principles on which I should have to act. More than once I reviewed the whole list of men with whom I should have to deal and to work, for I knew them all pretty well. Upon the policy needful for our restored State I felt no manner of doubt, and I was quite certain that I must not give way on the most important issues or on matters of principle;

but I closed emphatically the whole chapter of my personal dislikes.

PARIS, PADUA—AND HOME

Reaching Paris on December 7, I paid my first official visit to the President of the French Republic, M. Poincaré, in order to thank him by word of mouth for all the help he and France had given us; and, at an official dinner, I saw him again. Then I spent some hours with our troops at Darney, inspected them, visited the wounded and, on the way back to Paris, drafted my first Presidential Message. From morning to night I paid and received visits. The Foreign Minister, M. Pichon, showed the utmost cordiality, and I met a large number of the principal public men, including the President of the Chamber, M. Deschanel, and the Prime Minister, M. Clemenceau. Though Clemenceau had long interested me I had never met him in person. His acquaintances had told me that he had, at first, been somewhat pessimistic about the war and the future of France. Therefore it was, psychologically, the more noteworthy that he should have found the energy to work as he worked, not merely to conquer his own pessimissm and skepticism but to serve France. True, there is more than one sort of skeptic. Clemenceau's speeches and Parliamentary activity had attracted my attention long before, as had his literary work—his novel "Les Plus Forts" and his philosophy of history "Le Grand Pan," in which his alleged skepticism stands out in high relief. In the early stages of the war he was not particularly well-disposed towards us, and Austrian and Magyar propagandists spread the report that he was pro-Austrian. When he became Prime Minister on November 16, 1917, a part of the French press reproduced Magyar statements that he would be pro-Magyar because his daughter was alleged to have married a Magyar and his sister-in-law was a Viennese. But the vigorous, matter-of-fact way in which he dealt with the affairs of Prince Sixtus of Parma belied these stories; and, as he had disapproved of my policy in Russia because I refused to take our army to

Roumania, I was all the better pleased to hear him admit that events had proved me to be right. Besides, it was Clemenceau himself who had made the agreement about our Legions with Dr. Beneš as early as December 1917 and January 1918.

With Clemenceau's right-hand man, M. Philippe Berthelot, I discussed every question of importance that was likely to affect the post-war order in Europe and in the Near East. He was an interesting personality, not merely on account of his political position but as a keen observer of the course of world events. He favored consistently the removal of Turkey from Europe, in accordance with the original Allied plan. The eminent journalist, M. Gauvain; Professor Denis; Colonel House, who had invited Dr. Beneš to take part in the Armistice Conference; the American Ambassador, Mr. W. G. Sharp; the British Ambassador, Lord Derby; the Serbian Minister, M. Vesnitch; and Dr. Trumbitch, with whom I discussed in detail our future cooperation with the Southern Slavs, were among the men whom I met or with whom I renewed acquaintance in Paris.

There, too, the outlines of the Little Entente were agreed upon. I negotiated first with the Roumanian statesman, M. Take Jonescu, who presently brought the Greek Prime Minister, M. Venizelos, to me. In accordance with the situation then existing, we contemplated a close understanding with the Southern Slavs and the Poles, as well as with the Roumanians and the Greeks, who had made a Treaty of Friendship with Serbia at the time of the Balkan wars. Though we were fully aware of the obstacles in our path, and particularly of the territorial disputes between the Southern Slavs and the Roumanians, we agreed to clear the ground for ulterior cooperation during the impending Peace Conference. The idea of the Little Entente was, so to speak, in the air. It had been developed by our joint work with the Roumanians and the Poles in Russia, by our close relations with the Southern Slavs in all countries during the war, by common enterprises like the Rome Congress of the Oppressed Hapsburg Peoples, and by the organization of the Mid-European Democratic Union in America. On the basis of this experience,

I put forward in my book, "The New Europe," the demand that, alongside of the big Entente, similar groups should be formed, above all, among the Little States of Central Europe.

Before leaving Paris I was able once more to thank M. Briand—whom I met in the by no means unpolitical drawing-room of our friend, Madame de Jouvenel—for having been the first among Allied statesmen to accept our political program. And, once again, France was the first Allied State to accredit a Minister to our Republic in Prague. He was M. Clément-Simon who, appointed on December 12, started for Prague with me on December 14. The British military attaché, Sir Thomas Cunninghame, who had been appointed to Prague and Vienna, also accompanied us. We went by way of Italy, where, on the frontier at Modane, a General awaited me with an invitation to stay with King Victor Emmanuel at Padua. In fact, the King himself received me at Padua railway station and I was his guest until the morrow. Thus for the third time in my life I met a Monarch—if I except Prince Alexander of Serbia whom I had seen in London. The first was the Emperor Francis Joseph, who made a point of appearing to be the greatest aristocrat in Europe, and posed accordingly as a Monarch everywhere and in everything, whereas the King of Italy was strictly constitutional and unaffected. The second was King Ferdinand of Roumania. At Padua there was a question whether toasts should be exchanged at dinner. Both King Victor Emmanuel and I thought it superfluous, though had I thought otherwise the King would have submitted the text of his toast to his Government. It was my first lesson in constitutionalism.

An inspection of our troops stationed near Padua—the Infantry one day, the Cavalry on the next—ended my work abroad. It was in Italy that my voluntary exile had begun, and in Italy it came to a close. I started for home on December 17, a detachment of our Italian Legionaries, under General Piccione, accompanying me. On the journey my thoughts dwelt on my impending task. The traveling through Austria compelled me to reflect once again upon the disappearing Hapsburg Empire;

and as we passed through Brixen on December 18, all my ideas on Havlíček and Czech policy revived. Havlíček had taught me much; and his words "A reasonable and honest policy" rang in my ears the whole way from Brixen homewards.

It was on Friday, December 20, that we reached the Bohemian frontier. Many a tear was shed by the exiles who thus reached home again after years of wandering, and more than one kissed our Bohemian soil. The Head of the administrative district, a Czech whose accent proved him to have been born a German, made a first official report; and then the members of my family and the political delegates could be greeted. Friday has always been for me a special day of destiny. I do not know whether other men have such days but, in my case, the weightiest and happiest events have often happened on Fridays. I escaped from Austria in December 1914 on a Friday; President Wilson's final answer to Austria and our national Declaration of Independence were issued on a Friday; and on a Friday I set my foot once again on Czech earth after four years' labor abroad.

We stayed that night at Budějovice, or Budweis, so as not to reach Prague at night. Next day we went on through Vesely, Tábor—full of Hussite memories—Benešov and, at last, reached Prague.

What were my feelings as the people of Prague gave me so splendid a reception, and as I drove through the streets in a democratic motor-car instead of the gilded carriage that would have been too reminiscent of times that were past? Was I glad, was I joyous? Seeing the rejoicing, the wealth of costumes, colors, banners, decorations and flowers, answering the warmth of the greetings, what were my thoughts? The heavy work awaiting me, the work of building up our restored State decently and well, constantly weighed on my mind; nor did this train of thought cease when, in the afternoon, I pledged myself solemnly "In honor and conscience to act for the weal of the Republic and of the people, and to respect the laws."

Then, having visited my wife in a nursing home, I slept for the first time in the Castle, that is to say, I spent a sleepless night. Next day, Sunday, December 22, I delivered my first message in the Castle, reviewing briefly what we had done abroad. It had been submitted to and technically revised by the Council of Ministers. The Castle, not the Parliament, was chosen as the scene of this ceremony, although the choice raised the question whether the gathering in the Castle was or was not a National Assembly. The question was solved by incorporating the Message in the report of the Parliamentary Committee appointed to draft the reply to it, and by including it also in the verbatim report of the Assembly's proceedings.

CHAPTER IX

THE RISE OF THE CZECHOSLOVAK REPUBLIC

THERE is much truth in the saying that States are preserved by the same political forces as those which engendered them. For this reason I shall sum up the story of our work abroad in a systematic account of its political and juridical significance, so as to show how our Republic arose and how we attained independence.

Generally speaking, our independence is a fruit of the fall of Austria-Hungary and of the world conflagration. In vanquishing Germany and Austria, the Allies won our freedom and made it possible. At the Peace Conferences the victors established a new order in Western and Central Europe. We took part in these conferences from beginning to end and signed the Treaties, since the Allies, recognizing and accepting our program of liberation, had admitted us during the war into the areopagus of belligerent nations in whose hands the decision lay. And our former enemies presently recognized our independence in their turn by signing and by giving constitutional ratification to the Peace Treaties.

Yet it was only by our resistance to Austria-Hungary and by our revolt against her that we earned our independence. As President Poincaré tersely said, we won it by fighting in France, Italy and Russia. The peculiarity of our revolt lay in its not being carried through by force of arms on our own soil, but abroad, on foreign soil. As a people we were bound to take part in the war. Otherwise independence would not have been attained—assuredly not in the degree in which we attained it. Herein lie the meaning and the political value of our Legions in Russia, France and Italy. They secured for us the goodwill and the help of the Western Powers, while the march through Siberia gained us the liking of the Allied public at large and the respect even of our enemies.

Together with the Legions, those of our soldiers who helped to break up the Austrian Army by active and passive resistance lent essential aid to the cause, especially those who, in resisting, forfeited their lives. Every execution of such men dug deeper the grave of the authorities in Vienna and Budapest, for it proved that our people was locked in a life and death struggle with them. And every such execution we brought to public knowledge abroad, arraigning Austria openly and charging her with persecution and cruelty. In the young sculptor Sapík the spirit of the people was finely revealed. Mobilized and sent to the Russian front, he said, in bidding farewell to his friends at Prague, "I know I shall fall, but I will fire no shot against Russia." Hardly had he reached the front when he fell—having kept his word. Of such as he there were many thousands. The civilians, too, who were executed under the Austrian military terror; or who, like Dr. Kramář and Dr. Rašín, were condemned to death and imprisoned; and those whose property was confiscated or who were made to suffer in other ways, all bore their part in the work of liberation—they and the nameless souls in all classes of the Czech people for whom Austrian persecution made bitterer still the bitter time of war. Our freedom was truly bought with blood.

Other factors in the struggle were the diplomatic action and the propaganda of our National Council abroad. We formed the Legions, developed them into an army, and turned their share in the war to political account. The National Council abroad was the organ of men at home who discerned the nature of the world war and took the fateful decision either to carry on our revolt in foreign countries or to support it effectively by subterranean action at home. Everywhere, even in Russia, the main task was to break down traditional pro-Austrianism; and in this we succeeded.

We, who were abroad, managed besides to convince the Allies of our historical and natural right to independence. We re-

vealed to them the true character of the Hapsburg absolutism.
We showed that, under cover of constitutional appearances, a
minority ruled over a majority in Austria-Hungary and that
things in Austria and Hungary were as anachronistic and
anomalous as was the Caesarism of Prussia and Russia. This
the Western peoples understood as regards Prussia and Russia,
and it was our business to persuade them that the Caesarism of
Vienna was no better, nay, in many respects, worse. We dwelt
upon the cruelty of Austria toward those of her peoples who
were not of her mind, upon her dependence on Germany and
pan-German policy, and upon her heavy share of war guilt; and,
by showing what part our people had taken in the development
of European culture, we justified our claim to independence.
Even among the masses of the Allied peoples our four years'
propaganda spread these truths and drove them home.

Pro-Austrianism did not consist merely of a liking for
Austria and Vienna, but was inspired by the traditional view
that Austria was a dam against Germany; and though the war
was in itself a refutation of this view, it still prevailed. As I
have shown, it was very strong in all Allied and neutral countries, and it was no easy matter to overcome it, the less easy
because many of us had long sought to persuade the world that
Austria was a necessity. Besides, an intense pro-Austrian propaganda worked against us. Our victory was therefore the more
remarkable. The Allies knew less than we about Austria-
Hungary, and they were totally unacquainted with the complicated racial and economic conditions in Eastern Europe. Our
long experience and study of Eastern Europe enabled us therefore to put forward a positively-conceived policy against Austria
and Germany. Indeed, as I have said in referring to my first
official interview with Briand, we supplied the Allies with a
political program. This is no exaggeration, as our friends in
France, England and America admit. Nor did we give them only
our program. We gave them programs for the liberation of other
peoples and for the reconstruction of Europe as a whole. Of
this, proof may be found in my work "The New Europe" which

was handed in French and English to all the Allied delegates to the Peace Conferences at the end of the war.

Moreover, in our propaganda and action abroad, we were financially independent of the Allies. We declined even the friendliest offers of assistance. This is one of the reasons why we disavowed the attempt of the Russian Government to create its own paid "Czech National Council." The only case in which I took an English subsidy was in that of our American Secret Service, as I was entitled to do because it was doing special work exclusively for the Allies. True, we maintained our Legions on credit, but we kept them independent. Though I knew that I was thus mortgaging the Budget of our future State, it seemed to me the only right course.

Several instances of financial dependence which came under my notice strengthened me in this decision. The surprise which it caused some political men in Allied countries proves how weighty it was. They thought we disposed of immense funds, derived from financial resources at home. Thus our revolutionary prestige was enhanced in their eyes. I heard, however, that Austrian agents denounced us to the French as being subsidized by Austria, and there were even people who maintained that we were tools of Germany! The ways of Austrian and German propaganda were truly wonderful. My standpoint was and is that we had a right to a State of our own but that we must vindicate this right ourselves, win our independence anew and preserve it by our own strength. We needed to ask for nothing and we asked for nothing except the friendship and the help of all the Allies. It was, is, and always will be our duty to work strenuously and to be ready for self-sacrifice. This was not only a matter of principle; for, in practice, it meant that our National Council and our army stood on their own feet and were by no means mere political instruments of the Allies.

THE WORK AT HOME

At home there was the same fighting spirit. Our revolt abroad would have been impossible if the people in general had not assented to it from the outset and throughout the war. It is true that, for the first three years, there was no unitary movement embracing all political leaders, parties and members of Parliament. Political leadership was paralyzed by the Government—Klofáč, and afterward Kramář and Rašín, were imprisoned and Stříbrný was mobilized—so that the nation was deprived of visible guidance by its political organizations. Nor, until the end of the war, was armed revolt at home contemplated by the principal parties. It could not be, and there was no need of it; but the whole people took their stand against Austria and showed their ripe sense and their determinatoin in passive and, at the right moment, in active resistance. If our Allies expected an insurrection, and took us to task from time to time because it did not break out, they were wrong and unjust. It was enough that the mass of the nation declined to capitulate to political and military terrorism. Individuals sealed their resistance with their blood. The bulk of the people maintained discipline and, by work, kept themselves healthy and their spirit unbreakable. There were moments of depression (as I realized during the first four months of the war); some individuals and groups lost heart, though rather on account of uncertainty than from fear.

Our people seem to me to have shown remarkable organizing ability and political sense in developing cooperative societies for the supply of food, so that hunger should not weaken their resolution. The work was done chiefly in Bohemia and Moravia, and, to some extent, among the Czechs in Vienna where, however, supplies, especially of meat, were managed by the State. Those of our friends abroad who were, at times, tempted to think our people too passive, failed to understand the worth of this painstaking work in little things; and the action of charitable organizations like the "Czech Heart" was political as well as philanthropic.

The education which our people had enjoyed since our national renascence, came out in this work of detail and in their general discipline. The efforts of Dobrovsky, Jungmann,

Kollár, Palacký, Šafařík and Havlíček as well as those of Rieger, Sladkovský and their younger disciples, together with the influence of our literature, art and, above all, of our schools, had spread a political culture and a national consciousness of which the result was an imposing unanimity. Encouragement and strength were derived from Smetana's music, for Smetana himself had, in his youth, taken part in the revolution of 1848 and his operas foreshadowed our liberation. His "Libuša" is more than a prophecy; it is the musical festival of a nation inwardly set free. Or, to take another example. In those days at Prague Palacký's writings were sold out. Thinking people immersed themselves in his national program and in the testament of the Father of the Nation—an eloquent proof of political maturity. The quality and the level of our education I measure by the fact that neither at home nor, I believe, abroad, was a traitor to be found. Štefánik's probably baseless suspicion I have already mentioned; and I need only say that whereas, according to the latest estimates, 235 Germans were condemned for high treason, only 140 such cases are recorded in Allied countries.

Nor should the influence of our national institutions for physical and moral culture, such as the Sokols and other associations, be overlooked. A nation is an organized whole. These agencies, together with our political parties, organized it. Yet it needs a center for union and cohesion if not for leadership. In our case leadership was supplied by the press, particularly by those journals which, with tactical skill, withstood the military terrorism. By purposeful adroitness they revived sinking spirits, using language incomprehensible to the enemy though comprehensible to every Czech; and the necessary point of cohesion was provided by a few political leaders working in unison. The so-called "Maffia" played an important part from the outset, directing the struggle at home, keeping up communications with us abroad, maintaining the fighting spirit and, at the same time, disseminating news from the Allied world.

As regards the political parties themselves, the lack of unity, the personal and political dispersion that were so noticeable before the war, continued for some time after the war. Attempts to bring them together in 1915 having failed, the "Czech Association" was formed towards the end of 1916 out of members of Parliament and the old "National Committee." In July 1918 a new "National Committee" arose. It included representatives of all parties; and we abroad hoped it would lead to more consistent and unified action against Austria. In what precise relationship it stood to the "Socialist Council," set up in September 1918, is not yet clear. The Socialist Council seems to have been at once an effect of the Russian Revolution and an expression of the desire to unite the Socialist masses.

Between the political mood of the people and the policy of the responsible members of Parliament, difficulties and some antagonism naturally arose as the military situation developed. To the disavowal of our work abroad in January 1917 I have already referred—showing that it coincided with the beginning of the Emperor's peace negotiations—as well as to the political haziness revealed by the omission of a demand for the liberation of Slovakia and for its union with our State from the original drafts of the Declaration prepared for the first sitting of the Austrian Reichsrat. This omission was, however, made good in the final text of the Declaration on May 30, 1917. I know only too well that it was no easy matter to provide for the inclusion of Slovakia. The Slovaks were unknown, the pro-Austrians and the pro-Magyars exploited against us the statements of some of our leading men and made play with our official policy which restricted our aims to the historical rights of the Lands of the Bohemian Crown. And it is noteworthy that one of our historians also opposed our union with Slovakia.

Nor should it be forgotten, in judging the policy of our members of Parliament, that, during the early years of the war, Austria and Germany were victorious and that Russia, from whom so much had been hoped, was the source of many a disappointment. Thus it is comprehensible that not a few of our members should have been ready to halt and that the policy of liberation should have been regarded with some degree of skepticism. An Austrian General is reported to have said of the Czechs: "They join the colors like lambs; they fight like lions; and, when we lose, they are as happy as sandboys." This is a little wide of the mark but it indicates, nevertheless, some degree of indecision and uncertainty on the part of a dependent people groaning under military terrorism.

Perhaps, too, some members of Parliament felt more or less doubtful of our capacity for independence—doubts not always inspired by Austrian terrorism but by political reflection. Though we reported frequently upon the encouraging prospects abroad and urged our people to hold fast, the isolation of our leaders at home from the outside world and the pressure of Vienna upon them neutralized in part the effect of our reports, which may indeed have been thought exaggerated. But the people at large did not waver, even if they were more hopeful at some moments than at others. They wanted complete independence, independence of Austria and the Hapsburgs, as I was sure they wanted it when I went abroad. This desire was justified by our whole evolution under Austria. It could not be freely expressed in the early war years because Austria and Germany were still strong and triumphant; but, by the spring of 1917 when the power of Vienna and of the new Emperor were declining, hearts were beating high in Prague. Then, soon after the disavowal, our writers bestirred themselves. Firmer, albeit still prudent, manifestations followed. Among the workmen, led by the metal workers of the Daněk factories, there was marked political excitement. "Hunger" demonstrations were organized, and a deputation was sent to the Lord Lieutenant demanding the liberation of Dr. Kramář and of Dr. Adler. Some of these workmen were drafted into the army but the others placed themselves at the disposal of our members of Parliament.

From the summer and autumn of 1917 onwards we felt abroad that our members of Parliament were working more decidedly and unitedly against Austria. The declarations they issued on January 6 and April 13, 1918, stood us in good stead.

Little by little, the new National Committee secured the assent of all parties to the demand for a completely independent Czechoslovak State—which was our program abroad; and, when the time was ripe, the leaders of the National Committee gave formal and solemn sanction to this program at Geneva, while other leaders carried through the revolution at home in the same sense, even though they adapted themselves tactically to circumstances in the decaying Austrian State.

Our foreign colonies likewise did their duty. As a branch of the nation in distant lands and other continents, each colony lives amid different surroundings and under other conditions. Yet, despite their isolation, despite these differences, they were united in the endeavor to secure national independence. Each gave its mite. Political and personal antagonisms were got over with comparative ease, not even the Dürich affair doing lasting damage. The mistakes of some individuals and groups did but serve to bring out more clearly the general discipline of our people.

DE FACTO AND DE JURE

It is now necessary to examine in some detail the circumstances in which our State arose *de facto,* politically and materially, and those which gave it *de jure,* lawful, formal existence, that is to say, how our historical and natural right to an independent State was recognized by the Allies and afterwards by the Central Powers, and how our revolution abroad and at home was legalized.

In my work abroad I was always careful to cast our political program into a juridical form, since I had in mind the legal and international problems that would arise at the Peace Conference. Our right to independence I endeavored to define as exactly as possible so that foreign public opinion might become familiar with it. This was, indeed, the kernel of our propaganda. Starting from the historical rights of the Lands of the Bohemian Crown, which entitled us to the complete restoration of our State, I explained that, *de jure,* our State had never ceased to exist, and I invoked also our national right to independence and unity with especial reference to Slovakia. As I was fully aware that, like our National Council abroad, I was a revolutionary instrument, I expected the official representatives of other States to take their stand upon the Legitimist principle in dealing with me. They did so at first, even in regard to our prisoners of war, though not always consistently or in a hostile spirit. But much tact, and utilization of the growing feeling against Germany and her Allies, were necessary in order to establish regular relations between our National Council and the Allied Governments. Express recognition came later. The Allies were waging regular war against Austria-Hungary and observed international usage and wont. But when this usage was violated by the German invasion of Belgium, by the support given to the anti-English agitation in Ireland and by the propaganda in America against Austria, the Legitimist principle faded and we were recognized *de facto* and, presently, *de jure*. The work done by Voska in America and by Dr. Osuský and others in Switzerland in revealing these German and Austrian maneuvers was therefore of great value.

As time went on, our propaganda spread knowledge of our historical rights; and our natural rights and the justification of our revolt were also recognized by the more advanced public men and parties. Our efforts to gain freedom appealed to Western opinion. I, as a member of Parliament, was looked upon not only as the representative of my own constituency but as that of the whole people. When I said that I was acting in agreement with the majority of our political parties and of their leaders, my statements were believed. My status as a mandatory was everywhere regarded as important; and as early as 1914 my friends Steed and Seton-Watson had thought it essential in England. Even when negotiating with Dr. Beneš on the subject of our recognition in 1918, Mr. Balfour, as British Foreign Secretary, still felt some doubt whether our National Council was sufficiently representative of the whole nation. My knowledge of Western Parliamentarism had led me to submit my political program to all our party leaders before I left Prague and to ask for their opinion and assent; and though I was not in a position formally to answer for these parties or to get written confirmation from them, their assent entitled me to regard myself as authorized by them; and in 1915 I had applied directly to them for this authority.

After our National Council abroad had been regularly constituted in 1916, it gained influence in proportion as we organized our army and, by taking part in the war, became to some extent a military factor. The army convinced everybody that we were in earnest. The National Council became a *de facto* Government which, like our army, was progressively recognized by the Allied Governments. The various formulas of recognition show how far the National Council (afterwards the Provisional Government) was recognized *de facto,* and how far *de jure.* It is interesting to compare these formulas for, if right is understood as a political expression of actual events, they reflect in no small measure the political and military situation. Indeed, the table of recognitions given in the appendix shows how closely they kept pace with our military progress. Their significance depends upon the circumstances out of which they arose and the importance of the persons who granted them. Certainly President Wilson's recognition of us was very weighty because of the constitutional position of the American President and of his special relationship to his Government. In England, Italy and France, governments are stronger than in America, and there is no authority corresponding to the President of the United States. The Kings of England and of Italy and the President of the French Republic have not the same responsibility as he for acts of the Government. Therefore, in these countries, it is recognition by the Government that counts. All the Allies felt the great importance of America and it was for this reason that Wilson's final answer to Austria had so potent an effect.

The formulas of recognition were not merely unilateral promises, prudently worded. Some of them were regular bilateral treaties. All of them were preceded by negotiations between our National Council, or Provisional Government, and the Allied

Governments. The recognition of the National Council—in the first instance only of my own person—and of our National program, began unofficially through individual public men, such as the American Senator Kenyon who, on May 25, 1917, declared in Congress that the independence of the Czech nation must be a condition of peace. Similar individual declarations were made in the French Parliament, in England and in Russia. Then came the recognition of our rights by individual Ministers and, finally, by Governments. Some political men and lawyers were perturbed by the circumstances that our National Council, or Provisional Government, was established abroad, not on the territory which we claimed for the Czech State, and that our army had likewise been created and was operating outside our country. I answered by citing the analogy of the Serbian Government at Corfu; and, in the long run, the Allies made no bones about the matter.

The dates of the various recognitions and the conditions under which they were granted must also be borne in mind. France took the initiative at the beginning of 1916 and again in 1917; and though, as a Monarchy, England is more conservative, she willingly accepted our National Council and recognized our State rights. This is why I value so highly Mr. Asquith's early decision to take the chair at my first lecture in London University; and the formal declaration upon which Mr. Balfour agreed with Dr. Beneš, involves very complete recognition. Monarchical Italy got into touch with me very early at Berne and maintained contact with Štefánik and Beneš. If Sonnino's and Orlando's formulas of recognition were marked by some reserve on account of the Southern Slav question, the Italian Government gave ready support to the formation of our Legions, and we are indebted to it for the organization of our reserves after the conclusion of the Armistice.

Yet the negotiations with the Allied Governments for recognition were often long and difficult. There is, for instance, a great difference between recognizing a right to independence and direct recognition of the independence itself; and there is a certain difference between the recognition of our National Council and the subsequent recognition of it as a Provisional Government. Of this the negotiations with Mr. Balfour are an example. To the account which Dr. Beneš has already made public I may add that the British Minister's reluctance to recognize the National Council directly as a Government was happily overcome by the word "trustee" which Mr. Steed suggested to Dr. Beneš.

THE LEGAL BIRTH OF OUR STATE

The question arises when and how our State arose, and how long it has been in existence. How and when was it internationally recognized, what is the international legal significance of the various recognitions, and which of them are internationally and juridically decisive?

It is no easy matter for international and constitutional lawyers to answer these or other questions relating to the birth of new States. The world war created political and legal conditions which lay beyond the scope of recognized international jurisprudence in regard to all the new States. In our case, the general situation and our position in Austria-Hungary made our independence legally and internationally contingent upon recognition by the Allies in the first place. Mr. Temperley, the English historian of the Paris Peace Conference, dates the decisive validity of the recognition of our State from the admission of Czechoslovak plenipotentiaries to the plenary sitting of the Paris Conference on January 18, 1919; but he is uncertain whether November 5, 1918—when the representatives of our National Committee returned to Prague from Geneva, where they had established a direct connection with our Paris National Council and Provisional Government, ought not to be regarded as our State birthday. He attaches so much importance to this "direct" connection because several of the formulas of recognition which the Paris National Council had received undeniably possessed State-creative authority. Such authority he finds in the declarations of Mr. Balfour (August 9), of President Wilson (September

3), of M. Pichon (October 16), and of Baron Sonnino (October 24), 1918.

Seton-Watson accepts Temperley's view of the State-creative value of our admission to the Peace Conference, but he ascribes approximately equal importance to the British, American and above all the French recognitions. Others see State-creative force in the recognition of the Provisional Government and of the National Council. The difficulty lies in the circumstance that an independent State usually arises on the territory inhabited by its citizens. In our case, however, the Government and army abroad were recognized and therefore the State or, at least, the principle of State independence. Thus the reality departed from previous theory and usage. A further complication lay in the revolution at home. On October 28, 1918, the Prague National Committee proclaimed itself expressly as a Government "from this day onwards"; and both it and the first Statute announced the formation of the Czechoslovak State. This first Statute, albeit with some amendments, was put on the Statute Book and marked the beginning of a special independent legislative authority.

The position was therefore that, after receiving recognition from many quarters, the National Council abroad proclaimed itself as the Government of the Czechoslovak State and was recognized as such both by the Allies and by the chairman and the representatives of the National Committee at home. But, on the other hand, the National Committee at Prague also proclaimed itself as a Government. So, for a time, we had two Governments, one abroad recognized by the Allies, and one at home set up by right of revolution. The establishment of these two centers of action was due to the peculiar character of our revolt against Austria, which was carried out abroad and at home. But the important thing was that both centers, both *de facto* Governments, worked hand in hand and that no antagonism arose between them such as, for instance, arose between the Polish Governments in Warsaw and in Paris. As soon as our home Government was set up, it naturally became the head of the administration, and derived from this position its character and its authority, while the embryonic Government abroad had its own military and diplomatic work to do, particularly in connection with the peace negotiations. The problem was then to unite the two Governments.

When, therefore, did our State begin? Some writers conclude that it began on October 14, 1918, when the transformation of our National Council abroad into a Provisional Government was notified to the Allies. The French Government was the first to recognize it on October 15, and this recognition Seton-Watson regards as decisive. I agree with him and hold that our State has existed *de jure* since that day. On the other hand, the view was held that its existence dates from the Washington Declaration of Independence on October 18; but the history of the Declaration proves that it was the act of a Government already in being. Hence the decisive character of the date on which this Government was recognized. At home, the National Committee proclaimed itself as a Government on October 28, the date now generally accepted as the birthday of our State. But the Allied Governments negotiated with the Provisional Government abroad as the true representative of the nation and of the State from the moment they had recognized it. Their recognition, given during the war, was valid after the war and above all for the Peace Conference, as is eloquently proved by the inviting of Dr. Beneš to take part in settling the terms of the Armistice with Germany on November 4. Consequently, Dr. Beneš was looked upon as the representative of an independent Allied State, and he signed with the others the Minutes of these historic proceedings. The international significance of this document comes out most clearly if we consider the conduct of the Great Powers towards other States which were in process of formation, especially Yugoslavia and Poland. Serbia was invited to the Peace Conference as an independent Allied State; but it was long before Croatia—which was looked upon as a part of Austria-Hungary—was recognized as a portion of Yugoslavia. Hence the difficulty of securing recognition for Yugoslavia as distinguished from Serbia; whereas Slovakia was regarded by the Allies from the outset as a component part of our United State, although Slovakia, like Croatia, had belonged to Hungary. In the case of Poland the Moraczewski Government at Warsaw, which Dmowski's and Paderewski's Polish Committee in Paris did not recognize, was only granted express recognition in February 1919. Meanwhile our Provisional Government had been exercising its functions abroad from the very beginning of the peace negotiations.

When the Armistice negotiations began, the French Government drafted a plan for the Peace Conference. Dr. Beneš sent me a report upon it, and the French Ambassador in Washington, M. Jusserand, handed it to the American Government on November 29. It distinguished between Czechoslovakia and States like Yugoslavia which were in process of formation. Nobody doubted that these States would be formed—indeed, the Allies regarded their formation as part of the peace program—but there is a difference between a program, a promise, and real complete recognition. Our National Council abroad had been recognized by the Allies as the supreme authority over our army abroad— this is what I had worked for so hard in Russia—and therefore as a Government, if only a Provisional Government. And a Government is the Government of a State. Its status is shown, moreover, by the fact that Dr. Beneš, as Foreign Minister in it, appointed our first diplomatic representatives before the revolution took place at home, and that these representatives were acknowledged by foreign Governments. And though, later on, I, as President, gave Dr. Kramář, the Prime Minister, when he went as a delegate to the Peace Conference, the same credentials as Dr. Beneš received, Beneš had taken part in the peace negotiations before getting his credentials, and all the official Allied documents referred to him as Minister.

As a matter of fact the French Government and political circles in Paris were disquieted by the proclamation of the National Committee and by the events of October 28 at Prague, because it was imagined that the Prague Government was pro-Austrian and that it had been set up against the Government abroad. News of the revolution may have reached Paris by way of Vienna and have described it as a pro-Austrian undertaking. The delegates of the Prague National Committee, who left for Geneva before the revolution, evidently knew nothing of what had happened at Prague on October 28. But at Geneva they understood the significance of the Allied recognition which we had received—especially from President Wilson—and, in their agreement with Dr. Beneš, they approved of the Provisional Government abroad and of all it had done. They also expressly addressed Dr. Beneš as Minister. Thus they confirmed the declarations of the Chairman of the Czech Association on October 2, and of the Prague National Committee on October 19, that the question of Czechoslovak independence was international and not susceptible of settlement in Austria. But under pressure of the home situation, the National Committee was obliged to take action on October 28 and to proclaim itself a Government; and, as we shall see, the Government abroad was presently liquidated.

A distinction must be made between the actual existence of our State and its earlier official beginning as determined by international recognition. The fact of the revolution at Prague and in the whole country on October 28, speaks in favor of the date October 28, 1918. The whole nation saw in the revolution the beginning of a State independent of and detached from Austria and the Hapsburgs. And, finally, the formal circumstance that, on October 28, the nation publicly declared itself independent on its own soil speaks in favor of that date. Indeed, many authorities on constitutional law regard this circumstance as the necessary condition of the creation of a State. And though, as I have said, I hold that our State exists *de jure* since October 15, 1918, I decide *de facto* for the date of October 28 on the grounds just given. The question has its practical as well as its theoretical side, for it might affect the beginning of our obligation to pay reparations. Though not a political institution, the Reparations Commission decided, on April 15, 1921, that Czechoslovakia became a co-belligerent through the revolution of October 28, 1918.

Juridically, these questions have not yet been thoroughly studied. In studying them constitutionally and politically lawyers will find many an interesting and surprising problem, in our case as well as in those of other States which arose after the war. Precise juridical formulation of the actual conditions was not immediately feasible; and critics will discover more than one gap in the negotiations for the Armistice and the Peace Treaties. As in all revolutions, we have as yet no exact account of what happened. Events followed so swiftly one upon another and were in themselves so indefinite that it is no easy matter to describe them with scientific precision.

THE REVOLUTION AT HOME

Yet, for present purposes, it suffices to take the official documents and the public statements of the revolutionary leaders. During the night between October 27 and 28 special editions of the Prague newspapers announced that the Austro-Hungarian Foreign Minister, Count Andrássy, had accepted President Wilson's peace conditions. Dr. Rašín and Dr. Soukup declared this acceptance to be "the dying words of Austria-Hungary and the end of the Hapsburg Monarchy"; and on the same day, Dr. Rašín's manifesto appealed to the nation "not to dash the hopes of the civilized world which, with blessings on its lips, remembers thy glorious history culminating in the immortal deeds of the Czechoslovak Legions in Siberia and in the West. . . . Keep thy escutcheon bright as thy national army has kept it. . . . Belie not the faith of our liberators, Masaryk and Wilson, that they have won freedom for a people fit to govern itself. . . ."

Thus Dr. Rašín repeated what our representatives had declared in Vienna on October 2, when Staněk, the Chairman of the Czech Association, had made a speech recognizing the National Council abroad and our Legions in the name of all Czech members of Parliament. He said to the Austrians, "You wished to exclude us from the peace negotiations, but now, against your will, you will find Czechs taking part in them, as representatives of the Czechoslovak brigades. With them you will have to negotiate upon the Czech question, not with us; and hence we decline to negotiate with you. This question will be solved elsewhere than in Austria. Here there are no factors competent to solve it." And, in its proclamation of October 19, after the manifesto of the Emperor Charles, the National Committee in Prague identified itself with the declaration of the Czech Association, refused to discuss the Czech question in Austria and said: "The Czech question has ceased to be an Austro-Hungarian internal affair. It has become an international question and will be solved together with all world questions. Nor can it be solved save with the assent and in agreement with the internationally-recognized portion of the Czech nation beyond the frontiers of Bohemia."

The great importance which Dr. Rašín and Dr. Soukup assigned to President Wilson's answer to Austria-Hungary and to Andrássy's acceptance of it is clear; and from Dr. Rašín's account of the revolution in his "Maffia," we see how anxiously he had awaited the complete capitulation of Austria. He saw it in Andrássy's Note. Upon this capitulation the revolution followed immediately and, by it, the whole character of the revolution, especially its calm and bloodless course, was decided.

It has been argued that the revolution was somewhat belated and that it ought to have taken place immediately after the manifesto of the Emperor Charles on October 16, or after Wilson's answer which was published at home on October 21. I myself expected some demonstration on the part of our people after the Declaration of Independence in America which, like Wilson's answer, counteracted the Emperor's manifesto. In fact the statement issued by our National Committee in Prague upon the Emperor's manifesto was such a demonstration; and it seems to me now that the policy adopted by Dr. Rašín, in agreement with the whole National Committee, was right. The decision to await the complete capitulation of Austria corresponded to the disparity between Austrian military power and our own feeble forces at home. Had action been taken immediately after the Emperor's manifesto and the upheaval in Vienna, we should have needed a violent revolt, and that was beyond our strength; and if negotiations had been carried on with Vienna for the transformation of the Bohemian Lands into a National State—even as a merely tactical move—obligations of some sort would have been incurred and a bad impression would have been made abroad. The subsequent negotiations, under different conditions, with the Lord Lieutenant in Prague were less compromising and less open to misunderstanding.   The collapse of the Austrian forces on the Italian front might perhaps have served as a starting-point for a revolt; and I admit that a more radical group, if it could have been organized, might then have turned the situation to account. But by marking time for a while until Austria-Hungary had capitulated to Wilson, success was more surely and easily attained. In basing their action upon the Austrian acceptance of Wilson's program—an acceptance the more significant because it came from Andrássy, a Hungarian politician—Dr. Rašín and his friends clearly linked the revolution at home with the highest achievement of the Provisional Government abroad, and thus made their action on October 28 a synthesis of our whole revolution.

From Dr. Rašín's and Dr. Soukop's report in the Year Book of the Czechoslovak National Assembly, it appears that the National Committee negotiated, on October 28 and 29, with the Austrian military and civil authorities, and that a "Convention" was concluded with the military Command in Bohemia on October 28.   The Austrian military representatives accepted the "cooperation" of the National Committee and undertook to do nothing against its will.   Consequently, it was agreed on October 29 between the Lord Lieutenant and the members of Parliament, Soukop, Stříbrný, Rašín and Svehla, that the National Committee should be "recognized" as an executive organ of the Sovereign Nation (not of the State) and that it should be "associated" with the work of public administration.   In view of its brevity and vagueness this report needs to be completed and explained by those concerned.   What did they "agree" upon and what was the meaning of "cooperation" and of "association"?   How long were these arrangements to last, and with what object?

Obviously, the Lord Lieutenant in Prague, Count Coudenhove, as a representative of the Austrian Government, negotiated with the National Committee on the basis of the Emperor's manifesto, and perhaps on that of Dr. Lammasch's program for the establishment of Federal States which the Emperor had sanctioned on October 22. As an Imperial Lord Lieutenant he could not negotiate for the establishment of a Republic and a State independent of Austria and the dynasty. As is known, Count Coudenhove hints that the National Committee referred, in their dealings with him, to the Emperor's wish to set up local national governments. This would certainly have meant a Federal State within the framework of a new Austria. But his interpretation is not confirmed by the documents dated October 28. The text of the first Czechoslovak Statute and of the revolutionary manifesto differ from the Emperor's manifesto. He demanded the territorial integrity of Hungary, whereas the first Statute and the manifesto of October 28 speak of the "Czechoslovak" State and of the provincial authorities, with evident reference to Slovakia. On the other hand, it is true that the Emperor's manifesto mentions "Czechoslovaks." But the Statute declares that the form of the State shall be settled by the National Assembly and by the Provisional Government in Paris. This is in contradiction with the Emperor's manifesto which leaves no room for doubt that the form of our State was to be federal. (The first Statute and the revolutionary manifesto approximated more nearly to Dr. Lammasch's program.) And, in the preamble to the Statute, the Czechoslovak State is declared to be independent. Juridical independence is not a precise concept, yet it is in opposition to the absolute vagueness of the constitutional program contained in the Emperor's manifesto. There may be a difference between the wording of the Statute and of the revolutionary manifesto, and what the National Committee may have said, for tactical reasons, to Count Coudenhove. On this point we must await an authentic report. Meanwhile it may be admitted that the wording of the Statute and of the manifesto is indefinite. In the preamble to the Statute the National Committee describes itself as the executive organ of State sovereignty, but its first clause restricts the idea of sovereignty to sovereignty in home affairs. The form of the State is reserved for settlement by the National Assembly and the National Council, or Provisional Government, in Paris; but both are vaguely described as "organs of the unanimous will of the nation." In the revolutionary manifesto, the National Council calls itself, indeed, a Government, though it also calls itself, somewhat inexactly, the "only qualified and responsible organ."

While the revolution was proceeding at Prague, certain members and delegates of the National Committee were negotiating with Dr. Beneš at Geneva, the negotiations deriving their significance from the fact that they were conducted by Dr. Kramář who was chairman of the National Committee. The points of agreement to which they led, on October 31, are more definite than the Prague documents of October 28. Some of these points have been published, others not. I possess Dr. Beneš's official report upon them; and I am now more fully acquainted with the Austrian diplomatic reports—for, as I have said, the Austrians watched the proceedings closely. In point of fact, the Geneva Agreement recognized the Provisional Government in Paris and its work. It recognized, too, Dr. Beneš as Minister and the Republican form of the State which the Provisional Government abroad had proclaimed. This recognition refers to the Washington Declaration of Independence in which the Provisional Government laid down the fundamental principles of our reborn State. The ties with Vienna, Budapest and the Hapsburg dynasty were very definitely cut.

Though nothing has hitherto been published on this point, the Republican form of State was thus agreed upon at Geneva. Apparently, the delegates from Prague were not authorized to proclaim the Republic openly. The National Committee may have felt uncertain because of rumors in Prague that the National Council abroad had negotiated with Prince Arthur of Connaught and other hypothetical aspirants to the Prague throne. In Geneva this uncertainty was dispelled. Dr. Beneš informed the members of the National Committee there that no arrangements of any kind had been made about the throne, and he called upon them to sanction what he had done abroad, including our proclamation of the Republic. I possess the text of the telegram which Dr. Beneš sent from Geneva to the French Government upon the agreement; it mentions first of all the adoption of the Republican system—an excellent move in view of the attempts of Vienna to influence the Allies even after the revolution in Prague. But the agreement itself was declared to be confidential lest reprisals be taken. The delegates even thought of returning to Prague by way of Germany; and between Prague and Vienna negotiations went on to assure their safety on the journey home.

After their return to Prague the political position was cleared up. The ties with Austria and the dynasty having been formally severed at Geneva, the form of the State was settled at home in accordance with the decision of the Provisional Government abroad. Mr. Temperley has laid stress upon the political and juridical significance of the return of the delegation from Geneva to Prague and dates from it the existence of our State. Indeed, the way the delegates were received in Prague shows that our public opinion knew what the Geneva negotiations meant.

The relationship between the Provisional Government and a Government eventually to be constituted at Prague was naturally considered at Geneva. Though the records hitherto published do not show how the question was settled, the unpublished points of the agreement provided that the two Governments should be amalgamated, Dr. Beneš and Štefánik, the two Ministers in the Provisional Government, entering the Prague Government. I ceased to be Prime Minister and Minister of Finance as soon as I had been elected President and the Government had been finally established.

It may be asked why the revolution was not carried through completely on October 28 in the whole field of State and provincial administration. What happened was that on October 28 the National Committee took over the War Wheat Institute, the Lord Lieutenancy, the Provincial Administrative Commission and the Provincial Military Command; or, rather, negotiations were begun for the transfer of the Lord Lieutenancy, and only half, not the whole of the Military Command was taken over. It was no accident that the War Wheat Institute came first. The question of supplies was very weighty, and by securing the Wheat Institute the National Committee got control over the troops which depended upon it. This, I think, was a good plan. On October 29 the police headquarters, the Provincial High Court and the Public Prosecutor's Office were seized. On October 30 both the Lieutenancy and the whole of the Military Command were taken, after the military had attempted to regain control. This was the most dangerous moment in the revolution at home. The dynasty and the Austrian State were founded upon the army, and the Military capitulation had therefore great significance. On October 30, too, came the appointment of Tusar, a member of Parliament, to negotiate with Andrássy in Vienna; and the Slovak declaration of union at Turčansky St. Martin. After the return of the delegation from Geneva on November 5 the form of the State was finally settled. As leader of the delegation and chairman of the National Committee, Dr. Kramář announced publicly, in a speech before the railway station, that we should have a free, popular Democratic Republic; but not until November 14 was the revolution formally and materially completed. It took a fortnight to overcome technical difficulties and to bring the whole administration of the State and of the province actually into the hands of the National Committee.

Whenever a full account of the revolution is written, it will need to describe what went on in the various parts of the country. Revolutionary Committees, acting under orders from Prague, were formed in the administrative districts of Bohemia, while at Brno, or Brünn, and throughout Moravia, the Moravian members of the National Committee kept step with Prague and were in constant telephonic communication with the capital. Practically and theoretically some weight attaches also to the question whether the sovereignty of the Czechoslovak State prevailed throughout Slovakia from October 28 onwards. On this point there have been, I know, differences of opinion between various

Departments of State, and the Supreme Administrative Tribunal has had to deal with them.

THE QUESTION OF THE REPUBLIC

The question whether our State should be a Republic or a Monarchy is in itself important. Before the war our constitutional program was monarchical. If individuals in other parties be left out of account, only the Social Democrats were, as a party, Republican; but even their republicanism was more theoretical than practical. There was no real, direct republican propaganda. I was republican in principle when I went abroad in December 1914, but the issue did not then seem to me urgent; and, in the very last resort, if Russia had not collapsed, I should have been prepared to support the election of some foreign dynasty, though not the Russian if it had been possible to avoid it. Hence the importance of ascertaining how and when, abroad and at home, the republican form was chosen, for the question of form is independent of the question of the State itself. The first Statute of October 28 leaves the form in suspense.

Abroad, as I have said, I reported to the Allies that the majority of our people were monarchists. This was in 1914 and 1915. But, in my memorandum to the French Government and to the Allies in February 1916, I declared officially in favor of a Republic. Consequently we proclaimed the Republic, finally and solemnly, in the Washington Declaration of Independence, and this Declaration was accepted at Geneva and in Prague.

Among us, as elsewhere, the Russian Revolution had turned feeling decisively towards a Republic. The first demand for it was openly put forward in the meetings of workmen which the Czech Socialist Council organized at Prague and in a number of provincial towns and in villages on October 14, 1918; and though Dr. Rašín states in his "Maffia" that Austrian military dispositions prevented this from being done in Prague itself, the Socialist proclamation was disseminated among the people in leaflet form. Upon the views of the leading members of the National Committee the only evidence is a report written by Lammasch according to which Dr. Kramář stated, on his way to Geneva (October 22), that while he personally was monarchist, the majority of the Committee were republicans. But Kramář's royalism was not Hapsburgian. At Geneva he, like all the members of the delegation, was anti-Austrian and anti-Hapsburg, though he still favored a monarchy under a Russian dynasty. As Chairman of the National Committee, his view carried weight and it certainly influenced his party colleagues and perhaps some other members of the National Committee. Yet he, too, accepted the Republic under the impression of Dr. Beneš's account of the situation abroad. This is how I interpret his public speech on his return from Geneva. General Štefánik was also inclined to favor a monarchical form of the State though he agreed, after some hesitation, to the proclamation of the Republic in the Washington Declaration of Independence.

The most radical of the draft Constitutions which were submitted to the National Committee at Prague in 1917 had foreshadowed a personal union with Austria, that is to say, self-government under one and the same monarch; but it must be observed that these drafts were written under Austrian pressure. It was not until October 14, 1918, that serious discussion of the Constitution and the form of the State began, on a juridical basis which Dr. Pantuček had worked out. His report upon this discussion is weighty because it shows that even before October 28 the leading members of Parliament had taken all political eventualities into account, and it is obvious that there was no longer any question of our remaining within the Hapsburg Monarchy but only of establishing a State entirely independent and republican in form.

THE POLICY OF VIENNA

When describing in an earlier chapter the closing phases of my work in Washington I gave some account of the chief manifestations of Austrian policy. The history of this policy is of moment in judging our revolution in Prague, and I propose now to complete it in the light of documents subsequently received.

In Vienna it had not been forgotten that, at the opening sitting of the Austrian Reichsrat in 1917, the Czech Parliamentary Association had demanded the transformation of Austria-Hungary into a League of States; and the manifesto issued by the Emperor Charles on October 16, 1918, was intended as an appeal to our people, to the Southern Slavs and, at the same time, to President Wilson. Thoroughly informed by Professor Herron, President Wilson stood fast, and I checkmated the manifesto by declaring our independence on October 18. Next day, Wilson's answer to Austria struck Vienna like lightning. Dr. Redlich, the former Austrian Minister, relates that when it reached Vienna on October 19, it caused a panic at Court and in the Ministry for Foreign Affairs. It was, as he says, the death sentence of the Hapsburg dynasty. Dr. Lammasch was then sent for. He worked out his plan to turn Austria into a Confederation or League of States. The Emperor sanctioned it on October 20. For Austria it was radical, and calculated to appeal to Wilson. All the Hapsburg peoples were to take part in the Peace Conference where territorial questions would be decided, even the question whether the new States should be united in a Confederation or not.

But the Magyars raised obstacles. The Hungarian Prime Minister, Dr. Wekerle, rejected Lammasch's plan, clung to the Emperor's manifesto, demanded a personal union between Hungary and Austria and promised the Croats merely a revision of the Hungaro-Croatian settlement of 1868. Though people in Vienna were furious, the Magyars would not give way. Viennese policy sought to gain the support of the Czechs and especially that of the Southern Slavs, albeit with the intention of playing the Croats off against us. This time, however, the old tactics of *divide et impera* failed to work.

Towards the end of October, when the Austro-Hungarian army on the Italian front went to pieces before its final defeat, the position of Austria became desperate. On October 26 the

Emperor Charles telegraphed to the Emperor William his "unalterable decision to conclude a separate peace within 24 hours and to ask for an immediate armistice." This was done; and, during the night from October 27 to October 28, Count Andrássy, who had been appointed Austro-Hungarian Foreign Minister, accepted President Wilson's "death sentence." Deadly fear prevailed in Vienna, above all, fear of Bolshevism. The Russian precedent and the collapse of the army struck the Court, the Government and the Army Command with paralysis. This is clear from the confessions of the Austrian Commanders, and it explains the conduct of Vienna after Wilson's answer and the defeat in Italy.

As recently as October 14 the Austrian authorities had replied by reprisals and persecutions to the republican demonstrations of the Socialist Council at Prague and in Bohemia. An official report shows how terror-stricken they were. The Lords Lieutenant of Bohemia and Moravia sent to Vienna full accounts of every meeting and every speech, and looked upon the republican demonstrations as an unpardonable political crime. This was before Wilson's answer. After it, Vienna was stunned, as the story of Dr. Beneš's last dispatch to Prague strikingly proves.

This dispatch, or report on the situation abroad, was written on September 11. It was received in due course at Prague by Dr. Šámal who handed it to the Executive of the National Committee. But to make quite sure that it would reach its destination, Dr. Beneš wrote it out again, in fuller detail, and sent it by a female messenger from Switzerland to Prague. She was arrested, and the document fell into the hands of the Austrian War Office on the very day when the Emperor sanctioned Lammasch's policy. Though the report actually contained the name and address of the person to whom it was to be delivered, the Austrian authorities took no steps against him. On the contrary, it gave the delegates of our National Committee passports for Geneva and finally decided to accept Wilson's program.

It is in the light of this change in the standpoint of Vienna that the course of the revolution in Prague must be judged.

Even when Andrássy's capitulation had brought on the revolution, the position was not thought dangerous. True, the Minister of the Interior showed some anxiety about the fate of the Germans in Bohemia, but he expected that their National Committee would, with the help of the Government, find means of getting special treatment for them. On October 29 the Austrian Cabinet authorized the Lords Lieutenant in Bohemia and Moravia to negotiate with our people; and, on receiving reports of the arrangements made with our National Committee in Prague, the Ministry of the Interior instructed the Lord Lieutenant of Bohemia not to oppose political demonstrations. Similarly, on hearing the first news from Prague on October 28, the Vienna War Office ordered the Military Commands at Prague, Brünn and elsewhere to negotiate with the National Committee in case of need; and, during the following night, it expressly authorized them to accept the National Committee's proposals. Vienna was informed by the Military Commands in Prague and elsewhere, and by the civil authorities throughout Bohemia and Moravia, that the Austrian coats of arms were being torn down and the rosettes removed from the officers' caps—but no surprise was shown. In any case, it seems to have been thought, the new States would want their own coats of arms and emblems. In fact, all the local army headquarters were instructed to sort out the Austrian regiments according to their racial composition so far as this could be done peacefully and without revolt.

So excited and bewildered was Vienna that the Supreme Military Command submitted to the men in the field, on October 29, the question whether they favored a republic or the dynasty. At all costs quiet and order were to be preserved lest Bolshevism supervene. Disorder and indignation might easily give rise to a revolutionary movement, especially as hunger had prepared the way for it. This was one reason why Vienna asked our National Committee in Bohemia to supply the troops with bread. But the predominant motive was the desire not to offer the Allies a spectacle of distraction and disintegration. Even after the revolution, the Austrian authorities did their utmost to gain the favor of Wilson and the Allies; and, to this end, they needed the argument that the Austrian peoples and the army were calm. Hence also the remissiveness of the Prague Military Command when it received its orders from Vienna—a remissiveness which suited our National Committee and was supported by it. It agreed to work with the Military Command for the purpose of maintaining order, feeding the men and securing the departure of the non-Czech troops. In the name of the National Committee, Tusar, the Czech member of Parliament who had already been appointed a plenipotentiary by the Czechoslovak Government, appealed at the beginning of November to the Czechoslovak soldiers in the Austrian army to remain obedient to their Austrian superiors since they would be brought back into the territory of our State as soon as railway communications should permit and the necessary arrangements could be made.

The Austrian authorities did not realize that their remissiveness in dealing with Prague was a two-edged sword. They did not see that, if they could point to the tranquillity and order in the Bohemian Lands, foreign countries could hardly fail to understand that our National Committee had succeeded in establishing the new State calmly and prudently. Thus their tactics failed, despite the feverish activity of Austrian envoys and emissaries who, with the help of pro-Austrian politicians, were at work not only at the Vatican and in neutral countries, but in London, Washington, Paris and Rome. Baron Chlumecky was busy in Switzerland. His task was to get the support of the Vatican and to open relations with Paris, while Count Albert Mensdorff was instructed to deal with London direct and also to pull strings in Paris, since Austria was no less eager to turn France than England against us. In Paris, it was, however, taken as an insult that Count Andrássy should have been selected to carry on the negotiations which were in progress in Switzerland toward the middle of October, since he had been no less pro-German than Tisza throughout the war; nor did Count Mensdorff or Baron Chlumecky succeed in their main purpose, which was to get hold of Clemenceau. Neither Clemenceau nor anybody connected with

French governing circles was accessible to their suggestions. The Austrians were too tactless; and the agreement at Geneva between our Prague Delegation and Dr. Beneš upset their last diplomatic undertaking. Dr. Beneš demanded that all links with the Hapsburgs should be snapped, and the delegation snapped them emphatically. On his return to Paris he made good use of their action; and when he was invited, as the Foreign Minister of the recognized Czechoslovak Government, to take part in the Armistice negotiations with Germany, the attempts of Austria to open secret negotiations were frustrated.

The Allies had expected Austria definitely to break off her alliance with Germany, just as in 1917 England had awaited a clear Austro-Hungarian declaration in regard to Belgium, and France an unequivocal pronouncement upon Alsace-Lorraine. Had these things been done, peace negotiations would have taken place earlier. Austria might perhaps have saved herself if she had cut adrift from Germany and had turned against her. To such lengths even Viennese insincerity was not prepared to go, less on account of moral scruples than out of fear of the Magyars and of the Austrian Germans; and when, at the last moment, Austria accepted Wilson's conditions and decided to make a separate peace, France, in particular, thought her action insufficient.

Yet, by acting swiftly and vigorously on the basis of Lammasch's policy, the Austrian Government might have gained considerably. I doubt, however, whether Lammasch had any real influence. He proposed that all the Hapsburg peoples should be represented at the Peace Conference, which should settle territorial questions and decide whether or not a League of Hapsburg States should be formed. On such a basis the Viennese thesis might have been advanced with some effect and supported, as regards us, with arguments *ad homines*. Play might have been made not only with the pro-Austrian statements of the Burgomaster of Prague, Dr. Groš, but with the disavowal of the National Council abroad by our members of Parliament, and with their declaration in favor of a League of Hapsburg States at the moment when the Reichsrat was reopened. The Prague revolution would have been no obstacle, for Count Coudenhove would certainly have put forward his assertion that our National Committee had invoked the Emperor's wish to set up local national Governments when they began negotiations with the Lord Lieutenancy in Prague; and Tusar's appeal to our soldiers would have formed yet another term of the Viennese political syllogism.

All the weightier, therefore, was the fact that at Geneva the delegation of our National Committee and its chairman, Dr. Kramář, had agreed with our first Foreign Minister, as the representative of a Government which the Allies had recognized, upon a clear and definite anti Austrian program which Dr. Beneš could lay before the Allies. This Geneva agreement made it impossible for Austria to turn to account things that our people at home had done under her military pressure, or the tactics which our people had adopted at the moment of the Prague revolution.

In point of fact, Austria herself, the Emperor as well as the Government, had admitted our right to independence, practically and juridically, during the later years of the war. Of this, all the promises and efforts, in 1917 and 1918, to reconstruct Austria are obvious signs, as is the wish of the Emperor Charles, which the Lord Lieutenant, Count Coudenhove, had encouraged, to be crowned King of Bohemia at Prague. His wish was thwarted by members of the Austrian Government and also, it seems, by threats from our people that the coronation would be a fiasco. Still more significant is the fact that Austria herself accepted the declaration made on October 18 by President Wilson that the Czechoslovaks were entitled to an independent State and that this acceptance was signed by an Hungarian politician, Count Andrássy, in his capacity as Austro-Hungarian Minister for Foreign Affairs. True, this acceptance, like the previous manifesto of the Emperor himself, was an attempt to keep the Czechs within the Hapsburg Monarchy. In the same way the granting of passports for Geneva to the delegation of our National Committee was an effort to win Czech favor by amiability; and the reproach addressed by the Austrian Germans to the Austrian Government on this account ignored the situation which had arisen in Vienna after Wilson's reply. Moreover, the former Austrian Minister, Dr. Joseph Redlich, shows that when the Austrian German parties formally established the new Austrian State on October 21, they went ahead of the other Austrian races in dismembering the Empire; and he admits that the Emperor's manifesto of October 16 had given these races a legal basis for their action. The truth, on which it is necessary to insist, is that Vienna and Prague were pursuing divergent political aims.

The bonds that bound us to Austria were finally severed in the first sitting of our National Assembly on November 14. Dr Kramář proclaimed the dethronement of the Emperor Charles and the establishment of our Republic. No vote was taken and, as the Statute Book shows, no law was passed. Acclamation was so spontaneous and unanimous that a formal vote seemed superfluous.

On November 4 the National Committee in Prague had been asked, on behalf of the Emperor Charles, to give him permission to settle at Brandeis on the Elbe. There was a disposition to grant the request on condition that he should abdicate and abandon all claims to the Bohemian Lands. In the Year Book of the National Assembly there is, to this effect, a brief note that aroused my curosity, for it would surely have been a mistake thus to expose the ex-Emperor to temptation. It appears, however, that the note is incomplete and that no formal reply was made to him since the National Committee had been informally approached through third parties. An informal answer was therefore sent through the same channels. In much the same way the Magyars thought it expedient to approach the Slovaks, and the Hungarian Government went so far as to invite Dr. Milan Hodža, who had been a Slovak member of the Hungarian Parliament, to take part in negotiations at Budapest.

THE GERMANS OF BOHEMIA

Another problem of a special kind was raised by the separatist tendencies of the Bohemian Germans. After the revolution in

Prague, as I have said, they sought to organize four German districts—"German Bohemia," "The Sudetenland," "South German Moravia," and "The Bohemian Forest Region." But neither in political nor in administrative importance were these efforts comparable to our own revolution. Indeed, their rudimentary character seems to me a proof of the organic connection between the Czech and the German parts of the historic Bohemian Lands.

At that time we held part of the German regions in military occupation. Between our troops and their German fellow-citizens a number of agreements were made. At Reichenberg, for instance, the seat of the "Government of German Bohemia," a municipal authority and a Czech-German administrative commission, in the ratio of seven Germans to four Czechs, were set up by reciprocal agreement on December 16, 1918. At Eger there was, according to German accounts, an arrangement which the people of Eger interpreted as confirming their particular constitutional rights. They claim that our historian, Palacký, recognizes these rights; and it is certainly interesting to observe how Čelakovský describes the evolution of constitutional law in the Egerland and its "Bohemification." The Peace Treaty of St. Germain declares, however, that the Egerland belongs to the historical Bohemian State—a position which Austria also recognizes by her ratification of the Treaty. A thorough examination of the juridical aspects of the occupation of our German territory would nevertheless be expedient.

Nor is our relationship to the Germans of Bohemia our only constitutional problem. Political men and theorists have long busied themselves with a constitutional definition of the union of Slovakia with our State. Theoretically it is a question of distinguishing more precisely between "historical" and "natural" right. We invoked both of them during the war; and in view of Slovakia, I had long endeavored to harmonize them. Many of our public men, under the influence of a reactionary German conception of the historical rights of the Bohemian Lands, ignored our natural right to union with Slovakia; and, though I admitted historical right, I always upheld natural right alongside of it. Indeed, when I left Prague in 1914 I firmly intended to work for union with Slovakia. The Allies gave us plenary powers to unite Slovakia with our Republic on December 4, 1918, the first delimitation of the Slovak frontier being undertaken on February 19, 1918, after discussion between Dr. Beneš and the Allied military authorities (Marshal Foch and General Weygand) and with the French Foreign Minister, M. Pichon, and M. Berthelot. Our frontier with Poland was likewise determined by the Allies, small Austrian and Prussian areas being included in our territory. In principle, the recognition of the right to independence is far weightier than the question of frontier delimitation or that of the status of racial minorities. In the cases of Poland and Yugoslavia, frontiers were also delimited locally by special commissions. The frontiers of Sub-Carpathian Russia had further to be settled, as well as its constitutional position and its organization as a self-governing territory assigned to us by the Peace Conference in accordance with the wish of its people in America and at home.

ALLIED SINCERITY

The question is sometimes raised how far Russia and how far the Western Allies contributed to our liberation. From all that I have written it is clear that the Russian share in it was much smaller than that of the West. In saying this I do not forget that, at the beginning, and in 1916 and 1917, Russian armies helped the Allies and us also; as did Serbia who, though a small nation, rendered no less service to the Slav cause. I remember, too, that we were enabled to organize our army in Russia and to bring it into action, though not by merit of Russian policy. The plan of the Central Powers was that Germany should crush France while Austria, with German help, should defeat Russia. In executing it, our Czech and Slovak soldiers were sent to the front against Russia—and thus the subsequent developments were rendered possible. The merit of Russia in them was passive rather than active. Russia was no more able to liberate us than she had been able to free the Serbians and the other Balkan peoples of whom she solemnly proclaimed herself the protectress on the outbreak of war. Like us, the Serbians believed in the Tsar's promises; and, like us, they and the Southern Slavs were compelled to link their fate closely with that of the Western Allies. Official Tsarist Russia was Byzantine, not Slav. Our liking for Russia was chiefly a liking for the Russian people, and this liking was strengthened, not weakened, by the war.

It was instructive to observe our Legionaries in Russia. Contact with Russian officialdom soon dispelled the vague abstract notions about Russia and the Slavs which had been current among us. But they got to know the Russian people, the Russian peasants, and fell in love with them. They saw the defects, the great defects, of all Russian Governments; yet they saw, too, the natural influence of the huge Russian Empire upon the Russian character. They became acquainted with Southern Slavs, Poles and Ukrainians; they passed, indeed, through a good Slav school. On the other hand, the Russians learned from them that Czechs and Slovaks existed. Until then, none save students of Slavonic and a section of the Russian educated class had known anything about us. The peasants had heard only of Bulgars and Serbs as Orthodox peoples, and of the Poles as Catholics.

Sometimes, in controversial writings upon the revolution of October 28, it has been claimed that the Western Allies used or misused us as a means of compelling Austria to make a separate peace, and it has therefore been argued that our work abroad was, after all, not so very important. This argument is baseless. It is conclusively refuted by the fact that the Allies did not make a separate peace with Austria, and by their various recognitions of, negotiations with, and whole behavior toward us. Wilson's answer to Austria would alone suffice to dispose of it entirely. I was present when his answer was sent and know from experience how it originated, psychologically and politically. Wilson was totally incapable of the sort of cunning which is, by implication, ascribed to him; and we know how his answer disintegrated Austria and encouraged our people at home. The

Austrian "capitulation," of which Dr. Rašín spoke, sufficiently controverts a theory that so light-mindedly casts aspersions on the Allies. Their aims were lofty; and though there were among them individuals, groups and tendencies working for other ends, the Allies, despite all difficulties, carried through their democratic mission against reactionary absolutism. Among us also, the idea, the idealists, not the super-cunning, triumphed at the last.

I myself have dwelt upon the dangerous character of the negotiations of the Emperor Charles with the Allies through Prince Sixtus of Bourbon-Parma—if it is to these that the opponents of the Allies allude—and have shown that they were incompatible with the recognition which we had already received. I have shown, too, that they broke down in consequence of their own inherent impracticability; and that neither the French nor the Italian Foreign Minister was in agreement with them. I have dealt also with the endeavors of Austrian diplomacy to work upon pro-Austrian feeling abroad, even at the time of our revolution; and I am entitled to say that I have been thoroughly critical in my account of Allied policy during the war. Despite the reserve imposed upon me by the position I hold, I am persuaded that I have not departed from reality and truth.

Or, again, the opponents of the Allies may insist upon the point of detail that the Congress of Oppressed Hapsburg Peoples, which was to have taken place in Paris on October 15 as a sequel to the Rome Congress of April 1918, was postponed at the request of the French Government. Dr. Beneš, who was to have taken part in the Paris Congress, reported to me at the time that, on October 5, the Allies received the request of the Central Powers to open negotiations for an Armistice, and that on this account, the Allied Supreme Council had been convened in Paris. At this Council Lord Robert Cecil asked, on behalf of England, that the Congress of the Oppressed Peoples might be postponed so that it should not coincide with the meeting of the Council. Apparently the Allies did not know what questions would come before the Council or what the result of the Congress would be. But it cannot be taken amiss that they should not have wished their proceedings to be troubled by external pressure.

Even had the support we received from the Allies abroad only been given as a tactical move with the object of hastening the capitulation of Austria and an anti-German peace, we should certainly not have been left in the lurch, for it was our policy and our Legions that had brought Austria to the plight in which the Allies wished to see her. We should not have gone empty-handed. The Allies would have been bound by their recognition of us. The German Chancellor's "Scrap of Paper" could not have had its counterpait in Paris. Of that we had taken good care.

INTENTIONS

In the last resort, judgment on historical events and on individual acts and deeds depends upon the intentions, the plans, the convictions and the motives of the persons, parties and peoples by whom history is made. It is not enough merely to register outward facts and details and to say, while looking with satisfaction on the result: "We have our Republic. Why worry about the manner and the hour of its birth?"

For my part I have described fully the plans, aims and motives of our work abroad, and I hope that a similar account may be given of the revolutionary movement at home. If our political maturity and our national character are to be rightly judged it is very important to establish—in relation to the collapse of Austria and to the revolution wrought in the world—exactly what was done at home during the war years, what happened at Prague on October 28, 1918, what were the purpose and the sense of our own revolution and what the feelings and the decisions of the leading men, the political parties and the people at large.

The main question is whether the revolution at home was passive or active. Was it deliberately brought about, was it desired; or were the downfall of Austria, the breakdown on the

Italian front and in the interior merely turned to account, in haste, at the twelfth hour? If it was desired and intended, how long and by whom had it consciously been worked for at home? After four years' bitter experience, were our people prepared, at the end of the war, for a real overthrow of the Hapsburg State system, for a real, albeit a bloodless, revolution? It is not enough that many desired freedom. What did we do to gain it?

It is a question of our national conscience and consciousness. In my own case, I have explained repeatedly why I had pondered, year in and year out, the problem of revolution. It was no empty toying with ideas. I sought to analyze myself, our national character and even the soul of the Russians—for we were pro-Russian—so as to be clear in my own mind whether our and the Slav humanitarian program were merely passive, whether we should simply seek to defend ourselves against harsh oppression, or whether we should be capable of political action, independently, of our own free will and deliberate choice, from inward resolve, not alone under pressure—whether, in a word, we could be our own masters? This is why I went so deeply into the question how it came about that Chelčický and his Bohemian Brethren could exist alongside of Žižka. Was Chelčický a passive nature and is his passive quality also in our nature, in our blood, in our character, in our soul? Or was Chelčický an effect of the opposite extreme in Žižka; was he passive only in tactics, not in virtue of a principle inherent in his and our character? In Palacký's view, even Žižka and the Hussites acted only in self-defense. Does this mean that we were, in fact, guided, urged, compelled from outside, and that we only became heroes under stress of adversity?

In truth, Chelčický was not passive. He was, on the contrary, very active, radical, determined and uncompromising, no less active, no less radical than, and quite as fearless as Žižka. He and Žižka are the obverse and reverse sides of the same hard Bohemian coin. Chelčický's mistakes arose from a wrong conception of human nature.

It was from this standpoint that I watched, for instance, our lads in Russia and Siberia. We had an army, and were masters of it, and of ourselves. We could do what we liked —but did we always do as we should have wished and were we always on the alert? When things went badly, we were certainly weak. On the other hand, I have often heard thoughtful soldiers say that our men were most up to the mark under enemy pressure. How far is this true?

It may be argued that we once lost our independence and failed to preserve our State; further, that our Hussitism, our Bohemian Brotherliness, our whole Reformation—and a Reformation reveals what is inmost in moral and national character— were crude, ill-starred politically, and ended in defeat and subjugation; and that, in its political aspects, the Lutheran Reformation was more constructive. Again and again, as I thought of these things and of our national humanitarianism, I concluded that care for humanity does not proceed from any inborn passiveness but that it forms the true basis for a successful practical policy. This is proved by our re-conquest of independence, the re-establishment of our State. To me, the controversy upon our revolution of October 28 seems in reality a question of our State-creative capacity, our power of political construction, our activity in political leadership and ability to lead—a question whether we can be and, in the long run, remain, our own masters and the masters of our State.

To-day, as in the time of Hus, it behoves us to understand the whole position in Europe and in the world as well as at home. Our geographical situation and our history alike enjoin upon us a European and a world policy, despite the smallness of our nation and precisely because we are small. In the world as it is to-day can we keep permanently the independence we have won? Are we capable, intelligent, prudent, determined and tenacious enough to keep it? This is the kernel of the dispute about October 28.

Before and after the outbreak of war I, for my part, answered this question in the affirmative. I went abroad to begin revolutionary work in the conviction that the nation and its leaders at home would know how to put an Allied victory to good purpose, and that we should all work to realize our maximum political aims. The excellent way in which our revolution was carried through is a pledge of the future success. And my answer to the definite question whether we owe our freedom mainly to the work abroad or to the work at home, is that there was originally no difference of opinion about it. Dr. Rašín, in his manifesto of October 28; in the utterances of Dr. Kramář, the leader of the Geneva Delegation and chairman of the National Committee; and, I believe, in the general feeling of the people—as expressed by the way it welcomed the Geneva Delegation, hailed my return and that of the first detachment of the Legions—witness was borne that the work abroad was decisive. But this work was rendered possible by the general resistance of the people at home to Austria-Hungary, and by the revolution after Vienna had capitulated to President Wilson.

CHAPTER X

DEMOCRACY AND HUMANITY

HOW we made our State anew, by what means and with what aims, I have now shown. Henceforth we must think how to preserve it. Once before we lost our independence—all the more reason for us to take our bearings carefully and conscientiously in the new European situation created by the Peace.

It is no part of my task to deal in detail with home and foreign policy. Rather have I to expound the main principles on which I believe our restored State should be conducted. Its very re-establishment shows that the worth of these principles has been proved in practice. The policy pursued for four years abroad—the policy that gained us independence—must be continued. Foreign policy though it was, its principles are applicable also to our home policy. These principles are tersely expressed in the title of this chapter. It remains to illustrate them more systematically; and if, in so doing, many a problem of political science will be touched upon, I shall avoid far-reaching theory since I am speaking as a practical man. It is not merely as a theory of my work abroad and of my share in the world war and the revolution it wrought, but as an organic sequel that I regard this concluding portion of my report.

The war was, indeed, a world war, not solely a Franco-German struggle for Alsace-Lorraine, or a conflict between Germans and Russians or Teutons and Slavs. Such issues were but parts of a great fight for freedom and democracy, a fight between theocratical absolutism and democratic humanity. For this reason the whole world, literally, joined in the war which, by its duration, became a world revolution. Between it and the Thirty Years' War the analogy is obvious, both in point of length—the rapidity of modern communications and the technical perfection of the military machine compressed more than thirty years into the compass of four—and in point of character, substance and meaning. The Thirty Years' War was fought for the re-ordering of Europe after a religious revolution. In the Four Years' War it was a question of ordering Europe and the world anew after a political revolution—in high degree it continued what the Thirty Years' War had begun.

In the World Revolution three mighty theocratical monarchies fell—Orthodox Russia; Catholic Austria-Hungary; Lutheran Prussia-Germany. When the conflict began over the Austro-Hungarian attack on Serbia and the German attack on Belgium, who could have foreseen the overthrow of these three Empires, pillars of masterful theocracy and of monarchical aristocracy? Before the war, 83 per cent of mankind lived under monarchical and only 17 per cent under republican systems. To-day, the preponderant majority is republican; the minority, monarchist. In 1914 France was the only great Republic in Europe. The others were Switzerland, Portugal, San Marino and Andorra. To-day there are eighteen Republics, among them the two largest States, Germany and Russia.

Equally significant is the spread of self-government in various States. The Irish Free State is now a self-governing Dominion within the British Empire; and twenty-one Republics and autonomous territories are united in Soviet Russia. For administrative reasons several small States were suppressed in Germany after the war; but, in the new Austria, a strong autonomous and federalist tendency is noticeable. It was a similar tendency toward self-government that led to the division of the three Great Empires into smaller independent entities. Centralization ended by rendering monarchical absolutism impossible. The large, thinly populated States, created by occupation and expansion in an earlier age, were susceptible of extensive administration. Under modern conditions, extensive administration no longer sufficed and had to give way to the intensive administrations of independent

States. There are now thirty-five States in Europe. Before the war there were twenty-five.

"BALKANIZATION"

Thus the war set up a new order in Europe, in Central Europe particularly. Seven new or reborn States may be reckoned— Finland, Esthonia, Latvia, Lithuania, Poland, Danzig and Czecho-slovakia. Changes occurred in six older or existing States. Germany lost her non-German regions (with the exception of Lusatia); France regained Alsace and Lorraine; Belgium got a bit of the Rhineland; to Italy were added parts of what had been Austria; Bulgaria lost territory on the Aegean; Denmark recovered some Danish districts from Germany; Albania was delimited anew. Six States were radically transformed—Austria, Hungary, Yugoslavia, Roumania, Greece and Turkey.

The profoundest changes took place in Russia and in Central Europe; and it is here that the main difficulties of reorganization have arisen. Upon the precise area of "Central Europe," opinions differ. The whole of Germany, Switzerland and Italy are sometimes reckoned as belonging to it. But if Western culture, not geography alone, be taken as a guide, Western Germany, Switzerland and Italy belong to Western Europe, as do Bohemia and German Austria. The dividing line of culture runs to the west of the former territory of Russia, and leaves also Galicia, Hungary, Roumania and the Balkans to the east. The older, consolidated States lie in the West. Their special problems are how to improve administration and to decide whether the form of the State shall be monarchical or republican. In their cases, territorial and racial troubles are unimportant, at least in comparison with those of Central and Eastern Europe.

It was in the zone running from North to South, between the former territory of Germany and the former territory of Russia, that the small new States arose, corresponding in extent, on the whole, to the territories inhabited by their several races. Austria-Hungary, in particular, was split up into its ethnical component parts. Proportionately there are more small States in Europe than in any other continent. Asia is divided politically rather than racially; and though there are as many races in the seven hundred States of India as there are in Europe, they are all more or less under English influence. Africa, too, is divided politically. In America the number of races is comparatively small, and Australia is, in reality, British. The variety of national States in Europe expresses the intensive differentiation of culture which has gradually succeeded to her former undifferentiated and extensive condition. Thus Europe now comes first in the number of her independent States. The two Americas come next. There are fewer in Asia, though it is the largest continent; and fewer still in Africa.

Big peoples, like the British and the American, who are wont to apply continental standards of judgment and are not greatly troubled by questions of language, are wont to look upon the liberation of small peoples and the creation of small States as a bothersome process of political and linguistic "Balkanization." Yet circumstances are what they are, determined by Nature and History. Turkey, Austria-Hungary, Germany and Russia simplified half Europe by methods of violence, mechanically, and therefore, temporarily. As remedies for "Balkanization," freedom and democracy are preferable.

The problem is whether the big peoples which have hitherto threatened the small peoples and each other will accept the principle that all nations, big and small, are equally entitled to their own individualities in political organization and in culture. Recent political evolution has been favorable to the little peoples. Against a German mastery over Europe the whole world rose in self-defense. The Allies proclaimed the principle of equal rights for small nations, and President Wilson defended those rights with his watchword "self-determination." The Peace Treaties codified the fundamental features of this idea. True, the old jealousies between the Great Powers are not yet removed; and new causes of bitterness have been added to the old bitterness engendered by defeat and by the non-fulfilment of some of the victors' wishes and purposes. Nevertheless the Peace Treaties have created juster conditions throughout Europe, and we are entitled to expect that the tension between States and races will decrease.

Despite all antagonisms, there is, moreover, ground for hope that the lessons of the war will strengthen the prospects of peace. What may be faulty in the new order will be susceptible of pacific adjustment as occasion arises. All difficulties notwithstanding, it is possible to detect the beginnings of a free federalization of Europe in place of the absolutist mastery of one Great Power or of alliances of Great Powers, over the Continent. In a new Europe of this kind the independence of even the smallest national individuality can be safeguarded; and the League of Nations suggests an instructive analogy to what a united Europe may become.

Before the war, doubt was long and often felt whether our nation or any small nation could be independent—the doubt which inspired Palacký's well-known saying that Austria was necessary as a federation of races. Great as is my deference to Palacký, and carefully though I have ever borne in mind the difficulties and the special problems of little peoples, I believe nevertheless our own independence to be possible. This belief engendered my whole policy and tactics. It moved me during the war to begin the struggle against Austria-Hungary. I held our independence feasible on condition that we should always be ready and be morally fit—as Havlíček demanded—to defend our fredeom, that we should possess enough political understanding to follow an honest and reasonable policy at home and abroad, and that we should win sympathies in a democratically strengthened Europe. If the democratic principle prevails all round, one nation cannot suppress another. The history of Europe since the eighteenth century proves that, given democratic freedom, little peoples can gain independence. The World War was the climax of the movement begun by the French Revolution, a movement that liberated one oppressed people after another, and now there is a chance for a democratic Europe and for the freedom and independence of all her nations.

THE GROUPING OF SMALL PEOPLES

Natural as it would be for small peoples to draw near each other or to form alliances, such groupings cannot always be equal, in point of unity and central control, to larger neighboring peoples. Alliances may arise for various geographical and economic reasons or out of political friendship or under stress of common danger. And though it is not to be expected that all the little nations, as such, will join hands, since their interests are too various, some of them seem likely to form lasting groups, such as the Little Entente. The Northern States—the Finns, the Ests, the Latvians and the Lithuanians and even the Poles— may discuss their common interests. In any case it is expedient to remember that, if the Poles were included, there would be more than 100,000,000 inhabitants in the zone of small nations. But, geographically, this zone stretches from the North to the South of Europe, and its very length tells against the association of all the peoples that dwell in it. The Finns and the Greeks, for instance, might hardly perceive, at first sight, the community of their interests.

Austria-Hungary was often thought to be a natural federation of little peoples. The Turkish danger was alleged to have drawn Czechs, Austrians and Magyars closer together. Even now, a Danubian Federation is spoken of as though the Danube were a natural link between the peoples living on its banks or on those of its tributaries. Austrian historians and geographers have claimed that the Austrian Lands were bound to each other by geographical ties, and the Magyars have said the same of Hungary. Our historians have shown, on the other hand, that our Kings of the Přemyslide dynasty supplied the impulse to the creation of Austria before any Turkish danger existed, that the danger itself was temporary, and that, geographically and orographically, our Republic forms a more organic whole than the former Austria and Hungary ever formed. Assuredly, it is no less organic than they were. Nor are geographical conditions decisive in the world to-day. Modern technique has robbed natural frontiers of much of their former importance, unless they are mighty mountains, the broadest streams, or seas or deserts. Economic necessities, the need for security, and differences of culture have become stronger factors. Indeed, the disintegration of Austria-Hungary must be explained in the same way as its formation; and if historians explain how naturally the Hapsburg Monarchy was formed, they should also explain how naturally it went to pieces.

The Turkish danger gave the Hapsburgs no right to oppress their peoples by absolute rule. Now, these liberated peoples desire to repair, by intensive effort in their own States, the harm they suffered under extensive Hapsburg absolutist control. The social and historical forces which made and unmade Austria-Hungary will go on working. Such of them as were fruitful and healthy can be fostered and brought into play. It is possible and desirable that lively intellectual and economic intercourse should persist between the States among which the Hapsburg inheritance has been divided, and it is reasonable and timely that persons and goods should circulate more freely. Progress has already been made. The excitement and enmity of the war years are subsiding. We have concluded a commercial treaty with Austria based upon the common economic interests arising from our earlier connection, and upon the fact that a large number of our citizens live in Austria. Indeed, four of the Succession States have drawn closer to each other—Czechoslovakia, Yugoslavia, Roumania and Austria. Our friendship with the Southern Slavs, which began long before the war and has been strengthened by the Little Entente, expresses a reciprocal need. Both of us depend upon the East and the South and upon the sea. For us and for the Southern Slavs, Austria is important as a country of transit.

This circumstance suggests further possibilities. Many interesting tasks devolve upon the Southern Slavs, one of the weightiest being the part they may play in the Balkans. Geographically and historically their influence on the new Balkan order must be considerable. They are the biggest Balkan nation and, if only for this reason, what remains of Turkish rule in Europe cannot be liquidated without them. Before the war various attempts were made to form a Balkan Federation. There was a beginning of fraternization between the Serbian and the Bulgarian *intelligentsia*. To-day an alliance between the Bulgars and the Southern Slavs is again spoken of. There is, indeed, no reason to perpetuate the bitter antagonisms between the two peoples, all the less because the Croats and Slovenes, who are now included in Yugoslavia, had no part in them and should be able to exert a moderating influence upon Serbs and Bulgars alike. A federation between the Southern Slavs and the Bulgars would comprise some 17,000,000 souls whose numbers might be doubled in a few decades. The Southern Slavs—may the name be an omen!—will certainly reflect upon the problem of Constantinople and its solution; and the possibility of pursuing a big policy might help to check the foolish dissensions between Serbs and Croats. In saying this I do not forget the Greeks' relationship to Constantinople, on the one hand, and to the Serbs and Bulgars, on the other; nor do I overlook Italian aspirations in the Balkans and in Asia Minor, or the fact that Constantinople still interests the Great Powers, albeit now in minor degree.

So complicated are the circumstances of our position in the heart of Europe that we are bound to keep our eyes about us and really to take account of the whole world. Therefore I repeat what I said long before the war—that our policy must be a world policy. When Bismarck declared that whoever was master of Bohemia would be master of Europe, he understood, from his imperialist and pan-German standpoint, the position of our nation and our State in the very center of the Continent. We do not need to be the masters of Europe. It is enough that we should be our own masters. Yet we may learn from Bismarck's discernment how important the East is for us, precisely by reason of the Prussian-German "Urge toward the East," and that we should therefore desire the new order in the Balkans to be based on the national facts of ethnography and on the history of civilization there. In both respects the Balkan Slavs may hold a decisive position.

For the same reason we have yet another weighty interest in common with the new Austria. In its reduced dimensions, the Austrian Republic or—to give it its German name—*Osterreich*—has regained its original meaning as "Ost-Reich" or "Eastern Realm." It will, I presume, maintain its independence alongside of Germany but without joining Germany, as is desirable both politically and from the standpoint of Austrian culture. I agree with the Austrian politicians and men of learning who insist upon the special character of Austrian Germanism, defending it against the Germanism of Germany and particularly against Prussianism. The independent existence of Austria for a thousand years argues in favor of her maintaining it under the new conditions. Hence, in regard to Austria, a Republican Austria especially, our policy can and should be entirely friendly. In other words, we ought seriously to ponder the Austrian "Idea," even in the new situation, and to develop Palacký's conception. In any case the evolution of the new Austria demands alertness and political maturity on our part.

In the Austro-Hungarian Monarchy we lived alongside of Poles, Little Russians or Ruthenes, Roumanes and Magyars. With the Poles, Little Russians and Roumanes our relations were, even then, friendly in politics and in culture; and in Hungary, the Roumanes and the Slovaks went hand in hand. Now all of them, including the Magyars, are our neighbors and it is natural that we should wish to stand on a neighborly footing with them. Not only do the union of Sub-Carpathian Russia (the former Hungarian Ruthenia) with us, and the Little Russian minority in Slovakia, give us a particular interest in the Little Russians, but Poland, Roumania and Hungary are quite especially important because they border on Germany,

Russia and Austria—yet another reason for a policy of friendship.

GERMANY AND CZECHOSLOVAKIA

Palacký and other of our leading political men descried the chief obstacle to our independence in our numerical weakness as compared with our German neighbors. While there are but nine or ten millions of us, there are more than 70 million Germans of whom 60 million live in Germany alone. After the Russians, the Germans are, numerically, the strongest people in Europe. They surround us on three sides. Three millions of them dwell in our own State and a goodly number in other States. Treitschke thought it the mission of the Germans to colonize the East. Indeed, in olden times, their tendency was towards the East and South-East; and as it is not to be expected that a dictated peace will destroy a tradition and alter tactics that are centuries old, we have constantly to reckon with German pressure. Our historians, including Palacký himself, claim that the main feature of our history has been "a constant contact and struggle of Slavdom with Romanism and Germanism" and "an overcoming and assimilation of alien elements." Should the Magyars remain pro-German, Palacký thought, this position would be aggravated. In this I agree with him, though I should be inclined rather to insist that we have a more positive task than to carry on a merely negative struggle with the Germans, and that the progress of civilization and the strengthening of democracy render it more and more important.

German pressure upon us has, it is true, been somewhat eased by the maintenance of Austria as a separate, independent State. But it is not certain that the Austrian question has been finally solved—and prudent and far-sighted politicians must take account of all possibilities, not closing their eyes to contingencies that may be disagreeable. Our gravest problem is our relationship to the Germans in Germany. We must endeavor to make it "correct" and, in time, even cordial. The Germans have no reason for enmity. They can and must transform their

"Urge toward the East" into peaceful rivalry. We, too, like all European nations, look East and South. By the war, Germany has actually gained. She has become a Republic, she is racially more homogeneous and is consequently able to pursue pacific, democratic aims. Culture as well as strength weighs in the balance of our relationship to Germany, for, from the beginning of our evolution, Germany has influenced our civilization ecclesiastically, economically, and in art and literature. Hence the question of our independence of Germany is also a question of culture in the widest sense of the word. And it is obvious that good relations with Germany presuppose a reasonable political system of economic and intellectual cooperation with our own Germans.

Nor should optimism hide from us the difficulties inherent in our position in Europe and in our very history. To me it seems as though many of us only realized these difficulties after the establishment of our own State, though, in reality, they are nothing new and we ought to have been prepared for them. I have ever been conscious of them, even when I decided to work and to fight for our freedom and independence. Like the destiny of all nations, ours will be determined by natural and historical realities, not by the fantastical schemes and desires of the undiscerning. Therefore it is the task of our educated public men and our statesmen clearly to perceive our position, constantly to watch with observant eye our development and that of our neighbors, and to act accordingly. While we are not the smallest nation in Europe—we come ninth in point of population, and twenty-three smaller peoples come after us—our central situation and our numerical weakness compel us to be prudent and vigilant—vigilant, not crafty, for the era of political cunning is closed, nor has cunning ever brought a people real advantage.

From the knowledge that we withstood the pressure of our expansive neighbors we may draw strength—it is a potent argument—and consolation from the fact that, in a fateful hour, we found allies and protectors and, despite our hard fight, contrived to restore our lost independence. Yet the memory that, in a world-situation essentially similar, we, like our Slav neighbors, the Poles, once lost our independence, obliges us to redouble our circumspection and foresight. Neither should we forget that, toward the beginning of the Middle Ages, the Slavs extended to the Saale and to the Northern Elbe, although we have to-day a clearer and more accurate view than Kollár and his contemporaries held of what befell the Slavs of the Elbe. We need to know our strength and to estimate it soberly, seeking examples among the other nations great and small, copying no model heedlessly but rather pursuing with consistent resolve our own well-thought-out policy, working ever to increase our inner virtue as Havlíček defined it. Then we shall be able calmly to say: "We would not be subdued, and never and by none will we be subdued." I always think of little Denmark who in 1864 manfully and honorably refused to be intimidated by two giants, Prussia and Austria, notwithstanding the expectation of defeat. At the end of the world war Denmark got back what she had wrongfully lost, and got it without fighting.

The Influence of the West

For our political independence we have chiefly to thank the West—France, England, America and Italy. Though, in former times, our relations with Germany were so intimate that, for a while, our Kings stood at the head of the Holy Roman Empire, we were linked with the West—that is to say, with France, England and Italy, not with Germany alone—from the beginning of our development in Europe, whereas our relations with the Byzantine and Russian East were intermittent and episodical. The influence of the other Western nations upon us was less pronounced than that of the Germans, but French and Italian influences, especially in art, were noticeable among us in the early days. It was on a Western model that our King, the Emperor Charles IV, established Prague University. In the Reformation, the entire people threw in its lot with Western civilization, just as the whole of the West had followed in the steps of Hus who had himself been powerfully influenced by England. Our Reformation set up ideals which the West presently realized; for, as Palacký rightly observes, in our Reformation are to be found the germs of all the ideas and movements that developed afterwards in the West. Comenius was bound by spiritual ties to the West; and upon him, as upon Hus, English influence was beneficent.

Notwithstanding the one-sided German pressure to which we were subjected by the rule of Austria, we drew more fruitful inspiration from England and France precisely because we sought it of our own free will; and, at the time of our so-called renascence, we were greatly encouraged by the ideas of the French Revolution, both in the domain of politics and in that of general culture. Thus it was natural and logical that, in the world war, we should side against our oppressors and with France and the Allies generally. We could do no other. Except the Bulgars, all the Slav peoples were likewise on the Allied side—though some of the Poles wavered for a time—and the Southern Slavs, the Poles and the Ruthenes, not we alone, were exposed to Austro-Hungarian and Russian oppression. Like us, too, the other Slav nations tended westward, toward France in particular, as the history of Polish and Russian culture sufficiently proves.

In our special case, it was chiefly the Monarchy of the Hapsburgs that estranged us from the Central Powers. It had carried through the violent Counter-Reformation, it had broken political faith with our people, restricting their independence, Germanizing them, and becoming, after the French Revolution, the chief inspirer of reaction. Once the proud rulers of the Holy Roman Empire, the Hapsburgs had sunk to the level of being a mere vanguard of the eastward march of pan-Germanism. But German pressure upon the Slavs, and the fact that behind the Hapsburgs stood the Hohenzollerns, contributed also to determine our attitude towards Germany.

Yet, if we owe the restoration of our independence to France, England, America and Italy, our policy is nevertheless untrammeled, particularly in regard to Germany. The relationship between France and Germany is painful, but it will improve. We shall gladly do what we can to end an estrangement which we have no reason to desire. Alsace-Lorraine was, and is, not the chief and essential cause of Franco-German antagonism, as the pan-Germans themselves recognized when, before the war, they were wavering between East and West, looking now towards Asia, now towards Africa, in their uncertainty whether Russia or England was Germany's real adversary. Mr. Temperley notes with some satisfaction in his "History of the Peace" that Germany showed less hostility to us than to some other peoples; and, in their report upon our revolution, Dr. Rašín and Dr. Soukup relate that the German Consul-General at Prague informed them forthwith (November 2) that the German Empire recognized the Czechoslovak State and had no thought of taking our German territory. I know that, in Russia, our men felt quite differently about the Germans than about the Austrians and Magyars. The Germans and we were at war, yet we respected each other, as the agreement at Bachmatch and other minor incidents prove. Our resentment of Austro-Hungarian oppression was more direct, more personal; and, for this reason, our political relationship to the new republican and democratic Germany may well be other than it was to the old Austria-Hungary and to Prussia.

For my own part I may say that, though I was working for our political independence even before the war, I never showed hostility to the Germans of Germany or even to the Germans in Austria. Then and afterward I took a definite stand against Austrian Hapsburgism and Prussian Germanism, siding openly with the Allies during the war, but saying no word of insult to the Germans or to the Austrians as a nation. My bearing, as I have good ground to know, was recognized and respected even in German official circles. Nor was my policy affected by the knowledge that the Austrian military authorities and some circles in Germany wished to suppress my adherents by force and, above all, to have me arrested, even before the war, because they thought me dangerous.

My own mental training was by no means solely German.

I sought Western culture because I found German literature and philosophy insufficient. Intellectually, I was rooted in the Classics, and in French, English, American and Russian literature; and if I was more deeply versed in them than most of my fellow-countrymen, I believe that, on the whole, my personal development corresponds to theirs. Mine was determined not by political prejudice but by critical comparison of German culture with that of other peoples, and by a desire for independence and synthesis.

Our Relations with the East

With the East we had far less intercourse than with the West. Though we knew too little of our relationship to the Byzantine Empire and to early civilization, we do know that, after the short Byzantine era, our whole future development was decisively influenced by the West. In politics as in culture we were in touch with the Poles and, politically, with the Magyars, but it was not until the end of the eighteenth century that we had any intellectual relations worth speaking of with the Russians and the Southern Slavs. In consequence of the one-sided German and, subsequently, Magyar policy of Austria, her Slav peoples had to establish relations of their own. Thus, as Havlíček put it, alongside of the great pan-Slav movement that embraced Russia, Serbia, Montenegro and Bulgaria, a minor pan-Slav movement arose. Pan-Slavism could find no political expression in the absolutist epoch before 1848, but it made a demonstration for liberty in grand style at the Slav Congress of Prague in 1848; and when the subsequent reaction had died away, the Slav peoples of Austria came into closer touch with each other in the Vienna Parliament.

Kinship of blood and speech naturally led to reciprocity in culture, for the Slav languages are more deeply and closely akin than the Romance or the Germanic languages. In point of blood and speech, pan-Slavism is more natural than pan-Latinism or pan-Germanism. Kollár, who was a pupil of Herder, declared

Slav reciprocity to mean sheer humaneness and enlightenment. He looked upon the terms "Slav" and "human being" as identical, and upon Slav political ideals as the ideals of pure democracy which were supposed to have been cherished, in more or less mythical prehistoric times, by "dove-like" Slav peoples. He imagined that the peculiar and more exalted culture of the Slavs would redeem even the declining Western nations, in whose place the Slavs would become the leaders of mankind. In much the same way the Russian Slavophils, including the Poles, proclaimed simultaneously the Messianic mission of the Slavs, the redemption of mankind by Slav, Russian and Polish culture, though Russian culture was Orthodox, and Polish culture Catholic. Not until later, and then to some extent as a reaction against pan-Germanism, did the original pan-Slavist theories take on a political complexion.

Scientifically, the Slav Messianic theory is as untenable as are the Messianic yearnings of pan-Germans and others; and, alike in their philosophical and political forms, I always looked upon them skeptically, just as I regarded Western culture with a critical eye. We have no right to talk, as the Slav and the German Messianists did, of the "decline of the West." Nor, for my part, do I accept Spengler's philosophy or the theory of the decline of the Germans. Deeper knowledge points to a synthesis of culture, to the influence of all nations, Slav and non-Slav, upon each other. Our whole history and our geographical position demand such synthesis; and my answer to the old saying *Ex oriente lux* is that light comes likewise from the West. In truth, this synthesis is already going on, in philosophy and science, in mechanics and in the externals of civilization generally. In literature and art we know how long and how eagerly the Slavs have been absorbing Western culture, while, in the West, Russian literature has been gladly read, never with more avidity than in recent years. As the French novelist, Paul Adam, said years ago, "The Empires of the East and of the West must espouse each other."

Before the war, as I have shown, the reciprocal influences

of Western literature were strong in France, England, America and Italy. Even after the war the outlook is promising. Such Europeanism supplements and develops the healthy germ in Kollár's doctrine of reciprocity. It excludes only romantic Messianism and Chauvinism. In so far as it draws attention to the good qualities and special aptitudes of peoples, Messianism, that is to say belief in a national mission, has some merits. Sober critics will not exclude it wholly from their purview but will rather assign proper value to all living forms of culture. Thus they may prepare an organic synthesis, each nation fostering its own special genius and qualities under the influence of every vivifying factor in civilization.

This general rule has to be adapted and applied to individual cases. It is hard to say precisely what foreign influences have affected us most deeply and permanently, and still harder to decide which of them was most congenial and in what measure. For this we should need to know what our own national character consists in, how far our national being and striving are on right lines, what makes up the value of our culture and what foreign influences are suitable to it. When we were under official compulsion to adopt the German language and German culture, we naturally resisted them and welcomed other influences and examples, especially French, Slav and Russian. Our chief task is now to work out a critical, scientific philosophy of nationality and culture. It is not enough to love our Fatherland and people; we need to love them consciously, or, as Neruda once put it, to think out a sound program of culture all round. My pleading for such a program before the war led to conflict and controversy about the real value of our nationality. Now that we are free, I do not doubt that it will be more systematically taken in hand. Our historians, our critics of art and of literature, our sociologists and politicians are obliged to find their bearings and to answer the question what we are giving to the treasury of mankind, and what we need to take from other nations so as to be able to give greatly.

THE SLAV PROBLEM

It is from this standpoint that I judge the demand for "a Slav policy." My own policy has always been Slav, even during the war, though I conceived its essence and its aims otherwise than they were, and still are, currently defined among us. Freedom has brought us new Slav tasks—problems that are at once political and administrative as well as questions of culture—such as the union of Slovakia with the historic Bohemian Lands and the right treatment of Sub-Carpathian Russia and of the Polish and Little Russian minorities in Slovakia.

Like all the Slav peoples (with the exception of the smallest of them, the Serbs of Lusatia) we possess to-day a State of our own. Hence our political relationship to them is clearer and more practical than it was under Austria-Hungary. Of the official, economic and political relations, the Government will, of course, be in charge; but reciprocity of culture depends upon educated circles and educational institutions, not upon the Government alone. Such relations are now unhindered, and freedom may render them more efficacious than they were before. The independence of the Slav peoples makes it possible more fully to realize Kollár's ideal. We shall continue the cooperation with the Southern Slavs and the Poles which, as I have related, arose during the war; and though our relations with Bulgaria were somewhat troubled by the war, the cloud has passed away. Of Russia I have spoken at great length, explaining that, while our sympathies flowed strongly towards Russia from the beginning of our national rebirth, we had few real ties with her. By the end of the eighteenth century she was playing an important part in Europe, and her greatness naturally often led our people to conceive pan-Slavism as pan-Russianism. But the liking of the Russians for us was less lively than our liking for them. Under Tsardom, their Government and bureaucracy were Conservative and legitimist. Tsar Nicholas I rejected pan-Slavism for legitimist reasons. The sympathies of Russia had long lain with the

Orthodox peoples. As they were living under the hostile and non-Christian rule of the Turks, their liberation—including the conquest of Constantinople and of the Straits—became a Russian official policy. The Liberal section of the Russian public, on the other hand, would have nothing to do with the official policy and entertained none of the pro-Slav feelings which, in Russia as elsewhere, were propagated by a limited circle of Slavonic students and historians through whom knowledge of the Slav peoples and fellow-feeling with them spread to wider circles. Yet, even among the Russian masses, this fellow-feeling concerned only the Orthodox Slavs, the Serbs and the Bulgars. It drew strength from the ancient relationship of the Russian Church to Byzance.

Towards the Catholic and Liberal Slav races, official and Conservative Russia showed, on the contrary, reserve and even antipathy. From the time of Peter the Great, if not earlier, Russia had made friends with Prussia and Germany. The Russian Germans held, moreover, a strong position at Court. In the eighteenth century, when the Russian nobility was inclined to adopt French culture, Russian intellectual life became an odd Franco-German mixture. Subsequently, during the nineteenth century, German influence became more powerful and Socialism presently reenforced it among the younger generation. Until quite recently Russian knowledge of the culture and literatures of other Slav peoples was insignificant.

As her position in Europe and Asia demanded, Russia, a Great Power, proudly pursued a world policy in which the Balkans and Turkey played a notable part. Financial and political exigencies led her into the alliance with France, and ultimately into the Entente with England after long rivalry in the Balkans and Asia.

It was in these circumstances that the world war broke like a storm upon us. By it our former uncritical pro-Russianism was refuted and, I hope, dispelled. Our Slavism must not be blind. I, for my part, repudiate the pan-Russianism which, in the name of Slavdom and Slav policy, centers all hopes upon an imaginary Russia and is too often a mere pretext for Nihilist pessimism. All of us must hope that Russia will recover from her disintegration, but recovery and consolidation can only be the work of the Russians themselves. The work cannot be done by other peoples from outside. Loans, trade and other outward agencies of European civilization may help her. They will not redeem her, for only she can save herself. France and other nations have gone through revolutions and crises. They had to help, and helped, themselves. We can do little for the Russians. What we could do we did during the war, and are still doing it. It was because I understood how profound was the crisis in Russian political life and culture that I adopted my policy of non-intervention. I believe that Russia will come to her senses, consolidate herself and play once more a great political part, greater than under Tsardom. We and the other Slavs need her, nay, the whole world needs her. Russophil we remain, but in future we shall be more thoughtfully, more practically, Russophil, following in the steps of Havlíček who was the first political man among us to grasp the real distinction between Tsarism and the Russian nation.

Now and again a voice from Poland is heard to proclaim that the Polish nation will be the leader of the Slav peoples since, next to Russia, it is the greatest among them, and possesses the needful groundwork of Western civilization. We must wait and see whether Poland can play this part. I myself doubt if she is sufficiently qualified for it. Others again, in sundry Russian and Slav quarters as well as among ourselves, have, since the war, often extolled Prague as the capital of the Slav world. If they mean Prague as a center of Slav culture, I may agree with them. Geographically, Prague is easily accessible to those of the Slavs who look westwards. In culture, we possess the right foundations and might take the lead, especially as we have gone ahead of the other Slavs, thanks, chiefly, to our Reformation. The fact that we alone among the Slav peoples feel sympathy with all of them, without regard to the ecclesiastical and other differences which divide them so sharply from each other, entitles us, in a sense, to act as leaders. But a postulate of such leadership is that we should consolidate ourselves spiritually and mentally and should rightly adjust our bearing towards the non-Slav nations.

Our policy must above all be Czech, truly Czech, that is to say, truly a world-policy and therefore also Slav. In the conduct of foreign affairs we have a tradition, young though it be. Its bases and principles were worked out during the war in the light of experience gained in dealing with most of the States of the world. The political success that attended it—a success due to a sober and practical conception of the whole situation—speaks in favor of its continuance.

The Problem of Minorities

In some degree our foreign policy is determined by regard for our racial minorities. Save in the smallest States such minorities exist, inasmuch as a strictly ethnographical delimitation of frontiers is impracticable. Nationality, as expressed in terms of race, played little or no part in the formation of the majority of existing States. Indeed, the principle of nationality acquired State-creative power only in the modern era and, even then, it was not alone decisive.

No two minority questions are alike. Each presents peculiarities of its own. Our German minority in Czechoslovakia is a case in point. It is comparatively large, for it numbers three millions out of a total population of thirteen. Eleven European States count fewer than three million inhabitants. Our Germans are, moreover, mature in culture and are economically, industrially and financially strong. Politically, they suffer from the drawback that, under Austria, the Vienna Government looked after them to such an extent that their own political sense was not whetted. But at their back stands the great German people, and they are neighbors of Austria who is a neighbor of Germany.

Our claim that the German minority should remain with us is based on our historic right and on the fact that the Germans of Bohemia never attached value to union with Germany while they were under Austrian rule, or even in the time of the Bohemian Kingdom. It was modern pan-German propaganda that first gained adherents among them. During the war they sided with Austria and Germany against us. After the war, and particularly after the revolution in Prague, they sought to organize their own territory politically, but the very attempt proved the impossibility of coordinating their scattered and disconnected regions under one administration. The fact that they set up a variety of German units speaks for itself.

A Czech proposal, which was taken into consideraton at the Peace Conference, was once made to cede a part of German Bohemia to Germany. The idea of delimiting the new States as far as possible according to nationality had no lack of supporters in England and America. Yet, on mature reflection, many political men with whom I discussed it, recognized that the discontinuity of important sections of our German territory, no less than its economic interests, told in favor of our historic right; and, at the Peace Conference, these considerations prevailed.

Soberly judged, it is to the interest of our Germans themselves that there should be more rather than fewer of them among us. Were we to cede one and a half or even two millions of them to Germany, the remaining million would have far greater reason to fear Czechization than the three millions fear it now. And, if we consider the position between us and our Germans as it was under Austria and as the pan-Germans would like to have it to-day, the question arises whether it is fairer that a fragment of the German people should remain in a non-German State or that the whole Czechoslovak people should live in a German State.

The authority of President Wilson and the principle of self-determination have been invoked by our own Germans as well as by those of Austria. True, "self-determination" was not recognized in Germany, nor did Austrian Germans like Dr. Lammasch, Dr. Redlich, and others admit it, not to mention Czernin and other Austro-Hungarian Ministers. Before the war our people, too, proclaimed it; but, in point of fact, it has never been clearly defined. Does it apply only to a whole people or is it valid also for sections of a people? A minority, even a big minority, is not a nation. Nor does "self-determination" carry with it an unconditional right to political independence. Our Germans may "determine" to remain with us, as the Swiss Germans have "determined" to stay outside Germany. Individual rights are not the sole governing factors in the question whether a whole, or parts of a whole, shall be independent; the rights of others enter into it, economic rights no less than the claims of race and tongue; and in our case, Czech rights as well as German, and considerations of reciprocal advantage, especially in the economic sphere.

Hence it was urged at the Peace Conference that to exclude the German minority from Bohemia would damage the Czech majority—a decision the more warranted because the German people in general derives great political benefit, greater than it would if it were wholly united, from the circumstance that a notable part of it lives outside Germany proper, forming an independent State in Austria, holding a preponderant position in Switzerland, and possessing minorities in Czechoslovakia and elsewhere. Even since the war a number of German political men and historians have, indeed, proved that, from the standpoint of culture, the German people gains by its membership of different States. The same reasoning applies to the French—in France, Belgium and Switzerland—and to the English. Naturally, the Germans outside Germany are entitled to political freedom and to a due share in the administration of the States to which they belong. Those States, for their part, are entitled to demand that their German citizens shall not be an aggressive vanguard, as the pan-Germans would have them be, and that they should make up their minds to work together in peace with the peoples among whom they have lived for centuries and to whom they are bound by ties material and spiritual.

Our Germans, as I pointed out in my first Presidential Message, originally came to us as colonists; and the significance of this German colonization would not be lessened even if it were true that a few Germans were already living in the country. Yet this does not mean that, as colonists, our Germans are second-class citizens.   They were invited to come by our Kings who guaranteed to them the right to live their own lives in full measure —a weighty circumstance, politically and tactically, for the Germans as well as for us.   I, for my part, acknowledge and deliberately adopt the policy of our Přemyslide Kings who protected the Germans as a race, though I do not approve of the Germanophil leanings of some of the Přemyslides.   I have nothing against the association of the name "Přemyslide"—which, from our verb *přemysliti,* means "thoughtful"—with the Greek Prometheus, but rather perceive in the name of our first dynasty a reminder that our whole policy, not alone in regard to the Germans, must be well-pondered, thoroughly thought out or, as Havlíček demanded, reasonable and upright.   The settlement of the conflict between us and our Germans will be a great political deed, for it implies the solution of a question centuries old, the ordering of our relationship to a large section of the German people and, through it, to the German people as a whole.   To this end our Germans must de-Austrianize themselves and get rid of the old habit of mastery and privilege.

Politically, the Germans are the most important of our minorities, and their acceptance of our Republic will simplify all the other minority questions.   Alongside of the Germans we have a few Poles, more Little Russians (in Slovakia) and still more Magyars.   To them also the rule applies that the rights of race must be safeguarded.   Local self-government and proportional representation may, in a democratic State, serve this purpose well.   Each minority, too, must have elementary and secondary schools of its own.   In civilized Europe the number of high schools and universities is now determined by a definite ratio to population and educational needs.   In Germany there are approximately one university for every three million and a technical high school for every six million inhabitants.   In Czechoslovakia three million Germans have a university and two technical high schools.

For us, who live in a country racially mixed and so curiously situated in the center of Europe, the language question is of great moment, politically and educationally. The official language in a multi-lingual State must be determined by the requirements of the people and by the smooth working of the administration. The State exists for the people, not the people for the State. As a political entity and a unitary organization, our State and its army will use the Czech or Slovak language in accordance with the democratic principle that the majority decides. But, while the State will be Czechoslovak, its racial character cannot be settled by the official language alone. National character does not depend solely on language; and the national character of our State must be based upon the quality of a comprehensive educational policy consistently pursued.

Before the war I took part in the controversy upon the question whether the authorities should be unilingual or bi-lingual. In present circumstances I think it more practical that they should be bi-lingual though, during the transition period, it may be better, in some bi-lingual offices, that officials should work in one language only. Experience will presently show whether a unilingual system is feasible. In practice the question is one of knowing the languages spoken in the country. It is in the interest of racial minorities to learn the State language, but it is also in the interest of the majority to be able to speak the languages of the minorities, especially that of the biggest minority. The teaching of languages in the schools will be arranged on this basis. The German language is politically important for us. Our officials must know it, and know it well so as to understand even popular dialects. German is a world-language; and, if only on this account, is valuable as a means of education and culture. German must be taught in the Czech and Slovak secondary schools and in the higher classes of the elementary schools. In the corresponding German schools, Czech must be taught. In Slovakia an analogous rule applies, though perhaps to a more limited extent, to Slovak and Magyar. Time and experience will show whether the learning of these languages should be made compulsory or not. It must be remembered, if the complexity of our language question is to be understood, that in addition to our home languages we need Latin and Greek in our Classical high schools besides a knowledge of French and English, Russian and Italian. If they are true sons of Comenius, our pedagogues will have to simplify and to perfect our methods of teaching, so that the learning of languages may be made as easy as possible.

Chauvinism is nowhere justified, least of all in our country. A noteworthy fact, which I often mention to Germans and foreigners as characteristic of our people and of our revolution, is that despite all the Austrian acts of oppression during the war and the intolerant demeanor of a large number of our Germans, no violence was done to the Germans in Prague or elsewhere on October 28, 1918. So filled were our folk with the positive idea of creating a State that they thought no evil and took no reprisals. One or two excesses on the part of individuals prove nothing to the contrary. From the first, the leaders of the revolution wished the Germans to cooperate with them; and, at the Geneva Conference between the delegates of the Prague National Committee and Dr. Beneš a proposal was adopted without discussion, as something self-evident, that a German Minister should be included in the Government. In a democracy it is obviously the right of every party to share in the administration of the State as soon as it recognizes the policy of the State and the State itself. Nay, it is its duty to share in it. I know further that the National Committee in Prague simultaneously negotiated with the Germans and sought to gain their goodwill. The Germans affirm that the Lord Lieutenant of Bohemia, Count Coudenhove, was asked on October 29 to join the National Committee as a German representative. In the same spirit our National Committee at Brno, or Brünn, promised the military command in Moravia to invite two Germans to join it. After the revolution, the Czech leaders offered to set up a special Department of State for German affairs—a conciliatory and far-sighted step.

Chauvinism, that is to say, political, religious, racial or class intolerance, has, as history proves, wrought the downfall of all States. A modern Portuguese historian whose name I forget but whom I read in London, shows convincingly that chauvinistic imperialism wrecked the Portuguese World-Empire. The same lesson is taught by the fall of Austria and Hungary, Prussia-Germany and Russia—they who take the sword shall perish by the sword. We shall solve our own problem aright if we comprehend that the more humane we are the more national we shall be. The relationship between the nation and mankind, between nationality and internationality, between nationalism and humaneness of feeling is not that mankind as a whole and internationalism and humaneness are something apart from, against or above the nation and nationality, but that nations are the natural organs of mankind. The new order in Europe, the creation of new States, has shorn nationalism of its negative character by setting oppressed peoples on their own feet. To a positive nationalism, one that seeks to raise a nation by intensive work, none can demur. Chauvinism, racial or national intolerance, not love of one's own people, is the foe of nations and of humanity. Love of one's own nation does not entail non-love of other nations.

It is natural that, as a general rule, nationality should be determined by language, for language is an expression, albeit not the only expression of the national spirit. Since the eighteenth century, students of nationality have recognized that it is expressed rather in the whole of a nation's intellectual effort and culture. Conscious fostering of nationality implies therefore a comprehensive policy of culture and education. Literature and art, philosophy and science, legislation and the State, politics and administration, moral, religious and intellectual style, have to be national. Now that we have won political independence and are masters of our fate, a policy conceived in the days of our bondage can no longer suffice. Emphasis was then laid upon our linguistic claims. Now our national program must embrace the whole domain of culture. To the synthesis of culture towards which educated Europe is now striving, I have already referred. It is in countries of mixed race that this synthesis can best begin; and to all racial minorities among educated peoples a weighty and honorable task is thus assigned.

Democracy at Home

We restored our State in the name of democratic freedom, and we shall only be able to preserve it through freedom increasingly perfected. In home affairs as in foreign democracy must be our aim.

Democratic States have hitherto kept up, in greater or lesser degree, the spirit and the institutions of the old régime out of which they arose. They have been mere essays in democracy; nowhere has it been consistently applied. Only the really new States, the States of the future, will be founded, inwardly and outwardly, on liberty, equality and fraternity. Our position is not solely that our State must be democratic; it cannot be undemocratic. In comparing it with America I have said that we have no dynasty, no national aristocracy, no old militarist tradition in the army, and no Church politically recognized in the way the older States recognized it, particularly the absolutist, Caesarist, theocratic States. Apart from the positive worth of a republic and of democracy in themselves, these considerations influenced my decision upon the form of our State, though I knew that the education we had received for centuries and the example of absolutist, purely dynastic Austria had left their marks upon us. In the past our democratic aims were negative, a negation of Austrian absolutism. Now they must be positive. What we took as our ideal must become reality—and it will not be easy.

Democracy, the sovereignty of the people, differs not only in degree but in its whole quality from aristocracy, especially from monarchical aristocracy. The republican democratic State is founded not upon Divine Right, nor upon the Church, but upon the people, upon humanity. It is a government of all for all, not of rulers and ruled but of administration, self-government and the coordination of all State-creative forces. The democratic ideal would be direct government and administration by the people; but, given the growing dimensions of nations and States, democracy can only be indirect, exerting its functions through Parliament, by means of representatives elected under universal suffrage. Yet this Parliament, and the Government responsible to it, ought not to be rulers after the old fashion. They must ever bear in mind that their authority is derived by delegation from the electors.

Democratic constitutions provide for referenda which allow the democracy at large to come quantitatively into play from time to time, at least as regards legislation. And democracy necessarily protects individuals, for freedom is its aim and essence, and it was begotten of modern individualism. Hence the election and selection of its representatives is a means of assessing their value; for democracy takes account of competence and capacity, albeit with the difference that the authority it confers does not connote political or class privilege but signifies political and administrative fitness and expert quality. Its task is therefore to organize the authority of its elected leaders—not rulers—through the freedom and cooperation of all, and to educate such leaders for itself. It does not imply mere leveling without distinction of quality, but individualization and consequent recognition of capacity. Organizing ability and administrative knowledge are needed in the conduct of a democratic State, the ability and capacity to bring unity, *e pluribus et multis—unum*, out of diversity; and, allied with them, political sense, comprehension of the goal towards which a nation and a State and, indeed, the world are tending. The difference between "politicians" and "statesmen" is everywhere acknowledged. Democracy, too, relies upon science and upon all-round education, for it is itself a constant striving for political education and for the education of the people; and education is, in high degree, self-education.

As democracy grows stronger the urgent problem arises even in republics, how parliamentary institutions are to be arranged and amended, not alone technically, for institutions by themselves are not enough. Democracy needs personalities to direct the administration of the State, individuals who are capable of creative political work. To-day there is talk of a crisis in parliamentarism. In varying degrees people are discontented with it. But elected representatives are essential to democracy, and even the

Russian Bolshevists have had to set up their—undemocratically elected—parliament and parliaments despite their dislike of parliamentarism and democracy. The true reform of Parliament will be effected by reforming the electors, by their own political education and higher morality. Yet present systems of franchise and the parliaments they produce may be susceptible of many improvements if the objects are kept in view of ensuring that the candidates elected shall be politically competent, and that the parliamentary organization itself shall be simplified. Parties may secure the right, in given circumstances, to call for the resignation of one or more of their representatives and to replace them by others. The size of legislative assemblies may be reduced; and, under proportional representation, means might be found to reduce the number of legislators while maintaining the relative strengths of parties. Yet the advantage of having a large number of members of Parliament is that the broad masses of electors are rendered more familiar with the parliamentary system and that both Parliament and Government are brought into closer touch with the electorate. Whatever the form of a Parliament may be, education and morality on the part of its members are essential postulates.

Alongside of the reform of the parliamentary system stands the reform of officialdom, of the bureaucracy or civil service. The monarchical, Caesarist bureaucracies of the past were aristocratic, a means of ruling. Democratic bureaucracy will work administratively for the people. In the Austrian Empire the lowest of the State Railway officials lorded it over the public, as though to serve them were an act of grace; but, under a truly democratic system, the highest official is himself a free citizen, one of the people working for the people. Bureaucratic delays are to be avoided, affairs to be settled promptly and officials taught not to shun responsibility. Superfluous scribbling has to give place to oral procedure and the whole apparatus of administration to be unified and simplified. A democratic bureaucracy must be upright and clean-handed. Even in the Austrian Empire, civil service reform was long talked of. In our Republic it is all the more urgent. Even after the substitution of the double-tailed Bohemian lion for the two-headed Austrian eagle, something remains to be done. Democracy and the Republic are more than negations of monarchy and absolutism; they are a higher, more positive stage of political development.

Outwardly, in foreign policy, the work of democracy is to organize and strengthen, by methods of friendship, relations between States and nations. Democratic foreign policy all round means peace and freedom all round. The old diplomacy was dynastic and there is an insistent demand for a new diplomacy. Our citizens' new diplomatic representatives will be educated, honorable and free from class spirit; frank, yet tactful and discreet, serving their own nation without trickery in their dealings with other States and nations. The notion that diplomacy is necessarily compounded of cunning is obsolete. Men are beginning to understand that, between nations as between individuals, falsehood is stupid, and that it complicates and retards matters needlessly. Even in politics the method of truth is the most practical. The old régime was a world of illusions and its diplomacy was therefore illusionist.

If the new diplomacy is to be a diplomacy of the whole people its representatives must be accredited to peoples, not merely to heads of States. Logically this would imply that a diplomatic envoy should uphold the interests and the policy of his country in foreign Parliaments. Relations between States and nations might thus, in course of time, be usefully supplemented by inter-parliamentary intercourse.

Dostoyevsky claimed that the yearning for union with mankind—pan-Humanism—is a Russian and a Slav characteristic. But this yearning is to be found in all men and races. They cannot bear isolation. What I have often called "world-humanity" is but another name for the inborn desire and striving of men for general friendship and union. Like individuals, nations need sympathy. The course of history runs in the direction of a more unitary organization of mankind as a whole, a trend accentuated by the evolution of democratic States. The League of Nations is now the weightiest and widest international institution and is becoming a real organ of internationality. Alongside of it stand a goodly number of organizations like the Red Cross and the Postal Union. The "Statesman's Year Book" enumerates twenty-five such, but the "Handbook of International Organizations" gave a list of 437 others, even in 1922. The very conception, substance and dimensions of State sovereignty are undergoing transformation. In the era of what was still, at bottom, theocratic absolutism after the Reformation, the conception of sovereignty was strictly circumscribed, for at that time States were self-contained and, to use a current expression, self-sufficing, by reason of the sparseness of their population and of the lack of means of communication. Nowadays, international relations have developed in such a degree that no State can live regardless of others. Nationally and internationally, the independence of a State is to-day only relative. States are inter-dependent, the reciprocity of their relations is increasing and is being organized, even juridically, in ever clearer and more definite fashion.

ECONOMIC DEMOCRACY

Genuine democracy will be economic and social as well as political.

Economic questions are so important to-day because war and revolution have, by destroying the wealth and the accumulated resources of nations, brought about a condition of want that is economically primitive. The crisis throughout Europe, nay, throughout the world, necessitates economic reconstruction, but it is a mistake to take this situation, which arose out of the war, as confirming the Marxist doctrine of historical materialism and as a sign that our task is solely economic. The war and the social and economic position which it entailed prove, on the contrary, that, as Marx rightly said, hunger is no policy. Indeed, the crisis of the war and post-war periods has involved Socialism itself in a crisis.

The very creation of new republics and democracies proves

that the war stimulated rather than weakened the striving for social and economic justice. Democratic equality admits of no social nobility; but, as I said in speaking of Russian Bolshevism, I do not think Communism an ideal solution of the problem of economic equality. In the present stage of its evolution, democracy is seeking to get rid of misery and of the most glaring disparities of wealth. Yet, even in the economic domain, it must not merely level down. It must differentiate. The productive aspects of Capitalism are less open to criticism than its effects in enabling unproductive, non-earning, idle men to appropriate the fruit of others' hard and honest work.

The theorists of political economy, from Adam Smith onwards, deduce economic activity from selfishness, which is assuredly a potent motive. But they forget the human desire to exercise special aptitudes and faculties in various kinds of work and production. Inventors and men of enterprise are not merely selfish. The best of them are interested in their undertakings and inventions. They organize, direct and perfect the making of things. The social and economic anarchy, of which Marx rightly complains, arises in part because the right men are not put in the right places or given work, economic and other, according to their talents. Whether Socialism would mend matters remains to be seen. I am not opposed to the socialization of a number of undertakings—socialization, not merely nationalization or State control—such as railways, canals, coal mines and means of communication. I can imagine a gradual, evolutionary socialization for which the ground would be prepared by the education of workmen and of leaders in trade and industry. To this end well-ordered State finances will be needed and closer and apter control of the whole financial system, including the banks; and, above all, better social legislation, and unemployment insurance in particular.

One of our special problems is land reform. All parties demanded it before the war. During the Counter-Reformation the covetous Hapsburgs and their alien nobles built up huge estates by means of confiscation. Our country is rich and the social and economic task of our democracy is correspondingly great. It has also to care for the physical and mental health of the nation. Not in Czechoslovakia alone but in all belligerent countries the war weakened the vitality of the people. Most intensely were the effects of impoverishment and of psycho-physical exhaustion felt among the small nations. Some of them come within the range of ordinary observation, others are revealed by medical statistics. For instance, we are losing from tuberculosis nearly six times as many lives as are lost in England. In France and Serbia, two countries whose physical sufferings during the war were severest, the proportions are the same as among us. Moreover, our condition of public health and our high death-rate from tuberculosis have to be considered in conjunction with our big total of suicides, in respect of which we come fourth, if not third, among the nations.

Those who assume that health and longevity are assured by well being and by a sufficiency or a superfluity of nourishment need to be reminded that men do not live by bread alone. Wealth and food are not the only decisive factors. We are beginning to understand that it is as bad to eat too much as to eat too little. Experts in dietetics declare that too much meat is eaten, that we are suffering from albuminism as well as from alcoholism. Indeed, it is no paradox to say that civilized mankind does not yet know how to eat. Bodily and mental health are preserved by moderation and morality; and to live healthily a man must have a purpose in life, something to care for, someone to love, and must conquer the fear of death that assails him alike in moments of acute danger and at hours of petty anxiety about health. Civilized man is ever seeking health and happiness, yet is unhappy and unhealthy. With all his civilization he is pitifully lacking in culture.

Wide and weighty tasks await our Departments of Health and Social Welfare with whose work the problem of emigration is bound up. Since a high proportion of our people emigrate to America, particularly from Slovakia, we shall need a model Emigration Office, after the Italian pattern, to watch over our emigrants, inform them of the position in the countries to which they go and, generally, to manage and direct their movements. Study of the causes of emigration may show that it is possible to counteract them by colonization at home, by organizing labor and by checking excessive propaganda on the part of steamship companies. A truly educative policy will pay conscientious heed to every aspect of social welfare and public health.

THE THRALDOM OF HABIT

Democracy, in a new democratic republic, needs a new man, a new Adam. Man is a creature of habit. If we desire a really modern, consistent democracy we must break with our old political habits, and must abjure every form and kind of violence. Above all, we must de-Austrianize ourselves.

A democratic republic is a matter of principle. It does not simply mean replacing a Monarch by a President. Democracy is the political form of modern social organization, of the modern outlook, of the modern man. To proclaim and to practise the equality of all citizens, to recognize that all are free, to uphold inwardly and outwardly the humane principle of fraternity is as much a moral as a political innovation.

As I have shown when writing of Russia men are wont to make their earthly and heavenly gods in their own image. They are anthropomorphist. Politically and religiously they fashion their ideal of the future, in this world and the next, after their own capacities, their own good and bad qualities, their own usages and habits. All of us and all political parties have something of this folly in us for, in the last resort, anthropomorphism is what men are accustomed to think and to do. They find it hard to do anything new; and, at best, they change what is old as little as they can. Most of them are guided, in theory and practice, by analogy—to use the term in its logical and epistemological sense—not by creative understanding. But true philosophy and science demand that men should think, that they should gather wide experience, observing and comparing the present and the past, and verifying their deductions from experience by further experience so that haste may not lead them to fantastic conclusions. In art, as in politics and life, there is a difference between fantastic imaginings and the power of imagination, pure imagination as Goethe called it, for precise imagination is a very necessary means to right and exact thinking. A thinking man, ponderate in action, is he whose power of imagination can take him beyond himself, free him from the circumstances to which custom has bound him—a man who, by feeling and thought, can enter into the lives of other men and other times, immerse himself in the spirit of his race, of Europe, of humanity. Only thus can he create something and become a new man. Even then he will be modest and remember that men are no Titans, let alone gods.

From what I have called "anthropomorphism," from slavery to habit, politics and parliamentarism suffer in especial degree. Few political men are able to rise above themselves, to escape from being self-centered, to view themselves with a critical eye. And, as most people belong to some party or other, the party spirit prevails in Parliament, identifying the interests of party— that is to say of a few individuals and sometimes of a single individual—with the interests of the whole community. Thus Parliaments represent parties, coteries, and strong and influential—I will not say "leading"—personalities, rather than the nation, the people, the masses.

POLITICAL EDUCATION

As a cure for the evil of political anthropomorphism, democracy demands the political education of citizens and electors. I say education, not erudition, and certainly not a one-sided and exclusive school education. Needful as are schooling and schools, they alone cannot bestow understanding, talent or political sense. A strong and healthy brain is better than a school certificate. Often have I protested against what I call "schoolmaster politics." I mean the schoolmaster spirit in priests and officials as well as in professors and teachers; for all who have to deal with the young, or with obedient, dependent, unresisting folk, tend too frequently to be absolutist, self-willed, cranky and childish when they become members of Parliament and Ministers or attain public office and dignity. One of the weightiest democratic problems is the relationship of the academically-educated class to parties which, like the Socialists and Agrarians, represent the economic and class interests of great masses. It is in high degree the problem of the middle classes and of liberalism.

The so-called *intelligentsia*, the product of secondary schools and universities, which represents science, philosophy and general culture, is not organized as a class. Nevertheless it plays an important political part, particularly through the publicists in its ranks; and though the *intelligentsia* as a whole has not always been in the public eye, because its activity is educational rather than political, its leading members have everywhere made a stand against absolutism and theocracy. In the universities, at least, most of its members are apt to be conservative and to grow accustomed to a quiet, regular life.

In all democratic countries, and not least in the republics that have succeeded to monarchical or aristocratic systems, leading positions are now being taken in politics and in the public services by men devoid of higher education. How to preserve the special knowledge that is required in government, administration and in Parliament is a problem that arises in every democracy as soon as the center of parliamentary gravity shifts towards the great popular parties. Practically, the question is one of retaining under the parliamentary system the necessary number of educated specialists for the work of government and administration. Yet it is true that the academically-educated and capable official is often inferior to the experienced organizer and party leader in knowledge of men and in practical capacity for dealing with parties, Parliament and the Government; for political sense and statecraft are not to be acquired solely by schooling or even by administrative experience. Moreover, the problem of the educated comprises that of the semi-educated. Semi-education, as a transitional phase of our period of transition from theocracy to democracy, is the peculiar curse of our society and our era. Democracy has therefore to find means of turning semi-education into education.

Men are too apt to let words do duty for ideas and things— the "good round words" against which Havlíček rightly protested in politics, a "roundness" that should not be confounded with the natural inclination toward general ideas that accompanies the development of thought. In politics, even more than elsewhere, concrete thought is rare. To most people, collective concepts like "nation," "mankind," "State," "Church," "masses," "Party," "intelligentsia," "bourgeoisie," "proletariate" convey no clear, vertebrate ideas. There is nothing for it but to try to be concrete and to express general ideas as concretely as possible, while guarding, on the one hand, against misleading catchwords, and remembering, on the other, that in politics and in practical life watchwords are indispensable.

Laws also are general and abstract—frameworks to which substance is given by practice and experience. Hence the problem how far the Executive and the Court shall go in applying legal principles and in discharging what are, in effect, law-making functions alongside of those of legislative bodies. Here again we touch upon the need for education in juridicial, political and social matters and for sociological thought—a need which increases the urgency of popular education, the organization of the schools, the training of publicists, of officials and, not least, of political leaders. In the secondary schools the conflict between aristocracy and democracy has long been noticeable in the form of a dispute between Classical and Scientific education, the partisans of the former being confronted with a demand for a more practical and economically useful kind of school. In this demand there is some exaggeration. The object of schools is to teach the young to think, to accustom them to sound methods and to a scientific spirit, not merely to give them practical training and as much knowledge as possible. Whether the pupil presently forgets much of what he has learned is not the main point. He may forget mathematics and other necessary and useful branches of study as well as Latin and Greek. What matters is that he shall be able to find his bearings easily when he specializes and adopts a career. The secondary schools should certainly provide general and philosophical education; and, from the democratic standpoint, it is very important that secondary schooling should be of a unitary type as a step toward social unity.

The defects of our school system reflect the transitional character of our period. All that I have said of the disjointed, uncoordinated, incomplete, anarchical features of our modern era is reflected in the schools from the highest to the lowest. For some time past their influence upon the health and upon the nerves of children and students has rightly been a subject of investigation. But we have to think of mental and moral influences quite as much as of physical; and, in the pathology of education, suicide among children forms a special chapter. In the schools, that is to say, in our children, are reflected the conflict between Church and State, between philosophy and theology, between old and young. It is a fight for an outlook upon the world and upon life. And it is from this point of view that we should judge the claim of our school teachers that they themselves should receive higher academic training; for those very teachers who, amid their fatiguing work, strive to educate themselves more highly, are the most painfully conscious of the inadequacy of their own education.

DEMOCRACY AND PUBLICITY

From the democratic principles of liberty and equality it follows that democracy is based upon publicity. In this it differs from aristocracy. Hence, too, the great importance of public opinion in modern life. Freedom of opinion is a form of political freedom, and a condition of it. In practice, journalism and the daily press are extensions of parliamentary control over Governments if not substitutes for it—a circumstance that is sometimes used as an argument against parliamentarism. Moreover, the freedom of the press ensures the right to criticize public men and the whole apparatus of the State. Criticism is at once a postulate and a method of democratic policy just as it is a postulate and method of science and of the scientific spirit. The right to criticize is a right of political initiative. Thus the daily press enjoys a real albeit not a codified right of initiative and of referendum. In this right lies its great responsibility.

Politics and journalism are so intimately related that they penetrate each other; but the difference between them should be clearly understood. While newspapers, daily papers especially, are points of crystallization for tendencies, groups and parties, they have their own particular business interests. It is often a question how far the interest of a party or of a group coincides with the interest of the State; and the wish to increase the circulation of a party newspaper may easily lead to demagogy and partisanship. In the haste of working for the day, nay, even for the minute, the precision of journalistic judgment and of reporting is apt to suffer—a drawback that explains the general desire for the reform of journalism and for the education of journalists.

The right and the duty of democratic public opinion leave, or should leave, no room for concealment or secretiveness. Moral progress in public and private life can only be achieved by eschewing falsehood and prevarication. The watchwords of realism in literature and art—"Truth and Truthfulness"—apply also to politics and respond to the same mental and moral needs. Standards of truthfulness or, in other words, of intellectual cleanliness in politics and life differ from age to age and from country to country. Though the old aristocratic régime had its special code of honor, it ignored truthfulness. Absolutism in Church and State, which kept the people in subjection, was founded upon authority, secrecy and secretiveness; and the right means of combating it are democratic freedom, openness and truthfulness.

Among us, as elsewhere, politics are usually thought to be the art of getting the better of somebody else by cunning and deceit. But democracy should mean moral renovation in politics, in education and throughout the whole range of public and private life. Every nation speaks two languages, that of truthfulness and that of mendacity. Dostoyevsky thought that Russia could attain to truthfulness by dint of lying. Neither in the case of Russia nor in our own do I believe it. I desire for democracy an education inspired by ethical ideals.

DEMOCRACY AND THEOCRACY

My main historical and political contention is that democracy grew out of theocracy, and that it is the antithesis of the aristocratic system which theocracy most effectively organized.

Primitive men, savage and barbarian, naturally violent and selfishly ruthless, were socially organized by aristocrats, as a rule by absolute rulers and priests, whose cooperation was represented in higher stages of development by State and Church. (In Slavonic languages the words for "priest" and "prince" are closely related—"Kněz" and "Kniže.") Religion held the upper hand. It governed the whole existence, the thoughts and deeds of men, directing politics and the life of the State. Originally, it was mainly made up of belief in supernatural beings who were supposed to intervene in human affairs with friendly or hostile intent. Man was not self-sufficing. In fear he created not only his gods but all kinds of demigods, Kings, Emperors, hierarchs and princes of the Church. Later on, priestly organizations became more unified, and the development of the Church kept pace with the transformation of polytheism into hierarchical theological unity. In much the same way the greater States were evolved. Various forms of theocracy took shape among the Egyptians and the Jews, the Greeks and the Romans. In Rome, religion was preponderantly a State institution; and out of the Roman and Greek theocracies grew the medieval Roman and Byzantine theocracies which attained their climax, their unity of doctrine and organization, in Catholicism.

The Reformation split up this great theocracy and strengthened the State. Whereas, in Protestant countries, the Reformation was fostered by the State while, in Catholic countries, the State carried through the Counter-Reformation, the effect was in both cases to strengthen the State and to substitute its absolutism for the absolutism of the Church. Against the absolutism of the State, revolutions broke out, some of which have lasted down to our own time; and the State became constitutional by the transition to democracy and republicanism. Thus, in history and in substance, democracy stands in antagonism to theocracy; and hence the age-long process of de-ecclesiasticization that has steadily taken place in all domains of social life and, finally, even in the religious domain itself.

To avoid misunderstanding, some definition of terms is necessary. The word "theocracy" means "Divine Rule"; though, politically and in practice, theocracy was a hierarchy, a rule of the priesthood. So long as men held fast to a belief in divine revelation, to priestly doctrine, to theology, they were convinced that the Deity governed men and society. Vico, the first great sociologist, called the olden times the "era of gods and heroes," to which the human era presently succeeded; and Comte likewise called the earliest period of human development "theological" which gave place, after an intermediate metaphysical stage, to the scientific, "positivist" modern era. To-day Vico's distinction between the era of gods and heroes and the era of man is expressed in the terms "aristocracy" and "democracy." The foundations of all aristocracy were religious or, at any rate, priestly. Politically and in administration it was an oligarchy, with monarchism as one of its forms.

Medieval theocracy was the exemplar and culmination of social aristocracy and monarchism, the priesthood being an aristocratic institution, inasmuch as priests were fundamentally differentiated from laymen. The Pope was the Vicegerent of God, the absolute infallible leader of the priestly hierarchy and, through it, of lay society. But the Reformation broke priestly rule and undermined, at the same time, religious and political absolutism, even though at first it strengthened the State in the struggle against the Church.

Modern men see more clearly the true nature of religion. They understand the difference between religion and morality. They do not reject religion but they distinguish between its ethical and religious elements, and organize their social life on an ethical basis, since morality, love, and human sympathy are less exposed to skeptical incredulity than the transcendental theological ideas upon which theocracy was established. The evolution of the Church and Churches, of theology and philosophy, shows how their weightiest ideas have been transformed, how they have lost power; whereas the bases of morality, the positive feelings of human beings for human beings, have been proof against skeptical intellectual processes. Hence the notable fact that, in the modern era, ethics have been studied and fostered by philosophers and laymen alike, by Hume and Kant, until they have become, even in politics, the groundwork of men's outlook on life.

This does not mean that religion is unwarranted, undesirable or unnecessary. It means that modern men desire a free and individual religion in harmony with their reason. Religion is a powerful bond of union between men, yet a bond to be freely accepted, not enforced. Men have their roots in eternity; but, on earth, the surest tie between them is their inborn love of their fellow-men. Herein lies the significance of the historical process of emancipation from the Church, of the separation of Church from State, and of the innumerable efforts to solve the problems of religion and of religious organization.

In setting up democracy against theocracy I do not forget that democracy has evolved and is still evolving, or that there are various degrees of democracy and of democratic outlook. A democracy may be more or less republican, more or less de-ecclesiasticized. It may take the form of constitutional monarchy, and even then there may be differences such as existed between the English system and that of the former Austro-Hungarian Monarchy. What was sound in the old relationship between Church and State will remain in a new and higher form under a democratic system; and a genuine democratic policy will also prove its worth *sub specie aeternitatis*. Spiritual absolutism, the various forms of Caesaro-Papism and of temporal absolutism by which religion has been misused, will give place to a more exalted morality, a higher degree of humanity and a loftier religion which will freely guide the whole of public life. The ideal is Jesus, not Caesar. I say it is our task to make realities of the religion and the ethics of Jesus, of His pure and immaculate religion of humanity. He saw in the love of God and of one's neighbor the fulfilment of the whole Law and the Prophets, the foundations of religion and of morality. All else is accessory. The spiritual absolutism that shared temporal rule with the State, was evil. It was the spirit of the Roman Empire. Julius Caesar, like Augustus and his successors, attached high importance to moral and religious reform; but modern man is no longer satisfied with a religion that the State dictates for political reasons. Therefore we need Jesus, not Caesar.

The Reformation was an attempt to realize the religion of Jesus according to the Gospels. By suspending the priesthood it undermined ecclesiastical and political aristocracy. The codification of the rights of man and of citizens was a direct consequence of the Reformation which, in its Calvinist rather than its Lutheran form, positively strengthened democracy and parliamentarism and, in Protestant countries, prepared believers for political responsibility by laicizing the ecclesiastical administration and by educating them to religion and moral independence. In Catholic and Orthodox countries, on the other hand, the strengthening of democracy was negative rather than positive. Their peoples were merely encouraged to resist the Church and absolutism. Perhaps for this reason such countries are apt to be more radical and revolutionary in politics and religion than Protestant countries—a result of the deep antagonism between ecclesiastical doctrine and modern science and lay morality. Moreover, the antithesis between Catholicism and Protestantism has led to striking differences in the evolution of political parties. The prevailing tendency in England and America has hitherto been for political opinions to be represented by two great parties, and religious opinions by a large number of Churches and sects, that is to say, for individualism and subjective independence to be expressed religiously, ecclesiastically; whereas, in Catholic and semi-Catholic countries, including Germany, ecclesiastical unity is maintained by the help of the State, while individualism and subjective independence find expression in a variety of political parties.

Another effect of the religious and political revolution through which the world has passed in the modern era, with its recognition of the rights of men and citizens, has been the growth of international relations and of international law. Even in ancient times, intercourse between States was regulated by treaties which were the origin of international law. Of this organized internationalism only the germs were to be found in the Roman Empire; but, under the medieval theocracy it gained strength in marked degree by reason of the Catholicity and centralized organization of the Christian world. In its legal aspects, however, internationalism has made the greatest strides in the modern era, of which international law is really a product. During the past century, as I have said, a whole series of important international institutions and conventions have been established and, since the Great War, this tendency has been accentuated. President Wilson, indeed, looked upon the League of Nations as the main feature of the Peace.

Readers will find historical evidence for what I have said in Jellinek's book on "The State." Though, as a jurisconsult and authority on political science, he often fails adequately to express the unifying concept that informs his work, it emerges nevertheless, in substance and method, from his comprehension of the rise and fall of theocracy, of the gradual emancipation of the State from the Church, of law, and of modern civilization. The democratic State is a new State. The whole of its purpose and organization are based upon a new, non-theocratical outlook. Hence its newness. The old State, for instance, troubled little about schools and education; the Church directed and administered the education of the entire community, whereas the modern State has taken over the functions of the theocracy and has gradually come to control the whole field of education. A new lay morality having arisen as a result of the Reformation, of Humanism and of the Renaissance, the State assumed even the philanthropic functions of the Church and transformed them into social legislation. In comparison with the new State, the old was a little thing. Its thinking was done by the Church. If, under theocracy, scholastic philosophy was the handmaid of theology, the old medieval State was the servant of the Church. When the State was emancipated from the Church it had to begin to think, to take over, to extend and to increase the former ecclesiastical functions. This is why the democratic State is new.

The Value of Morality

I know with what superiority "practical" and "realist" politicians look down upon the claim that the groundwork of the State, no less than that of the Church, should be moral.

It is easy to forget that society has always been based upon ideas and ideals, upon morality and a philosophy of life, and to overestimate the value of its material and economic foundations. From the beginning of its historical evolution the State leant, for this reason, upon the moral authority of the Church. This was precisely the origin of theocracy, which developed into democracy. De Tocqueville, whose book "Democracy in America" I have mentioned, lays stress upon the religious foundations of the American Republic and upon their significance even in the present time; and rightly so, for a written Constitution, a Parliament, a bureaucracy, the police, the army, trade and industry cannot guarantee democracy nor can the State ensure it if its citizens lack uprightness and are not agreed upon the weightiest ethical principles of life. We, for our part, need clearly to understand what the making of a new State implies. Long, long ago we lost our dynasty, our State and our army. The people were estranged from the aristocracy and the Church. We had no Parliament—only a feeble substitute for it in the provincial Diets. Now that our State is restored to us, by what institutions, in virtue of what political ideas are we to organize it, how are we to make good this lack of tradition and of authority? Are a bureaucracy and the police, the power of compulsion, enough to establish and to preserve a republican, democratic State? Does a Parliament, with its racial and party divisions, suffice for the purpose? In Austria-Hungary, the Monarch embodied the old theocratic tradition, and was hallowed by belief in Divine Right. The Church cited St. Paul's injunction in support of Monarchical and of State authority; and the bureaucracy, the nobility and the army were trained in the spirit of loyalty. What is the fount of authority in our young Republic, and on what grounds can it claim recognition from its own citizens and from foreign States and nations? Our citizens, at home and abroad, acknowledged the authority of the revolution in the first moment of general enthusiasm over the conquest of independence. How will it be in a workaday world?

Unlike Chelčický, I do not belittle the outward authority of the State, but I cannot deify it and its power. When I took upon myself the obligations of the Presidential office, well knowing what my daily administrative tasks would be, it was clear to me that no State or policy can prosper unless the groundwork be moral. As St. Paul wrote at the beginning of the 4th chapter of the second Epistle to the Corinthians: "Therefore, seeing we have this Ministry, as we have received mercy, we faint not; but have renounced the hidden things of dishonesty, not walking in craftiness nor handling the word of God deceitfully; but by manifestation of the truth commending ourselves to every man's conscience in the sight of God." That is the program of the Republic and of Democracy *sub specie aeternitatis*.

The ethical basis of all politics is humanity, and humanity is an international program. It is a new word for the old love of our fellow-men. The word "love" has to-day come so largely to mean the relations of the sexes that modern men are chary of using it in a religious sense. Hence, under the influence of Humanism and its ideal of humanity, words like humanity, sympathy and, eventually, altruism, gained currency in philosophical writings. But there is a difference between Humanism and humanity; for humanity is, in reality, nothing but love of our fellows, though new social and political conditions have caused it to be formulated afresh.

Humanity is not mere sentiment. Even Jesus said "Love thy neighbor as thyself." Man is naturally selfish. The question is whether he is solely selfish or whether he feels love or sympathy for his neighbor immediately, directly, not for selfish reasons. Psychological analysis has persuaded me that human beings do feel immediate, selfless, unselfish love for their fellows; and, it was in order to strengthen this conviction that I translated Hume's Ethics. Selfishness may be the stronger motive. If so, it is the more necessary to ennoble and deliberately to foster our inborn love of mankind; and, if selfish justification be needed, experience shows that, in the last resort, love of our fellow-men is worth while; for it, and the social order which it inspires among normal human beings, satisfy us most fully. What does not pay, in the last resort, is guile.

Nor does the injunction to love imply the total suppression of selfishness though, like love itself, self-love needs to be educated and trained. There is a wise and prudent, just as there is a foolish egoism, and selfish folly is more harmful than foolish humanity. Some people's ideas of egoism, or selfishness, are vague. It is not always selfish for a man to care chiefly for those about him, his family, his own people. It is there that he can work best, and use his energy to good purpose most easily and constantly. A reasonable man will therefore work for those whom his influence can reach—love must be work for the beloved. Humanity does not consist of sentimental yearning for the weal of the whole world; nor is the energy that is born of talent, precise knowledge, devotion to an idea—Plato's Eros—a form of selfishness.

It is wrong to assert that humane, human feeling ends by

being swamped in morbid susceptibility. Rather the contrary —it calls for reason and practical sense. Precisely because I realize the significance and, in some degree, the priority of feeling, I insist upon reasonableness, education, enlightenment, science and learning. With Dante, I demand *Luce intellettual piena d'amore*. Some think that the real meaning of love of our neighbor lies in the command that we should love our enemies. Assuredly, we can love our enemies; but, until men have attained this moral height, they might do worse than observe the humane and practical injunction to be just to their enemies.

Who are our neighbors? The Jews had been bidden to love their neighbors, but they conceived them as their own people. Jesus and his followers included other peoples. We interpret the humanitary principle extensively, that is to say politically and juridically, not merely intensively or ethically. Much as we may love our own people, we condemn Chauvinism and cherish the ideal of finding some unitary organization for Europe and for mankind at large. We desire a world-policy. We do not conceive internationalism as anti-national or super-national, and we do not pour out our souls in bootless love for some distant folk in Asia. Mankind is for us a concrete, practical idea, an organization of nations, for there can be no internationalism without nationality. I repeat, the more national we are the more human we shall be, the more human the more national. Humanity requires positive love of one's own people and Fatherland, and repudiates hatred of other peoples.

Nor is humanity identical with passive pacifism, peace at any price. Defensive war is ethically permissible and necessary. Humanity opposes violence and bars aggression. It is active, not passive; it implies efficacious energy; it must not be a mere word upon paper but a deed and a constant doing.

Between morality on a big scale and on a small there is no distinction. It is a false notion that political men need take no thought of ethical principles when the interest of the State is involved. A man who lies and deceives in public life will be a liar and a deceiver in private life. Only a decent man will be decent in all things. Havlíček judged rightly in making no distinction between private and public morals. No State, no society can be managed without general recognition of the ethical bases of the State and of politics; and no State can long stand if it infringes the broad rules of human morality. The authority of the State and of its laws is derived from general recognition of ethical principles and from general agreement among citizens upon the main postulates of philosophy and life. Once again—Democracy is not alone a form of State and of administration. It is a philosophy of life and an outlook upon the world.

The Greeks and Romans declared justice to be the foundation of States; and justice is the arithmetic of love. The law, written and unwritten, enables the State gradually to extend the injunction of love to all the practical relations of social life and, in case of need, to enforce compliance with it. Hence the old dispute about the relative value of morality and law. Though an ethical minimum, the law, as the embodiment of public right, carries great weight by reason of its definiteness and practical adequacy. In practice, the State approaches the ethical maximum—the ideal—through the ethical minimum—the law; and human evolution brings the minimum ever nearer to the ideal.

Among the Greeks and the Romans natural law was looked upon as the moral basis of all law, a view which the medieval Church developed in accordance with the theocratical principle. After the fall of theocracy this view or doctrine was changed, not abrogated. To-day we formulate natural law in human terms, ethically, not religiously. In my view—which I state briefly for the benefit of those who are familiar with the problems and controversies of the philosophy and science of law—the ethical principle is not susceptible of formal but only of practical definition. Kant's "Categorical Imperative" is, for instance, inaccurate. The standpoint which I take up has a fundamentally important bearing upon politics, State and political science, and law. While I reject all attempts to cut the State, law, jurisprudence and politics adrift from an ethical anchorage, and to attribute to them an origin, a justification and a non-ethical purpose supposedly derived from some necessity of merely social association, I admit that a distinction must certainly be made between morality and law, as concepts, and that the distinction is warranted by historical evolution. Moreover, in so far as morality was and is sanctioned by religion and represents an essential factor in religion, law has acquired independence by reason of the separation of the State from the Church and the establishment of the State's own independence. But jurisconsults are wont to seek the grounds for this independence of the State and of its law in some sort of non-ethical principle, since they are not aware that they are still working with the old theocratic concepts which have simply been formulated anew. My standpoint is deliberately and consciously antagonistic to modern attempts to derive the sanction of the State and of law from some fundamental, non-ethical principle. I maintain that the postulate of the scientific method "entia non sunt multiplicanda praeter necessitatem" applies also to the domain of political and legal science, and claim that the State is natural cooperation in an organized form. In the contrary argument I see a relic of theocratic doctrine reduced to a fictitious conceptual entity by juridical abstraction and by a kind of scholastic reasoning which has hitherto run on theological lines.

THE GOOD AND THE BEAUTIFUL

In considering the foundations of the State and of politics, the connection of the State and the Church with art and æsthetics should not be overlooked. Philosophers have long discussed abstractly the relationship between the True, the Good and the Beautiful; but our interest lies in the more concrete relationship between the Beautiful and the politically Good. If morality is the groundwork of politics, the relationship between the Beautiful and the morally Good has a bearing upon politics also.

The ordering of society is sometimes judged artistically and æsthetically. Figurative reference is made to the "structure" and the "architecture" of the State, and there is an artistic element in the demand for political and social harmony. Upon one aspect of the connection between politics, art and beauty—to wit, eloquence—the Greeks reasoned concretely; and hitherto a good speaker has generally been looked upon as a good politician. If eloquence and rhetorical art are more nearly akin to demagogy than to politics, we must not forget that even demagogy appertains to politics. Where does the one end and the other begin? And again, if the Greeks made no clear distinction between demagogy and democracy, and if democracy is reproached with demagogical tendencies, are we not entitled to ask whether Kings and Emperors by the Grace of God never made use of this very demagogy for their own purposes?

Of animadversions upon demagogy there is no lack, but their authors cling, as a rule, too closely to traditional aristocratic forms and condemn the healthy popular style of political agitation and discussion. I myself had to overcome the prejudice of the intellectual man accustomed to the academic and theocratic rostrum. By delving into the history of political eloquence, I discovered that it was especially the French Revolution which, despite exaggerations on both sides, humanized political style in speech and writing. One of the problems of democracy is how to put true and noble human quality into politics and the administration of the State. A strong word at the right time and in the right place frightens none but nervous æsthetes. A good word is a deed. What else is literature? A good word cannot be lost. It is as though it were governed by the law of the conservation of energy. Plato, Jesus and all the great spiritual leaders of men speak to us still.

The thoughts of statesmen and legislators need to be expressed in appropriate language, for in politics, legislation and military affairs style is a weighty matter, and art may be helpful. Nor is the value of a good official style to be overlooked either from the standpoint of grammar or from that of æsthetics. In our case particularly it would be a notable adjunct to democratic policy and administration. In a democratic State symbolism and ceremony need also to be carefully considered. How to turn a purely monarchical edifice, like the Castle of Prague, into a democratic building and to manage the gardens and parks in democratic fashion is, for example, a problem that ought to interest the best artistic minds. As the optical, sensuous expression of an idea, ceremony has great educational significance. Poets, too, have ever been the creators and wardens of national and political ideals. I, to whom the connection between politics, statecraft and poetry has always appealed, have sought deliberately to refine my power of imagination by reading the best poetry, and have striven, as a realist in art, to attain Goethe's "precise imagination." The statesman is akin to the poet. In the true Greek sense of the world he is a "creator"; and, without imagination, no creative, world-wide policy on big lines is possible.

DEMOCRACY AND ANARCHY

Genuine democracy demands of every citizen a living interest in public affairs and in the State, just as the Church demands living faith from believers. In old Austria, all of us were more or less in opposition to the State and ended by thinking it enough to "call upon the Imperial and Royal Government" to do this or that. In other words we left the administration of the State to our masters and quarreled merrily among ourselves. Very few thought of educating the people politically to take an active share in the life of the State, despite their opposition to it. We looked upon the State as our enemy, and upon participation in the Government as treason. Now that we have our own State, are there among us enough men and parties with an adequate political sense of what it means? Have they a sufficient living practical interest in it to be able to discard the old negation and positively to create a new order of things?

Whereas the old Austrian State required the people to recognize and obey the absolutism of the reigning aristocracy and bureaucracy, democracy demands that all should take interest in and understand administration and public life. In a democracy, not one man but each and all are the State; and

"State sense" implies renunciation of the political indifference which was so widespread in the absolute State as to be an essential part of it. Unsupported by general interest, the Republic becomes *de facto* an aristocratic, bureaucratic State, the expression of a minority, for the nature of a State is not determined by its form alone.

In essence, democracy is opposed to every kind of anarchism or political indifference, no matter whether anarchism springs from "advanced" views or from mere antipathy towards political organization. The anarchism of many honest folk, like that of Tolstoy, is really a child of the absolutism that estranged men from the State and from political life. In its opposition to democracy, anarchism invokes liberty, the fundamental idea of democracy itself. Some anarchists seek to prove that the State is a transient institution which has arisen within the known period of human history and will again disappear. Marx and Engels worked out this view in detail, and the Communists now make use of it against the Social Democrats. Other anarchists repudiate any sort of State, claiming that it is in itself unnatural, violent and incompatible with freedom. To this category of anarchists belong the exaggerated individualists, the Titans, who think the State a hindrance to them, an unworthy stumbling-block. There is, besides, an ethical and religious anarchism—that of Chelčický and of Tolstoy. In our own case the fact that, having no State of our own, we organized ourselves racially and set ourselves, as a people, above the Austrian State, engendered a certain inclination to be anarchical. Even Kollár reflects Herder's view that the State is an artificial and the race a natural institution. This may be true in so far as the State is narrower than the race and cannot comprehend its whole life, despite the State's constant endeavor to secure centralizing control over it.

Against all forms of anarchism I, for my part, consistently uphold Democracy and the democratic State. Everybody feels a natural yearning for freedom, a yearning which the State must respect; but the study of history has taught me that society has always been organized in some form of State, that social life and cooperation have likewise been organized, and that individuals have ever been bound to each other, more or less consciously, in a community. This organization has been either set up by force or by reciprocal understanding on the basis of social need, fellow-feeling and reason; and though the early forms of society were largely fashioned by the despotic force of strong and capable leaders, so that States took on a military character and relied on the army, it is none the less true that even primitive States arose for moral reasons and through understanding. Save perhaps in germ, there was at first no such thing as Rousseau's "Social Contract." It evolved by degrees as civilization progressed. But the religious influences that played a part in the most primitive forms of society invalidate the view that the State arose solely by force. The most primitive religion contains an ethical element. It is true that the primitive society was no democracy but rather an aristocracy and a form of monarchical absolutism; yet, however strong a single leader may have been, he could never have made a State by his own strength alone if his community had not in some way agreed with him.

Nor do I accept the so-called patriarchal theory—so often upheld by Slav politicians and theorists—according to which the State arose as an extension of the family and was, as such, justified and good in itself. With the family the State had nothing in common. Other forces engendered it. The State is but the organizer of social life, which is something essentially different from family life. The latest studies of primitive peoples convincingly confirm this view. Aristotle said that man is by nature a political creature. Into this political "nature," by which theorists explain the State, elements of reason entered from the first; and the functions and organization of the State vary according to time and circumstances. Now and again, one "estate of the realm" or social class monopolizes power and uses the State for its own ends; at other moments special economic conditions or a particular form of culture set their stamp upon the State, which ever seeks the support of the most powerful social forces, religious, scientific or financial. A strong personality may even get the power of the State into his own hands. Each of these contingencies implies misuse of the State. Indeed, its whole history proves its imperfection; but its imperfection is no better warrant for anarchism or "astatism" than a defective school system would prove the worth of illiteracy. Social life is impossible without some central, centralizing and controlling authority. If anybody wishes to call this authority by some other name than that of "the State" he is welcome to do so. It is the thing that matters, not the word; though, in politics, the part played by words, "round words," is by no means small.

Certain it is that the State, even the democratic State, is no divine, omniscient, omnipotent institution such as Hegel conceived. It is human, sometimes very human, with all the weaknesses and imperfections of the men who organize and direct it. It is neither so bad and unreasonable as the anarchists say, nor so good and lovely as its semi-official apologists pretend. Taking it all round it is not worse than any other work of man; and it is a necessity.

The same applies to the laws. The law is the codification of administrative principles. In administration there is much that is purely technical, an outcome of the State machinery. Yet a law possesses moral significance inasmuch as justice and right are required of it and of the State itself. The foundations of right, its security and its protection lie in morality, that is to say, in humanity. I reject the pan-German doctrine that might creates right, in so far as might is identified with violence. But I accept the democratic contention that as little as possible should be demanded of the State, as meaning that democracy requires of every citizen public spirit and a sense of the law. Democracy is based on individualism, not on capricious individualism but rather on the effort to strengthen individuality and the sense of individual responsibility. Democracy means self-government, which means self-control, and self-government begins at home. Look at England. How is it that we find in her case a quite respectable democracy despite her aristocracy and Monarchy? Because of the public spirit of her citizens, because they do not look with indifference upon the State and the administration, because they display strong individualism politically, as well as in ecclesiastical and religious matters. The English citizen helps himself whenever he can, and therefore the State helps him. He does not call for the police in season and out of season. In England, self-government is self-administration, self-control.

Only by virtue of this general, living interest in the State, and by the constant development and extension of public spirit is democracy possible, for democracy implies a natural right to take the initiative in every domain of public life, no matter whether the right be formally expressed in law or not. Right exists *de facto* in a free State. Nor is it entirely true that the main object of political and State-creative activity is to organize. I think, for instance, that our German neighbors have over-organized themselves. By force of habit, any and every organizations tends to become a mechanical form. We need living organizations. How are we to get them if we are not ourselves alive? Life is change, constant change, constant growth. An active people will make living organizations, new and ever new in the State and in society.

DEMOCRACY AND REVOLUTION

Democracy was begotten of revolution. Our own Republic and democracy are no exceptions to this rule. Revolution is justified in self-defense for which the necessity arises when every other means has failed. In revolution, as in war, self-defense is morally permissible. Revolution is permissible when —as during the World War—administrative and political chaos threaten; and it is justified if it brings reform and improvement. But democracy does not mean perpetual revolution. The war, and the upheavals it brought on, stimulated revolutionary fancies. But war fever and the excitement of revolution die down. Men are compelled to resume steady and peaceful work; and, for some of them, it is not easy. Political and social Utopianism, such as the notion that the State is omniscient and all powerful, has swollen the demands upon it so inordinately that disillusionment has entailed dejection and weariness; and, as usual, men are apt to blame others, not themselves, for failure. We shall have to overcome the revolutionary spirit as we overcame militarism. Bloodshed is an evil inheritance of the past. We desire a State, a Europe and a mankind without war and without revolution. In a true democracy, war and revolution will be obsolete and inadequate, for democracy is a system of life. Life means work and a system of work; and work, unostentatious work, is peace. Work, bodily and mental, will get the better both of the aristocratic and the revolutionary spirit. Even Marx and Engels had to revise the view of revolution which they put forward in 1848, to recognize that machinery, invention, technical progress, applied science and work are the surest and most efficient means of social revolution, and to declare themselves in favor of Parliamentarism.

Democracy, say its opponents contemptuously, consists of perpetual compromise. Its partisans admit the impeachment, and take it as a compliment. Compromise, not of principles but of practice, is necessary in political life as in all fields of human activity. Even the extremest extremists as, for example, Lenin when in power, make compromises. The policy of cultured and conscientious statesmen and parties is not, however, to reach a compromise between opposites but to carry out a program based on knowledge and on the understanding of history and of the situation of their State and nation in Europe and in the world. This means, once again, a world policy. The object is deliberately to pursue a clear aim, not to seek the golden mean. Honest men eschew compromises of principle though they may accept compromises in detail and in method. However firm and consistent it may seem to be self-opinionated in small, secondary, indifferent matters, it is merely petty and doctrinaire. For the maintenance and development of democracy the thought and cooperation of all are needed; and, as none is infallible, democracy, conceived as tolerant cooperation, signifies the acceptance of what is good no matter from what quarter it may come. What is hateful is the readiness of puny, short-sighted men, without aim or conviction, to make compromise an end in itself, to waver between opinion and opinion, to seek haltingly a middle course which usually runs from one wall to another.

DEMOCRACY AND DICTATORSHIP

I defend democracy, moreover, against dictatorial absolutism, whether the right to dictate be claimed by the proletariate, the State or the Church. I know the argument that dictatorship is justified, since conscience and right, reason and science, are absolute; and I am not unfamiliar with talk about the dictatorship of "the heart." Logic, mathematics, and some moral maxims may be absolute, that is to say, not relative as they would be if all countries, parties and individuals had a special morality, mathematics and logic of their own; but there is a difference between the epistemological absolutism of theory, and practical, political absolutism. The most scientific policy depends upon experience and induction. It can claim no infallibility. It offers no eternal truths and can form no warrant for absolutism.

Absolutism did not consist in the existence of a monarch but in his assertion of infallibility. In emancipating itself from ecclesiastical guardianship, the State claimed something of the absolute authority which had been proper to the Church and to the Pope. Of this infallibility the style "by the Grace of God" is an expression; but whereas the Pope could invoke revelation and tradition reaching back to Christ, the theories of State and monarchical absolutism were only a reflection of the principles and practice of the Church. A curious sign of waning belief in the absolute authority of the French Kings may perhaps be found in the attempt of Marcier de la Rivière, shortly before the French Revolution, to appeal to Euclid as an absolutist; for it shows how, in defense of absolutism, theorists stuck at nothing in order to demonstrate the infallibility of the ruler, his right to dictate and his freedom from control.

Resistance to absolutism is characteristic of democratic progress throughout the modern era which has been marked by a long series of religious, literary, social and political revolutions. Even in the Roman era dictatorship was rightly limited to war time, because, in war, one leader is better than a dozen; and, in so far as revolution resembles war, it, too, gives rise to dictatorships. They are, however, unsuited to normal times. Political leaders are not infallible. Four eyes see better than two, as I have learned by experience and study. Russian Bolshevism itself proves the inadequacy of dictatorship. Claiming to be the *non plus ultra* of political and social development, and declaring itself infallible, it established its Inquisition for the same reasons as Spain established hers. Democracy needs to be especially on its guard against political upstarts, for none but the uncultured or the half-cultured hold themselves infallible.

During my years abroad I thought we should need a temporary dictatorship for our revolution against Austria. In case it should prove possible to unite all our Legions in France, it seemed as though they might march with the Allied armies through Germany. The victors might dictate peace in Berlin as the Germans dictated it in Paris or Versailles. When I discussed this idea with President Wilson, I imagined that our men would reach the capital of Germany and march home thence. Even the capitulation of the Central Powers did not render it wholly fantastical. Marshal Foch meant to hold the Rhine and thought of making Prague a base for the liberation of Poland. In such an event a temporary dictatorship might have been necessary, pending the establishment of a constitutional Government by regular elections; and it seemed to me that, in the excitement of the revolution, solutions might be found for many a burning question, subject to subsequent approval or amendment by Parliament. My plans were made for all contingencies; and I need hardly say that the thought of a provisional centralized dictatorship, based upon the army, was not inspired by any hankering after absolute power or that it was conceived irrespectively of the assent of our leaders at home. I imagined that our leaders at home and abroad would act as a Provisional Directory, as a real Government ready to take responsibility. But things developed otherwise. After the revolution, which was carried through bloodlessly, thanks to the unexpected collapse of Austria-Hungary, the dictatorship of the revolutionary National Committee and of the National Assembly proved sufficient.

THE PROBLEMS OF A PRESIDENT

After my election to the Presidency of the Republic I pondered over the functions of a democratic President in the concrete, not in the abstract as I had done before. It had never occurred to me that I might be President, so entirely was I absorbed in the work of liberation. Though I had observed republican institutions in Switzerland, France and America, and had compared them with constitutional monarchies in England and in Italy by way of verifying the practical accuracy of views derived from study, I had conceived my future position as that of a writer and a member of Parliament striving to consolidate and develop our new Republic. I had not even thought of retaining my professorship. Indeed, I had busied myself with the purely theoretical question whether the Presidency of a Republic is not a relic of monarchism. In republican Rome, I reflected, there were two Consuls; and, in Japan, two Emperors. Nor, even in a Monarchy, does one man ever govern a great State alone. It is not practically possible. A monarchy is a kind of oligarchy. Some form of Directory would respond most closely to the letter of democratic principle; though it would be inevitable that, in a Directory of several Presidents, one of them would exercise most influence and wield the chief authority.

Like other peoples, we shall evolve gradually and get away from monarchism little by little. Though the necessary conditions for a Republic exist among us, a strong royalist feeling for Crown and Kingdom was formerly fostered, only the

Socialist parties and a section of the intellectual class being republican in principle. Under Austria, the whole of our education was undemocratic; and, in politics, habit is stronger than reason. Now, under the Republic, the President and all other Republicans have to become truly republican and democratic, for the republic is a form, democracy is the thing itself. The form, the written Constitution, does not always guarantee the substance. Yet, in public life, what matters is the thing itself, the substance. It is easy to write a fine Constitution, less easy to apply it finely and consistently. There are cases in which a monarchy may be more democratic than a republic. Each of the four main types of republic—the Swiss, the French, the American and, to a certain extent, the pre-war German Federal Constitution (the last-named being a striking example of the difference between form and substance)—corresponds to the circumstance and to the evolution of its respective country. No institution can be mechanically and unorganically transferred to another land. But, as regards the Presidency, the Swiss and German types offer no guidance. The American and the French types remain. I have already said that, after the American War of Independence, the position of the King of England was taken as a model for that of the President of the United States. Washington was an aristocrat by birth. As President, he decorated his house at Mount Vernon with statues of Alexander, Caesar, Charles XII, Marlborough, Prince Eugene of Savoy and Frederick the Great. His successors were more democratic. In America the President chooses his Government outside Parliament, whereas the French Government is formed of members of Parliament. In our case I should favor a mixed system under which the President would select a definite number of Ministers, half of them, perhaps, or a majority, among members of the Chamber of Deputies and the Senate, and choose the others outside Parliament though naturally in consultation and agreement with the political parties. By this means the Government might gain expert quality, for it is one of the recognized defects of the Parliamentary system that most members of Parliament are merely party men, and few of them are specially qualified.

There is a sound idea in the American custom of appointing a special non-Parliamentary Commission to draw up the Budget, powerless though the Commission is in practice—the idea that Parliamentary parties should not mismanage finance. Party spirit is not always identical with public welfare; nor do parties remain in touch with the electorate as closely as they ought. One of the chief causes of their inertness is that they pay too little heed to the organization and education of their supporters in what I may call "peace time," that is to say, during the intervals between general elections. They only grow vigorous when an election is in sight or when conflicts and schisms arise in their own ranks. Democracy means constant and positive work of detail. In my view, parties ought not to be allowed a long period for mere electoral agitation. The general election should follow upon the end of a Parliament as soon as the technical arrangements can be made.

ENDS AND MEANS

The main principles that guided me abroad will guide me also as President. True, they are only a framework. Their practical application will depend upon circumstances and upon the persons with whom I shall have to work; and, in a democratic Republic, it is the duty of every citizen to work for the public weal. Under popular government all have a right to take the initiative, all are called upon to act, all are responsible —though, even in a democracy, many are called and few are chosen.

The difficulty of passing from an aristocratic and monarchical to a democratic system arises from the failure of monarchical aristocracy to accustom citizens to bear responsibility and to take decisions. Monarchism and Caesarism have left something of aristocracy and absolutism in many of us. To give orders is not always identical with leadership. Our Republic has to educate its citizens in democracy. And, for the sake of our whole future, it is important that the main lines of our development should be laid down from the outset. The general direction is weightier than the details. We have to decide upon principles and tactics so as to create a sound tradition, to march with firm step towards our national goal, and not to oscillate about "a golden mean." My own principles and aims have grown organically out of our history in which I have steeped myself. My guide and master was Palacký, the "Father of the Fatherland," who gave us a philosophical history of our nation, understood its place in the world, and defined our national objective. He perceived that, in virtue of our geographical situation and of our past, we are a part of the world as a whole; that we need to realize this position and to act in accordance with it. He saw that Europe and mankind were tending towards unification, and he told us what part we were to play in the "centralization of the world." He added:—

The miraculous power of steam and electricity has set up new standards. The old barriers between countries and peoples are disappearing more and more, the families and tribes of humanity are being brought nearer together, into closer reciprocal contact. . . . International rivalry has reached a degree hitherto unknown. It will grow and grow. Those who stand out of the race will decline and presently be past saving. I ask myself whether our people, gifted beyond others, is to stand aside, through neglect or incomprehension on the part of its leaders, whether it shall take no part in the emulation which can alone assure its life in future.

It is time for our people to awaken and to seek its bearings in the spirit of the new era, to glance beyond the narrow limits of its home and, without failing in love of its country, to become more zealously and withal more circumspectly a citizen of the world. We must take part in world trade, take advantage of the general progress, surrendering nothing of our old faith and uprightness yet discarding our old, easygoing habits, the weakness and indifference that begot our poverty and faintheartedness. We must tread new paths and renovate ourselves by industry—farmers, men of learning and officials not less than manufacturers, merchants and artisans. To the former comfortable cheapness of life we have said farewell for ever. No longer can we be coarsely ignorant of the needs of a civilized age. Whatever the Government of our State, taxes will not be lighter; and, if we would not decay and fall into penury, we must redouble our zeal and seek to stand as equals alongside of other nations whose spirit of enterprise has spread their sway to the uttermost parts of the earth.

Palacký insists that this world policy, in the true sense, must be based on humane principles. He continues:—

My last word is a warm and heartfelt wish that my beloved people in Bohemia and Moravia, whatever their station, may never cease to be true to themselves, true to truth and true to justice. . . . In the glorious era of Hus, the Czechs outdid all other European peoples in education and spiritual eminence. . . . Now they still need to educate themselves and to heed the dictates of enlightened reason. This is the only counsel I would bequeath to them. . . . Whenever we have triumphed it has been more by the might of the spirit than by physical power; and, whenever we were vanquished, it was through lack of spiritual vigor, moral courage and boldness. It is wholly wrong to imagine that the military wonders our fathers wrought in the Hussite Wars came from blind and barbaric raging and smashing, not from high enthusiasm for an idea, for moral sturdiness and lofty enlightenment. When, in a like struggle, two hundred years later, we sank almost to the grave, it was because we no longer towered in spirit above the enemy but, being more like unto them in demoralization than unequal to them in strength, we put our hope in the sword and in force. . . . Not until we conquer and rule by the power of the spirit, in the struggle that Providence has laid upon us from time immemorial, can we be assured of a lasting future.

Time and again Palacký animadverted upon our moral failings. In considering why we were Germanized, he compared us with our German neighbors, with whom we have always to measure ourselves, and concluded that we ourselves were in some measure to blame for our decline. He did not believe that, by race and blood, the Germans are our superiors of spirit or finer of intellect, but he thought them less prone to our faults, which he thus described:—

Among the various defects of our people, the worst and the greatest is one for which there is no Czech name though it has long gnawed at our roots—intemperance, self-indulgence in the broadest sense. Czechs, and Slavs generally, bear themselves far better in woe than in weal. They are tender and capable, zealous and inventive, active and tenacious; but they are also sensuous and vain, inconstant, exuberant, and covetous. They find getting easier than keeping; what they gain to-day is squandered to-day or to-morrow. In placid sensuousness our fair sex knows no bounds. Nowhere in the wide world is the goddess Fashion so passionately worshipped or so many sacrifices made to her. Nor is this a modern trait. . . . Dalemil was the first and Comenius the last to ascribe the downfall of our people to vanity and exuberance. Against these failings King George and other Fathers of the country worked fruitlessly by law and precept. Six hundred years ago the Czechs began to earn and alas! to deserve the nickname of "an apish people" because they aped and imitated everything they saw among their neighbors. In this the Germans are more coolheaded, more sober, more prudent. A German knows how to make a fortune and how to husband it. After having gained a competence abroad he is not ashamed once more to live a peasant's life in Bohemia. Fond though he is of good food and drink, he looks further into the future and lusts less after dainties, jewels and luxury. . . . The suffocation of national feeling among us is not the only cause of our misfortunes. Other causes are our blind cleaving to home earth, our lack of enterprise abroad, a desire for novelty that seeks rather to enjoy than to create, that is more passive than active, nay, even our easy-going good fellowship that abhors violence and suffers wrong more readily than it wrongs a neighbor. . . . To get rid of this ancient, evil spirit we must first know and recognize its nature, for it is a matter of life and death; knowing it, means can be found to exorcize it and save our lives. To this end vigorous will is needed, firm and persistent rather than fiery. Not by noisy raving will it be achieved, only by quiet, true-hearted effort, sincere and steady, as undeviating under temptation as under terror. Reasonable moral education must be brought to a higher level so that our people may understand itself and ensure its future. Any other remedy is but a pitiful palliative. . . . To all patriots I appeal that they should strive to give our people nourishing spiritual and moral food. Then they will muster enough sound sense henceforth to eschew poisonous infections.

THE HUMANE IDEAL

It is no accident but a natural consequence and continuation of our history that our political independence should have been restored in the form of a democratic Republic. Negatively the ground for it was prepared by the loss of our former independence, by our subjection to an alien dynasty and its anti-Czech system, its foreign army, its alien nobility, and a Church that was forced upon us. All these things estranged us from monarchism and its institutions. Positively, too, our past had prepared us for democracy. The foundations of the modern humane and democratic ideal had been laid by our Hussite Reformation in which, as Palacký shows, the Bohemian Brotherhood Church was especially significant, inasmuch as it surpassed in moral worth all the other Churches and the earlier attempts at religious reform. The Bohemian Brethren rejected the use of all force by State or Church, so well did it understand the intimate connection between Church and State which was the essence of medieval theocracy. Chelčický's extreme view was mitigated by his successors, as was the evanescent Communism of the Taborites; and though King George opposed the Brotherhood, he proclaimed the ideal of universal peace and was thus in agreement with the Brethren's fundamental doctrine. Comenius, the last Bishop of the Brotherhood Church, built up his conception of humanity upon education and the school, and sought by means of them to carry out his national and pan-human program. He still speaks to us through Leibnitz and Herder whose influence upon Dobrovsky and Kollár Professor Denis has finely demonstrated; and their successors, Palacký, Šafařík and Havlíček likewise expressed the needs of their time in accordance with our national ideal of humanity.

In resisting the absolutism of an Austria inspired by the Counter-Reformation, we were the more disposed during the eighteenth century to welcome the "Era of Enlightenment" and the French Revolution because Rousseau, the intellectual leader of the Revolution, who had been brought up in Swiss Calvinism and Republicanism, took the ideas of the Reformation as his starting-point. Thus the thought of the West inspired our national rebirth. As Marx has justly observed, the men of the French Revolution trod the path which the Reformation had marked out. The "Era of Enlightenment," the doctrine of humanity and the guiding principles of the eighteenth century are a sequel to the Lutheran and Calvinist Reformation and to our own Hussite reform. I do not claim that the humane ideal is specifically Czech. Nor do I assert that we Czechs and Slovaks are endowed by nature with a particularly gentle, tender, dove-like disposition. On the contrary, I think we are pretty hard, notwithstanding a peculiar receptive softness in our temperament that is not identical with kindliness or warmth of feeling. The humane ideal is pan-human and each people seeks to apply it in its own way. The English expression of it is mainly ethical; the French, political (by the proclamation of the Rights of Man); the German, social, or Socialist; and our own, national and religious. To-day it is universal, and the time is coming when all civilized peoples will recognize it as the foundation of the State and of international relationships.

Two questions have emerged from the lively discussions upon our national program before and after the war. The first relates to the humanitarian ideal in itself, and the second to the doubt whether it is founded on religion. On the first, I hope that what I have written will clear up some misconceptions. On the second, it will be difficult, if not impossible, to reach agreement with those who reject the ideal altogether or deny its religious basis. Those who do not admit that morality, religion and "ideology" generally have any serious political meaning; who claim that "moralizing" and religion represent an "obsolete standpoint" and are good for children, women and sentimentalists, whereas practical, "realist" politicians eschew sentimentality and work with practical realities, decline altogether to accept the humane ideal. Yet even between "realists" of this sort there are differences. Neither Bismarck nor the pan-Germans disdained religion. They repudiated the humane ideal, but they either, like Bismarck, attached great value to ecclesiastical religion or, like Lagarde, to the new pan-German religion.

Among ourselves as well as in Germany the doctrine of humanity is controverted in the name of nationalism. For instance, I read recently the following statement by one of our Legionaries: "We gained freedom because we promised the Allies that we would form a dam against German Imperialism. Not on account of our glorious past, or of our mature culture and economic development, nor because we are the people of Hus, Comenius and Palacký was our nation set free, but because our representatives abroad contrived to spread the conviction that our national independence would strengthen the Allies against the German Imperialist danger. We made this engagement and we must keep it. We shall keep it if our State is nationalist and the whole spirit of its public administration is Czechoslovak."

This is a wrong and one-sided view. It is my right to say what I promised the Allies. I fought pan-Germanism very vigorously and insisted on our right to independence. But I never asserted, and could not assert, that we should form a dam, that is to say, the only dam, against German Imperialism. My object was to awaken the Allies to a full understanding of the pan-German plan and to convince them of the common danger; but I sought also to convince them that, as the people of Hus and Comenius, we were entitled to aspire to freedom and to ask for their help. The number of our Legionaries' bayonets certainly came into the reckoning. From the outset I myself called for bayonets, not in a merely nationalist or chauvinistic spirit, but persuaded of our good right to defend ourselves, to justify our independence morally and legally, and to make it clear that we were upholding something of value in culture and civilization.

To have talked in England and America of bayonets, of nothing but bayonets, would have been suicidal short-sightedness, for the idea that bayonets alone count is precisely what the Great War refuted. Our whole propaganda abroad was, indeed, a refutation of chauvinistic nationalism. If nationalism means love of one's own people, I have nothing to say against it. The "national idea" thus conceived is a noble and worthy political force that welds individuals into a self-sacrificing whole; and humanity is made up of organized national wholes. About love of one's own people there can be no dispute. Only the quality of such love, its aims and the tactics by which they may best be realized, can be open to discussion. It is Neruda's deliberate and dis cerning love of our nation that appeals to me, not the indiscriminate love that assumes everything to be right and righteous merely because it bears a "national" label. Notwithstanding Havlíček's strong protest, there are still too many speculators in patriotism, just as there are not a few well-meant but weak and impracticable "national" programs.

Neither in politics, literature nor journalism have the leaders of any people been content to appeal solely to the number of their bayonets. They have always offered other proofs of their people's worth. Even the pan-Germans sought to justify the primacy of the German nation by the excellence of its science and philosophy. The French extol their political continuity since Roman times, praise the State-creative skill with which the central administration was built up and the French idea of State sovereignty carried through. A Frenchman will point to the contests of the Kings of France with the Papacy—that is to say, against theocracy—and, above all, to the Great Revolution, its policy and ideas (even should he refer to Napoleon he will lay stress on the Republic and democracy); to the French contribution to the literature, civilization and culture of the world and, latterly, to the part taken by France in the World War and in the Peace. In his chain of reasoning the French bayonet by itself appears as a very minor link.

In the same way the Englishman will mention the State-creative capacity with which the greatest World Empire has been built up; and precisely he will insist that it was built up by policy and administration, not by the sword. He is proud of his Reformation, be he Anglican or Independent, and will explain what services the English Revolution rendered to democracy. He will cite the weighty fact that the form of his State, "Constitutional Parliamentarism," has been adopted throughout the world—a world that speaks more English than any other language. Nor will he forget his literature or his unique Shakespeare. And all other nations will agree upon the value of English and French culture, accepting them without repugnance. Germans, Italians, Russians, Dutchmen, Danes and Norwegians have likewise their own stories to tell the world. For us the question is what we have to tell it. What will be its idea of us?

Politically, we shall be able to show that we founded our State, a fairly big State, in very ancient times, and that we possessed, and possess, State-creative capacity. This was proved not only by Charles IV and King George but, before their time, by the effort to form a Great Moravian Empire and by the organization of the realm of the Přemyslides—a State created by a native dynasty and administration in the very neighborhood of the Germans who had crushed the other Slav States. We shall instance the administrative ability shown in our Doomsday Book and other institutions; but we shall lay especial emphasis upon our school system in earliest periods, and upon our having founded the first university in Central Europe. Our Hussite Reformation will, however, be our most valid title in the eyes of Europe. It was begun by a number of moralists, Štítný and others, before Hus. He and his successors continued it. It was mainly ethical. To theological doctrine it attached minor importance. In the Hussite wars we defended ourselves against the whole of a Europe marshaled by the Papacy. Žižka's saying, "The Czech is a captain" we shall not forget; nor shall we overlook Chelčický and his Brotherhood or Comenius as their offspring. If the English are able to invoke Shakespeare, the French Rousseau and the Germans Goethe, we can call ourselves the people of Comenius. Before the Battle of the White Mountain our Estates compelled the Emperor to issue a "Letter of Majesty," an Edict of Toleration, rare proof of the Czech striving against intolerance, all the rarer if it be compared with the keenness of eccleciastical strife in Germany. We shall remember the Battle of the White Mountain, the hostile Counter-Reformation, our national downfall and our national rebirth at the end of the eighteenth century, thanks to the steadfastness of a people which, outlasting all religious storms, remained unbroken in body and soul. We shall point proudly to our indefatigable resistance to Austria-Hungary—a resistance that was moral at heart, for we should often have been ready to recognize Austria politically—and, finally, we shall describe our part in the World War and assure Europe that we shall strive for democracy, peace and progress. In a word, Palacký's philosophy of our own and of world history is our best recommendation. From the beginning of the fourteenth to the end of the eighteenth centuries, the Czech question, the question of our existence, was in essence the question of religion and of humanity.

These were, briefly, the main arguments with which we upheld our title to fight for freedom, and showed why it was the duty of others to stand by us. National they were, but not nationalist in the sense of the Legionary whom I have quoted. Nor were they Liberal after the manner of many Liberals who reject the moral and religious foundations of the humane ideal. Among such Liberals some essay to ascribe our whole Reformation to the awakening of the national consciousness in a struggle against the Germans—a view so shallow and thoughtless that it needs no special refutation. Others admit that the humane ideal of the Reformers and the Reformation (and, subsequently, of Comenius) was, indeed, based on religious feeling yet allege that it was otherwise with the leaders of our national renascence. Though the more reasonable of them confess that Palacký, and possibly Kollár, may be looked upon as religious humanitarians, they insist that all the other leaders of our renascence were devoid of religious convictions and were

Liberals in the sense of insisting upon the importance of nationality and of upholding the contemporary Liberal principles of democracy and of freedom of conscience.

Recently, too, I read a Liberal explanation of my own humanitarian doctrine. It was described as that of a theorist, whereas our real national ideal of humanity was alleged to have been evolved as the weapon of the weak amid the circumstances of the modern era. Assuredly the small and the weak in the struggle against the great and strong will not straightway put their faith in iron but will see what can be done by reason and reasonable methods. Thus it has always been. Like Comenius before them, Kollár and Palacký taught the humane ideal on principle and as good discipline for the character, not on utilitarian or tactical grounds. We wished, and we wish truly to be human. A Czech "Liberal" is usually a Catholic, according to the ecclesiastical register, and is illiterate in religious matters. Since he cannot conceive religion apart from his Church, its ritual and its doctrine, he understands neither Palacký nor our other greatest writers, though their names are ever on his tongue. Nor, even if he be an historian, does he understand our history.

Sentimentalists, who dislike making up their minds on religious matters, who have little faith in themselves but cherish pleasant childhood memories of incense, ritual and church organs, appeal from Palacký the historian to Palacký the politician, arguing that he deprecated religious dissensions and, though a Protestant, was more than reconciled to the Catholic Church. Yet Palacký himself repudiated all belief in external religious authority, and declared: "I myself am incapable of ever becoming a Catholic." Not religious indifference caused him to lead the nation away from dogmatic disputes, but the feeling that they were harmful; and he agreed with Brother Lucas, who stood against Luther in defending the rights of reason in the interpretation of Scripture. Palacký undoubtedly had a religious conception of the national humanitarian ideal. His whole philosophy of history proves it, as his opponents recognize; and his writings suffice fully to establish the religious basis of our humanitarian outlook.

Can it be an accident that three of the chief leaders of our renascence were Protestants? Besides Palacký there were Kollár and Šafařík, both of them Slovaks and Protestants, who took our Reformation as their starting-point. Though, as I have observed, Kollár's grasp upon the principle of humanity was not so deep and conscious as that of Palacký, the decisive fact is that he too was a Protestant, and that both felt themselves to be children of the Reformation, ecclesiastically and religiously. Indeed, our Slovak Protestants in general were fully aware of their spiritual descent from Hus as well as from Luther. If we would understand the true significance of our renascence, we must comprehend that among us and throughout Europe the eighteenth and nineteenth centuries carried forward the ideas and the yearnings of the Reformation. We must perceive clearly what are the guiding ideas in history, how they develop and how, despite all changes of detail, they remain essentially the same. To take an example: Palacký was a disciple of Kant, and Kant was the philosopher of Protestantism. This does not mean that Kant expounded Luther's catechism—he rejected theology of all sorts—but it does mean that he accepted Protestant individualism and subjectivity, that he laid stress upon the ethical side of religion, repudiated authority in matters of belief and transformed the leading ideas of Protestantism into a philosophical system which was nevertheless incompatible with Protestant Orthodoxy. In much the same way Palacký, a Czech Protestant, transformed the Church of the Bohemian Brotherhood into an humanitarian system and, like Kant, discarded Lutheran Orthodoxy.

Our Liberal historians might learn a lesson from the philosophical Pope, Leo XIII. He, the restorer of Thomistic Scholasticism, condemned the Reformation and, in his encyclical "Diu Lemen illud" (1881), described the Reformation not only as the mother of modern philosophy but of modern politics, and, above all, of democracy. To the Reformation he traced the modern conception of right and law, and of Socialism, Nihilism and Communism. In subsequent pronouncements he thundered against "the Lutheran Rebellion" and demanded uniform Catholic education. Though I do not agree with the head of the Roman Church in his estimate of the ideals, aspirations and institutions of the modern era, and need hardly point out the exaggeration of placing Socialism and Nihilism on the same footing, I think Leo XIII was right in the main, that is to say, in claiming that the modern outlook on life, the modern State and modern democracy arose by and through the Reformation. It is in this sense that our renascence and modern development pursue the work of our Reformation, and that our "Awakeners" like Palacký, set out more or less consciously from the point at which our history attained its climax. None of our distinguished men and spiritual leaders was so careless of things religious as our "Liberals" pretend. Dobrovský, as a Freemason, deliberately opposed the Church, though not religion. Upon Kollár, Šafařík and Palacký we are agreed. Havlíček was a Liberal yet not religiously indifferent. The first and greatest of our poets, Mácha, was religious through and through, though tormented by skepticism; for him the problem of religion was the problem of life. Neruda was deeply religious, as every reader of his "Songs of Good Friday" must feel. Světlá and, more profoundly, Nováková sought traces of the Reformation among the people. And, among our contemporaries, how moral and religious are Holeček's and Čapek-Chod's analyses of character. Šalda even preaches a return to God. Nor are Svatopluk Čech and Vrchlický, though Liberals, exceptions to the rule; the former prayed to an Unknown, and the latter suffered throughout life from the problem that tormented Faust.

OUR RELATION TO CATHOLICISM

The Catholic historians and politicians who judge our Reformation from their religious standpoint are serious and consistent opponents of Palacký. In their eyes the Reformation was, and is, a religious and political mistake; the Catholicizing of our people by the Hapsburgs was its spiritual and national salvation; the Bohemian Brotherhood and Protestantism would have Germanized us; the Battle of the White Mountain was a blessing.

In Germany, England and elsewhere Catholic historians and public men look more objectively upon the origins and significance of our Reformation. Admitting the defects and errors of their own Church, and the need for reform at the end of the Middle Ages, they recognize at least the relative and temporary justification of Protestantism. If Providence directs the course of history, if there is order and purpose in the sequence of events, how can the Reformation and the rise of Protestantism be condemned in the lump without thought of the significance, for Catholics in particular, of so huge and lasting a movement throughout the world? Precisely from the theistic point of view, the Catholic opponents of Palacký take up an untenable position in their interpretation of history. Could there have been a Reformation if the Church had satisfied the people's needs? Did not the Reformation proceed from the bosom of the Church itself? The best Catholics have ever criticized the shortcomings of their own Church. Indeed, their critical literature, from the beginning down to the Reformation, would fill more than one library. But as soon as the movement for reform went on outside the Church, and new Churches were founded, the old Church became a Party of which the main object was to retain power by compromise or by force. Hence the "Compacts" made with us, hence the Inquisition, hence Jesuitism—and the Inquisition and Jesuitism carried through the Catholicizing process in our midst also. Yet, if the Church was inadequate I do not assert that the Reformation was adequate in all things and everywhere. Among Protestants, party strife soon replaced spiritual emulation; new theocracies, eager for power, sprang up against the old theocracy; the Churches that professed the religion of love resorted to violence and readily allowed themselves to be misused by temporal Powers.

Our Catholic opponents of the Czech Reformation, who maintain that the Catholicizing process saved the nation from Germany and Prussia, are able to invoke the authority of Bismarck, who is said once to have spent a sleepless night in trying to imagine what the course of history might have been had the Protestants won the Battle of the White Mountain. Bismarck may have wondered whether a Protestant Bohemia would have associated herself with the Protestant policy of Prussia against Austria. Austria would thus have remained an unimportant German borderland while, with the help of Bohemia, the Germans would have been masters of the Danube and the dream of Berlin-Baghdad might have been fulfilled with Czech assistance. We know how much weight Bismarck assigned to the geographical position of Bohemia in the mastery of Europe.

There is much virtue in "if"; but I have little liking for "ifs" in history. I prefer facts. Our Reformation fortified our nationality as never before. While Catholicism predominated, Germanization went on and the Hussite movement saved us from it. German historians bear witness that, among us as in Poland, the Reformation worked mightily in an anti-German sense. In our case as in others it fostered the national language and literature, because public worship and, especially, the reading of the Bible in the language of the country had far greater influence upon literature and national education than they have to-day. In endeavoring to raise the level of morality, the Reformation strengthened our national character; and victory at the White Mountain might therefore have invigorated and renewed the nation yet more, despite some initial penetration of the Germans among us during the Protestant era. Where is it written that the Evangelical Czechs would have let themselves be led tamely by Prussia, seeing that Protestant Prussia and pan-Germanism were defeated in the World War by Protestant England, Protestant America and revolutionary France? Comenius, who was the flower and fulfilment of the Bohemian Brotherhood, is, by himself alone, a proof to the contrary, as are all the writings and the activity of our exiles. The Hussites, the Brethren, and the Evangelical Czechs kept up lively intercourse with the Germans, who received them well, and also with the Dutch, the Swiss, the English and the Swedes; yet in all lands they worked for the liberation of their Fatherland. In defense of his people, Comenius carried on a true world-policy of education. And after the White Mountain the Catholic Hapsburgs catholicized us, not merely as they had done before but Germanized us by fire and sword, by confiscation and by the suppression of education; and the Catholic adversaries of the "Arch-Heretic," Hus, made the Czechs an object of general hatred as a people of heretics. It was Catholic, ultra-Catholic, Austria that fell politically under the sway of Protestant Prussia and became her obedient vanguard on the Danube.

Notwithstanding the Battle of the White Mountain and its sequel, Catholicism failed to take deep root among us. It was addicted to violence, its leaders were alien in blood and in creed—especially the Jesuits, who are alien even to-day—and, with few exceptions, its hierarchy was German and Hapsburgian, not Czech. The argument that the Czech defeat on the White Mountain was a national advantage is mistaken. It seeks to turn a religious into a racial question in order to appeal to patriotic sentiment. The Catholic historians and those non-Catholics who judge the Reformation solely as a strengthening of our national consciousness misunderstand the essence of religious feeling and the whole sense of our history.

To examine exactly how far Protestantism and how far Prussianism was a decisive influence in the evolution of Prussian Germany would be to go beyond my present purpose. The Lutheran Church unquestionably became a handmaid of the Prussian State; but half of Germany was Catholic, and there is no proof that the German Catholic or Center Party, despite its opposition to Bismarck, would have acted otherwise than Bismarck towards the non-German Catholics. The case of Luther, founder of German Protestantism, is significant. As long as he was a Catholic he opposed the Czechs. After leaving the Church he always stood out for a just and sober estimate of them, preached racial peace, extolled the moral purity of the Bohemian Brethren, and held them up as an example to the Germans by declaring that he and his followers were Hussites. Leading German thinkers, like Leibnitz, Herder and Goethe afterwards showed goodwill towards the Czech people and condemned the Hapsburg hangmen. Herder, in particular, embraced the ideas of Comenius and desired the restoration of Czech independence, while poets and writers such as Schiller, Lenau, Alfred Meissner and Moritz Hartmann gladly sought in our history material for their works.

An impartial history of our religious development will show the relationship between Catholicism and the Reformation in a light different from that which the adversaries of Palacký throw upon it. The facts that the Reformation affected us so profoundly (nine-tenths of the people are estimated to have accepted it); that it so long withstood the fierce pressure of Rome, the Hapsburgs and their German partisans in Bavaria and elsewhere, the last religious rising of the Moravian peasants taking place as late as 1775; and that the fight for religion and morality formed for four centuries the main substance of our history, prove that our Reformation arose from and responded to national character. True, our historians should inquire to what extent the spirit of Catholicism was national before and during the Reformation, and whether it did not suffer from the drawback that it came to us from abroad, from Germany, Italy and elsewhere. I know well that Catholicism is international. Yet its centralizing tendency did not prevent it from assuming a national complexion which theologians and ecclesiastical experts have noticed in France, England, Germany, Italy and other countries. Our lower Catholic clergy, who are recruited mainly from the people, had and have the same national sense as the people, and some of them took an active part in the literary work of our reawakening. But the Hierarchy, which determines ecclesiastical policy and life, was, like the training of the priests, with very few exceptions, non-Czech. It is a striking fact that, among us, Catholicism has never brought forth a Czech theology, and that it has not shown the same independence and individual character as in other lands.

The problem whether this or that religion and Church is best suited to the character of a people deserves to be more carefully studied. Half the Germans, for instance, are Protestant and half are Catholic; the English are chiefly Anglican, but most of them are thoroughgoing Protestants; and in France there is an important Protestant minority. I name these, the most cultured and most important nations, as evidence that nationality does not exclude ecclesiastical differentiation and that this very differentiation has been of value to those nations themselves and to mankind at large. On the other hand, the nations that did not pass through the Reformation and failed to differentiate themselves religiously, have not yet attained the same historical importance as the others. We belong to these others; and our history, especially since the fourteenth century, is one of the most living and spiritually valuable.

CHURCH AND STATE

What is the meaning of the Hapsburg Counter-Reformation for us to-day? Save for some tiny remnants our Reformed Churches—the Hussite Church and the Bohemian Brotherhood —were utterly destroyed. The Hapsburgs, encouraged and helped by the Roman Church, carried through the Catholicizing process with fire and sword, by confiscation and banishment. There is no other instance of the overwhelming majority of a Christian nation having had its religion thus changed. In France, Italy and Spain, where the Reformation was likewise violently suppressed, it had affected only a minority. In those countries, moreover, the Counter-Reformation was carried out by their own people, whereas, in our case, it was the work of an alien dynasty, hostile to us and to our spiritual traditions. In the light of these facts, every enlightened and educated Czech is bound to ask what this violent Catholicizing signified if, as Palacký held, our Reformation and the Bohemian Brotherhood

marked the highest point of our history. How is the comparatively rapid reversion to an older religious and ecclesiastical
form to be explained? Does violence suffice to explain it or
did the fault lie in the Reformation itself? If so, what was it?
Does the success of the Hapsburgs in forcing Catholicism upon
us reveal some failing in our national character, some lack of
endurance, of steadfastness, of political capacity? What meaning are we to ascribe to our Protestantism, in which—according
to the Emperor Joseph's Edict of Toleration—Hussitism and
the Bohemian Brotherhood, that is to say, Palacký's perfect
Church, were preserved in the guise of Lutheranism and Calvinism? If, as I hold, Palacký's philosophy of our history is essentially true, the cleft between Church and culture has, in our
case, peculiar national importance, an importance not solely
philosophical and religious as in the cases of other nations; it
means that our Reformed Church was suppressed by an alien
dynasty with the assent of the Catholic Church, and that the
Hapsburg Counter-Reformation yawns as an abyss between the
Reformation period and the present day.

No Czech historian can escape the problem of the Counter-
Reformation. From the very beginning of the national
reawakening the memory of our Reformation revived and
stimulated intellectual freedom. The names of Hus, Žižka,
Comenius and afterward of Chelčický, became dear to all.
Controversy began upon the meaning of the Reformation, the
Counter-Reformation and the religious question generally.
Palacký—with whom I do not agree on this point—looked upon
the division of the Church into Catholicism and Protestantism
as a result of historical theological evolution. He thought that
each form of belief responds to a need of the human spirit,
Catholicism representing the principle of authority and Protestantism the principle of reason. The difference between them
seem to him relative, not absolute; and he expected this rela-
tivity to develop not by the triumph of the one principle over
the other but by their reconciliation, harmony and interpenetra-
tion. The two Churches, he held, should tolerate, not oppose

each other, since disbelief would in future menace both of them.

As an explanation of the relationship between Catholicism and Protestantism I think this interpretation too general and abstract. Moreover, it is insufficient to cover our contemporary religious position. We are confronted with the special relationship between Protestantism and Catholicism in our own country, and have to judge the religious and moral value of the Hapsburg Counter-Reformation. Now that hundreds of thousands of our people are taking advantage of their religious freedom to leave the Catholic Church and to found another on the basis of the Reformation, the religious question is acquiring practical importance and is compelling thoughtful minds to revise the Liberal standpoint on the subject of religion. To assert, as some indifferentists do, that religion is out of date and that the dispute between Catholicism and Protestantism is consequently of no moment, is a view at once shallow and mistaken—and fatal to Liberalism everywhere.

Palacký's interpretation of the relationship between Protestantism and Catholicism cannot stand even against the strictures of our Liberals; for in Czech Liberalism there has always been some disposition to understand the religious side of our renascence, however little it grasped the essential nature of the Reformation and of religion itself. To what lengths this disposition could go may be seen in the case of the Young Czech Radical leader Sladkovský, who went over to the Orthodox Church and expected his followers and all opponents of the Catholic Church to do likewise. What I opposed in Liberalism was its religious indifference. I claimed and proved that religious feeling is not dead and that, in the last resort, we should not be able to ignore the Churches or to escape from the necessity of making up our minds about them. For my part, I declined to coquet with Orthodoxy, and urged that the religious question should be earnestly studied in order to prepare means of solving it. As a result, there arose the dispute upon the meaning of our renascence, the Hapsburg Counter-Reformation and the religious question.

In the name of "Progress" not a few demand that the religious question should be left severely alone. We cannot return to the Middle Ages, they say. This is a very foggy and unprogressive outlook. Nowhere does the religious question nowadays imply the mere adoption of old ecclesiastical forms. Protestantism and Catholicism are alike in a state of crisis. If we are to bridge the abyss of the Hapsburg Counter-Reformation and to establish new links with our national Reformation, we must continue its tradition in harmony with the spiritual needs of our time. If it be said that the present generation of Czechs no longer believe as Hus believed, and that Hus stood nearer to Rome than we stand, the answer is that though we no longer believe as Hus believed, he and his disciples are models of moral resolution, steadfastness and religious uprightness. Hus began the fight against the worldliness of the Church and the people followed him. His fight for higher morality and lofty piety, sealed by the sacrifice of his life, was a fight against the moral decadence of the Church, the priesthood and the Papacy. When, in the name of the Cross, Rome declared a European war against us, Žižka, sword in hand, upheld victoriously the living principles Hus had proclaimed. Even Chelčický recognized that the struggle against the temporal rule of the Priesthood necessarily involved hostility to the State which the Church was supporting, that is to say, simultaneous antagonism to the political and the ecclesiastical power; and, with a truly Žižka-like vigor, he took up the fight for the humane ideal against ecclesiastical and political violence. If he overshot the mark, his great idea survived him. Comenius, the last Bishop of the Bohemian Brotherhood which Chelčický founded, taught us that education and careful upbringing are indispensable to any thoroughgoing religious and moral reform. The examples of Hus and Žižka show that life is worthless without truthfulness and unless it be guided by conviction. Chelčický and the Brotherhood show that a system of life based on ecclesiastical and political force is evil. Comenius pointed the way to an exalted, all-embracing wisdom and humane sympathy. In the spirit of these masters we must go forward and hand on their torch to future generations. What names has the Hapsburg Counter-Reformation to compare with these four—Hus, Žižka, Chelčický, Comenius—names dear to our whole people and respected throughout the world? Over against a great idea it can set naught but naked force.

The relationship of religion to political and practical life I sum up in the command that we should seek first the Kingdom of God and His righteousness and that all other things shall be added unto us. A man and a people religiously convinced, a nation steadfastly determined to realize its ideals, will always reach their goal. This I have learned from life; this too is the teaching of our own history and that of all nations.

Our Reformation was a democratic revolution against theocracy. Its faults, the faults of a first attempt, do not prove its principles and essence to have been wrong; and, when I think of our Revolution of October 28, 1918, I reject the view that, merely because the Reformation was ultimately crushed by force, its overthrow shows it to have been a mistake and ourselves to have been politically inert and incompetent in statecraft. The task of finding a solution for the general religious crisis awaits us all, our thinkers and our Churches. Our Republic must ensure full liberty of conscience to every citizen so that discussion may be free and every conviction be expressed. Unlike Austria it must, moreover, carry through the separation of Church and State and, in education especially, the reforms which that separation implies.

No Church, least of all the Roman Catholic, has ever welcomed separation from the State even though religion may gain by it, as it has gained in many lands. Therefore we must be prepared for resistance. It will demand much diplomatic tact and clear definition of our educational policy. In order that the separation might be accomplished without conflict I decided before the end of the war that our Republic should at once be represented at the Vatican. I foresaw that, after the war, the ecclesiastical question would be acute. The object of separation is to set the Churches free from the State and the State free from the Churches, and to make religion a matter of unconstrained conviction. Under Austria, the Church relied on the police power of the State, whose officials were obliged to profess the official religion. In consequence the Church suffered and came to rely more upon the police than upon its doctrines and religious life. The State suffered likewise in that it relied upon the Church, not upon itself and its own worth. To "de-Austrianize" ourselves means, first of all, to separate the Church from the State.

The Law of Love

In old Austria there was no freedom of conscience. In our Republic it must be real, not merely recognized in legal Codes but practised in every domain of public life. It is a national demand, a demand that arises from our whole history. Our religious development as well as ecclesiastical conditions make it incumbent upon us to separate the Churches from the State. I foresaw that ecclesiastical convictions would be complicated by the union with Slovakia and by the inclusion of Sub-Carpathian Russia in our Republic; and because I anticipated that political freedom would, as it has ever done, tend to aggravate them, I wished to confine the separation question to the purely ecclesiastical and religious domain.

Within our borders we have several races and a considerable number of Churches and denominations. Alongside of our new Czechoslovak Church, Orthodoxy is spreading. The ranks of our Protestants have been swelled by the considerable number of Slovak Lutherans of the Augsburg Confession; as have those of the Catholic Uniates in Sub-Carpathian Russia. Thus we have Roman Catholics and Uniates, adherents of the Czechoslovak Church, Protestants, Orthodox, Unitarians and the Jews. Besides, many of our citizens are undenominational, members of no Church, yet holding private religious convictions of their own.

Under Austria-Hungary the Roman Catholic Church was predominant throughout the territories which now form our Republic. True, the native Protestants, Calvinists, and Lutherans of the Augsburg Confession were recognized by the State in the Historic Lands of the Bohemian Crown, though they enjoyed no official favor. Some foreign missions like the Baptists were more or less tolerated. In Slovakia the Protestant minority was, like the Catholic majority, racially oppressed by the Magyars, who sought also to Magyarize the Uniates in Sub-Carpathian Russia and to suppress the Orthodox movement. The Jews, on the other hand, had managed to gain the goodwill of the Hungarian and the Austrian Governments. How things have changed since the advent of religious freedom may be judged from such figures as are available.

A comparison of the official returns in 1910 and 1921 shows that, since the establishment of the Republic, the Czechoslovak Church has been founded and that in 1921 its members numbered 525,323, nearly all of whom left the Roman Catholic Church to join it. Its membership is now much larger. In addition, 724,507 Roman Catholics left their Church without adopting any other creed. The losses of the other Churches have been insignificant. In 1910 there were only 12,981 persons in the Historic Lands of the Bohemian Crown who professed no religion. Similarly, the Roman Catholic Uniate Church has lost heavily in Sub-Carpathian Russia, where under Hungary, in 1910, only 558 professed the Orthodox faith, whereas in 1921 the Orthodox numbered 60,986. In the regions inhabited by Czechs all the Protestant Churches show a strong increase of membership, quite apart from the adhesions to the Czechoslovak and the Orthodox Churches. Among the German population, on the other hand, the increase has only been normal. In 1910 there were 157,067 Calvinist and Lutheran Czechs as compared with 153,612 Germans. In 1921 the figures were 231,199 Czechs and 153,767 Germans. The smaller Protestant Churches also show an unusual increase—the Brotherhood from 1,022 to 3,093, the Free Reformed Church from 2,497 to 5,511, the Baptists from 4,072 to 9,360, besides 10,000 Unitarians and 1,455 Methodists. Altogether there were, in 1921, nearly 1,000,000 (990,319) Protestants in the Republic.

Even in the Historical Bohemian Lands and in Slovakia the Orthodox (including the Armenian Orthodox Church) have increased their membership, the totals being 12,111 in 1921 as compared with 2,502 in 1910; and the Old Catholics, who are mainly Germans, have grown from 17,121 to 20,255. On the other hand, the number of Jews has decreased from 361,650 to 345,342. Yet the Jewish communities show a strong religious life, Orthodox Eastern tenets being preponderant in Slovakia and Sub-Carpathian Russia, and more liberal tendencies in the West. Among the Jews Zionism and the Jewish National movement play an important part.

It is natural that the religious developments in our Republic should attract foreign attention, because among us Catholicism is losing ground, while e sewhere it is gaining in authority if not in extent. Even abroad it is beginning to be understood that the importance of the Czech question was not solely political. All our Protestant Churches are linked in various ways with our Reformation and with the Hussite tradition, just as, in Sub-Carpathian Russia, there is an analogous movement towards Orthodoxy. The Czech Reformed Church and the Lutheráns have united themselves in the Evangelical Church of the Bohemian Brethren, with which other denominations, including the Unitarians, are also associated. The new Czecho-slovak Church is Hussite. It is natural, too, that these Churches should seek contact with the foreign Churches to which they are most akin. The Czechoslovak Church is related to the Anglicans and the Old Catholics. It has, too, a certain kinship with the Polish Mariavites and, in some respects, with Ortho-doxy. The Orthodox movement is in touch with the Greek and Serbian Patriarchs. Orthodox, too, are our neighbors in Roumania and Russia. These varieties of ecclesiastical allegiance obviously strengthen the principle of religious toleration, a principle that sprang from the Reformation, though it was by no means immediately observed in the Reformation itself. On the authority of Augustine and of Thomas Aquinas the lives of heretics were forfeit in the Medieval Church—a barbaric doctrine that took time to overcome, as is proved by the case of Servetus, whom Calvin had burned at the stake in 1553. So gradually, indeed, did the spirit of toleration develop that Locke, who was one of its strongest advocates, would not tolerate atheism. Not until the French Revolution was the full right to freedom of conscience codified and practised in the religious field, but even then by no means in the field of politics.

In our Democratic Republic, freedom of conscience and toleration must not merely be codified but realized in every domain of public life. Palacký's philosophical interpretation of our history esteems the Bohemian Brotherhood as its consummation. The Father of our Nation and our historical past alike enjoin upon us pure Christianity, the teaching of Jesus and His law of life. Democracy is the political form of the humane ideal.

APPENDIX.—TABLE

DATE.	FRANCE.	ENGLAND.
August-September, 1914.		
October 2, 1914.	The French Minister of the Interior grants to trustworthy Czechs the same privileges as to citizens of Allied States.	
October 19, 1915.		The British Prime Minister, Mr. Asquith, agrees to take the chair at Professor Masaryk's inaugural lecture at King's College, London, and makes a written declaration. The Czechs in Great Britain are exempted from the disabilities of enemy aliens.

OF RECOGNITIONS

ITALY.	AMERICA.	RUSSIA AND OTHER STATES.
		The Russian Commander-in-Chief, Grand Duke Nicholas Nikolayevitch, issues a proclamation to the Austro-Hungarian peoples; the Tsar receives a first Czechoslovak deputation; the creation of a Czech Družina in the Russian army is sanctioned; the Russian Foreign Minister, Sazonof, receives a Czechoslovak deputation and declares that the restoration of the Bohemian Kingdom corresponds to the intentions of the Russian Government; the Tsar receives a second deputation and expresses the hope that Czechoslovak wishes will be fulfilled.

APPENDIX.—TABLE

DATE.	FRANCE.	ENGLAND.
1915 and 1916.	In Western Europe the Czechoslovak National liberation. A branch of the Council is established	
January 13, 1916.		
February 3, 1916.	The French Prime Minister, M. Briand, receives Professor Masaryk and agrees with his policy of liberating the subject Hapsburg peoples.	
April 17, 1916, to January 4, 1917.		
January 10, 1917.	In the Allied reply to President Wilson's Note tion of the Czechs and Slovaks from alien rule is	
March 24, 1917.		
June 13, 1917.	Conclusion of an agreement between Professor Masaryk and the French Minister, M. Albert Thomas, upon the sending of 30,000 Czecho-	

OF RECOGNITIONS

ITALY.	AMERICA.	RUSSIA AND OTHER STATES.
Council is set up and becomes the central organ of the movement for in Russia.		
		The Družina is transformed into a regiment of Czechoslovak Rifles in the Russian Army.
		The formation of a Czechoslovak Brigade in the Russian army is sanctioned; the Tsar agrees to the liberation of the Slav prisoners of war but presently withdraws his assent; the formation of a Czechoslovak division in Russia is sanctioned.
of December 21, 1916, asking for a definition of Allied war aims, the libera- declared to be a main condition of peace.		
		Milyukoff, the foreign Minister of the Russian Provisional Government, confirms the regulations for the formation of a Czechoslovak army.

APPENDIX.—TABLE

DATE.	FRANCE.	ENGLAND.
	slovak prisoners of war from Russia to France —the first Treaty of State concluded by the Czechoslovak National Council; a further agreement between the National Council and the French Government upon the formation of the Czechoslovak army being made on August 17, 1917.	
August 18, 1917.		
October 4, 1917.		
April 9, 1917, to February 16, 1918.		

OF RECOGNITIONS

ITALY.	AMERICA.	RUSSIA AND OTHER STATES.
		The Branch of the Czechoslovak National Council in Russia issues a loan of 20,000,000 francs for its army.
The Italian Government sanctions a formation of Labor contingents of Czechoslovak prisoners of war.		
		General Dukhonin sanctions the formation of the first independent Czechoslovak Corps in Russia; agreement between the Czechoslovak National Council and the Ukrainian Government; agreement with the Bolshevist Commander Muravieff upon the armed neutrality of the Czechoslovak forces, which are declared to form part of the French army, Muravieff guaranteeing its safe conduct to France.

APPENDIX.—TABLE

DATE.	FRANCE.	ENGLAND.
March 1918.		
March 21, 1918, to April 24, 1918.		
May 22, 1918.		On behalf of the Foreign Office, Lord Robert Cecil recognizes the right of the Czechoslovak nation to complete independence; and (June 3rd) the British Government declares its readiness to recognize the National Council as the supreme authority of the Czechoslovak movement and the Czechoslovak Legions as a belligerent Allied army.
May 29, 1918.		

OF RECOGNITIONS

DATE.	AMERICA.	RUSSIA AND OTHER STATES.
	Congress amends the Immigration Law so as to allow Czechoslovak Legionaries recruited in the United States to return thither after the war in the same way as the American volunteers in the Allied armies.	
Signature of Treaty between the N a t i o n a l Council and the Italian Government upon the creation of a Czechoslovak Legion in Italy; and solemn presentation of colors to Legion in Rome.		
	The Government approves of the resolutions of the Rome Congress of Oppressed Hapsburg peoples and (June 28th) supplements its approval by declaring that all the Slavs must be freed from German and Austrian rule.	

506   Appendix

DATE.	FRANCE.	ENGLAND.
June 3, 1918.	In the Allied War Council held at Versailles the American declarations, and declare their sincere	
June 29, 1918.	The Government recognizes the Czechoslovak right to independence and the National Council as the first basis of the future Czechoslovak Government; the President of the Republic presents colors (June 30th) to the Czechoslovak Legion in France.	
Aug. 2 and 3, 1918.	American-Japanese Agreement upon military in-representatives at Washington promise military	
August 9 to November 11, 1918.		The British Foreign Secretary, Mr. A. J. Balfour, issues a declaration recognizing the Czechoslovaks as an Allied nation; their Legions in France, Italy, and Siberia as a united Allied and belligerent army waging regular warfare against Austria-Hungary and Germany; and the National Council as the trustee for the future Czechoslovak Government. The British Government recognizes the National Council on this basis and concludes a diplomatic convention with it. The British Prime Minister, Mr. Lloyd George, thanks the National Council for the achievements of the Czechoslovak Legion in Siberia.

OF RECOGNITIONS

ITALY.	AMERICA.	RUSSIA AND OTHER STATES.
French, British and Italian Prime Ministers associate themselves with the sympathy with the Czechoslovak and Southern Slav struggle for freedom.		
tervention in support of the Czechoslovak Legion in Siberia; the Allied and material assistance to the Legion.		

APPENDIX.—TABLE

DATE.	FRANCE.	ENGLAND.
August 23, 1918.		
September 9 to October 7, 1918.		
October 14-18, 1918.	Dr. Beneš informs the Allied Governments that ment and accredits Czechoslovak representatives ment. On October 18th Masaryk, on behalf Washington. President Wilson informs Austria- visional Government, which Italy also recognizes in the Allied armistice negotiations in Paris; and appointed to Prague. Greece and Belgium recog- December 4th the Allies recognize the Czecho- the administration in the former Austro-Hungarian	

OF RECOGNITIONS.

ITALY.	AMERICA.	RUSSIA AND OTHER STATES.
	The Foreign Relations Committee of the Senate declares Czechoslovak independence to be one of the most important conditions of peace; and the American Government (September 3rd) recognizes the existence of a state of war between the Czechoslovaks and the Central Empires, and the National Council as the *de facto* Czechoslovak Government.	
		The Japanese Government recognizes the Czechoslovak army as a regular belligerent force and the National Council as its supreme organ. The Chinese Government recognizes (October 3rd) the Czechoslovak army in Siberia in the same way. The Russian Soviet Government recognizes (October 7th) the National Council as the *de jure* Government of the Czechoslovak State.

the National Council has constituted itself in Paris as a Provisional Govern-
to them. Next day (October 15th) France recognizes the Provisional Govern-
of the Provisional Government, proclaims Czechoslovak independence at
Hungary that the United States has recognized the Czechoslovak Pro-
on October 24th. On November 4th Dr. Beneš is invited to take part
on November 15th the first French and British Military Missions are
nize the Czechoslovak Government on November 22nd and 28th. On
slovak State, and authorize its troops to occupy Slovakia and to supervise
Monarchy.

INDEX

Absolutism, 356, 410, 467-8, 471, 476
Adler, Dr., 127, 375
Aehrenthal, Count, xvii, 44, 82, 97, 322-3
Agram High Treason trial, the, 72
Albania, 411
Alexander, Prince, 362, 365
Alexeieff, General, 138-9, 145 6, 154, 159, 167, 189, 202
Allies, the—
  author's estimate of, 21-2, 358-9, 368, 370; ties with, 52, 127; and Russia, 138, 191, 203; their contribution to Czech independence, 402-5, 420
Alsace-Lorraine, 211, 267, 409, 411, 422
America—
  funds raised in, 5, 8, 27, 58, 85; representing Western civilization v. Germany, 32, 45; Czech colony in, 51, 54, 224; to provide troops, 62; Czech propaganda in, 71, 75, 83; enters the war, 117-18, 125; and Japan, 192; the author in, 217-18, 224; democracy in, 225-9; and literature, 229-35; Yugoslav colonies in, 239; accepts the Rome Congress resolutions, 243; and the Bolshevists, 253; Lithuanians in, 254; change of view upon Austria-Hungary, 295-6, 304; share in victory, 328-9
"Americanism," 227
American Mission in Petrograd, 134
Americans, pro-German, 237
"Anabasis," the Siberian, 275-83, 316
Anarchism, 462-4
Andrássy, Count, 385-7, 391, 395, 397-9
Anglo-French Entente, the, 71, 109
Anti-Austrian policy, 34
Anti-Bolshevist movements, 190-2
Aquinas, Thomas, 36-7
Armistice, the, 310
Austria—
  and Serbia, 2, 32, 240; and the Russians, 12, 19; and the Sokols, 13; estimate of her army, 21; and the

Austria (continued)—
  Czechs, 22-3, 29-30, 32-4, 58-63, 96, 127, 135, 189, 393-401; and Italy, 39-40, 43-4, 55, 266; and the question of war guilt, 64; and intrigues in Switzerland, 67-8; impending collapse of, 117; makes a peace move, 125, 205, 211, 267, 290; and the severance from Hungary, 263-275, 393-400; and England, 266; and America, 308-9, 311, 394; her poets, 343; her military terrorism, 369-70; the new, 417-18
Austria-Hungary, the breaking up of, 263-275, 309, 369, 387, 396, 398
Austria-Hungary, the oppressed peoples of, 242, 248-50, 291, 295
Austrian Germans, the, 26
Austrian Italians, the, 39
Author on his training and work, the, 318-24
Averescu, General, 187

Bahr, Hermann, xvi
Bakhmetieff, M., 238, 353
Bakunin, 181
"Balkanization," 411-14
Balkan policy of Vienna, 2, 290
Balkans, the, 10, 19-21, 44, 290
Baráček, M., 48
Barbarism, Bolshevist, 176, 181
Belgium, 1, 309, 411
Belgrade, Austrian evacuation of, 11
Belligerents, author's estimate of the, 20-2
Benckendorff, Count, 5, 54, 119
Beneš, Dr., 8, 27-9, 34, 49-50, 71-3, 78-80, 83-6, 95, 98, 104, 119, 125, 188, 191, 214-15, 238, 243, 268, 292, 310, 318-19, 362, 383, 389-90, 395, 398-9, 404
Berchtold, Count, 2, 64-5
Berlin-Baghdad scheme, 32, 116, 148, 485
Bernstorff, Count, 125

Berthelot, General, 134, 186, 193
Berthelot, M. Philippe, 364, 402
Bethmann-Hollweg, Herr, 32, 100, 123, 211-12, 324
Biliński, M., 64-5
Bismarck, 31, 337-9, 341, •351, 356-7, 416, 477, 485
Bohemia, xvi, xix, 5, 7, 79, 92-3, 127, 141, 144, 148, 152, 213, 222, 311, 372, 387, 416, 429-31, 473, 485
Bohemian Brotherhood Church, the, 475, 484-5, 491
Bohemians, the German, 400-1, 430
Bolshevism, 175, 178, 180-4, 190, 195, 198, 201, 395, 396, 441
Bolshevist propaganda, 177, 182
Bolshevist Revolution, the, 170, 173-84, 190, 194
Bolshevists, errors of the, 194
Boroevitch, General, 128
Bosnia, 23, 244, 246
Bosnia-Herzegovina, annexation of, xvii
Bottomley, Horatio, 91
Bouček, Dr., 28
Branch of the Paris National Council, the Russian, 164, 197-8
Brest-Litovsk, Peace of, 184, 192-3, 196, 279, 285
Briand, M., 96, 148, 164, 204, 211, 267, 270, 287, 365
Brusiloff, General, 116-17, 138, 144, 153, 154, 158-60, 163, 167
Buchanan, Sir George, 134
Bulgaria, 10, 32, 50, 53, 94, 244, 290-1, 358, 411, 416, 427
Bülow, Prince, 43, 56
Burian, Count, 56
Burrows, Dr., 86, 361

Caillaux, M., 209
Cantons, the Swiss, 69-70
Capitalism, 331, 441
Capitalist system, the, 179, 330
Caporetto, 242, 266
Carducci, 38
Carlotti, Marquis, 134
Cartier, Baron, 238
"Čas," the, 12, 27, 49, 322
Catholicism, 36-7, 44-6, 57, 106-8, 148, 219-20, 264, 346, 452-3, 483-96
Cavell, shooting of Miss, 65
Cellere, Count, 238

Červinka, M., 165
Charles, the Emperor, 128, 267-74, 294, 299, 307, 310-11, 386, 399-400
Chauvinism, 434, 457
Chelčický, xx, 322, 406, 462, 475, 491-2
Chicago, 218-20, 224, 232
Chlumecky, Baron, 397
Choc, M., 4
Church, the Czechoslovak, 493-4
Churches and the revolutionary process, the, 332-5, 352-5, 450-6, 492-3
Cinema spirit, the, 113-15
Clausewitz, 326-7
Clemenceau, M., 205, 209-11, 215, 247, 268-71, 290, 363-4, 397
Colonies, Czech, 74-6, 121 9
Comenius, xv-xvi, xx, 8, 34, 59, 92, 474-7, 480-1, 487, 491-2
Comert, Pierre, 134
Communism, 178-9, 183-4, 483
Comte, 105, 110, 349
Constantinople, 19, 144, 416
Constitution, the Czechoslovak, 221
Corfu, Declaration of, 206, 241, 245-48
Cossacks, the, 13, 186, 190
Coudenhove, Count, 387-8, 399, 434
Crane, Mr. Charles, 8, 224, 235
Croatia, 23-4, 39-42, 53, 144, 147-8, 245-8
Croats, the, 240, 394
Crown Prince, the German, 362
Culture, English, 113
Czech Association, 127-8
Czech Colonies, 74-6, 121-2, 124, 149, 223, 376
Czechoslovak army in Russia, the, 153-89
Czechoslovakia, xx, 22, 124, 128, 289, 302
Czech publications in other countries, 51-2, 127
Czechs, the—
   and Austria, xv, 22-3, 28-30, 58-63, 126-7; and Germany, 31, 417-19, 422; league in Russia, 33; national revival of, 37; societies in Switzerland, 50; co-operation with Southern Slavs, 52; and Russia, 143, 145-7, 152-60, 191, 253, 426-7; and Italy, 215; and their Constitution, 221; and the Yugoslavs, 241; and the Poles, 250-1; in Siberia, 275-8; and the German Bohemians, 400-1

Czech soldiery, the, 3-5, 24, 170-4, 375
"Czech Throne," the, 14, 75, 143
Czernin, Count, 35, 128, 205-6, 210, 213, 217, 267-8, 272

Dalmatia, 39, 54-5, 146, 244, 246
D'Annunzio, 38, 102
Danzig question, the, 275
Dardanelles, the, 57, 93, 115-6
Declaration of Independence, Czecho-slovakian, 294, 309, 366, 386
Declaration of January 6, 1918, the, 217
De jure recognition of Czechoslovakian State, 377
Delcasse, M., 56, 147
Democracy, 335, 349, 356, 358, 436-44, 447, 451, 460, 496
Democracy, American, 225-7, 454
Denis, Professor, 7, 11, 51, 55-6, 58, 64, 73-4, 97, 99, 475
Denmark, 411, 420
Diamandy, M., 134, 186
Dictatorship, 467-8
Dieterichs, General, 168, 204
Discipline of the Czech people, 336-7
Dmowski, Roman, 120, 250-1
Dostoyevsky, 347, 439, 499
"Družina," the, 33, 58, 62, 149-50, 154, 156, 163, 169, 171-2, 283-4
Duchesne, General, 56
Dukhonin, General, 167-8, 189
Duma, the, 139
Dürich, M., 51, 76-7, 83, 99, 148, 155, 157, 163-4, 192, 244

Ebert, Herr, 310
Edict of Toleration, the Emperor Joseph II's, xv
Ekaterinburg, 280
England, 45, 54, 66, 71, 86-96, 110-15, 122, 148, 193, 206, 209, 212, 288, 421-2, 478-9, 487
Entente, the Little, 188, 364, 414-5
Erzberger, Herr, 45, 210-11, 310
European Powers and Bolshevists, 201
European situation, the, 28
Evolution of modern Russia, 16
"Expressionism," German, 344, 348

Fasciotti, Baron, 186

Ferdinand, Archduke Francis, 1, 25
Feyler, Colonel, 56
Finland, 208
Finns, the, 414
Foch, Marshal, 9, 102, 209, 213-4, 269, 310
"Fourteen Points," President Wilson's, 265, 293-4
France, 43, 57-8, 66, 71, 96-9, 104-8, 127, 144-5, 153, 160, 166-8, 176, 188, 193, 197, 204, 206, 209, 267-71, 329, 365, 411, 421, 442, 478, 488
Francis Joseph, the Emperor, 127-8, 210, 365
Frederick, Archduke, 5, 7, 26
French disciplinary system in the Czech army, 166, 169
Friedjung, Dr., xvii
"Frightfulness" in war, 65
Frontier questions, 402

Garrigue, Charlotte, 323
Gasparri, Cardinal, 45, 264
Geneva, 47, 389-90, 393
German army, the, 20-1
German-Bolshevist relations, 193-6
German minority in Czechoslovakia, the, 432
German mobilization compared with Austrian, 3
German propaganda—
in Switzerland, 57
in America, 259-61
Germany, 30-2, 40, 43, 50, 63-66, 117-9, 176, 187, 193-4, 206, 211, 228, 252, 263, 289, 299-300, 310-11, 324-9, 332, 335-44, 356-60, 410, 418-9, 473, 484
Gettysburg, 225-6
Giers, M. de, 41
Gioberti, 37
Giolitti, Signor, 44
Goethe, 337-9, 341-3, 360, 461
Goremykin, M., 139
Goritchar, Mr., 39
Gorky, Maxim, 134, 141
Gothein, Professor, 32
Great Britain, Czechoslovak Treaty with, 288
Greece, 10, 208-9, 309, 411
Greene, Sir Conyngham, 201
Grey, Sir Edward, 54, 86
Grillparzer, 343

Groš, Dr., 72
Gutchkoff, M., 157

Hajn, Dr., 4, 23
Hapsburgs, the, xv-xviii, xx, 6, 26, 29, 66, 153, 299, 309-10, 351, 357, 385, 394, 398, 415, 421, 441-2, 486-7
Harper, Professor, 134
Hartmann, Eduard von, 63
Havlíček, Karel, 19, 29-30, 222, 322, 366, 373, 413, 420, 458, 475, 483
Hebbel, 342-3
Hegel, 337-8, 340, 348
Henderson, Mr. Arthur, 134
Herron, Professor, 304-7, 394
Hertling, Count, 213
Hertz, Dr., 307-8
Hindenburg, General, 212
Hinkovitch, Dr., 239, 248, 250
Hlaváč, M., 35
Hoetzendorf, General Conrad von, 44, 65
Hohler, Mr., 238
Holland, the author in, 7-8
Hollar, Wenceslas, 92
Horký, 76
House, Colonel, 221, 224, 235, 298, 300-1, 364
Humanity, 455-7, 476-7
Hungary, 209-10
Hurban-Vajanský, Svetozar, 220, 222
Hus, John, xi, xx, 58-9, 67, 82, 92, 174, 322, 366, 407, 421, 473, 477, 479, 492, 495

Imperialism, 32, 40, 63, 99, 331, 343, 416, 417
Imperium, Roman, 357
Intelligentsia, the, 445
International, the, 133
Irish, the, 90-1
Irredentists, the, 39, 255
Ishii, Count, 238
Isvolsky, M., 97-8, 143, 148
Italy, 21, 35-40, 43-4, 55-6, 99, 103-4, 120-1, 146-7, 188, 210, 215, 240, 242, 246, 266, 301, 330, 411
Italy, the author in, 35-46, 365

Janin, General, 133, 142, 285

Japan, 192, 201, 203, 205-6
Jassy, 186-8
Jewish National Home in Palestine, 209
Jews, the American, 236
Jews, the German, 25
Jusserand, M., 238, 298, 312

Kaiser, the, 31-2, 56, 211-2, 310, 317, 324, 326, 351, 356
Kalina, M., 4, 13
Kant, 337-41, 344-5, 360, 458, 482
Karageorgevitch dynasty, the, 241
Károlyi, Count, 221, 305-6
Kastiliansky, Dr., 8
Kenyon, Mr, 224
Kerensky, 135, 138, 161, 170, 175-6, 182, 207, 211, 262
Kerr, Mr. Philip, 89
Kieff, 150-7, 162-5, 173-7, 184-5, 189-90, 197, 245
Kitchener, Lord, 6, 10, 115-6
Klecanda, M., 165, 197-8, 217
Klofáč, M., 4, 372
Koerber, Dr. von, 26
Kollár, 59, 106, 222, 373, 423-4, 426, 462, 475, 480-1
Koloušek, Professor, 22
Koniček, M., 53-4, 78, 99, 223
Korniloff, General, 158, 167, 189, 202
Kosák, Mr., 6
Kramář, Dr., 24, 26, 49, 51, 58, 76, 83, 99, 126-8, 155, 216, 362, 369, 372, 375, 383, 389, 391, 393, 399-400, 408

Lammasch, Professor, 67, 292, 306-7, 388, 394-5, 398, 430
Lamprecht, Professor, 32, 351
Lamsdorff, Count, 140
Lancken, Baron von der, 211
Language in Czechoslovakia, the problem of, 433
Lansing, Mr., 294-6, 298-9, 308-9, 312
"League" in Russia, Czech, 150-4, 157, 161, 164-5
League of Nations, the, 359-60, 439-40
Lenin, 67, 133, 167, 179-80, 182-3, 192-3, 253-4, 466
Liquidation of Austria-Hungary, 292
Literature, American, 228-234
Literature, English, 111-3, 207
Literature, German, 343-4

Little Entente, the, 188, 364, 414-5
Little Russian lands, 255, 259, 308
Lloyd George, Mr., 94, 116, 118, 191, 212, 242, 246, 249, 267, 276
Lomonosoff, M., 253
London, the author in, 85-95
London, Treaty of, 56, 120-22, 147, 240, 242-4, 301
Loret, Professor, 41
Lorkovitch, Dr., 23-4
Ludendorff, General, 207, 212, 273, 276, 290
Lumbroso, Professor, 43
Lusitania, sinking of the, 65, 119
Luther, 486-7
Lützow, Count, 48

Machar, J. S., 49
"Maffia," the, 28-9, 68, 95, 217, 373, 386, 392
Magyars, the, xix, 23, 32, 66, 146, 222, 264, 274-5, 357-8, 363, 394, 400, 414, 417, 423
Mamiani, 37
Manditch, Dr., 244
Manzoni, 38
Markovitch, Professor Božo, 52
Marne, battle of the, 10, 21, 56-7, 92, 315
Marxism, 131, 178-81, 196, 267, 330-1, 440-1, 466
Masaryk, Thomas Garrigue, xi-xx
Mazzini, 38
Mercier, Cardinal, 45
Messianism, 424-5
Mestrovitch, M., 39
Michaelis, Dr., 212
Mid-European Democratic Union, the, 254-6, 291
Mihailovitch, Lynba, 39, 246
Militarism, 348
Military outlook, the, 94-6
Milner, Lord, 132
Milyukoff, M., 53, 117, 119, 130, 132-4, 157, 160, 176, 193, 211, 244
Minorities, racial, 429
Miscalculations of Germany, 327-8
Moghileff, 164, 167-8
Moltke, General von, 325-6
Mommsen, 63
Montenegro, 52, 122, 244, 246-7
Moravia, 391, 473

Morris, Mr. R. S., 201
Moscow, 175, 177, 190, 196-200
Muravieff, M., 176-7, 185, 189, 200
Musicians, German, 339

National Committee at Prague, Czechoslovak, 291, 374, 380-2, 386-93, 395-6, 399
National Council, the, 77-9, 148, 155, 157, 163-5, 285-6, 288, 312, 369, 377-80
Nationalism, 331-2, 477
Neutrality in Russia, Czech, 188, 192, 197, 280, 428
"New Czechs," 77
Nicholas, Grand Duke, 12, 17-18, 55, 147
Nietzsche, 340, 344
Nivelle, General, 209
Northcliffe, Lord, 243
Norway, 133

Okhrana, the, 161
Orlando, Signor, 102, 215, 242-3
Osuský, Dr., 80, 83-4, 120, 215, 292, 304-6, 377

Pacifism, 60-1, 133, 291, 300
Paderewski, M., 250-1
Palacký, Francis, xvi, xx, 29, 59, 61, 373, 406, 413, 417-8, 472-7, 480-3, 487, 490
Paléologue, M., 143-4, 270
Pálffy, Count, 44
Pan-Germanism, xx, 17, 19, 31-2, 340-1, 351, 355, 358, 416, 430, 464, 477
Pan-Slavism, 32, 77, 99, 130, 155, 423, 426-7
Papacy, the, 36-7
Pashitch, M., 2, 65, 120, 147-8, 206, 242, 246, 248
Paunkovitch, M., 52-3
Peace Conference, the, 301-2
Peace feelers, 123, 210-12, 290
Peace proposals, 123, 126, 293, 300, 307-8, 395
Peace Treaties, the, 412-3
Peasants, the Russian, 183, 403
Pergler, Mr., 218, 237, 292
Pétain, General, 209

Petrograd, 148, 151, 174, 189, 193
Philosophers, the German, 351
Pittsburgh, Czechoslovak Convention at, 220-223
Poincaré, President, 368
Poland, 83, 135, 208, 241, 243, 250-3, 301, 308, 402, 428
Polish question, the, 253
Political strikes in Germany, 212
Popovitch, Professor, 39
Positivism, Comte's, 105, 349
Prague (1848), Slav Congress of, 423
Prague, the revolution at, 383-4, 393-6, 399, 405
President, the author as, 311-5, 362-3, 366-7, 455, 469-71
Pro-Austrianism, 369-70, 383-4
Professors and international politics, 318
Propaganda, 58-9, 71, 80-85, 91, 135, 164, 203, 235, 237-9, 251, 312, 371, 377
Protestantism, 452-3, 482, 486-92
Provisional Government, Czechoslovak, 292, 294, 387
Prussianism, 67, 337-8, 341, 356, 417, 486

Rašin, Dr., 28, 49, 58, 83, 126-7, 216, 369, 372, 385-7, 392, 404, 408, 422
Rasmussen, M., 41
Rasputin, 136-7, 142-3, 156
Reading, Lord, 238
Red Cross, the American, 277-8
Redlich, Dr. Joseph, 400
Reformation, the, 333, 335, 420-1, 449-50, 452, 482-3
Regency Council in Poland, 252
Reiss, Professor, 66
Religion, war and, 352-4
Religious question, the, 491-2
Republican, the author a, 392
Republic, the Czechoslovakian, 311, 368
Republic, the German, 310
Republics, spread of, 410
Revolution, 465-6
Revolution in Austria-Hungary, 309-10
Revolution, the French, 334, 353, 421, 476
Revolution, the German, 310-11
Revolution, the Russian, 117, 126, 130, 136, 140-1, 151-2, 156, 160, 166, 169, 173-84, 196, 216, 245, 269-70, 374, 392

Ribot, M., 271
Robertson, Major-General Sir William, 94
Rodd, Sir James Rennell, 43
Rodzianko, M., 130
Rolland, Romain, 60, 109
Roman-German tradition, 32
Roman Law, 36
Romanticism, 106-7, 342
Rome Congress (1918), the, 242-5, 247, 250
Rome, the author in, 38-47
Roosevelt, ex-President, 237
Rosen, Baron, 143
Rosmini, 37
Roumania, 10, 21, 110, 145, 186-8, 208, 364, 411
Russia—
    Czech faith in, xviii; her assigned part in the war, 6; advance to Cracow, 11; estimate of her army, 11, 93, 135-8; unpreparedness of, 13, 16; and the Czechs, 12-4, 148, 155, 188, 253, 427-8; and Austria, 12-3; the author's estimate of, 16-9; and Slavdom, 16-20, 427; enmity with the Poles, 17; Czech colony in, 53, 62, 76, 149-52; has no Slav policy, 55, 98, 142-4; counted on by the French, 56; feeble propaganda in, 62; Conservative influence on Czech colony, 76; and France, 98-9; demoralization of her army, 103; definitely defeated, 117; the Revolution, 129, 130, 136, 140, 151, 156, 160, 166, 216, 245, 269, 374, 392; secret treaty with France and England, 145; and the Družina, 149-50; will not recognize the Czech revolution, 159; Czech army in, 153-74, 276-89; and the Yugoslav question, 240; declares in favor of Italy, 244; and the Southern Slav question, 244-5; and Poland, 252-3; estimate of her share in the war, 329-30; her contribution to the liberation of the Czechs, 402
Russian Church, the, 141
Russo-Czech political relations, 13, 16-7
Russophilism, 12-9, 24, 51
Ruthenes, the, xix, 256-8

Safařík, 482-3

Salonika, Serbian revolutionary activities at, 245-6
Šámal, Dr., 28-9, 395
Sarajevo, 1-2, 64
Sarolea, Professor Charles, 90
Savinkoff, 135, 198-9
Sazonof, M., 7, 13-4, 17, 42, 55, 143-4, 146
Scheiner, Dr., 13-5
Schools, 446-7
Schopenhauer, 340
Secret Service, Czech, 260-2, 371
Self-determination, 432
Self-government, spread of, 410
Separatism, German, 311
Serbia—
Austro-Hungarian ultimatum, 1-2, 240; animosity to Bulgaria, 1-3; opposition to Austria, 4-7; Austrian reverses in, 11; author's estimate of her army, 21; relations with Croatia, 40; and the Vatican, 44; Czech colony in, 50, 52-3; and the Sarajevo outrage, 64-5; overthrown, 117; and Russia, 138, 146, 161-2; the centre of the Southern Slav world, 240; differences with Italy, 246; and the Geneva Agreement (1918), 248; share in the war, 330
Serbo-Croat-Slovene State, the, 241, 362
Seton-Watson, Mr., 6-9, 14, 42, 54, 72, 82, 86-9, 92, 122-3, 242-3, 245
Shokoroff, General, 168
Shulgin, M., 185
Siberia, 196, 199-200, 203, 278-9
Silesia, 251
Sitchinsky, M., 253
Sixtus, Prince, 210, 213, 267-9, 363, 404
Slav aspirations, 15-6, 33
"Slav Brethren," the, 142, 144, 146, 158
Slavs, the, 130, 142-9, 423-4, 426-9
Slovakia, 23, 34, 39, 142, 144, 152-3, 216, 222-4, 245, 308, 374, 391, 401-2, 442-1, 493-5
Slovaks, the, xix, 23, 221-4, 274, 308, 400
Šmeral, Dr., 4, 213
Smetana, 373
Sobolevsky, Professor, 245
Socialism, 440-1, 483
Socialist Party, the German Independent, 133
Socialists, the German, 8, 324

Sokols, the, 7, 13-5, 170, 373
Sonnino, Baron, 56, 101, 159, 242-3, 266-7
Sorokin, 135
Soukup, Dr., 4, 49, 385-7, 422
Southern Slav movement, the, xvi, 23, 39-41, 58, 120-2, 147, 239-50, 415-6
Soviets and the Czech army in Russia, 279
Spalaikovitch, Dr., 134, 244
State, the, 463-5
"Statism," 335
Steed, Mr. Wickham, 5-8, 54, 87-8, 115, 122, 242-3, 245, 259, 284
Štefánik, M., 28, 74, 77-80, 83-4, 96, 100-3, 132, 142, 150, 152-3, 156, 163-4, 166, 186, 188, 213, 237-8, 241, 243, 284, 292, 312, 373, 393
Štěpina, Mr., 15, 218
Stinnes, Herr, 137
Stockholm, Socialist International Conference at, 213, 216
Stoyanovitch, Dr. Nikola, 39
Stránský, Dr., 4
Stürgkh, Count, 117
Štúr, Ludevit, 220
Stürmer, M., 117, 136, 140, 143, 145, 152, 155-6, 218, 261, 327
Submarine warfare, the, 118, 132, 209
Suicide, 345-8
Sukhomlinov, M., 12
Superman, the German, 351
Supilo, M., 39, 52, 122, 146-7, 242, 244, 248-9
Supreme Command, the German, 325-9
Sussex, sinking of the, 217
Svatkovsky, M., 9, 41-2, 53, 98, 131-2, 270
Svehla, M., 4
Sweden, 133
Switzerland, 47, 52, 56-7, 67-70
Sychrava, Dr., 48, 51, 67, 72, 80, 215, 292

Take Jonescu, 186, 364
Tannenberg, 11
Tchelyabinsk, incident at, 275
"The New Europe," Seton-Watson's, 82, 123
Theocracy, 449-52
Thirty Years' War, analogy with the, 409-10

Thomas, M. Albert, 134, 166
Thun, Count, 24-5
Tisza, Count, 41, 309-10, 357, 397
Tokio, 201, 206
Tolstoy, 59, 60, 131, 141, 462
Treaty of 1909, Austro-German, 64
Treitschke, 64, 418
Trieste, 23
Triple Alliance, the, 357-8
Trotsky, 190, 193-4, 204, 279
Trumbitch, Dr., 39, 147, 206, 240-3, 246-8, 306, 364
Tsar, the, 12, 16-8, 24, 51, 57, 101, 131, 136-43, 154-6, 160, 163, 176, 181, 192, 223, 240, 280, 426
Tsarist Absolutism, 158, 207
Tsarista, the, 138-40, 156
Turkey, 10, 21, 32, 95, 208-9, 212, 358, 412-5, 427
Turkish danger, the 414-5

Ukraine, the, 171, 176, 184-5, 187-90, 192, 196, 200, 202, 208, 253
Unity of command, 209, 290
"Universal," the Fourth, 185

Valona, 44
Vandervelde, M., 134
Vatican, the, 39, 44-6, 104, 212, 264, 311, 361, 397, 492-3
Venizelos, M., 364
Vesnitch, M., 55, 97, 246, 364
Vico, 36, 450
Victor Emmanuel, King, 365
Vinogradoff, Sir Paul, 7, 89, 119
Vladivostok, 199-200, 275-7
Voinovitch, Dr. L., 39

Voska, Mr., 4, 33, 76, 84, 134, 259-62, 284, 377

War, author's analysis of the, 315-6, 324-35, 349-51, 356-60
War guilt, the question of, 63-7, 324
Warsaw policy, 253-4
Washington, Catholic Congress in, 220
Wasserman, 348
Wemyss, Admiral, 310
White Mountain, Battle of the, xii, 34, 361, 480, 484
Whyte, Sir Frederick, 89
William, the Emperor, 32, 139
Wilson, President, xi, 124-7, 130, 148, 201, 204, 213, 224-5, 227, 235-8, 241-2, 246, 249, 255, 265-6, 274, 277, 290, 293, 295-304, 308-9, 311-12, 378, 384, 387, 394-5, 397-400, 412, 430
Wiseman, Sir William, 238
Witte, M., 139-40

Young Czech Party, the, 30
Young, Mr. Fitzgibbon, 90
Ypres, 10, 21
Yugoslav Committee in London, 52, 120-1
Yugoslavia, 244-8, 295, 411, 416
Yugoslavs, Czech co-operation with the, 239-50

Zboroff, Battle of, 160-1, 167, 171, 174, 188, 217
Žižka, xx, 59, 174, 322, 406, 479, 491
Zupanitch, Dr., 39
Zurlinden, General, 56

25158930R00298

Printed in Great Britain
by Amazon